Out of the Shadow

Out of the Shadow

REVISITING THE REVOLUTION FROM POST-PEACE GUATEMALA

Edited by Julie Gibbings and Heather Vrana

University of Texas Press Texas

Printed in the United States of America
First edition, 2020

Requests for permission to reproduce material from this work should be sent to:
Permissions
University of Texas Press
P.O. Box 7819
Austin, TX 78713-7819
utpress.utexas.edu/rp-form

♾ The paper used in this book meets the minimum requirements of ANSI/NISO Z39.48-1992 (R1997) (Permanence of Paper).

Library of Congress Cataloging-in-Publication Data

Names: Gibbings, Julie, editor. | Vrana, Heather A., editor.
Title: Out of the shadow : revisiting the revolution from post-peace Guatemala / edited by Julie Gibbings, Heather Vrana.
Other titles: Revisiting the revolution from post-peace Guatemala
Description: First edition. | Austin, TX : University of Texas Press, [2020] | Includes bibliographical references and index.
Identifiers: LCCN 2019040184 | ISBN 978-1-4773-2085-3 (cloth) | ISBN 978-1-4773-2086-0 (library ebook) | ISBN 978-1-4773-2087-7 (ebook)
Subjects: LCSH: GuatemalaPolitics and government1945-1985. | GuatemalaHistoryRevolution, 1954Influence. | Social changeGuatemalaHistory20th century. | MayasGuatemalaSocial conditions. | Ethnic conflictGuatemala. | GuatemalaHistory1945-1985. | Collective memoryGuatemala.
Classification: LCC F1466.5 .O83 2020 | DDC 972.8105/2dc23
LC record available at https://lccn.loc.gov/2019040184

doi:10.7560/320853

To the Guatemalan revolutionaries of 1944–1954
and all other generations who drew and will
draw inspiration from them

Contents

Figures

Foreword

The Path back to the Future—the Enduring Legacy of the Revolution

Jim Handy

I first began working on understanding the Guatemalan Revolution when I began my doctorate in 1978. In the aftermath of the 1976 earthquake, highland communities engaged in energetic efforts at community, peasant, and labor organizing. It was no coincidence that the repression that had been relatively constant, if fluctuating, in Guatemala since the overthrow of Arbenz in 1954 escalated rapidly and began to focus increasingly on Mayan communities in the highlands. My writing was, therefore, necessarily always informed by two dreadful perspectives: the ongoing violence that needed to be exposed and explained,[1] and my own research on the revolution in the countryside and the untimely end of the Arbenz administration.[2] My own work, thus, was always infused with an appreciation for the connections between the revolutionary decade and its overthrow and contemporary struggles in Guatemala. Nonetheless, given all the horror and drama people endured in the ensuing decades, I was a bit cautious about suggestions that the revolution had deep resonance for generations of Guatemalans who had not lived through those heady ten years of spring.

Recent events and experiences have led me to understand more fully the relevance of the revolutionary era to contemporary Guatemala. Let me relate briefly a personal experience that helped me come to this understanding. In September 2013, I was invited to Guatemala City for a book launch of a Spanish translation of one my books.[3] It was to coincide with what would have been the one hundredth birthday of Jacobo Arbenz Guzmán. To my shock, the launch was held in the main hall of the old Museo of the University of San Carlos in downtown Guatemala, a huge room filled to the rafters. I suspected, of course, that this crowd had much more to do with an opportunity to celebrate Arbenz's life and remember the revolution than anything to do with my book—an impression that was reinforced when just before we began, Jacobo Arbenz Vilanova (the former president's son, in one of his rare public appearances in Guatemala) and his family entered the room to sit in the front row. The crowd went crazy. It was a long and emotional evening, imagining what could have been had Arbenz not been overthrown in 1954. After the event wound down, I spent many long hours listening to people who wanted to talk about what had happened in their community during the revolution, and to discuss their ongoing struggles for land. Very often these struggles involved land that had been provided to them during the revolution and taken from them after; most often they would start their discussion with a comment on how the revolution had "given back" their land and their struggles to reacquire it since. This was a very small and self-selected sample, but certainly for this group of people, the Guatemalan Revolution continues to have major significance in their lives and continues to be essential in understanding contemporary Guatemala and its problems.

One of the things that became apparent to me that evening was that there are important links between involvement in, and memories of, the revolution and continued activism in many areas. While some of the arguments made in the past about the continuing influence of the "revolutionary" decade have been exaggerated, there is significant evidence of rural organizers through the last few decades of the twentieth century who traced their activism to the revolution.[4] There is also clearly a sense of a more generalized continuity in the aspirations of a localized historical justice that was so apparent during the revolution, a continuity outlined in Cindy Forster's *La revolución indígena y campesina en Guatemala*.[5] My conversations with people that evening, and on numerous other occasions, suggest that in a concrete manner recovering land gained during the revolution—or land they believed they might have gained had the revolution continued—remained a concern for many in or from rural communities. In a more general sense, re-creating the hope people imagined existed during the revolution still holds particular relevance for many.

What exactly was it about the revolution that reverberates so strongly now? Few of the people in the room were either alive during the revolution or old enough during it to remember it clearly. Thus, what they are remembering is not their own experiences, but some distillation of those of others, some social memory. History and memory, as we know, are always re-created to serve contemporary needs, to address contemporary questions—to remember the future and imagine the past—as J. H. Plumb once said many decades ago.[6] How has the Guatemalan Revolution been imagined, remembered, to serve Guatemala's present and future?

Of course, the whole idea of revolution might be questioned. The changes that came may or may not have been deep enough, radical enough, or sudden enough to be termed a "revolution," defined most simply by the Oxford dictionary as "a forcible overthrow of a government or social order, in favour of a new system."[7] If there was revolution, there was clearly not just one. There were two presidents during that decade: Juan José Arévalo, from 1945 to 1951, and Jacobo Arbenz Guzmán, from 1951 until his overthrow in 1954. The two administrations were very different, with distinct agendas and plans and often very different priorities. The first was much more cautious about reform in general, and especially limited in its approach to reform in rural areas. The government of Arbenz was much more determined to extend the revolution to the countryside.

More important, as the chapters in this volume make clear and as the stories people told me in the *museo* that evening in September made even clearer, the "revolution" was felt differently, occurred at a different time, and led to radically different consequences in each community. The files that record the unfolding of agrarian reform after the passage of Decree 900 in 1952, located in the archives of the National Agrarian Department, make it even clearer that for many communities the important changes that came with the revolution revolved around the issue of control over land and that the complicated history of struggles over land mark the ebb and flow of the revolution. If there was revolution, it was not one revolution but multiple ones.

These administrations also had their failures: the result of misguided policies, or political infighting, or simple greed and ambition on the part of many politicians. The revolutionary administrations, like all government administrations, contained competing agendas, each government ministry anxious to advance its own particular administrative goals, reflecting different constituents. The Ministry of Labor in the Arévalo administration, particularly when led by Alfonso Bauer Paiz, was often more radical and more inclined to support organized labor than other ministries in that administration. During the Arbenz administration, those supporting the distribution of land to peasant farmers often competed with sectors of the government more interested in promoting agricultural modernization. On occasion, both administrations were torn apart when one or another powerful politician sought to extend his/her own influence. The fairly constant conflict between Augusto Charnaud MacDonald, an influential member of the Partido Acción Revolucionaria (Revolutionary Action Party; PAR) who eventually left to form the Socialist Party, and José Manuel Fortuny, an influential advisor to President Arbenz, helped make political discourse within the ranks of those supporting the revolution more bitter and less productive. Revolutionary politicians were by turns too timid and too impatient; they too often created policy through the adoption of inappropriate ideologies (both foreign and homegrown). Both administrations had difficulty imagining and articulating a role for Mayan culture in a revolutionized Guatemala. Reformers often believed they had a deeper and profounder understanding of Guatemala than they did. And, many of them were not able to rid themselves of ingrained conceptions about women, race, and peasants that helped undermine policies and programs.

For all of the conflicts, though, those ten years provide us with portraits of some amazing people. For every opportunist who sought primarily his or her own position and power, for every administrator too enamored with ideas of social engineering and economic modernization, there were many others who were devoted to the proposition that the revolution was meant to reduce poverty and deepen democracy. In the context of peasant and worker organization and agrarian reform, organizers such as Amor Velasco; Victor Manuel Gutiérrez, the longtime secretary general of the Guatemalan Labor Federation; and Leonardo Castillo Flores, the secretary general of the peasant league, worked tirelessly and selflessly to forward the goals of the revolution and improve the lives of Guatemala's poorest. They worked in or with two administrations that despite their errors, despite their misgivings, and most especially despite the often-violent opposition, accomplished some amazing things.

When I first started doing work on the Guatemalan Revolution forty years ago, the widely accepted understanding of the Guatemalan Revolution, at least in academic writing, was that the rural poor—especially campesinos and especially Mayan campesinos—had not only failed to embrace the revolution and its policies, but often actively opposed them.[8] The few instances of peasant and rural labor activism recognized in most of the literature were either in specific locales (the United Fruit Company plantation on the Pacific coast at Tiquisate or in particular large estates controlled by the government, called collectively Fincas Nacionales, where labor organization was more pronounced) and/or the result of the work of political agitators from Guatemala City: Carlos Manuel Pellecer, Clodoveo Torres Moss, and others. When Mayan peasants and rural workers engaged in protests, they were considered by many to be "easy instruments in the hands of unscrupulous men" as *El Imparcial*, the major newspaper in the country, phrased it in 1948.[9] I remember, particularly, as an example, a work by Brian Murphy written in the 1960s, entitled "The Stunted Growth of Guatemalan Peasant Movements," which offered an interpretation echoed time and time again in the literature.[10] Agrarian reform itself was both little understood and underappreciated—considered to have been carried out in an arbitrary and chaotic fashion and used primarily to support political agendas either nationally or locally. Of course, these interpretations fit the rhetoric of the so-called Liberación that came to power after Arbenz's overthrow and the US State Department, which was active in that ouster, but they were repeated surprisingly often by academics and proved to be remarkably durable.

We now know this not to be true. Almost all of the chapters here require us to be careful in our assessment of what the revolution actually meant in specific locales at specific times. They impress upon us the need to be nuanced in our understandings of who welcomed aspects of the revolution and who did not, which elements of revolutionary change Guatemalans in different communities embraced and which they opposed, and what long-standing historical, local, ethnic, and familial conflicts found expression through revolutionary policies. Nonetheless, the clear picture we have of the revolution in the countryside is one in which peasants, Maya and non-Maya, readily embraced aspects of revolutionary change. They quickly sought opportunities to increase and diversify their agricultural production. They dramatically took advantage of and engaged fully in electoral democracy, at the municipal and national levels. In most areas, campesinos and workers carried outside organizers along with them, urging quicker decisions under the Agrarian Reform Law and putting pressure on the government to act. Most important, in the context of the agrarian reform, campesino organization, agitation, and activism pushed the reform. It was the peasants' embrace of the opportunity to obtain land that ensured that the reform went beyond what the Arbenz administration had envisioned. Peasant and rural labor activism made it revolutionary.

In the process of what was not a "stunted growth" but a virtual explosion of activism and organization, something unique happened. National political organizations and entities not only needed to pay attention to rural associations, but were often driven by their demands. This influence occurred partly because of the fractured nature of national political parties and organizations: revolutionary parties fought for adherents and support, and peasant leagues and rural workers unions courted the same constituents.

This competition was both a strength and a weakness of the revolution. It also occurred because of the determination and strength of rural activists and because campesinos and rural workers would not be ignored.

This activity is also, I think, what helps me, tentatively, try to answer my first question: "What exactly was it about the revolution that reverberates so strongly now?" It seems clear that the Arbenz administration was pulled along, and at times immensely surprised, by the scope of the change that was happening in the countryside. Many in the administration were a little frightened about what was happening, and at times deeply troubled by some aspects of it. Constant rumors about an impending confrontation between Arbenz and agrarian organizers, including a rumor that Arbenz's own estate had been invaded by peasants, were, on the one hand, purposefully spread misinformation by landowners and conservative opposition, and, on the other, a reflection of serious tensions within the Arbenz administration. And there were, no doubt, some in the administration or with the ear of the administration who thought they might at some point take the reins of this revolution for their own ends. Again, Charnaud MacDonald's attempts to gain political control over the peasant league stand out as an example. But, mostly and to his historic credit, Arbenz did not succumb to those fears. Agrarian officials worked hard to apply the law according to the standards outlined in the decree, including seriously considering the landowners' appeals against original expropriations. But, most important, the administration lived up to its promises of supporting the organized peasantry and labor, occasionally protecting them when necessary, arbitrating among conflicting and competing demands. In the process, a revolution was in the making.

Of course, there are all sorts of other things that allow the revolution to continue to appeal to many in Guatemala. The fact that it was overthrown with a heavy dose of US intervention makes it easier not to take responsibility for its fall. Its untimely end means one never really needs to question when the revolution might have disappointed its followers given the contradictory demands of various revolutionary adherents. Perhaps of greatest significance, one gets a sense that—at least in the context of a serious opportunity to restructure landownership and power, and to lessen inequality—this might have been Guatemala's best chance to do so. Agrarian reform, while still important, will never again be able to shape the Guatemalan economy the way it would have a half century ago. But, my suspicion is that there is something else that makes the revolution appeal to many in contemporary Guatemala. To explore this, I might venture into a brief discussion of the relationship between history and social memory.

Rachel Hatcher reminds us that 3rd Avenida norte in Guatemala City has, like many other avenues and streets in the old town, an alternative, more romantic name.[11] La Tercera (Third Avenue North) is also officially known as La Calle del Olvido (The Street of Forgetting). This street seems to be a favorite locale for graffiti artists; their messages are all about not forgetting, with the names and sometimes pictures of the disappeared or dead often staring out on those walking by. Hatcher has commented on the almost obsessive compulsion to whitewash over this graffiti, not unreasonable for property owners unfortunate enough to be thus targeted. But, Guatemalan whitewash seldom completely erases the images. Instead what happens is a kind of pentimento effect, where old memories continue to be visible through the whitewash, slowly fading and being painted over by new graffiti meant to be more immediate.

The Calle del Olvido is not the only striking example. On the side of the Inter-American Highway between Los Encuentros and Chimaltenango, west of Guatemala City, a large sandstone cliff provides free billboard space for those with the equipment to access it. Before each election, political coalitions whitewash over their predecessors' fading messages and affix their own symbols encouraging votes. As the new whitewash fades, the symbols of past coalitions merge with those of the present. One is left with a kind of shorthand guide to Guatemala's often sad political history, each slowly disappearing symbol evoking memories of similarly faded hopes or, too often, realized dread. These persistent images strike me as an interesting illustration of the way memory and history work in concert to provide us glimpses of the past, obscured partly by attempts to erase them, and then obscured, recovered, or adorned with more vibrant memories of the past—how images of the past keep intruding on the present.

Memory, both personal and especially historic/social, is a slippery thing. As one of my colleagues, Chris Kent, has eloquently argued, what makes memory possible in the first instance is, perhaps, ironically, partial forgetting.[12] If I were to remember everything that happened to me yesterday and try to recount it to you, it would by definition take most of a day to do. Forgetting, in this example, happens in two ways: first, I (choose) not to recall it, and second, I (choose) not to recount it. As Michel-Rolph Trouillot has pointed out, in the process of creating "history" the chosen silences always outnumber, and sometimes overshadow, the remembrances.[13] But some things not remembered, not recounted, reappear, take on more tangible form, and are reinvigorated as part of social memory. Attempts to silence aspects of the past through purposeful forgetting are not always, indeed one might say not often, successful.

As Tzvetan Todorov has remarked: "Memory is a partial forgetting in both senses of the word."[14] What gets remembered and recounted in a society is never innocent, never completely accidental. Memory gets encapsulated or contained in specific understandings of the world, the group and its history. That containment is always linked to power but never simply a function of power. In a similar manner, Trouillot suggests, focusing on the way some historical narratives are made possible and some silenced allows us to understand more fully the role of power in crafting what is remembered.[15]

Social memory has been described as an expression of a hegemonic discourse that determines the way the past is or can be explained.[16] Alternatively, Steve Stern has suggested we might best think of a memory box in which all sorts of disparate and distinct events and memories get stored, but take shape around emblematic memories that provide the scaffolding for a society. Sometimes, this scaffolding is erected through the use of carefully selected "slices of history," employed to obscure broader understandings of the past.[17] In either conception of the role of social memory, it is clear that determining what gets remembered most vividly and what gets whitewashed, remaining partially hidden until it gets reintegrated into group memory, is always the result of a struggle over the power of remembering, the power of imagining. As Michel Foucault suggests, this determination is always in some ways part of that permanent provocation between power and "subjugated knowledges."[18]

The Guatemalan Revolution has a unique existence. Its memory was deliberately and partially silenced, but its existence was widely known and recounted. Although never held up as model (except briefly by the Méndez Montenegro government, the "Third Government of the Revolution" in the 1960s), many things the revolution openly aspired to—including promoting democracy and social justice and ending poverty—were and needed to be part of the governing discourse of all governments thereafter. No governments after the revolution argued that they were working to increase poverty, though they were all so good at doing exactly that.[19] All of these subsequent administrations employed rhetorical flourishes reminiscent of the revolution, while attacking all the concrete actions that allowed the revolutionary administrations to begin to deepen democracy and address inequality and poverty. While official discourse "rant(ed) deliriously" in attempts to hide the undemocratic and repressive nature of Guatemalan society after 1954,[20] memories of the Revolution remained vibrant partly because appealing to them was, and to a certain extent is still, oppositional, part of those subjugated knowledges in permanent provocation with official discourse. The memory of the Revolution gained strength because it stood so starkly in contrast to the administrations that followed who fostered inequality, heightened poverty, dispossessed peasants, repressed workers, and violently attacked democracy.

At moments of recovery from periods of intense social stress—moments of hegemonic rupture, as William Roseberry would suggest—the need for shared emblematic memories becomes even more intense, even more necessary to provide a sense of community, worth, and hope. In such moments, certain emblematic memories become more powerful, more useful in providing the scaffolding around which a sense of what kind of society is possible is imagined. In this sense, I think, the revolution has taken shape as an emblematic memory that reminds us what is, and was almost, possible. There is a sense that a path was lost with the overthrow of the revolution and that remembering the revolution may help Guatemala find its way back to a more promising future.

Notes

1. Jim Handy, *Gift of the Devil: A History of Guatemala* (Boston: South End, 1984).

2. Jim Handy, "Revolution and Reaction: National Policy and Rural Politics in Guatemala, 1944–1954" (PhD diss., University of Toronto, 1985).

3. Jim Handy, *Revolución en el área rural: Conflicto rural y reforma agraria en Guatemala, 1944–1954* (Guatemala City: Centro de Estudios Urbanos y Regionales de USAC, 2013).

4. Greg Grandin, *The Last Colonial Massacre* (Chicago: University of Chicago Press, 2004).

5. Cindy Forster, *La revolución indígena y campesina en Guatemala* (Guatemala City: Editorial Universitaria, USAC, 2012).

6. J. H. Plumb, *The Death of the Past* (London: Macmillan, 1969).

7. "Definition of revolution in English," accessed August 26, 2019, www.lexico.com/en/definition/revolution.

8. See, e.g., Robert Wasserstrom, "Revolution in Guatemala: Peasants and Politics under the Arbenz Government," *Comparative Studies in Society and History* 17 (1975): 443–478. Wasserstrom relied on the studies of six communities by anthropologists to arrive at his assessment. For these, see R. Adams, ed., "Political Change in Guatemalan Indian Communities: A Symposium," in *Community Culture and National Change*, ed. R. Adams, 1–54, Middle American Research Institute publication no. 24 (New Orleans: Tulane University Middle American Research Institute, 1972); and R. H. Ebel

and Harry S. McArthur, *Cambio político en tres comunidades indígenas de Guatemala*, Cuadernos del Seminario de Integración Social no. 21 (Guatemala City: Editorial José de Pineda Ibarra; Ministerio de Educación, 1969). The importance of Wasserstrom's argument is reflected in the fact that both Carol Smith and George Lovell subsequently reiterated this argument, citing Wasserstrom, in later works; see Smith, "Local History in Global Context," *Comparative Studies in Society and History* 26 (1984): 193–228; and Lovell, "Surviving Conquest: The Maya of Guatemala in Historical Perspective," *Latin American Research Review* 23 (1988): 25–57.

9. *El Imparcial* (Guatemala City), January 15, 1948, 1.

10. Brian Murphy, "The Stunted Growth of Guatemalan Peasant Movements," in *Crucifixion by Power: Essays on Guatemalan National Social Structure, 1944–1966*, ed. Richard Newbold Adams, 438–478 (Austin: University of Texas Press, 1970). A similar approach was demonstrated by Neale Pearson, "The Confederación Nacional Campesina de Guatemala and Peasant Unionism in Guatemala, 1944–1954" (MA thesis, Georgetown University, 1964).

11. Many of my ideas about this have been improved through frequent conversations with one of my former doctoral students, Rachel Hatcher. I highly recommend her book *The Power of Memory and Violence in Central America* (Cham, Switzerland: Palgrave Macmillan, 2018).

12. Chris Kent, "History: The Discipline of Memory—and Forgetting," *Structurist* 37–38 (1997/1998): 34–40.

13. Michel-Rolph Trouillot, *Silencing the Past: Power and the Production of History* (Boston: Beacon, 1995), 27.

14. Tzvetan Todorov, *Hope and Memory: Lessons from the Twentieth Century* (Princeton, NJ: Princeton University Press, 2003), 127.

15. Trouillot, *Silencing the Past*, 23–25.

16. William Roseberry, "Hegemony, Power, and Languages of Contention," in *The Politics of Difference: Ethnic Premises in a World of Power*, ed. Edwin N. Wilmsen and Patrick McAllister, 71–84 (Chicago: University of Chicago Press, 1996), esp. 81–82; and William Roseberry, "Hegemony and the Language of Contention," in *Everyday Forms of State Formation*, ed. Gilbert Joseph and Daniel Nugent, 355–366 (Durham, NC: Duke University Press, 1994), esp. 360–361.

17. Steve J. Stern, *Remembering Pinochet's Chile: On the Eve of London* (Durham, NC: Duke University Press, 2004), esp. 105–106; and Stern, *Reckoning with Pinochet: The Memory Question in Democratic Chile, 1989–2006* (Durham, NC: Duke University Press, 2010), esp. 268–269.

18. Michel Foucault, *Power/Knowledge: Selected Interviews and Writings, 1972–1977*, ed. Colin Gordon (Brighton, UK: Harvester, 1980), esp. 81–84.

19. I want to thank J. T. Way for this insightful comment.

20. Eduardo Galeano, "Language, Lies, and Latin American Democracy," *Harper's Magazine*, February 1990, 19.

Acknowledgments

Like most worthy intellectual endeavors, this project was born of naïve enthusiasm and extended far beyond any bounds we had previously imagined or expected.

In an autumnal New Haven coffee shop, we discussed the limitations of extant writing on the revolutionary period, with which each of us had been contending in frustrated solitude. Buoyed by this conversation, and encouraged by the tide of protests against then president Otto Pérez Molina, we realized that Guatemala and Guatemalanists were ready for a new reckoning with the meaning of the revolution. Even more, the time had come for a more diversified understanding of the so-called Ten Years' Spring. That there were actually many revolutions was patently clear, but what did this realization offer to scholars, scholarship, and the political community at the present juncture? For the next four years, we explored this question together, sharing coffees, walks, and countless Skype calls and emails. We drafted a list of scholars who might help us think through these questions, and thus our community of collaborators expanded. This volume is the result of an extended collaboration between the coeditors, the contributors, and many others who offered insights along the way.

We would like to thank our respective institutions, Southern Connecticut State University, the University of Florida, and the University of Manitoba. As this book was going to press, Gibbings welcomed the opportunity to move to the School of History, Classics, and Archaeology at the University of Edinburgh.

This volume would not have been possible without the generous support of the Social Science and Humanities Resource Council of Canada (SSHRC) Connections Grant. Contributors' chapters and our introduction benefited from several opportunities to meet and discuss our work. Contributors discussed initial papers at the January 2016 meeting of the American Historical Association in Atlanta, where Michel Gobat offered generous comments. We would especially like to thank Michel for his insights into periodization and Central American exceptionalism as crucial frameworks for the project. In the fall of 2016, we reunited in New Haven, this time with Jim Handy, for a small workshop on the meaning of the revolution and its relationship to the 2015 protests and contemporary politics in Guatemala. This workshop was supported by the Southern Connecticut State University Faculty Development Grant. Then, in May 2017, we gathered in Winnipeg with almost all the contributors for a three-day event to workshop individual chapters. This event was funded by the SSHRC, Research Manitoba, the University of Manitoba Institute for the Humanities (UMIH), and the Mauro Center for Peace and Justice. Generous support from several departments and the Dean's Office in the Faculty of Arts as well as the Geopolitical Economy Research Group of the University of Manitoba also enabled the multiday workshop. We would like to express our gratitude toward Jonathan Peyton, Esyllt Jones, Jorge Nállim, and Adele Perry for their invaluable comments on contributors' papers. In addition, we would like to thank the Canadian Museum for Human Rights for hosting the national debut of Isabel Acevedo's *El Buen Cristiano*. Importantly, the 2017 workshop was possible only with the insight and hard work of Paul Jenkins of the UMIH.

Jessica Kirstein meticulously translated the chapters by Jorge Ramón González Ponciano and Arturo Taracena Arriola. Two anonymous reviewers provided useful comments on the manuscript that ultimately refined and improved our work. In addition, we are grateful to Kerry Webb and her colleagues at the University of Texas Press, who encouraged this project and guided us toward its timely conclusion.

On a more personal note, we would especially like to thank Gil Joseph for his support of this project from the very beginning and his enduring commitment along the way, in spite of the obstacles placed in the way. We would also like to thank J. T. Way, who helped to shape the introduction, and this volume, in indispensable ways. Jim Handy also deserves special mention for his place at the origins of this project and his ever-present willingness to revisit the revolution alongside us. Julie would also like to thank Paul Jenkins for his boundless faith and generous support; Heather thanks David Kazanjian for his revolutionary spirit.

Finally, we thank each other for the kind of comradeship and intellectual interlocution of which most can only dream.

Out of the Shadow

Introduction

Revisiting the Revolution in Contemporary Guatemala

Heather Vrana and Julie Gibbings

Destiny

When the historian Piero Gleijeses asked the economist Alfredo Guerra Borges to reflect on his role in the first moments of Guatemala's Revolution against the dictator Jorge Ubico in 1944, Guerra Borges replied, "It wasn't a great conspiracy, and it wasn't a child's game. We were just a group of young men searching for our destiny."[1] The destiny to which Borges referred was both personal and part of a post–World War II democratic efflorescence that spanned the hemisphere. In Guatemala, the revolution in October 1944 inaugurated a ten-year period of democratic social reforms under two presidents: Juan José Arévalo (1945–1950), and Jacobo Arbenz (1950–1954). For the first time in Guatemalan history, the state enacted reforms designed to improve the social welfare of the population as a whole, such as the creation of the National Indigenous Institute, the Guatemalan Institute of Social Security, a modern Labor Code, and the agrarian reform, while balancing the imperatives of capitalist-oriented development. From where he sat in 1973, Guerra Borges emphasized Guatemala's famed "Ten Years of Spring" as a moment of personal and collective dignity. By then, the "destiny" Guerra Borges and his comrades had sought was all but dashed with the revolution's untimely end at the hands of a CIA-supported military coup in June 1954. Across the 1960s, unpredictable events—a series of military presidents, the betrayal of some of Guerra Borges's former comrades who joined the anticommunist repressive apparatus, and his own personal reckoning with the revolution's failures—had left their imprint upon the social memory of the revolution. Destiny, in this sense, did not simply describe the feeling that they were historical actors charting an unknown future in October 1944. It was also personal and collective code for the inescapable shadow of the revolution.

Guatemala's bloody participation in Latin America's Cold War, and particularly the 1954 military coup, cast a shadow that colored popular memory and scholarship of the revolution. In these pages, the contributors demonstrate how the period we think of as Guatemala's "Ten Years of Spring" resulted from competing memories, national and global histories, and political aspirations of different social and ethnic classes, not just across the 1940s and 1950s, but also in Guatemala's tumultuous post-1954 history. While the revolution ended as a state project in 1954, it lived on in Guatemalans' desires and fears, and it shaped their ideas of what was possible in their country. Most recently, the revolution appeared as a key frame of reference in the mass protests and national strike that led to the resignation of president Otto Pérez Molina in 2015. Protestors took to Twitter and other social media platforms, where they posted merged photographs of Guatemala City's central plaza filled with citizens in October 1944 and August 2015 to create a pastiche of possibility.

The purpose of this volume is to move scholarship out from the counterrevolution's enduring shadow by bringing to light the many revolutions that existed in the past and how they are mobilized in the present. To highlight the diversity of Guatemalan experiences during the revolution, the following chapters introduce new regions, frameworks, and actors that challenge the dominant historical narrative of the revolution. What has been understood largely in terms of diplomatic confrontation, military and intelligence intervention, or struggles over land during the agrarian reform becomes a much more nuanced history of many revolutions in many places with contradictory aims. The chapters collected here move beyond the 1954 coup as the determining event of the revolution and turn our attention toward the revolutionary governments' internal political, cultural, social, racial, and geographic dynamics. While we argue that *many revolutions took place in Guatemala*, we also underscore the importance of these contradictory memories in the present.

Writing the history of Guatemala's revolution has long been deeply intertwined with accounting for shifting memories and meanings of the revolution, the political history of post-1954 Guatemala, and Latin America's Cold War. Guerra Borges's interview with Gleijeses itself bears the imprint of two and half decades of political hopes, fears, and betrayals. Just the year before the interview, commanders of the Ejército Guerrillero de los Pobres (Guerrilla Army of the Poor; EGP) returned to Guatemala to launch a new armed revolutionary strategy that shifted the focus of recruitment from ladinos in the capital and eastern Guatemala to the Maya western highlands, and from an emphasis on class to an analysis of racism and colonialism. In response, the armed revolution was met by fierce counterinsurgency forces. Gleijeses's resulting book, *Shattered Hope*, reflected the weight of the memory of the 1944–1954 revolution, as well as the historical conjuncture in which it was researched and written: the rebirth of the armed revolution and the military's genocidal response. Unlike previous histories of the revolution, *Shattered Hope* excavated what Gleijeses called "the Guatemalan side of the story," and found that the US government's willingness to intervene in order to protect its "backyard" provided "no convenient villain . . . but rather a complex interplay of imperial hubris, security concerns, and economic interests."[2] This complex interplay resonated strongly for the Guatemalan Left in the early 1970s.

Without a doubt, Guatemala's revolutionary decade was a defining moment in the Latin American Cold War. Led by a coalition of largely urban reformers—students, teachers, middle-class professionals, and young military officers—Guatemala's October 20, 1944, revolution had its global and regional roots in the ideological struggles of the Spanish Civil War (1936–1939) as well as in the democratic efflorescence and global antifascism of World War II.[3] The coalition first forced the resignation of Guatemala's Napoleon Bonaparte–loving dictator, Jorge Ubico, in June 1944, and then that of his would-be successor, Juan Federico Ponce Vaides, in October, as it sought to end more than a decade of dictatorship and political repression. While the rebels' cause was furthered by Ubico's own pro-Franco propaganda, they advanced by aligning themselves to antifascism more generally, as Kirsten Weld has argued. "Being the ideological light of humanity's war against international fascism (that reached even Jorge Ubico and Federico Ponce Vaides)," one student activist declared, "it was the Atlantic Charter that guided the revolutionaries in Guatemala in the decisive battle against dictators."[4] In seeking to build a revolutionary Guatemala after deposing Ubico and Ponce Vaides, young student leaders along with an older generation of intellectuals charted a new course for the nation, which they outlined in the 1945 Constitution. Notably, the revolutionaries looked to the Spanish Republic and its efforts to break with the Catholic Church and the landowning class for inspiration.[5] While most agreed on the need for education, labor, and land reform, few agreed on how far those reforms should go.[6] The first president, Juan José Arévalo (1945–1950), a self-proclaimed spiritual socialist, believed more in gradual educational and moral reforms than in material redistribution.[7] The government implemented modest reforms, including the creation of the

National Indigenous Institute, the Instituto Guatemalteco de Seguridad Social (Guatemalan Institute of Social Security; IGSS), and a modern 1947 Labor Code. Above all else, Arévalo sought to implement moderate reforms while quelling escalating expectations among peasants and laborers for workers' rights and land reform. Long before the passage of Guatemala's agrarian reform law in 1952, laborers on nationalized plantations went on strike and demanded the redistribution of the former German properties among workers and peasants.[8]

In 1950, Juan José Arévalo was elected on a platform of agrarian reform and passed Decree 900, Guatemala's agrarian reform law on June 17, 1952. While this moderate agrarian reform allowed only for the expropriation of unused land and offered indemnification, its radical nature empowered rural peasants to direct the reform process through Local Agrarian Committees.[9] Many believed that the reform was necessary to transform Guatemala into a capitalist country. In his 1953 address to congress, Arbenz declared, "The Agrarian Reform Law begins the economic transformation of Guatemala; it is the most precious fruit of the revolution and the fundamental base of the destiny of the nation as a new country."[10] Others involved, including the United Fruit Company (UFCO), denounced the reform and Arbenz's revolutionary government as communist. Their fears were not altogether fabricated. Guatemala's homegrown communist party, the Partido Guatemalteco de Trabajadores (Guatemalan Workers Party; PGT), established in 1949, rapidly gained adherents among peasants and workers. Moreover, the revolutionaries' challenge to the Catholic Church and diplomatic recognition of the Spanish Republicans had proved decisive by sparking early opposition to the regime that found expression under the new Movimiento de Liberación Nacional (National Liberation Movement; MLN) Party.[11] Tensions over communist influence mounted within the nation until a group of disaffected military officers affiliated with the MLN received support from the United States to mount a military coup. The Liberation Army entered Guatemala from El Salvador and Honduras on June 17, 1954, and the next day bombed the capital from bases in Nicaragua. Without the support of the middle class and top military officers, on June 27, 1954, Jacobo Arbenz resigned. U.S. military support for the overthrow of a democratically elected president demonstrated that the "Good Neighbor" policy of nonintervention, launched by Franklin Roosevelt in 1933 and extended under Harry Truman, had definitively come to an end. However, the significance of the revolutionary decade and its conclusion cannot be fully understood without addressing what happened next.

A new era of U.S. Cold War interventionism was on the horizon. This was certainly one of the lessons that Fidel Castro's 26th of July Movement adopted in 1959, and it worked to fuel U.S. operatives' desire to purge Cuba of antirevolutionary forces during the first years of the Cuban Revolution. Likewise, the apparent failure of Guatemala's revolution helped to convince many Latin American leftists that a democratic road to revolutionary change was impossible, contributing to the growing appeal of the armed option in dialogue with the Cuban Revolution.

By the early 1960s, hopes of reform and what the PGT called "democratic restoration" were largely dashed. In April 1961, the PGT included the armed option as one of its tactics. About six months earlier, a group of young junior military officers had launched a failed revolt against Miguel Ydígoras Fuentes, a president they accused of corruption and usurping power. That Ydígoras Fuentes had offered support to the U.S. military in its Bay of Pigs invasion of Cuba was the final straw. Fleeing into the hills, the group re-formed and established Guatemala's first guerrilla group, the Movimiento Revolucionario 13 Noviembre (13th of November Revolutionary Movement; MR-13). The following year, the group merged with others who represented urban intellectuals, workers, and students to form the Fuerzas Armadas Rebeldes (Rebel Armed Forces; FAR). The U.S.-trained counterinsurgency gained force after the failure of Julio César Méndez Montenegro's Third Government of the Revolution (1966–1970). The hypocrisy of and disillusion with Méndez Montenegro's presidency only served to further divide citizens. Disagreements about strategy and tactics divided the Left, and failures to overcome regional and ethnic differences further impaired the guerrillas' struggle, while increasing cravenness on the part of the Right made such divisions increasingly deadly. For the next several years, in close consultation with the United States, the Guatemalan government, army, and National Police reorganized to more efficiently combat the insurgent threat, which had remained, to this point, largely urban and nonindigenous.

By the 1970s, the armed revolutionaries regrouped under new strategies that sought to be more inclusive of indigenous leaders and their communities. These strategies were enacted by the Ejército Guerrillero de los Pobres (Guerrilla Army of the Poor; EGP) and by the Organización Revolucionaria del Pueblo en Armas (Revolutionary Organization of People in

Arms; ORPA). As the decade drew to a close, and faced with the success of the Sandinistas in Nicaragua in 1979, the reactionary forces of the military and police became ever more brutal, carrying out spectacularly violent actions. Guatemalan soldiers opened fire on a crowd of peacefully protesting Q'eqchi' peasants, killing at least 140 and wounding 300 people. In January 1980, Guatemalan security forces set fire to the Spanish Embassy, where a group of K'iche' peasants and their allies were protesting the assassinations and disappearances of friends and family members in the department of El Quiché. Thirty-seven people died in the attack. These massacres foreshadowed an even more vicious violence to come. The Guatemalan government and military's counterinsurgent focus turned from the city to the countryside with a vengeance. Military and paramilitary forces ruthlessly targeted indigenous communities, committing atrocious massacres at places such as Río Negro, Dos Erres, and Plan de Sánchez, all in 1982.

In response to rural violence, the population of Guatemala City exploded far beyond its infrastructural limits. War refugees, including people escaping the economic disruption of the war, fled to the city center and the ravines around its borders to the north and west. Still others fled across the Mexican border. The guerrillas once again reorganized, this time under the umbrella organization Unidad Revolucionaria Nacional Guatemalteca (Guatemalan National Revolutionary Unit; URNG), which wrestled with the ongoing question of armed revolution. This was a period of "war by other means," which saw political struggles over the meaning of violence, and the rise of what Diane M. Nelson and Carlota McAllister have called "the discourses that attempt to account for [violence's] reasons and with forms of memorialization (and temporal lag) that themselves do violence."[12] War by other means drew on military, political, economic, spiritual, and social weapons, including memory of the 1944–1954 Revolution and its projects.

By the mid-1980s, a bipolar Cold War gave way to a complicated web of Third World loyalties and Soviet collapse. Around this time, the gradual foreclosure of peaceful opposition invigorated the power of mourning and human rights. Groups such as Grupo Apoyo Mutuo (Mutual Support Group; GAM) formed to support family members of people illegally detained and forcibly disappeared during the war. Student, worker, and campesino groups also oriented their protests toward the international politics of human rights. In 1985, military president General Oscar Mejía Victores permitted a Constituent Assembly to begin drafting a new constitution. The following year, presidential elections brought only the second civilian president in more than three decades to power. As president, Vinicio Cerezo continued the modest work of his predecessor. On December 29, 1996, representatives of the government and the guerrilla forces signed the final Accord for Firm and Lasting Peace, bringing the Guatemalan Civil War to an end more than thirty-six years after it started with the rebellion of military officers against Ydígoras Fuentes. Before long, the Historical Clarification Commission and the Oficina de Derechos Humanos del Arzobispado de Guatemala (Office of Human Rights of the Archbishopric of Guatemala; ODHAG) conducted interviews and research to ascertain the sources and dimensions of the war's violence. Estimates of the number of deaths and harrowing descriptions of organized surveillance, detention, torture, sexual violence, and assassination entered public discourse. So, too, did dissatisfaction with those estimates and accounts. One particularly vocal group was H.I.J.O.S. (Daughters/Sons for Identity and Justice against Forgetting and Silence), which was formed in Guatemala in 1999 by Wendy Santizo Méndez and several dozen other young people whose parents had been killed or disappeared. For the last two decades, H.I.J.O.S. has insisted: "Ni olvido, ni perdón [Neither forgetting, nor forgiveness]." In anticipation of the 2015 general elections, H.I.J.O.S. has also taken up images from the revolutionary decade as emblems of the nation's potential, promoting figures such as Jacobo Arbenz, Alaíde Foppa, Alfonso Bauer Paiz, and Rafael Piedrasanta in an imaginary slate of candidates for the presidency, vice presidency, and ministerial posts. These "campaign ads" assert, "La revolución florece [The revolution flourishes]." H.I.J.O.S. insists that struggles for a more just world, embodied in Guatemala's revolution, can never end.[13]

In Guatemala, the revolution signifies one of very few moments of democratic and social reform, in which the state took an active interest in bettering the lives of the majority of its citizens. As such, the revolution and its aftermath are central to popular memory and demands for social and historical justice. One need look no further than the 2015 mass protests against corruption that reached all the way to the president to see the power of these claims. During these protests and a national strike, Guatemalans drew on the rhetoric and even historical figures of the revolution in order to call for the resignation of then-president Otto Pérez Molina. The contest over the meaning of the past revolution has itself largely been about the present and future. The common Latin prefix "post-" denotes time, order, and rupture: afterward, after, or subsequently. In general usage, "peace" connotes "freedom from civil unrest or disorder; public order and security," "freedom from quarrels or dissension between individuals . . . a state of friendliness, amity, concord," "freedom from, absence of, or cessation of war or hostilities; the condition or state of a nation or community in which it is not at war with another."[14] Together, then, "post-" and "peace" signify a moment of rupture with a state of public order and security, after a cessation of hostilities, subsequent to a state of concord, and, in general, the end of freedom from insecurities. Thus the post-peace period began in the early 2000s, when drug trafficking and gangs, alongside repression of protests against mining and hydroelectric ventures, marked a new era of political violence. Shaped by this broader historical context, the scholarly literature about the revolution has been overdetermined by its untimely end. Owing to its tremendous importance, the history of the revolution—its meaning, virtues, flaws, and legacies—has been an endless source of debate. It is from this critical juncture that the scholars included in this volume write.

Under the Shadow of the Cold War

By now, this much should be clear: the dramatic nature of the CIA-supported military coup on June 24, 1954, and the equally dramatic descent into armed insurgency and counterinsurgency radically shaped subsequent interpretations of Guatemala's ill-fated democratic revolution.[15] In fact, we argue that it has done so to the detriment of our understanding of the revolutionary decade. After all, the teachers, farmers, doctors, politicians, students, and community members who brought the promises—and failures—of the revolution to fruition could not know how their efforts would end. Even more, while historical memory of the revolution may be inextricable from the shadow of the Cold War, examining the generative legacies of revolutionary projects (Nelson [chapter 9], Andersson [chapter 3], and Konefal [chapter 10]) will help scholars to understand why the revolution itself remains so powerful. Only now, in the post-peace era, has this become possible.

In this volume, we excavate some of the forgotten revolutions that have been overshadowed by the military coup and the Cold War while also attending to the revolution's enduring legacies and potency in the ever-shifting present. In the immediate aftermath of the revolution, members of the deposed revolutionary government and US-state agents sought to shape interpretations and justify their actions. Since the revolution's abrupt conclusion, three overlapping strands have emerged. The first strand, "foreign intervention," gave primacy to US involvement in the military coup and emerged among both proponents of the overthrow and its detractors. The second strand, "internal barriers to change," emerged among the

Left and blamed the revolution's untimely end on a questionable alliance between the radical Left and the bourgeois army and politicians. These interpretations were principally concerned with explaining, and even sometimes justifying (in the case of the "foreign intervention strand"), the 1954 coup. From the outset, then, the first two strands of revolutionary historiography were locked into an ongoing dialogue with both the overthrow of Arbenz and competing social memories about the revolution and the nation's political future. Clearly, both strands were deeply imbricated in the ideological battles of the Cold War, as Guatemala itself continued to be a major flashpoint for Latin American's Cold War. In varying forms, these two strands dominated scholarship until well after the signing of the Peace Accords in 1996. With the Truth and Reconciliation Commission's recognition of genocide and the emergence of the Pan-Maya movement, another "fragmented nation" strand of scholarship took shape among scholars who approached the revolution from the perspective of indigenous histories, the problem of racism, and regional differences. Influenced by social and cultural histories from below, this third, "fragmented nation" strand looked toward the ladino eastern region and the coasts, Mayas and others, including Afro-Guatemalans and Maya-Germans.

This volume proposes a new, fourth strand of scholarship that builds on these insights from the perspective of twenty-first-century post-peace Guatemala. In 2015, revelations of a corruption ring reaching the highest levels of government resulted in mass demonstrations and ultimately the resignation of President Otto Pérez Molina and Vice-President Roxana Baldetti. In the midst of these protests, demonstrators creatively invoked images and figures from the revolutionary decade. Newspaper editorialists narrated seventy-one years of uninterrupted revolutionary struggle beginning in 1944, protestors tweeted images merging the events of 2015 and 1944, and activists carried banners evoking the names of past revolutionary leaders. Unfortunately, the hopes and aspirations of a good number of Guatemalans were promptly dashed as the nation's first round of elections proceeded on schedule without what many considered to be viable candidates. The disjunction between the events of 1944 and the present was a source of frustration and sparked new forms of protest: absenteeism and spoiled ballots reached record levels. On social media, highly circulated images of the *voto nulo* (null vote) became a form of protest. These protests served as confirmation that Guatemala was in the era of post-peace.

The chapters in this volume accentuate the shifting memory and meaning of Guatemala's "Ten Years of Spring" in the present and the past.

Because of the momentous stakes of the revolution, the revolution itself lacks a fixed beginning and ending as different actors took up its promises and pitfalls as they searched for their own destiny. These chapters illustrate the many different revolutions and how each of these competing revolutions was shaped by distinct historical genealogies, significances, and legacies. Before outlining the chapters contained in this volume, however, it is useful to excavate in greater detail the three preceding strands, which we have called foreign intervention, internal barriers to change, and fragmented nation.

Historiographical debates about the revolution began at the very moment at which Guatemala's Ten Years of Spring came to a fateful end. The very same day that Jacobo Arbenz read his resignation speech, Juan José Arévalo, the first president of the revolution, published *Guatemala, democracia y el imperio,* a trenchant critique of the US intervention.[16] In many respects, this work launched what we have called the foreign intervention strand above. In his furious attack on the United States, Arévalo argued that the "Liberation" movement that ousted Arbenz had been organized by the CIA and that it was financed by the UFCO. The motive, Arévalo claimed, was not to destroy communism, but rather to nullify the Labor Code of 1947 and halt the expropriation of uncultivated lands held by the UFCO.[17] "Our crime," Arbenz explained in his resignation speech, "is having enacted an agrarian reform which affected the interests of the United Fruit Company."[18] In Guatemala, such interpretations rang true, and demonstrations led by students, labor organizations, and nationalists castigated the Eisenhower administration for coming to the defense of United Fruit.[19] One US-based proponent of Arbenz's overthrow, Daniel James, also published a response entitled *Red Design for the Americas: Guatemalan Prelude* within months of the overthrow.[20] In this vitriolic work, James justified the intervention by charging that the Arbenz government was utterly controlled by communists, from the political parties to Congress, the agrarian reform office to government information agencies. Like much foreign diplomacy scholarship of this hyperparanoid period, James's *Red Design* mistakenly equated nationalism and communism. As one reviewer wryly noted, James "paints the Communists as almost superhuman and diabolically clever persons, who never make mistakes and who are always successful."[21] As the subtitle to *Red Design* suggested, the book argued that the whole region was on the cusp of turning to communism. Debates about the relative influence of communism, the UFCO, and the role of the US government continued to dominate the literature until the early 2000s.[22]

In contrast to foreign-relations scholars who focused largely on diplomacy, the second strand launched a major critique of the revolution from within. The PGT launched this strand with a critique of the revolution as a largely elite-driven, or bourgeois, effort to *reform* rather than *transform* the nation. In June 1955, the PGT published *La intervención norte-americana y el derrocamiento del régimen democrático*. The PGT listed the United States, the "feudal landlords," foreign monopolies, and the army as the backbone of the reactionary forces that overthrew Arbenz's constitutional government. From this assessment, the PGT blamed the overthrow of Arbenz on a fatal error: the willingness of the Left to cooperate with the bourgeoisie and its failure to fully trust the working class. The new military regime banned the PGT, forcing many of its leaders into exile in Mexico. This interpretation, like the foreign intervention strand, subsequently shaped a new generation of scholarship that emerged alongside a broader rethinking on the Left.

In response to the political disappointments over the course of the 1960s, a new "revisionist" Left paradigm emerged in the 1970s that reexamined the debates between and within the "foreign intervention" and "internal barriers" strands but remained heavily focused on explaining the causes of the coup. Influenced by the broader field of Cold War scholarship, these scholars viewed inexorable US economic drives as mostly responsible for the character of the Cold War, drawing on revisionist diplomatic historian William Appleman Williams's observation that the United States generally opposed democracy in the so-called Third World.[23] Clearly, US actions were driven not by ideological commitments to "an empire of liberty" but by economic interests. The United States thus intervened in countless ways within Latin America to protect trade, markets, and North American business interests, like the UFCO. Dependency theory, in vogue across the region, also furthered this view, and the case of Guatemala worked well to exemplify its claims. José Aybar de Soto, in his *Dependency and Intervention*, explained: "The UFCO propaganda campaign in combination with such factors as the prevalent ideological climate in the United States and the close linkages with governmental decision makers, among others, led to a positive assertion of core interests that for all practical purposes constituted a defense of UFCO interests in Guatemala."[24] These revisionist arguments peaked in 1982 as the Guatemalan military launched its scorched-earth campaign, with the publication of *Bitter Fruit*, a journalistic account of how UFCO officials conspired with the Eisenhower administration to topple Arbenz.[25] By the late 1980s, then, scholars largely agreed that the Arbenz regime had not constituted a Soviet threat to the United States and that

US officials removed Arbenz either because they confused communism and nationalism or because they were acting in the interests of the UFCO.[26] Even as this scholarship reached a wider audience with *Bitter Fruit*, Guatemala's descent into a genocidal, scorched-earth campaign set the stage for new historical interpretations of the revolution.

While dependency theory and New Left revisionism gained force, Guatemalan historians intimately tied to the armed revolution also reassessed the revolutionary period. They returned to the original line of questioning opened by the PGT: Was the historic downfall of the revolution the result of an alliance with the bourgeoisie? These scholars, also in the midst of debates among the armed Left about colonialism in Marxist thought, largely agreed: the alliance with the bourgeoisie was a cause of the failure and resulted in a futile revolution. Exemplifying this thinking was Severo Martínez Peláez's classic interpretation of colonial Guatemala, *La patria del criollo*, which was originally conceived when the author was in exile in the late 1950s in Mexico. It held that the abolition of forced labor was "perhaps the only fundamental" result of the "ten years of faint-hearted revolution between 1944 and 1954." Martínez Peláez, who emphasized the primacy of class exploitation over racism, saw the Guatemalan Revolution as a moment of lost possibility in a history of creole domination and the colonial origins and survivals of inequality.[27] Carlos Guzmán Böckler and Jean-Loup Herbert disagreed with Martínez Peláez on the primacy of class over race, but they largely agreed with the exiled leftist on the failure of the revolutionary governments to overturn the colonial order. In *Guatemala: Una interpretación histórico-social*, Guzmán Böckler and Herbert conceived of 1524–1969 as a *período ÚNICO*—in capital letters—a single epoch defined by an unchanging system of colonial dominance. In Böckler and Herbert's view, the Ten Years of Spring was not a revolution, but a political movement dominated by Guatemala's "petit urban bourgeoisie" who advanced a "timid agrarian reform" that was ultimately crushed by that same class's own "vacillations and contradictions." When it failed to fight the 1954 invasion, the *burguesía de servidumbre* (servile bourgeoisie) proved its own lack of revolutionary spirit and subservience to colonial—and neocolonial—powerbrokers. Thus, Guzmán Böckler and Herbert concluded, Guatemala's bourgeoisie "remained within the *marco* (rubric) of the colonial system."[28] This concern with explaining the military coup, which had dominated foreign diplomacy and internal barriers strands since the revolution's end, often came at the expense of a deeper understanding of the revolution itself.

One contemporary work within the internal barriers strand, Richard Newbold Adams's *Crucifixion by Power* (1970), began to challenge this singular focus. Adams and other contributors to the volume argued that the revolution, preeminently nationalistic in character, introduced lasting social reforms and spurred grassroots political participation in ways never seen before. While the revolution's overthrow by the United States in 1954 ensured the continued "crucifixion" of Guatemala's popular sectors, Adams held that "the contemporary situation [of the late 1960s] in Guatemala is in great part due to changes that were actually accomplished during the revolution."[29] The argument that the legacy of the revolution could be seen in grassroots political participation, particularly in Mayan and peasant mobilization, and the promise of a democracy yet to come would later be taken up by scholars and citizens alike who sought to reimagine Guatemala's post-peace future.

Meanwhile, diplomatic historians of the foreign intervention strand were increasingly interested in a more complex understanding of the Cold War that took seriously foreign diplomats' concerns about communist infiltration, decentered US economic motivations, and recuperated the political agency and ideology of non-US actors. Many adopted the work of John Gaddis, who trumpeted a new synthesis in Cold War studies.[30] Gaddis recognized the structural patterns of the world economy, as dependency theorists had, but he also stressed the new political dynamics of the postwar international system and domestic pressure within the United States. Obsessed with attending to global power imbalances, and constrained by domestic partisan and bureaucratic politics, US diplomats, the new scholarship argued, sought to contain the communist bloc rather than to achieve economic hegemony.

In conversation with these scholars, a new generation of revisionist scholars addressed Guatemala's revolution as one of the seminal events of Latin America's Cold War. Piero Gleijeses's *Shattered Hope*, with which we started this introduction, focused anew on US diplomatic perception of the communist threat in Guatemala. His interviews with Arbenz's widow and high-ranking officials of the PGT showed that Arbenz sympathized with the communist view but was not controlled by communists; he also viewed the UFCO as a subsidiary problem. In direct contrast to *Bitter Fruit*, Gleijeses concurred with José Manuel Fortuny, a former leader of the PGT, when he summed up the insignificance of the UFCO on US intervention in Guatemala: "They would have overthrown us even if we had grown no bananas."[31] Rather, the real fear for US officials was that the agrarian reform would promote the organization of peasants in support of the administration and afford communists the opportunity to organize peasants as they had organized workers. Indeed, the PGT itself had also believed that organizing the agrarian reform through local committees would be the basis for a deeper radicalization. By fostering agrarian reform from below, the PGT believed they could sow the seeds of a collective society. Unlike scholars who sought to reveal US responsibility for the 1954 coup and Guatemala's descent into civil war, other scholars, such as Robert Pastor, continued to ascribe democratic motives to Eisenhower even as the bloody counterinsurgency waged on. As a result, these scholars were accused of papering over the human tragedy wrought by the CIA-orchestrated 1954 coup in Guatemala.[32]

In contrast to the postrevisionist foreign intervention strands of Gleijeses, other historians attempted to decenter foreign diplomacy and refocus on internal pressures and dynamics that led the middle class and military officers to abandon the revolution. This move was inspired, in part, by recent events, including the early 1980s' genocidal scorched-earth campaigns and a seemingly intractable state of war into the 1990s, but also the rise of the new identity-based Pan-Maya movement and the end of the Cold War. This new generation of scholars rightly focused on the 1952 agrarian reform as the historic moment that unraveled the revolution. Among this group, works by Jim Handy, Diane M. Nelson, Aura Marina Arriola, and Cindy Forster built on the insights of earlier studies of the internal barriers and foreign diplomacy strands while engaging in contemporary debates over the meaning of democracy, addressing gender, social class, and ethnicity.[33] Published in 1994, Jim Handy's pathbreaking *Revolution in the Countryside* was exemplary of this trend.[34] Unlike the PGT and the Left's earlier critiques, however, Handy emphasized the agency of rural peasants, who took up and pressed for reform from below. As they pushed the revolution to new heights, these peasants generated conflict as well as deep racist fears among military officers and the middle class, who began plotting against Arbenz. Unlike diplomatic historians, Handy followed the internal barriers strand to argue the revolution was doomed regardless of CIA support. Culpability for the coup and Guatemala's descent into civil war resided not in malevolent US imperialism, but in Guatemala's own divided and racist society. The US foreign relations scholar John Gaddis took Handy's argument even further when he wrote that the 1954 military coup was "a massive overreaction" at a moment fraught with anticommunist hysteria. By and large, he wrote off the episode as a response to "a minor irritant," one that "did little to alter the course of events inside Guatemala," whereas Arbenz's "quixotic" regime "had made so many enemies . . . that it probably would not have lasted in any event."[35] This position once more placed the blame for Guatemala's post-1954 descent into political violence on internal divisions among Guatemalans. The implications of the internal barriers argument troubled Guatemalans. When the Asociación de Amigos del País (Association of Friends of the Nation) commissioned a new general history of Guatemala during the peace process, *Revolution in the Countryside* was notably absent from the review of literature on the subject.[36]

As the Cold War drew to a close and Guatemala embarked on post–Peace Accord reforms, the revolution seemed little more than a hastily concluded, decade-long experiment. Since the late 1990s, Guatemala—and indeed, much of the region—has confronted neoliberalism, security, corruption, and dashed hopes for peace. These growing concerns make the need for deep change even more urgent, even as most Guatemalans do not desire a return to armed conflict. This new period has also been defined by deeper efforts to reckon with the past, in line with the proliferation of memory and human rights literature. This scholarship and its popular groundswell forced public recognition from the United States. In 1999, President Bill Clinton embarked on a four-day tour of Guatemala, culminating in an apology. In step, Clinton affirmed, "We are determined to remember the past, but never repeat it."[37] The publication of Nick Cullather's *Secret History*, which made hundreds of redacted pages of internal reports of the CIA in the years before the 1954 coup available to readers, illustrated scholars' desire to participate in the recuperation of memory of the revolution and its historic legacies.[38] The efforts of researchers for the Comisión para Esclarecimiento Histórico (Historical Clarification Commission; CEH) to uncover and account for human rights abuses during the civil war also revealed how memories of political action in local agrarian committees and the PGT during the revolution inspired later political action, action that shaped the logics and geographies of armed organizations during the civil war. Similarly, the human rights worker Daniel Wilkinson published a riveting popular history of the revolution that uncovered enduring silences about the agrarian reform and spoke to the intimate historical ties between that reform and political violence in the western highlands.[39] These political genealogies were also central to Grandin's *The Last Colonial Massacre*.[40]

As has always been the case in thinking about the revolution, contemporary political factors dialogued with the scholarly community's preoccupations and thus generated new insights into the revolutionary decade.

Within Guatemala, the past decade has witnessed vociferous debates about the meaning and legacy of the revolution among historians, as well as a proliferation of commemorations of the period's heroic actors (Handy [foreword] and Taracena Arriola [chapter 5]).[41] In this sense, the revolution remains an unfinished project that continues to inspire hope and dread, aspirations and deep fears. As new social actors on the Right and the Left emerge, memory of the revolution has once again become bifurcated: some, such as H.I.J.O.S. and the six-term Guatemala City mayor and president Alvaro Arzú, celebrated its democratic promise; others, such as the Comité Coordinador de Asociaciones Agrícolas, Comerciales, Industriales y Financieras (Coordinating Committee of Agricultural, Commercial, Industrial, and Financial Associations; CACIF) and, in a different moment, Arzú again, emphasized the consequences of its failures (Konefal [chapter 10]). As the organizers of a 2004 commemoration of Juan José Arévalo, noted: "Arévalo's trajectory demonstrates that another nation not only is desirable—but rather in some way or other—it is also possible."[42] This time, the decentering of the national frame through an emphasis on "the local" and "transnational" led scholars beyond the coup to once more seek to understand the meaning of the revolution itself, revisiting the question of internal versus external factors (Adams and Giraudo [chapter 7]).[43]

More recently, historians have revisited the question of communist influence by breaking down old divisions between diplomatic and social history, as well as internal versus external factors. As Gilbert M. Joseph has argued, this new wave of historians argued that what gave the Cold War its ideological force was "the politicization and internationalization of everyday life."[44] As such, foreign relations scholars who had wanted to assess the Guatemala's Ten Years of Spring not only gave primacy to the 1954 coup, but also assessed the revolution principally in terms of national interest, state policy, and the broad imperatives of the international economy rather than the lived experiences and political agency of marginalized peoples, particularly women and members of the poorer classes. More broadly, historians sought to move away from who was to blame in the Cold War and to understand from a decentered perspective what the Cold War meant for a variety of Latin American social actors. This more decentered moment has also spurred broader reflections on the memory and legacy of the 1954 military coup, while no longer attempting to assign blame.[45]

For other historians, the decentering of the Cold War has also allowed for an understanding of the multiple meanings and projects that comprised Guatemala's Ten Years of Spring. In this new wave of scholarship, scholars broke down old divisions between diplomatic and social histories and between the two strands that dominated Guatemalan historiography. In his sweeping history of the twentieth century, *The Last Colonial Massacre*, Greg Grandin was less preoccupied with what motivated the United States policymakers and more concerned with identifying what was being fought over in Latin America itself.[46] As such, Grandin drew upon the life histories of Maya activists to illustrate how this politicization and internationalization of everyday life shaped the course of twentieth-century Guatemalan history. This new scholarship was also reflective of a rethinking of indigenous communities, students, and the church in the wake of new understandings of the period of violence. Rather than treating communities as politically unified wholes, historians strived to understand the hierarchies and conflicts that constituted Maya communities and fissures within student and youth communities.[47] Taken together, these works moved away from the previous focus on the coup itself to look at continuities and excavate different genealogies, including antifascism, Guatemala's nationalization of German properties during World War II, and high modernism.[48]

As the chapters that follow make clear, revisiting the revolution offers crucial insights into populism (Sierakowski [chapter 1], Chassé [chapter 2], Andersson [chapter 3], Taracena Arriola [chapter 5], Konefal [chapter 10]), democracy (Chassé [chapter 2], Andersson [chapter 3], Carey [chapter 6], Nelson [chapter 9]), nationalism (Sierakowski [chapter 1], González Ponciano [chapter 5], Foss [chapter 8], Konefal [chapter 10]), and the transnational turn (González Ponciano [chapter 5], Adams and Giraudo [chapter 7], Foss [chapter 8], Nelson [chapter 9]). This volume moves beyond the coup as the determining event of the revolution. Likewise, it moves away from an overwhelming emphasis on diplomatic confrontation and military and intelligence intervention. Instead, it turns our attention toward examining what was being fought over, allowing different sets of actors to emerge, which permits us to understand the *many revolutions that took place in Guatemala*.

This more expansive focus, freed from the shadow of a bipolar Cold War, also permits us to place Guatemala's decade of social democracy within the transnational context of the "democratic spring" during and after World War II. As Kirsten Weld has stunningly detailed, Guatemala's revolutionaries and counterrevolutionaries were deeply inspired by the Spanish Civil War.[49] Likewise, due to German commercial and social power in Guatemala, a large number of people among the lower and middle classes were drawn to wartime democratic, antifascist discourse that was inflected by the Great Power conflicts.[50] Nationalist wartime propaganda, crafted in collaboration with Nelson Rockefeller's Office of the Coordinator of Inter-American Affairs, promoted democratic values and freedoms, often invoking strong, popular liberal traditions in Latin American politics and culture that referred back to the independence struggles that took place in the early nineteenth century and were cemented in 1920s. The revolution can be seen as a Guatemalan articulation of these postwar ideals. Inclusion and participation across social class in democratic processes—promoted by political actors as diverse as Mahatma Gandhi, Harry S. Truman, and Clement Atlee—found their articulation in the written and spoken addresses to the people offered by Arévalo and Arbenz. As Atlee nationalized public utilities and created the National Health Service, so did the creation of IGSS, the social security institute, in 1946 mark the first provision of social welfare by the state. In 1947, the Labor Code finally abolished nineteenth-century forced labor.

The revolution was also spurred by postwar economic growth and political mobilization across the region. In El Salvador, students, labor, and military officers successfully revolted against General Maximiliano Hernández Martínez, who had moved to extend his executive power and term in office. Costa Rica's brief 1948 civil war, too, was spurred by executive corruption. As in Guatemala, these wars also led to the revision of the constitution (though in El Salvador the reforms were short lived). Meanwhile, economic plans to promote growth through the diversification and modernization of agricultural production, based on the thinking of Raúl Prebisch and the United Nations Economic Commission for Latin America and the Caribbean (UNECLA), sought to strengthen Guatemala's connections to the world market. Of course, these are just some of the ways that revisiting Guatemala's revolution can illuminate issues of interest far beyond national, even regional, borders. In much of Latin America, the postwar democratic spring had played out during 1946 and 1947, and concluded by 1948.[51] But in Guatemala, it was just entering its most radical phrase with the passage of the Labor Code (1947) and the Agrarian Reform (1952). This raises the question not of why the revolution came to an end in 1954, but rather of why it endured so long.

As Guatemala and we, its students, emerge from the shadow of the Cold War, we are free to look with fresh eyes upon the *dates that disrupt* these long-held chronologies, assumptions, and preoccupations that guided an emphasis on a bipolar Cold War and the predominance of the 1954 military coup. They can be viewed as windows into alternative historical genealogies that are suggestive of a multiplicity of interpretations, meanings, and legacies of Guatemala's "revolutionary spring." Like the contributors' efforts to reveal the multiple revolutions that took place between 1944 and 1954, the following dates that disrupt are intended to be read from different angles and perspectives to reveal multiple different interpretations of the past. They have been chosen because the authors feel they are also "time knots": that is, historical moments that densely weave together the material and ideological remains of the past that endure and imprint upon the present.[52]

Dates That Disrupt

April 1920: On the eve of the ouster of Manuel Estrada Cabrera from his twenty-two-year reign of terror, over one hundred Q'eqchi' Mayas from Alta Verapaz wrote to the National Assembly requesting access to universal education; the end of compulsory military service, debt peonage, and forced labor; and the recognition of their rights as citizens of Guatemala.

March 1923: In the midst of the democratic opening surrounding the Unionista revolution, the Universidad Popular was inaugurated in Guatemala City. Designed by university students, including Miguel Angel Asturias, to provide night classes to the working class, it was closed by Ubico in 1932. In many ways, this university for the pueblo set a precedent for the autonomous university envisioned by students, faculty, and bureaucrats after 1945.

August 1944: General Juan Federico Ponce Vaides ordered the expropriation of large tracts of German-owned land and businesses. Through this maneuver he desperately sought to gain credibility and public support for his regime and an end to the groundswell of protest that ousted his predecessor, Jorge Ubico, from office. These expropriations would provide some of the experience and technical expertise that enabled the revolution's controversial Decree 900. More important, this nationalization mobilized rural peasants to demand the redistribution of German properties beginning as early as 1941. The basis of the 1952 land reform, the revolution's crowning achievement, lay in an autocrat's nationalist strike against foreign fascism.

December 1944: Guatemala's Legislative Assembly—guided by the revolutionary junta of Jacobo Arbenz, Francisco Arana, and Jorge Toriello—moved to terminate diplomatic relations with Franco's Spain in the name of the democracy. A month later, the junta terminated diplomatic relations with Spain.

March 1945: Standing before a crowd in the congressional chambers,

Arévalo addressed his citizens: "We are going to equip humanity with humanity. We are going to rid ourselves of guilt-ridden fear through unselfish ideas. We are going to add justice and happiness to order, because order does not serve us if it is based on injustice and humiliation." He continued, "We are going to revalorize, civically and legally, all of the men of the Republic. . . . Democracy means just order, constructive peace, internal discipline, [and] happy and productive work . . . a democratic government supposes and demands the dignity of everyone." The revolution abolished order "based on injustice and humiliation" and ushered in real democracy, which nevertheless required "internal discipline, [and] happy and productive work" and men who had been "revalorized." The revolution, in 1945, meant "[working] directly for a transformation of the spiritual, cultural, and economic life of the republic," a task laid out in the first-person plural *nosotros*. The speech vowed to teach civic values to all of those citizens who had lost or not yet acquired them. Reinforcing this reading, Arévalo added that Guatemalan democracy would become "a permanent, dynamic system of projections into society [by] tireless vigilance."[53] Individual self-improvement, supported by an active state, was Arévalo's "spiritual socialism."

December 1953: Anticommunists in exile published the "Plan de Tegucigalpa," a plan for government written by "a strong nucleus of men imbued with the feelings of Nation, Home, Religion, and Liberty, who [would] try to win for their *pueblo* the conquest of real democracy."[54] The plan was to be "government of the *pueblo*, by the *pueblo*, for the *pueblo*" and "attendant to the idiosyncrasies of Guatemala." In doing so, anticommunists sought not to distance themselves from the idea of social change, but to counter Arbenz's embrace of "foreign ideologies." Both Arbencista and anticommunist nationalisms were united by faith in the principles of liberalism, especially belief in equal liberty, the constitutional republic, political rights, and the responsibility of certain citizens to lead the nation.[55] Especially in its proposals for education, indigenous communities, land reform, and trade, the "Plan de Tegucigalpa" largely drew on or developed the core principles of the revolution. Primary education ought to be free and mandatory, and rural education centers would increase access to formal education for poor and indigenous communities; indigenous and ladino mestizaje was Guatemala's unique racial offering and would strengthen the pueblo; properties seized under the agrarian reform would be returned, but a "humanized" version of the modern trade system that included fixed minimum export prices, greater domestic investment in industrialized agriculture, and the provision of low-interest loans for campesinos would increase the number of private property holders and so encourage self-improvement. The echo of Arévalo's discourse upon assuming the presidency is clear. In so many respects, then, the democratic florescence of the revolutionary decade gave weight to anticommunist counterrevolutionaries' claims to democracy, sovereignty, and self-determination—ideas that were all but void during Ubico's reign.

June 25, 1956: On this day, Guatemalans awoke to headlines announcing a nationwide State of Alarm for thirty days. The State of Alarm limited public gatherings, expanded police purview, and instituted a travel curfew. For months, university students at the public Universidad de San Carlos had planned events in honor of the anniversary of Ubico's defeat. Counterrevolutionary leader Carlos Castillo Armas and his ministers and police force clamped down on the youths' activities in order to limit the commemorations. As the date approached, a secondary school student, a teacher, a *universitario*, or a professor would be arrested every few days. Police patrolled cafés, secondary schools, university buildings, and other places where students and intellectuals gathered downtown. The largest university student union, the Asociación de Estudiantes Universitarios (AEU), emphasized how the commemoration was simply a civic celebration: "The AEU could do no less than to honor the blood spilled in the name of freedom," since "the memories of an opprobrious dictatorship that cast out thought . . . [and] sincere and spontaneous, free and independent speech survive."[56] The AEU's brief statement reiterated the close ties between the pueblo and the university, reframing the revolution in terms of national unity. Strategically, it also located this solidarity in the past and in opposition to dictatorship. It upheld the notion that the universitario was the intellectual author of the revolution while the regular Guatemalan citizen provided the muscle and firepower. But by the end of the day, several students would be killed and dozens injured in a shootout downtown, just around the corner from the Presidential Palace. Despite claiming to further the democratic principles of the revolution, Castillo Armas's counterrevolutionary government proved that it was willing to shed blood to ensure the memory of the revolution was forgotten. Six years later, reacting to the student-led "Jornadas de Marzo y Abril," the government would reiterate its forcible forgetting.

March 1966: To the surprise of many, the civilian Julio César Méndez Montenegro won a bid as president under the Partido Revolucionario, essentially a revised version of Arévalo's Partido Acción Revolucionario (PAR). Branded as the "Third Government of the Revolution," Méndez Montenegro's lofty campaign rhetoric was undermined by one simple problem: in order to rule, he had to form a gentlemen's agreement with his opposing parties, Castillo Armas's Movimiento de Liberación Nacional (MLN) and the Partido Institucional Democrática (PID), another party that represented the interests of the military. While Méndez Montenegro held the title of president, in effect, he was limited to changes he could push forward with the military's support. However unintentionally, Méndez Montenegro did echo the military's crucial role in the overthrow of Ubico and its prominence during Arbenz's rule.

October 1974: On the occasion of the anniversary of the coup, a journalist for the national newspaper *El Imparcial* asked revolutionary minister of finance Jorge Toriello why the revolution had failed. Toriello replied that, to the contrary, the revolution was successful in that it had "charted the course for what was yet to come." He was referring to the numerous institutions—such as the modern national banking system, including the Bank of Guatemala and the Monetary Law; the IGSS; and many workers' and neighborhood cooperatives—that were rooted in the revolution. Contrary to the reporter's suggestion, Toriello (who had himself famously and publicly broken with Arévalo) highlighted the continuities of revolutionary and postcoup life.[57] Toriello was not alone in this. That same year, President Kjell Laugerud García had shocked and even appalled his colleagues in the far-Right MLN party by hosting fifteen hundred agrarian cooperativists for a lunch at the National Palace. Beyond supplying lunch, the Laugerud government provided money and equipment to cooperativists, part of his administration's ongoing efforts to modernize agricultural production and neutralize the appeal of the Left by promoting the military as an agent of social change. Notably, while it celebrated cooperatives, Laugerud's government also regularly arrested, assassinated, or disappeared leaders of leftist organizations. Even so, many of these leaders and organizations were among those celebrated by Toriello as holdovers from the revolutionary period. By the end of 1975, some ninety thousand Guatemalans had joined cooperatives.[58]

December 1985: Vinicio Cerezo, a civilian, was elected president by a wide margin in elections broadly believed to be free and fair. In January of the following year at Cerezo's swearing in, his predecessor, Brigadier General Oscar Mejía Victores, watched while the Christian Democrat decried the corruption and abuse carried out by a long line of military presidents. "We are a people who were thrown out of our house and today we are going home," he said. "A people who were denied expression, and many of us were persecuted for telling the truth."[59] Cerezo had survived several assassination attempts, but many other civilian political candidates (including Manuel Colom Argueta and Alberto Fuentes Mohr) were less lucky. Under Mejía Victores, Guatemala began a cautious and interrupted "return to democracy" and could hearken back to the early months of the revolution and the presidency of Laugerud when the military elite enjoyed a more prominent role. But it was with Cerezo's inauguration that, in his words, "we [Guatemalans] have recuperated our voices as citizens." This reclaiming referred to the period before the coup and, incidentally, the early years of his childhood. The coup occurred when he was twelve. He recalled, "I remember sitting in a tree watching the rebel planes fly over. . . . I thought to myself that this was going to mean very bad times for our family and for Guatemala. That was when I decided it was the right thing to dedicate myself to the cause of democracy." Perhaps subtly indicting Arbenz for too easily giving in to the counterrevolutionaries, Cerezo promised, "The only way they are going to get me out of the palace is to carry me out dead."[60]

December 1996: Former combatants of the URNG and representatives of the government signed the last of several peace agreements, finally ending the thirty-six-year-long Guatemalan Civil War. The revolution was not mentioned explicitly, but several agreements emphasize strengthening civil society and checking the power of the military. The Agreement on the Strengthening of Civilian Power and on the Role of the Armed Forces in a Democratic Society (September 1996) and Agreement on Constitutional Reforms and the Electoral Regime (December 1996) provided a plan for strengthening democratic institutions, achieving a balance of power between governmental branches, and restricting the power of the president, the military, and the police. By focusing on this strengthening of civil society and limiting human rights investigations and amnesties to the period of the "armed conflict," the agreements had the effect of turning back the clock to the official start of the war in 1960, if not the 1954 coup.

February 1997–February 1999: The CEH was a key piece of the Peace Accords, though it received its mandate from the 1994 Oslo Accords and so predated the 1996 agreements. The commission comprised three people, including two Guatemalans and a foreign leader to ensure impartiality. Its remit was to clarify the human rights violations and acts of violence committed in the thirty six year civil war. It would assemble a report that summarized all relevant factors in the war and make recommendations to support enduring peace, ultimately strengthening internal democratic processes. This final report was presented to the United Nations on February 25. The prominent role of the international body in navigating the difficult years following the end of the war set up a powerful counterargument for sectors who opposed the report. Some argued that the UN and, by extension, the CEH violated national sovereignty. This was a tragicomic second life for a key argument of democratic revolutionaries throughout Central America at midcentury. In 1944, revolutionaries opposed Ubico's willingness to sell Guatemala's natural resources to foreign interests above the best interest of Guatemalans. At the same time, the report offered an important moment of meaning making and historical memory, as researchers had to account for the origin of the civil war and its violence.

January 2012: Pepsi kicked off an ad campaign called "Guatemórfosis" to convince all Guatemalans that they are personal agents of change. Narrated by Ricardo Arjona, a Guatemala-born rock star who had catapulted to global fame over the past decade, and set to the backdrop of his song "Mi País," the Pepsi video informed young *chapines*, "Guatemala will change when you change." The whole campaign started from promoting a unifying social project of progress and change then devolved into a call for responsibility (and consuming Pepsi). It seemed, early in the second decade of the new millennium, that the memory of the social revolution had been relegated to the contests of the Cold War, *y ya*.

April–September 2015: Faced with the reality of a corrupted and dysfunctional state and ongoing human rights violations, a romantic view of Guatemala's revolutionary spring has been mobilized with mounting intensity. For months, many Guatemalans worked for a renewal of popular mobilization, and public intellectuals called for a new democratic revolution in the spirit of 1944. H.I.J.O.S., a youth group formed by family members of individuals disappeared by the government, played a prominent role in demonstrations and launched massive graffiti and poster campaigns. By contrast, the Comité Coordinador de Asociaciones Agrícolas, Comerciales, Industriales y Financieras (CACIF), representing Guatemala's most corrupt and entrenched oligarchy, dug in its heels and wielded formal and informal influence wherever possible. Perhaps at no other time had Guatemala's revolution been so vigorously debated, reimagined, deployed, and even deplored by so many Guatemalans.

June–August 2019: General elections saw more than two dozen parties propose presidential candidates. While some candidates were dismissed as ineligible, twenty-one candidates competed in the first round in June. At the same time, twenty-six parties proposed candidates for 106 legislative seats. For months, citizens lined up at locations throughout the major cities and in the countryside to ensure that their identification papers were in order. For the first time, citizens could effectively reject all of the proposed candidates using the *voto nulo*, the product of a 2016 electoral reform. If a majority of votes cast read voto nulo, the elections would be held with new candidates. The option reflected an incorporation of a key protest strategy from 2015 into the electoral process, but also tacitly acknowledged civil discord and dissensus. Voto nulo became the electoral form of post-peace as this book went to press.

Outline of the Chapters

Inspired by the groundswell of 2015, the contents of this book highlight the numerous tangible and intangible legacies of the revolution. Some are embedded in the structures of state, in plans for and visions of development, and in the economy. Others are reflected by the individuals-turned-symbols of famous revolutionaries whose lives and deaths loom large in the political imagination. In the neoliberal era and stripped of their idealistic, ideological underpinnings—dedication to social democracy, anti-imperialism and economic nationalism, the simple belief that "progress" was possible—and removed from the context of the modernist era of development and the geopolitics of the Cold War, these legacies articulate differently. Reflecting upon these changing legacies in popular memory, Jim Handy's foreword asked why the revolution reverberates so strongly in certain moments and proposes, by way of an answer, that "The Revolution" was in fact many revolutions.

Part 1, "New Regions," features three case studies situated in Guatemalan regions largely neglected by scholars: the Caribbean and Pacific coasts and the Petén. These case studies challenge the notion of a revolution based in a capital city, revealing instead how peripheral regions and their worker-citizens figured centrally into Arévalo's, then Arbenz's, revolutionary praxis. In "To Wrench our Rights from La Frutera: Race, Labor, and Redefining National Belonging on the Caribbean Coast," Ingrid Sierakowski reexamines the construction of ideas of racial, social, and political inclusion among workers on United Fruit Company plantations, foregrounding the Caribbean region as a space where new ideas of citizenship and national belonging were developed, then projected onto the national stage. In chapter 2, "The Coastal Laboratory: Milpa, Conservation, and Agrarian Reform," Patrick Chassé, in turn, locates the roots of the 1952 Agrarian Reform Law in a complex negotiation between modernization-minded government policymakers in Guatemala City and indigenous communities on the Pacific coast, who forced the state to experiment with a more holistic model of agricultural development that incorporated productivity, environmental health, and social well-being. Anthony Andersson picks up these themes in chapter 3, "Arévalo's Tomorrowland: The Revolutionary Crusade to Build and Defend the New Guatemala on the Petén Frontier," focusing on the Poptún colony in the forested Petén, where national politics and international science met racial anxieties about indigenous citizenship.

Part 2, "New Frames," reexamines three central, enduring revolutionary tropes: the so-called indigenous problem, youth support for revolution, and the revolutionary watershed. In chapter 4, "The 'Indigenous Problem,' Cold War US Anthropology, and Revolutionary Nationalism: New Approaches to Racial Thinking and Indigeneity in Guatemala," Jorge Ramón González Ponciano links the intellectual history of the revolutionary governments' indigenista programs, which sought to build a monocultural state, to ongoing class-race inequality. In chapter 5, "Youths and Juan José Arévalo's Democratic Government in Guatemala, 1945–1951," Arturo Taracena Arriola reexamines the narrative of friendly relations between Arévalo and the urban ladino youth sector. He traces the roots of the Partido Comunista de Guatemala (Guatemalan Communist Party; PCG) and Arévalo's growing anticommunism to three Arevalista youth organizations that ultimately turned against the president in search of a more radical revolution. In chapter 6, "Rethinking Representation and Periodization in Guatemala's Democratic Experiment," David Carey Jr., in turn, examines the limits of two bellwethers in the early revolution—the elimination of forced labor and the improvement of educational opportunities for indigenous people of Patzicía—arguing that the transition from dictatorial to democratic rule was a complex, protracted process that played out slowly and differently rather than being the watershed it has sometimes been portrayed to be.

Part 3, "New Actors," looks once more at how the revolutionary governments responded to the indigenous citizens they had come to view as a vital part of the national imaginary and of national progress, but from the perspective of outsider experts in medicine, public health, and ethnography. In chapter 7, "'A pack of cigarettes or some soap': 'Race,' Security, International Public Health, and Medical Experiments during Guatemala's October Revolution," Abigail E. Adams and Laura Giraudo trace the infrastructural and professional networks behind inter-American public health campaigns against onchocerciasis during Arévalo's administration. Adams and Giraudo demonstrate how these campaigns created US-Guatemalan international biomedical prestige for Guatemala and affirmed racial hygiene discourses, which directly and indirectly informed the handling of the now-infamous sexually transmitted disease (STD) experimentation on humans. In turn, in the analysis in chapter 8 of the Instituto Indigenista Nacional de Guatemala (National Indigenista Institute of Guatemala; IING), in "'Una obra revolucionaria': *Indigenismo* and the Guatemalan Revolution, 1944–1954," Sarah Foss assesses how ladino and indigenous institute ethnographers envisioned and enacted nation-building policies that dismissed biological understandings of race while reinforcing the state's enduring paternalism toward indigenous communities.

Finally, in part 4, "New Memories," Nelson (chapter 9) and Betsy Konefal (chapter 10) return us to the legacy of revolution for social and cultural struggles in the present. In chapter 9, "Water Power Promise: Revisiting Revolutionary DIY," Diane M. Nelson illustrates how one K'iche' community's quest for electricity in the 2010s reactivated community memories of prerevolutionary, revolutionary, and civil war struggles to survive, create, and live liberatory lives against state violence and capitalist accumulation by dispossession. In turn, in chapter 10, "Reclaiming a Revolution: Memory as Possibility in Urban Guatemala," Konefal examines how several generations of urban activists, armed revolutionaries, state officials, and politicians have used Día de la Revolución (Revolution Day) to shape social memory and express demands infused with historical import by laying claim to commemorative public spaces and historical events. These final chapters demonstrate how Guatemalan actors at the state and regional levels—in dialogue with transnational development institutions, NGOs, and civil society—have fulfilled many of the revolutionary leaders' dreams but in ways that those leaders would hardly recognize. In the final analysis, and in the absence of the felicitous achievement of what at heart were really the revolution's goals, it may be that the purest legacy of the revolution's spirit lives on not in infrastructure or politics, but in popular culture and memory.

Together, the chapters reframe our understanding of the Guatemalan Revolution by emphasizing new regions, new analytical frames, new historical actors, and new historical memories.

Ultimately, the chapters in this book bring together the work of a range of scholars to critically reflect upon approaches to the period and region. The authors include scholars working from new environmental and technological perspectives (Nelson [chapter 9], Chassé [chapter 2], and Andersson [chapter 3]), alongside those who address transnational networks (Taracena [chapter 5] and González Ponciano [chapter 4]), new approaches to medicine and public health (Adams and Giraudo [chapter 7] and Foss [chapter 8]) and the cultural politics of nationalism (Sierakowski [chapter 1] and González Ponciano [chapter 5]). Participants draw upon and combine a range of methodologies, including anthropology and cultural studies (Nelson [chapter 9] and Adams and Giraudo [chapter 7]), ethnohistory (Carey [chapter 6]), sociology (González Ponciano [chapter 5]), and oral history (Konefal [chapter 10]). Alongside recent critical works that have reexamined three other iconic Latin American revolutions—the Mexican Revolution, the Cuban Revolution, and the civil war in Peru—our analyses of the often-contradictory policies and practices of the revolutionary decade bring the revolutionary decade into closer dialogue with new research methodologies in the fields of history and anthropology and the study of revolutions elsewhere in Latin American and the world.[61]

In offering these diverse perspectives, the chapters examine actors and themes heretofore neglected from scholarly discussions: the role of foreign mining and hydroelectric companies in indigenous communities; the green revolution and agricultural industrialization; anthropologists', medical doctors', and forestry experts' efforts to manage the revolution from above; and the appropriation and redeployment of state policy and communist and anticommunist ideology by Mayas, Afro-Guatemalans, mestizo women, and schoolteachers.

Drawing from the committed research and vigorous disagreements that enlivened earlier debates over external versus internal factors in the revolution's demise, the comprehensiveness of the revolutionary project, and shortcomings with regard to indigenous communities, the contributors gathered here not only take stock of the field to date but also endeavor to weave a fourth strand. From the present conjuncture, whence former heads of state are hauled off to jail for corruption but not crimes against humanity and other *payasos* hold public office,[62] some might look back and see all social democracies of the twentieth century as a moment of exception amidst ongoing immiseration. But we reject that unthinkable possibility. Now is the time to revisit the revolution—for its lessons in social transformation and radical possibility.

Vámonos.

Notes

1. Piero Gleijeses, *Shattered Hope: The Guatemalan Revolution and the United States, 1944–1954* (Princeton, NJ: Princeton University Press, 1991), 3, 380, 399.

2. Gleijeses, *Shattered Hope*, 7.

3. Kirsten Weld, "The Other Door: Spain and the Guatemalan Counter-Revolution, 1944–54," *Journal of Latin American Studies* (January 2019): 1–29, https://doi.org/10.1017/S0022216X18001128; Julie Gibbings, *Our Time Is Now: Race and*

Modernity in Postcolonial Guatemala (Cambridge: Cambridge University Press, forthcoming [2020]).

4. Medardo Mejía, *El movimiento obrero en la Revolución de Octubre* (Guatemala: Tipografía Nacional de Guatemala, 1949), 5.

5. Weld, "The Other Door."

6. For discussion, see Heather Vrana, *This City Belongs to You: A History of Student Activism in Guatemala, 1944–1996* (Oakland: University of California Press, 2017).

7. Max Paul Friedman argues that Juan José Arévalo's spiritual socialism was rooted in the ideas of the German philosopher Karl Christian Friedrich Krause, "Transnationalizing the Guatemalan Spring: From Argentine *Krausismo* to Spiritual Socialism, 1919–1963" (paper, 2017 American Historical Association meeting, Denver, Colorado).

8. Gibbings, *Our Time Is Now.*

9. See Greg Grandin, "Everyday Forms of State Decomposition: Quetzaltenango, Guatemala, 1954," *Bulletin of Latin American Research* 19, no. 3 (2000): 303–320.

10. Cited in Jim Handy, *Revolution in the Countryside: Rural Conflict and Agrarian Reform in Guatemala, 1944–1954* (Chapel Hill: University of North Carolina Press, 1994), 78.

11. Weld, "The Other Door."

12. Diane M. Nelson and Carlota McAllister, "Aftermath: Harvests of Violence and Histories of the Future," in *War by Other Means: Aftermath in Post-Peace Guatemala*, ed. Diane Nelson and Carlota McAllister, 1–48 (Durham, NC: Duke University Press, 2013), 4.

13. Heather Vrana, "'Our ongoing fight for justice': The Pasts and Futures of *Genocidio* and *Justicia* in Guatemala," *Journal of Genocide Research* 18, nos. 2–3 (2016): 245–263.

14. Entry s.v. "post-" and "peace," *Oxford English Dictionary*, 3rd ed., accessed May 10, 2019, http://www.oed.com.

15. This volume argues the opposite of some recent revisionist scholarship of the revolution, see, esp., Timothy J. Smith and Abigail E. Adams, eds., *After the Coup: An Ethnographic Reframing of Guatemala 1954* (Urbana: University of Illinois Press, 2011).

16. Juan José Arévalo, *Guatemala, la democracia y el imperio* (México, DF: América Nueva, 1954).

17. See Guillermo Toriello, *La batalla de Guatemala* (México, DF: Cuadernos Americanos, 1955).

18. Cited in Stephen M. Streeter, "Interpreting the 1954 US Intervention in Guatemala: Realist, Revisionist, and Postrevisionist Perspectives," *History Teacher* 34, no. 1 (2000). 63.

19. See overview in Streeter, "Interpreting the 1954 US Intervention in Guatemala."

20. James Daniel, *Red Design for the Americas: Guatemalan Prelude* (New York: John Day, 1954).

21. Harry Kantor, "Review of Red Design for the Americas: Guatemalan Prelude. By Daniel James," *Western Political Quarterly* 8, no. 1 (1955): 127.

22. See, e.g., Carlos Samayoa Chinchilla, *El Quetzal no es rojo* (Guatemala: Arana Hermanos, 1956); Jorge del Valle Matheu, *La verdad sobre el "Caso de Guatemala"* (Guatemala: n.p., 1956); Clemente Marroquín Rojas, *La derrota de una batalla: Réplica al libro "La batalla de Guatemala" del ex-canciller Guillermo Toriello* (México, DF: n.p., 1957).

23. See William Appleman Williams, *The Tragedy of American Diplomacy* (New York: Norton, 2009). For an overview as it relates to Latin America, see Gilbert M. Joseph and Daniela Spenser, eds., *In from the Cold: Latin America's New Encounter with the Cold War* (Durham, NC: Duke University Press, 2007).

24. José Aybar de Soto, *Dependency and Intervention: The Case of Guatemala in 1954* (Boulder, CO: Westview, 1978), 237.

25. Stephen C. Schlesinger and Stephen Kinzer, *Bitter Fruit: The Untold Story of the American Coup in Guatemala* (Garden City, NY: Doubleday, 1982).

26. Immerman, on the other hand, defended the view that Arbenz regime did not constitute a Soviet threat to the United States and argued that US officials removed Arbenz not because of the UFCO but because US officials confused communism and nationalism. When Arbenz enacted land, the United States intervened to stop the spread of communism. Richard H. Immerman, *The CIA in Guatemala: The Foreign Policy of Intervention* (Austin: University of Texas Press, 1988).

27. Severo Martínez Peláez, *La Patria del Criollo: An Interpretation of Colonial Guatemala*, trans. (shortened from original) Susan M. Neve and W. George Lovell, ed. W. George Lovell and Christopher H. Lutz (Durham, NC: Duke University Press, 2009), xviii, 278, 280.

28. Carlos Guzmán Böckler and Jean-Loup Herbert, *Guatemala: Una interpretación histórico-social* (México, DF: Siglo XXI Editores, 1970), 57, 88, 171, 172, 174, 175.

29. Richard N. Adams, ed., *Crucifixion by Power: Essays on Guatemalan National Social Structure, 1944–1966* (Austin: University of Texas Press, 1970), 193.

30. John Lewis Gaddis, *The United States and the End of the Cold War: Implications, Reconsiderations, Provocations* (Oxford: Oxford University Press, 1994); and Gaddis, *The Long Peace: Inquiries into the History of the Cold War* (Oxford: Oxford University Press, 1989). See also Gaddis, *The Cold War: A New History* (New York: Penguin, 2005).

31. Gleijeses, *Shattered Hope*, 27.

32. Robert A. Pastor, "A Discordant Consensus on Democracy," *Diplomatic History* 17, no. 1 (1993): 117–128, see critique in Grandin, "Off the Beach: The United States, Latin America, and the Cold War," in *A Companion to Post-1945 America*, ed. Jean-Christophe Agewn and Roy Rosensweig, 426–445 (New York: Blackwell, 2002).

33. Jim Handy, "'The Most Precious Fruit of the Revolution': The Guatemalan Agrarian Reform, 1952–54," *Hispanic American Historical Review* 68, no. 4 (1988): 675–705; Handy, "'A Sea of Indians': Ethnic Conflict and the Guatemalan Revolution, 1944–1952," *The Americas* 46, no. 2 (1989): 189–204; Diane M. Nelson, *A Finger in the Wound: Body Politics in Quincentennial Guatemala* (Berkeley: University of California Press, 1999).

34. Handy, *Revolution in the Countryside*.

35. Gaddis, *The Cold War*, 178.

36. Luján Muñoz, Jorge, and Daniel Contreras P, eds., *Historia general de Guatemala: Época contemporánea, de 1945 a la actualidad*, vol. 6 (Guatemala: Asociación de Amigos del País, Fundación para la Cultura y el Desarrollo, 1997).

37. John M. Broder, "Clinton Offers His Apologies to Guatemala," *New York Times*, March 11, 1999.

38. Nick Cullather, *Secret History: The CIA's Classified Account of Its Operations in Guatemala, 1952–1954* (Stanford, CA: Stanford University Press, 2006).

39. Daniel Wilkinson, *Silence on the Mountain: Stories of Terror, Betrayal, and Forgetting in Guatemala* (Durham, NC: Duke University Press, 2004).

40. Greg Granin, *The Last Colonial Massacre: Latin America in the Cold War* (Durham, NC: Duke University Press, 2004).

41. See Carlos Sabino, *Guatemala, la historia silenciada (1944–1989)* (Guatemala: Fondo de Cultura Económica, 2007); J. C. Cambranes, *Guatemala: Sobre la recuperación de la memoria histórica (entrevista a dos voces)* (Guatemala: Editora Cultural de Centroamérica, 2008); and Edelberto Torres-Rivas, *Guatemala: Un edificio de cinco pisos* (Guatemala: Catafixia Editorial, 2017).

42. Lucrecia Méndez de Penedo, "Presentación," in *Actas de Encuentro: Juan José Arévalo, presencia vivía: 1904–2004* (Guatemala: Universidad Rafael Landívar, 2004), 10.

43. Greg Grandin's *The Blood of Guatemala: A History of Race and Nation* (Durham, NC: Duke University Press, 2000) marked a crucial turning point in indigenous historiography, when he noted how Maya elites opposed the revolution. For works that center new historical actors or regions in their analyses, see also Grandin, *The Last Colonial Massacre*, and Grandin, "Everyday Forms of State Decomposition, 303–320; Vrana, *This City Belongs to You*; J. T. Way, *The Mayan in the Mall: Globalization, Development, and the Making of Modern Guatemala* (Durham, NC: Duke University Press, 2012); Patricia Harms, "'God Doesn't Like the Revolution': The Archbishop, the Market Women, and the Economy of Gender in Guatemala, 1944–1954," *Frontiers: A Journal of Women Studies* 32, no. 2 (2011): 111–139; Robert H. Holden, "Communism and Catholic Social Doctrine in the Guatemalan Revolution of 1944," *Journal of Church and State* 50, no. 3 (2008): 495; Cindy Forster, "The Macondo of Guatemala: Banana Workers and National Revolution in Tiquisate, 1944–1954," in *Banana Wars: Power, Production, and History in the Americas*, ed. Steve Striffler and Mark Moberg, 191–228 (Durham, NC: Duke University Press, 2003); Forster, "Violent and Violated Women: Justice and Gender in Rural Guatemala, 1936–1956," *Journal of Women's History* 11, no. 3 (2003): 55–77; and Smith and Adams, *After the Coup*.

44. Joseph and Spenser, *In from the Cold*, 10.

45. Abigail E. Adams, "Antonio Goubaud Carrera: Between the Contradictions of the Generación de 1920 and U.S. Anthropology," in Smith and Adams, *After the Coup*, 17–48.

46. Grandin, *The Last Colonial Massacre*.

47. Grandin, *The Last Colonial Massacre*; Julie Gibbings, "Mestizaje in the Age of Fascism: German and Q'eqchi' Maya Interracial Unions in Alta Verapaz, Guatemala," *German History* 34, no. 2 (June 1, 2016): 214–236, https://doi.org/10.1093/gerhis/ghw017; Arturo Taracena Arriola, *Etnicidad, estado y nación en Guatemala* (Antingua, Guatemala: Centro de Investigaciones Regionales de Mesoamérica, 2004); Grandin, "Everyday Forms of State Decomposition"; Vrana, *This City Belongs to You*.

48. Way, *The Mayan in the Mall*; Gibbings, *Our Time Is Now*.

49. Weld, "The Other Door."

50. Gibbings, *Our Time Is Now*.

51. This distinguishes Latin America from much of the rest of the world, particularly postcolonial Africa and the United States, where post–World War II democratic

nationalism and internationalism produced significant political outcomes. On Latin America, see Leslie Bethell and Ian Roxborough, eds., *Latin America between the Second World War and the Cold War: Crisis and Containment, 1944–1948* (Cambridge University Press, 1997); Bethell and Roxborough, "Latin America between the Second World War and the Cold War: Some Reflections on the 1945–8 Conjuncture," *Journal of Latin American Studies* 20, no. 1 (1988): 167–189.

52. Gibbings, *Our Time Is Now*; see also Dipesh Chakrabarty, *Provincializing Europe: Postcolonial Thought and Historical Difference* (Princeton, NJ: Princeton University Press, 2001).

53. Juan José Arévalo, *Discurso al asumir la Presidencia de la República de Guatemala* (Guatemala: Tipografía Nacional, 1945), 237.

54. *Boletín de CEUAGE* 1, no. 1 (June 1953), Centro de Investigaciones Regionales de Mesoamérica (hereafter CIRMA).

55. See Vrana, *This City Belongs to You.*

56. "Lucha Cívica de Junio es del Pueblo proclama la AEU," *El Imparcial*, June 23, 1956, CIRMA.

57. Way, *The Mayan in the Mall*, 61, 70–71, 233n5.

58. Ibid., 133–134, 255n30; see also Inforpress Centroamericana, *Central America Report*, December 13, 1974, 129; Inforpress Centroamericana, *Central America Report*, March 14, 1975, 89–90; and Inforpress Centroamericana, *Central America Report*, November 17, 1975, 329.

59. Marjorie Miller, "Guatemala Ends Military Rule as Cerezo Becomes President," *Los Angeles Times*, January 15, 1986.

60. "Man in the News: Marco Vinicio Cerezo; Not a Friend of Generals," *New York Times*, December 10, 1985, A3.

61. See Gilbert M. Joseph and Jurgen Buchenau, eds., *Mexico's Once and Future Revolution: Social Upheaval and the Challenge of Rule since the Late Nineteenth Century* (Durham, NC: Duke University Press, 2013); Carlos Aguirre and Paulo Drinot, eds., *The Peculiar Revolution: Rethinking the Peruvian Experiment under Military Rule* (Austin: University of Texas Press, 2017); and Lillian Guerra, *Heroes, Martyrs, and Political Messiahs in Revolutionary Cuba, 1946–1958* (New Haven, CT: Yale University Press, 2018).

62. President Jimmy Morales was famous before holding public office for his portrayal of a clown on television.

PART I
New Regions

CHAPTER I

"To Wrench Our Rights from La Frutera"

Race, Labor, and Redefining National Belonging on the Caribbean Coast

Ingrid Sierakowski

In July 1949, a group of "anti-Arévalistas" confronted Samuel MacPherson, a known supporter of President Juan José Arévalo, as he walked home in the banana enclave town of Morales, Izabal. According to a letter written by one labor leader, "the honest and defenseless Samuel MacPherson . . . was insulted and attacked by a gang of enemies of the people and trusted United Fruit Company employees."[1] The last names of MacPherson's assailants—Dedett, Smith, Vanegas, Jiménez, and González—suggest that they were a racially mixed group of black West Indians, mulattos, and ladinos, while the victim was himself also likely of West Indian descent. In previous decades, conflict on Guatemala's Caribbean coast had revolved around xenophobia and racism against black migrant workers. During the Guatemalan Spring, however, political struggle in the banana plantation zone raged instead over the power of the United Fruit Company (UFCO) itself—with people of all races and backgrounds on both sides.

"Sadly, the majority of them are the bad type of Guatemalans who only bring dishonor to our beautiful Guatemala," lamented Julio Barrios, the letter's author, of the group that had assaulted MacPherson.[2] In doing so, he made no mention of their race nor challenged their claim to Guatemalan nationality, but rather questioned their patriotism in light of their willingness to ally with United Fruit. Barrios's characterization of the men as "enemies of the people" hinged on their reputation as "trusted UFCO employees," who did not join labor unions or subscribe to the mounting revolutionary nationalism of the era. Notably, while those involved in the attack represented a diverse cohort of enclave workers of varied ethnicities, theirs was a politically charged confrontation *among Guatemalans.*

While studies of the Guatemalan Spring (1944–1954) consistently emphasize the United Fruit Company's sway over national politics, these accounts largely ignore the role that the company's plantation workforce played in this history.[3] This chapter reexamines how racial, social, and political inclusion was constructed during the democratic opening, foregrounding the Caribbean region as a space in which new ideas of citizenship and national belonging were ushered in, experienced, and projected onto the national stage. Located on the Atlantic coast, the province of Izabal was largely peripheral to the nation's history prior to the arrival of the US-based United Fruit Company and its subsidiary, the International Railways of Central America (IRCA). The Caribbean lowlands experienced a boom period in the early 1900s, as new railways, port facilities, and banana plantations were established in the area. United Fruit and its subsidiaries soon monopolized the country's export facilities upon which Guatemala's coffee producers came to rely. Along with these transnational companies came a substantial influx of West Indian migrants who performed the grueling task of growing, harvesting, and loading bananas onto mules, trains, and ships. The descendants of these black workers, as we will see, later contributed to the political and social transformations of the Guatemalan Spring, reframing questions of race, national inclusion, and social citizenship in ways that resonated beyond the confines of the enclave.

During the democratic opening, enclave workers helped to galvanize national sentiment against the United Fruit Company and the International Railways. Their local struggles for better wages and labor rights became inextricably linked to the larger campaign of the Guatemalan government to break the companies' stranglehold over the country's economy. Plantation and port workers' struggles for labor rights thus commanded a high degree of importance on the national stage. Within the enclave, plantation and port workers helped spur a new form of national belonging that hinged on an individual's contributions to nation building. Fundamentally, it was these contributions that would come to define the era's revolutionary nationalism, a process characterized by inclusive and participatory politics that sought to bring to fruition the promises of the democratic opening. By taking on the "imperialist" American corporations—considered the primary obstacle to national sovereignty—these workers strived to solidify their own inclusion and sense of belonging across racial boundaries in a country that had once spurned their forefathers. After decades of being relegated to the margins of the nation-state, workers on the Caribbean coast saw these old patterns shift dramatically during the 1940s and wasted no time in finally asserting their rights against those of United Fruit's economic interests. This chapter traces the process through which workers of varied racial backgrounds eventually sought to make the foreign United Fruit Company unwelcome, in a nation they had come to claim as their own.

Race, Migration, and Work in the Enclave

Prior to the Guatemalan Spring, Izabal had remained a world apart from the rest of the country. In the broader Guatemalan imaginary, the Atlantic coast was characterized as an archetypal export enclave, a veritable "state-within-a-state" where the multinational corporation was sovereign, with both capital and labor imported from abroad. The United Fruit Company, or La Frutera, as it was generally known, initially depended on black foreign labor to begin agricultural production and to build its rail and port infrastructure. La Frutera recruited hundreds of English-speaking black British West Indians, often hailing from the island of Jamaica. Many of them had previously been contracted to complete similar projects in Costa Rica and Panama.[4] A smaller number of Chinese merchants and East Indian workers (then known as *culíes*, or "coolies") also arrived in Guatemala often by way of the British Caribbean.

With time, ladino Guatemalan workers were also increasingly hired and forced to compete with the earlier generation of West Indian laborers for cheap wages. These ladino men arrived not only from Guatemala's eastern provinces—such as Zacapa, El Progreso, Chiquimula, and Jalapa—but also from the neighboring Central American republics of Honduras and El Salvador. In the Guatemalan racial lexicon, as Richard Adams has noted, "the term Ladino may cover a number of different ethnic groups even though it is more specifically applied to the Spanish American culture bearer."[5] Thus, a person categorized as ladino can be of white (European), mestizo (mixed European and indigenous) descent, or, in some cases, an indigenous person who no longer practices the culture (language, dress, and customs) of her or his ethnic group. However, sharp racial hierarchies inherited from colonial, postcolonial, and liberal state formation in western Guatemala provided few ready-made answers when it came to Caribbean blackness. Unlike former plantation colonies that relied upon chattel slavery from their inception, dark skin and African features never played a preponderant role in Guatemalan discourses of race, which instead fractured the population along indigenous-ladino lines. In the fluid social space occupied by black and racially mixed workers at the docks and banana plantations, many found themselves assimilated into the rather unfixed category of "ladino."

The presence of a distinct ethnic group, the Garifuna (pl. Garinagu), on Guatemala's Atlantic coast, further complicates the Caribbean mosaic. Although often categorized as ladinos by census takers, at the local level, the Garifuna were universally recognized as comprising their own social group. Known as *caribes negros* (black Caribs), they were generally referred to as *morenos* ("dark-skinned people") in Izabal. Originally from the island of St. Vincent, the community emerged from the intermixing of runaway black slaves and Arawak and Carib indigenous groups. Their unique language, culture, and religious customs preserved links to their Caribbean past and to other Garinagu fishing communities along the Central American coast in Honduras and Belize.[6] Although members of the Garifuna community rarely signed on to work on the inland banana plantations, over time, many males were hired at the docks in Puerto Barrios.[7]

Once black West Indian workers began to organize strikes for better wages, the United Fruit Company shifted away from hiring foreign laborers to increasingly recruiting Guatemalan ladino migrants.[8] However, rather than dismiss all black workers, La Frutera chose to isolate them from the new ladino arrivals, erecting a key barrier to worker solidarity. By promoting English-speaking West Indians into managerial positions, United Fruit fostered racial tensions between workers from different backgrounds and prevented unification on both the banana plantations and the docks. These policies fanned discontent and xenophobia within the plantations to such an extent that on one infamous occasion in 1914, deadly violence flared up between Guatemalan ladinos and black Jamaican migrants.[9] The company's "divide and conquer" strategy of racial segmentation worked largely as intended, drawing a clear line between Guatemalans and foreigners, which coincided exactly with the racial divide.[10] For the men and women who lived and labored in the port and docks, regardless of skin color, the United Fruit Company's monopoly power was part of their day-to-day lives. La Frutera, or El Pulpo, as United Fruit also came to be known, dominated their world, from the fields of the oldest banana plantations located in the towns of Quiriguá, Morales, and Bananera in Izabal, to the nation's primary deepwater port and the terminus of the railroad at the town of Puerto Barrios.

Work and Repression under Dictatorship

While racial tensions and discrimination against black workers dated from the nineteenth century, during the Great Depression, xenophobia led to the passage of openly racist immigration legislation. In 1931, soon after dictator General Jorge Ubico came to power, the government enacted strict laws barring entry to "individuals of the yellow race" and "individuals of the black race" *por razones étnicas* (on purely racial grounds).[11] Many West Indian workers now had to weigh their options, for if they traveled abroad they risked being denied reentry into Guatemala. Matters were even more complicated for immigrants who had formed families with local women: their children of racially mixed black and ladino descent were Guatemalan citizens. Ironically, given the anti-immigrant legislation passed by the government, the 1930s witnessed increasing coexistence among diverse working-class populations at the community level. Neighbors of various backgrounds who resided in the United Fruit Company's housing yards on the plantations in Bananera and Morales, or in neighborhoods such as Banns, Roundhouse, and El Rastro in Puerto Barrios, often came together to beseech the help of local magistrates in obtaining needed services, though officials generally denied their requests. Archival documents, especially local censuses, convey the widespread process of interracial coupling, signaled by the large number of locals with mixed Spanish and English names and surnames.[12] This dynamic was largely the product of the gender imbalance in Izabal, where men greatly outnumbered single females. By this period, nearly all single women in the area were ladina migrants from Guatemala and elsewhere in Central America, who worked as laundresses, cooks, and market vendors.[13] It was these migrant working-class women who paired up with plantation and dockworkers in both formal and common-law marriages. As a result of these unions, new generations of Spanish-speaking racially mixed *Guatemalan* children grew up in a markedly diverse social milieu. By the mid-1940s, therefore, Guatemalans in the enclave had already experienced decades of engagement with people of different races, whether as coworkers, neighbors, or family members.

The experiences of working-class families contrasted sharply with those of the small number of white Americans who also resided in the enclave. La Frutera provided them with comfortable, modern facilities, low-wage domestic servants, and schools in their secluded housing *colonias*, or neighborhoods. Their families also had access to better wards at the company hospital, which was segregated in accordance with Jim Crow.[14] For enclave workers, the Americans' privileged presence came to symbolize everything that was denied to them as Guatemalans. United Fruit managers were generally addressed as "Misters," a term that became a stand-in for white. The term also helped affirm worker deference and the implicit recognition of the racial and social hierarchy that separated them from their bosses.[15] By the eve of the revolution, the primary racial cleavage in Izabal was no longer one of black immigrant versus ladino migrant, but rather all workers of color against the tiny number of American managers.

Given the enduring alliance between bosses of the United Fruit Company and Ubico's military authorities, enclave workers had no recourse in challenging the awful conditions and treatment they faced at the docks or on the plantations. Workers remembered terrible workplace accidents, which could have been prevented had more safety mechanisms been implemented by United Fruit. For instance, stevedores described how in 1943 they witnessed their friend being fatally struck in the head by a falling slab of mahogany. The white manager at the docks, Mr. Percival, admonished them for halting their work. Percival allegedly shouted, "Nothing to see here," and ordered them back to work.[16] Even local officials delayed recovering the body, apparently abiding by Mr. Percival's demands. For the workers, the disregard for their coworker's life signaled that their manager was more preoccupied with securing the ship's cargo than their very humanity. They lamented their powerlessness under Ubico's regime, as they well knew how those who attempted to rectify these conditions could face arrest or even murder. They had the example of their *compañero* Juan Colíndres, who was executed by firing squad in 1938 for organizing clandestine meetings to establish a labor union at the docks.

During this period, Ubico empowered the military police to repress all criticism of his regime in Izabal as elsewhere in Guatemala. In 1933, Daniel Hemsley of Puerto Barrios was accused, along with another black man, of "expressing awful things about the President" allegedly "calling him a thief who steals from the poor."[17] Ubico, it seems from these apparent criticisms, was despised not only for instituting repressive policies, but also for his role in exploiting the most disenfranchised. Fortunately for Hemsley, Elvira Smith, the owner of the bar where he purportedly voiced those criticisms, and her Chinese immigrant husband testified on his behalf, eventually securing his release. It is important to note here the enduring presence of this racially diverse group of people, some of whom owned small businesses, even during the high tide of xenophobic legislation. In sum, Ubico's dictatorship had essentially denied disgruntled enclave residents and nonwhite workers of all backgrounds the right to fully air their grievances. When the dictator fell and local power holders were forced to vacate their posts, spaces for social and political participation were immediately filled by those whose voices of protest had long been marginalized.

"Our Beloved Nation": Enclave Citizens and the New Politics of Inclusion

When Ubico was ousted from power in 1944, Izabal's banana plantation and port workers poured out into the streets to demonstrate their support for the new revolutionary junta. In the presidential election held the following year, Arévalo carried the province in a landslide, according to published election results. During Arévalo's administration, unionized workers participated actively in the democratic process, backing progressive candidates and even running union leaders for local office. At this time, particularly within labor organizing, the rhythm of social and racial integration increased dramatically. Banana and port workers began to find their common voice *as workers* and to see their claims for national inclusion and social citizenship imbue them with power in new ways. For those who had been loyal to Ubico's regime, however, this shift signaled a dramatic sea change. Former municipal military officials saw themselves out of their posts, as the new democratic government filled the political vacuum with new cohorts of elected officials. Many of those displaced in the transition to democracy looked askance at the rise of lower-class ladino, black, and mulatto workers within local posts.[18]

As new discourses of democratic and social rights emerged, enclave residents appealed to local officials for support in their efforts to eke out a decent living. As early as November 1944, Puerto Barrios' seamen wrote to migration officials requesting longer travel visas and exemption from paying the required fees. The racially diverse group of men who signed the petition suggested, "If we take on these jobs and leave the country, it is with the sole objective of improving our economic conditions, for if we had another way to achieve this, we would not abandon our beloved nation."[19] While coming together across racial lines was not new for enclave workers, that these twenty-eight workers were granted full cooperation from government officials was rather unprecedented. The contrast between the responses of these officials and those of the Ubico era could not be starker. As they stated in their response, "It is our duty to look after the well-being and improvement of *our citizens*," making no distinction between the petitioners.[20] Of importance, both the workers and the bureaucrats had begun to use a new language of revolutionary nationalism and inclusive citizenship in their calls for social and economic improvement.

However, these emergent transformations did not necessarily mean that shifts in conceptions of race and inclusion among elites were a given. Those tasked with writing the country's new Constitution, for instance, initially struggled to expunge racist notions embedded in legislation inherited from the dictatorship. Although some of those responsible for the new Constitution represented elite interests, new voices won out as immigration restrictions were abrogated. As one member reminded the constitutional committee in reference to previous labor policies and antiblack restrictions, "The state has to protect the workers; it does not have to consider their race."[21] The 1945 Constitution explicitly stated for the first time that "racial discrimination is unacceptable in a democracy," declaring "illegal and punishable any discrimination by reason of affiliation, sex, race, color, class, religious beliefs, or political ideas."[22] One of the key ways in which grassroots movements sought to assert these inclusive ideals was through the construction of a new discourse of revolutionary nationalism. For the people of the enclave, it would be through their struggles in the labor movement that this process began to take shape.

By the time the country's first Labor Code was enacted in February 1947, banana and dockworkers in Izabal were among the national labor movement's most militant and vocal members. They joined teachers, students, rail workers, and shoemakers as some of the most organized sectors of the early democratic opening. They quickly mobilized and pushed for union recognition and equitable labor contracts, giving real meaning to the reforms underway.[23] In its 435 articles, the code regulated numerous aspects of working conditions, such as setting an eight-hour workday.[24] The workers' unions received official recognition, bargaining rights, and labor courts to settle workplace disputes. The new Labor Code, however, was far from all encompassing. Among agricultural workers, for instance, labor unions could only be organized on farms and plantations that employed over five hundred workers. While this meant that those who worked on small farms could not form their own labor unions, it also permitted the workers on large plantations (such as those owned by the United Fruit Company) to become the first to push for their demands for better wages and conditions.

The Sindicato de Empresa de Trabajadores de la United Fruit Company (United Fruit plantation workers' union; SETUFCO), with its headquarters in Bananera, became the very first labor union in Guatemala to officially register under the new Labor Code. Only twenty-three years old when he filed the paperwork, Alaric Alfonso Bennett, a black worker of West Indian descent, added his name to the national labor registry on behalf of SETUFCO as its secretary general. A key labor leader on the plantations of the Caribbean coast, Bennett led thousands of workers, the majority of whom were ladinos with no apparent black ancestry.[25] Signing the registry for the Union Sindical de Trabajadores de Puerto Barrios (stevedores' union in Puerto Barrios; USTPB) was José Domingo Segura, a racially mixed ladino of partially black ancestry. During this period of social upheaval, Segura guided the port workers' union, with a membership of over a thousand workers, through some of the most heated labor battles with United Fruit. Their work stoppages paralyzed the nation's commerce, which depended on exports of coffee and bananas. In these early efforts, Segura gained some renown in Puerto Barrios as the leader of USTPB, and later, as a member of the Partido Guatemalteco del Trabajo (Guatemalan Communist Party; PGT). In leading thousands of workers of various national backgrounds and racial hues, Bennett and Segura helped demonstrate that the United Fruit Company could no longer apply its "divide and conquer" strategy of racial stratification to prevent worker solidarity as it had once done.

At the local level, the work of labor unions not only entailed addressing immediate workplace concerns but also quickly moved into the political realm. Unions such as SETUFCO and USTPB soon became a significant voting bloc in Izabal, electing prolabor congressmen to represent their interests in the halls of power. The descendants of black and mestizo migrants now took their place in the country's highest legislative body. In 1947, they helped elect Dr. Guillermo Melbourne, a mulatto, as their representative to the National Congress.[26] Two years later, the enclave's workforce reached another milestone, electing labor leader Alaric Bennett as a diputado for the Partido de Acción Revolucionaria (Revolutionary Action Party; PAR), the largest progovernment party. Of significance, as a man of black, Jamaican descent, Bennett was placed into power by a majority mestizo population. But his election also had special significance for the enclave's West Indian and Garifuna populations, which enthusiastically cast their votes for the twenty-five-year-old. In Puerto Barrios and Livingston, many wrote in their ballots variations on the phrase "for Bennett, the black man" ("por el negro Bennett," or "por Ben el negrito").[27] Rather than limited to local elites, literacy in the province was accessible to a significant portion of the enclave's citizens, for about 41.6 percent of the population could read and write, a rate markedly higher than the national average (28 percent).[28] Like

Melbourne's election, Bennett's rise to power demonstrated the visible political integration of the enclave's black and racially mixed population on a national scale. As Bennett declared upon taking his new post, as "the first congressman of color," he suggested that before the democratic opening, "there had been racial discrimination—very little, to be sure—but now it has completely ended."[29] "In Guatemala," he said, "we are experiencing a true democracy without any kind of discrimination."[30]

In Bennett's understanding, "a true democracy," labor union rights, and racial harmony were all part and parcel of the same revolutionary process. According to one sociological study of this period by Mario Monteforte Toledo, the social integration in Izabal was much in evidence. Like Bennett, Monteforte Toledo found very little racial prejudice against Izabal's people of color: "There is no discrimination against them except as a social class but without any ethnic implication. They tend to abandon black cultural patterns and acquire those of the poor Ladinos . . . who they live together with on a daily basis without segregation. Mulattos should not be considered as a specific ethnic group, but as part of the working class in general."[31] While Monteforte Toledo suggests the inclusion of blacks under the category of ladino, he also conveys some problematic perceptions of difference, alluding to their "black cultural patterns."[32] Albeit contradictorily, his work reveals the continuing presence of mulattos and blacks in the enclave in a way that counters recent scholars' studies that assert they were pushed out of the nation after the 1930s.[33] As we have seen here, especially in the early years of United Fruit's presence in Izabal and through the implementation of Depression-era xenophobic legislation, the process of social integration was not so swift or painless.

Upholding National Sovereignty from Below

During the late 1940s, much of the mass organizing that took place in the enclave brought together ladino, black, and mixed-race workers organized together *as Guatemalans*. Increasingly, these organized sectors came to frame their demands not just as their own, but as those of the nation itself. While the number of foreign born had dwindled in the two decades since the passage of immigration restrictions, the enclave largely continued to be a space of migrant labor. By the early 1950s, the majority of the residents of Izabal—nearly twenty-eight thousand out of a total of fifty-five thousand—had migrated to the province from elsewhere in Guatemala.[34] These recent arrivals—mostly ladino campesinos from the Oriente—could make few primordial claims to belonging to the place vis-à-vis those of foreign extraction. In fact, they were relative newcomers to the coast when compared to black workers who had immigrated from the West Indies decades earlier, their locally born children, or the Garifuna, whose presence predated the country itself. What brought these workers together was their common struggle against the United Fruit Company, whose interests were seen as increasingly inimical to the laborers' well-being and the interests of the nation as a whole.

In contrast to workers' defiance of La Frutera, Guatemalan agricultural producers and other elites often sided with United Fruit. During the early contract campaigns in 1948–1949, the country's powerful coffee exporters openly showcased their dependence on United Fruit. They called on the government to curb any labor agitation that could prompt La Frutera to pull out of the country, as it had threatened to do if workers continued launching strikes. Urging the government to end an important banana and port workers' strike in 1949, for instance, they insisted that the country was "incapable of staying afloat" without the United Fruit Company: "We lack the internal material capabilities and the industry to keep our ties to the outside world," they argued.[35] With elites' continuing alignment with foreign interests, United Fruit workers took up the banner of national sovereignty and made the company's Caribbean domains into an epicenter of political conflict as they refused to scale down their actions. By countering workers' militancy, upper-class landowning elites were exposed as feeble and unwilling to take action against El Pulpo. From the unionists' perspective, the contract campaigns afforded the unions, as they put it, the "means to wrench our rights from la Frutera," which in turn helped them affirm their inclusion like never before.[36]

Just as the country's landowning elites were seen as allied with United Fruit, port and banana workers who sided with the company bosses and opposed labor unions—regardless of their race—were cast as "enemies of the people." As we saw in the opening of this chapter, conflicts between pro- and antiunion factions took on a nationalist tone. Similarly, USTPB labor leaders expressed contract demands not merely in financial terms, but as a patriotic challenge to foreign "companies that deny exploited workers their bread and want to trample over the sovereignty of Guatemalan laws."[37]

Enclave workers were not alone in casting their grievances against the United Fruit Company as a struggle fundamental to the nation's progress. Their plight garnered the support of other labor unions and progressive politicians in Guatemala City, especially given United Fruit's notorious reputation and its refusal to abide by the newly established labor laws. Banana plantation and dockworkers also found clear allies in leaders such as Víctor Manuel Gutiérrez, who headed the powerful Confederación General de Trabajadores de Guatemala (Guatemalan General Labor Confederation; CGTG).[38] In his speeches to UFCO workers, Gutiérrez did not mince words about El Pulpo. "This is a company," he stated in 1951, "that now aspires, in its boundless ambition to further drain the blood of our land."[39] As we will see, the enclave and its workforce soon found themselves at the very center of the democratic opening's most consequential program of nationalist economic development.

Land Reform and Defining Belonging in Izabal

Based on his campaign promises, President Jacobo Arbenz's economic program reflected the wider popular feelings regarding the disproportionate power of foreign transnational companies over the country. As Arbenz saw it, eradicating this dependency, particularly breaking the United Fruit Company's monopoly power, was a fundamental precondition for the economic development of the country.[40] Organized labor had played an important role in helping to elect Arbenz, and its continued backing also gave him the political capital to follow through on his proposals. First and foremost on the reform agenda was a large-scale land reform, which aimed to break up unused *latifundio* lands held by "feudal" estates and the United Fruit Company.[41] These lands would be distributed to the country's poor and landless peasantry, who would then bring them into production for the domestic market.[42] In addition to implementing the land reform, Arbenz also pursued infrastructure projects that challenged the company's monopoly over transportation and export facilities. A new Atlantic highway linking Guatemala City to the Caribbean coast and a new deepwater port in Santo Tomás in Izabal, for instance, would compete directly with IRCA's railway line and Puerto Barrios' docks.

Perhaps because of its history of labor mobilization and unequal concentration of landownership in the hands of white foreigners, Izabal became a bastion of agrarian reform. From the early years of the democratic opening, the labor movement had denounced the country's severe land concentration as a central obstacle to national economic development. The 1950 agricultural census exposed that UFCO holdings utterly dominated the province to the detriment of small- and medium-sized estates. According to the census numbers, a minuscule 1.3 percent of the farms held 94 percent of the productive land in the province. In fact, the 12 largest properties alone accounted for nearly 80 percent of all arable land in

Izabal, while the smallest 5,083 farms collectively amounted to just 4.3 percent.[43] The United Fruit Company's fifty-nine farms in Izabal comprised over 2,356 *caballerías* (approximately 263,000 acres), of which at least two-thirds (1,559 caballerías) had been left fallow.[44]

Under Arbenz, the land reform gave enclave workers new tools to chip away at the power of La Frutera. It was no surprise that on May Day 1952, leading up to the signing of the land reform, enclave workers came out in droves to show their support. Outside of Guatemala City (where thirty-five thousand people participated), the places where the population turned out en masse to the demonstrations were the UFCO company towns of Tiquisate, Puerto Barrios, and Morales. More than five thousand marched in Puerto Barrios, while in Bananera nearly sixteen hundred plantation workers joined in, despite United Fruit's alleged "threat to lay off anyone who participated."[45] When Congress passed the land reform law (Decree 900) on June 17, enclave workers were among the first to establish agrarian committees and begin petitioning for UFCO lands.

By October, agrarian committees from Quiriguá, Los Amates, Morales, and Puerto Barrios began officially petitioning for pieces of United Fruit's enormous expanses of abandoned land in the Motagua District.[46] In Quiriguá, for instance, once the center of United Fruit operations, the new agrarian organizations enlisted more than five hundred members, including many plantation workers active in SETUFCO, the banana workers' union.[47] As occurred throughout the enclave, the Quiriguá agrarian committee included a diverse mix of landless/land-poor social groups: farmworkers, *arrendatarios* (renters), recent migrants, urban wage laborers, and even a handful of female members.[48] Emblematic of the catchall nature of the membership criteria was the fact that the "campesino" union's founder, Dudley James, was actually a black West Indian employee at the UFCO hospital.[49] Spanish, English, and Mayan surnames (Sosa, Caal, Smith, Kenedy, Choch, Díaz, etc.) appeared alongside one another as fellow committee members on the petition forms submitted from Puerto Barrios.[50] While the United Fruit Company fought back against the expropriations, by June 1954 a whopping 40 percent of all productive land in Izabal was in the process of being reallocated to landless workers and peasants.[51]

Although it did not fit the stereotypical image of the rural "campesino" reclaiming ancestral lands through the agrarian reform, the enclave's diverse workforce was never divorced from the process of harvesting the land.[52] Indeed, those populating the port and banana plantations were considered—for all intents and purposes—to be both wage laborers and landless campesinos. By mobilizing around a campesino identity, they became prime candidates to obtain land from the United Fruit Company's vast uncultivated holdings. Even those who worked as stevedores, mechanics, or train operators stood to benefit from access to a plot of land. Having another means to sustain their families would have provided laborers with economic alternatives and increased their bargaining power vis-à-vis United Fruit. With these profound transformations under way, as new forms of revolutionary inclusion were being constructed, international and local opposition to Arbenz's government increased precipitously.

United Fruit's high-level contacts within the State Department and the US Central Intelligence Agency (CIA) allowed the issue of land expropriation to be cynically elevated into a national security priority for the United States. Funds from the United States paid for extensive anticommunist propaganda that flooded the country during the period. Groups such as the Comité Cívico Nacional (National Civic Committee; CCN), for instance, professed that they had joined the anticommunist struggle "for our God, for our homes."[53] The CCN vehemently opposed land redistribution, even attracting some local landowners from Izabal who crossed the border to El Salvador and Honduras to join the growing number of dissidents who were training for an uprising.

Counterrevolution and the Defeat of the Guatemalan Spring

For much of 1954, with intensifying threats of foreign invasion, Izabal was placed on high alert. As Colonel Carlos Castillo Armas's CIA-sponsored Liberacionista Army was gearing up to invade the country from neighboring Honduras, locals were spurred into action.[54] Comités de Defensa de la Soberanía Nacional (Committees for the Defense of National Sovereignty) recruited farmworkers, dockworkers, teachers, land reform beneficiaries, and members of the Civil Guard in Puerto Barrios to patrol the borders, waterfront, and rail lines.[55] With the backing of some dozen progovernment organizations, the Defense Committees established their headquarters at the port workers' union building near the docks. From their stance, Castillo Armas's forces aimed to undo all that they had achieved. For these activists, the looming invasion threatened to turn back the clock to a time when those in power silenced their voices and sided with the interests of United Fruit.

In June 1954, with the country besieged by the counterrevolutionary invasion, labor and peasant confederations denounced what they saw as a foreign plot against the Guatemalan government. At the time, these

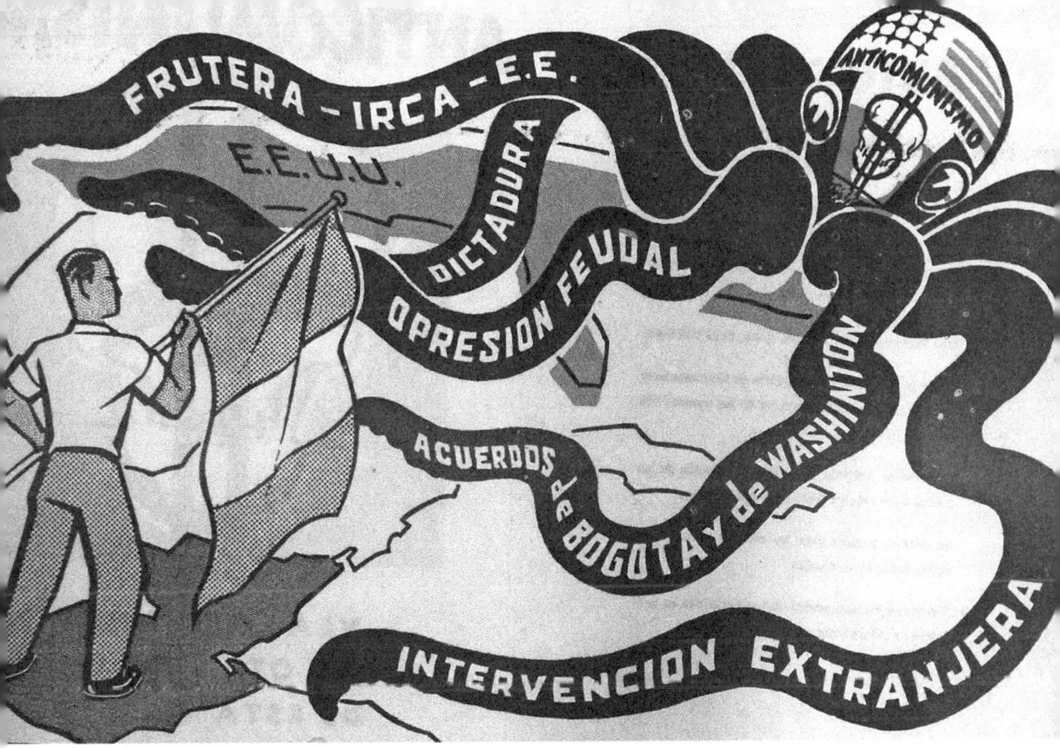

FIGURE 1.1. *"El Anticomunismo" pamphlet, ca. 1954. From Folder: Cooperation of Admin. Parties, Box 6, Guatemala Documents Collection, Manuscript Division, Library of Congress, Washington, DC.*

popular organizations did not know the extent to which the invading army was trained and funded by the CIA. To many, though, as figure 1.1 shows, it was glaringly obvious that behind the attack stood the United States government and El Pulpo. When a contingent of Liberacionista troops attacked Puerto Barrios, the Defense Committees successfully defended the city, providing the revolutionary government with one small victory in the battle for Guatemala. Tragically, however, another armed contingent successfully occupied the plantation towns of Morales and Bananera, the heart of the multiethnic labor movement, where locals were caught off guard. The counterrevolutionaries rounded up many Arbenz supporters and carried out a massacre of the top SETUFCO leadership.

Former labor leader and *diputado* Alaric Bennett was singled out for particular cruelty by the invaders. Although many stories regarding the specific details of his murder have circulated since his death, most coincide on the intense violence inflicted on him as his mutilated body was exhibited for all to see in the town of Bananera.[56] His attackers made an example of him. Bennett was a high-profile figure who symbolized the multiracial popular challenge to the United Fruit Company as well as the Guatemalan Spring's promise of social and political inclusion. His death seemed reminiscent of the xenophobic violence inflicted against black West Indian migrants four decades previous. It was meant to send a message to the people of the enclave: to those who followed him as he led the banana workers labor union and to those who once enthusiastically cast their ballot for him in 1949. The counterrevolutionary forces thus sought to erase the inclusionary achievements of the land and labor movements of the previous decade with this and other acts of spectacular violence.

The targeting and assassination of Bennett offered a glimpse of the nature of Castillo Armas's emerging regime and the brutality of the repression that was to come. In response to the murder of UFCO labor leaders in Bananera and the growing chaos enveloping the country, President Arbenz tendered his resignation on June 27, 1954. Soon thereafter, the United States formally recognized the dictatorship of Castillo Armas. Over the coming months and years, in Izabal as elsewhere in Guatemala, labor unions were banned, the land reform was violently rolled back, thousands were jailed or killed, and the entire democratic process was effectively demolished. The first years of the counterrevolution proved to be devastating for the enclave's labor movement, as even those activists who survived the violent repression receded from view, forcibly silenced by both fear and their defeat.

Conclusion

Viewed from the Caribbean coast, the Guatemalan Spring looks more diverse, participatory, and inclusive than when examined from other perspectives. As we have seen, a sizeable sector of the population embraced the key social and political transformations of the democratic opening. Notably, at the helm of these efforts were labor leaders of black and mixed-race ancestry such as Alaric Bennett, who led the banana workers' union, and José Domingo Segura, who led the dockworkers in Puerto Barrios. With the rise of trade unionism and democratic politics, the descendants of migrants were able to acquire new forms of social mobility and political power *as Guatemalans*, consolidating their sense of national belonging and citizenship. These were the very sorts of transformations that the CIA-backed Liberacionistas sought to undo.

The brief histories recounted here suggest that citizens of the enclave took advantage of the mechanisms afforded to them by the democratic process and sought to forge new forms of inclusion within the nation's existing political structure, from the bottom up. For them, reclaiming the nation's sovereignty coincided with their long-standing efforts "to wrench our rights from la Frutera," to return to the evocative phrase of the USTPB. In the end, the Guatemalan citizens of the enclave represented more than a particular political ideology. Instead, the movement's revolutionary nationalism—a key process the enclave's citizens had helped forge—represented an alternative conception of national belonging. While revisionist literature on the Guatemalan Spring has sought to downplay the importance of the United Fruit Company's interests in the overthrow of Arbenz, the unprecedented transformations that took place in Izabal and the ferocious reaction that they provoked stand in contrast to that frame.

The experience of Izabal reaffirms the central importance of the conflict over La Frutera within the course of the Guatemalan Spring, just as it also reveals the ways in which race, national inclusion, and social citizenship lay at the very core of the period's popular activism. By pushing for inclusion from below, the Atlantic region's plantation, rail, and port workers helped thrust the issue of national sovereignty and the United Fruit Company's monopoly control to center stage. As we reconsider the changes brought about by the Guatemalan Revolution, it is imperative that we bring into focus the role that the labor movement played in helping redefine the nation's democratic opening. Driving this period of mass reform were the concerted efforts of the government and the social movements alike. The reformers' intent had been to create new opportunities for inclusion for those whom one revolutionary bureaucrat simply called "our citizens" in response to a workers' petition from late 1944.

Notes

1. Julio T. Barrios, Secretary of Propaganda, SETUFCO to SAMF, August 1, 1949, box 21, folder: SAMF, Guatemala Documents Collection (GDC), Manuscript Division (MD), Library of Congress (LC), Washington, DC (hereafter GDC, MD, LC).

2. Ibid.

3. See Piero Gleijeses, *Shattered Hope: The Guatemalan Revolution and the United States, 1944–1954* (Princeton, NJ: Princeton University Press, 1992); and Guillermo Toriello Garrido, *La Batalla de Guatemala* (México, DF: Cuadernos Americanos, 1955). A clear exception to this trend is Cindy Forster, *The Time of Freedom: Campesino Workers in Guatemala's October Revolution* (Pittsburgh: University of Pittsburgh Press, 2001).

4. Jason M. Colby, *The Business of Empire: United Fruit, Race, and U.S. Expansion in Central America* (Ithaca, NY: Cornell University Press, 2011); and Colby, "Progressive Empire: Race and Tropicality in United Fruit's Central America," in *Making the Empire Work: Labor and United States Imperialism*, ed. Daniel E. Bender and Jana K. Lipman, 289–311 (New York: NYU Press, 2015).

5. Richard N. Adams, *Cultural Surveys of Panama, Nicaragua, Guatemala, El*

Salvador, Honduras (Washington, DC: Pan American Sanitary Bureau, Regional Office of the World Health Organization, 1957), 270.

6. Nancie L. Solien González, *Sojourners of the Caribbean: Ethnogenesis and Ethnohistory of the Garifuna* (Urbana: University of Illinois Press, 1988).

7. Frederick Douglass Opie, "Black Americans and the State in Turn-of-the-Century Guatemala," *The Americas* 64, no. 4 (April 2008): 583–609.

8. Colby, *The Business of Empire*; Douglas W. Kraft, "Making West Indians Unwelcome: Bananas, Race and the Immigrant Question in Izabal, Guatemala, 1900–1929" (PhD diss., University of Miami, 2006).

9. Paul J. Dosal, *Doing Business with the Dictators: A Political History of United Fruit in Guatemala, 1899–1944* (New York: Rowman and Littlefield, 1993), 119–120; Douglas W. Kraft, "Making West Indians Unwelcome," 131–135.

10. Indeed, this strategy worked across the circum-Caribbean, as several scholars have outlined. See Colby, *The Business of Empire*; Aviva Chomsky, *West Indian Workers and the United Fruit Company in Costa Rica, 1870–1940* (Baton Rouge: Louisiana State University Press, 1996); and Philippe I. Bourgois, *Ethnicity at Work: Divided Labor on a Central American Banana Plantation* (Baltimore, MD: Johns Hopkins University Press, 1989).

11. Asamblea Legislativa, Decree 1745, Article 2, May 31, 1931.

12. Censo de varones de 15 años de edad, en alto, Puerto Barrios, Paquete 4, 1930; and Puerto Barrios local census, Paquete 1, 1944. Jefatura Política de Izabal (JPI), Archivo General de Centro América (AGCA), Guatemala City (hereafter JPI, AGCA).

13. Even into 1950, single men in Puerto Barrios outnumbered single females six times over. See Dirección General de Estadística, *Sexto censo de población, 1950* (Guatemala City: Tipografía Nacional, 1953), 35. An earlier census of 1921 had the ratio of males to females in Puerto Barrios at 2:1: *Censo General de la República, 1921* (Guatemala City: Tipografía Nacional, 1921), 232. For a work that documents the experience for a similar enclave context in Costa Rica, see Lara Putnam, *The Company They Kept: Migrants and the Politics of Gender in Caribbean Costa Rica, 1870–1960* (Chapel Hill: University of North Carolina Press, 2002).

14. Charles D. Kepner, *Social Aspects of the Banana Industry* (New York: AMS Press, 1936), 170.

15. "La UFCO no quebrantará la combatividad ni la unidad de Muelleros de Puerto Barrios," *Octubre*, December 13, 1951, 4.

16. Ibid., 5.

17. Daniel Hemsley case documents, February 15 and 20, 1933, Paquete 2, 1933, JPI, AGCA.

18. Rosendo Pérez Ventura, for instance, served as Regidor Segundo (second alderman) in Morales before the October 1944 Revolution. He was also identified with the United Fruit Company and participated in Colonel Carlos Castillo Armas's invasion in 1954. Nomina de juntas municipales, May 15, 1944, Paquete 3, 1944, JPI, AGCA.

19. Notarized request from Catarino Blanco, Octavio Castro, Hugh M. Dockery, and twenty-five others, November 9, 1944; Oficial de Migración, November 10, 1944. Both in Paquete 3, 1944, JPI, AGCA.

20. Oficial de Migración, November 10, 1944, Paquete 3, 1944, JPI, AGCA. Emphasis added.

21. For the back-and-forth between the members of the Constitutional Commission committee on these issues, see *Diario de sesiones de la Comisión de los Quince encargada de elaborar el proyecto de la Constitución de la República* (Guatemala City: Tipografía Nacional, 1953), 113.

22. For the new laws, see Artículo 21, *Constitución de la República de Guatemala*, 13. Also, "Decreto 10, Ley de extranjería," in *Labor revolucionaria: 333 decretos del Congreso de la República*, vol. 15: 9–10 (Guatemala City: Tipografía Nacional, 1947).

23. "CTG a los trabajadores de la ciudad y del campo," October 1946, Item 606, Taracena Flores Collection (TFC), Latin American Collection of the Benson Library at the University of Texas at Austin (Benson-UTA), Austin, Texas (hereafter TFC, Benson-UTA).

24. *Código de trabajo: Promulgado por decreto no. 330 del organismo legislativo de Guatemala. En vigor desde el 1 de mayo de 1947, año III de la revolución* (Guatemala City: Unión Tipográfica, 1947).

25. The union registered June 9, 1947. The Puerto Barrios dockworkers (USTPB) registered in October of that year. The workers from the Sindicato de Empresa de la Compañía Agrícola de Guatemala (Workers from the United Fruit Company union in Tiquisate on the Pacific Coast; SETCAG) and the Sindicato de Acción y Mejoramiento Ferrocarrilero (the rail workers union for action and improvement; SAMF) all officially registered that same year. Mario López Larrave, *Breve historia del movimiento sindical guatemalteco* (Guatemala City: Editorial Universitaria, 1979), 31.

26. "Nuevos diputados al Congreso," *Diario de Centro América*, February 24, 1947. For reference to his mixed race, see Alfonso Bauer Paiz and Iván Carpio Alfaro, *Memorias de Alfonso Bauer Paiz: Historia no oficial de Guatemala* (Guatemala City: Rusticatio Ediciones, 1996), 180.

27. "El primer diputado de color, Alaric Bennett, de Izabal, da declaraciones," *Nuestro Diario*, March 1, 1949; "PAR superó sus votos en Izabal," *El Imparcial*, January 18, 1949, 1 and 6.

28. Dirección General de Estadística, *Sexto censo de población, 1950*, 125.

29. Alaric Alfonso Bennett, quoted in "El primer diputado de color," *Nuestro Diario*, March 1, 1949.

30. Ibid.

31. Mario Monteforte Toledo, *Guatemala: Monografía sociológica* (México, DF: Universidad Nacional Autónoma de México, Instituto de Investigaciones Sociales, 1959), 91.

32. Although Monteforte Toledo's study was published in the late 1950s, it is interesting to note that both Bennett and Melbourne must have crossed paths with Monteforte Toledo, as they were all serving in the National Congress during that period.

33. Colby, *The Business of Empire*; Kraft, "Making West Indians Unwelcome."

34. Dirección General de Estadística, *Sexto censo de población, 1950*, 92 and 110. Although the statistics cannot be confirmed, Monteforte Toledo's study estimated that there were three thousand blacks and six thousand mulattos in the northeast region of the country—the product of the mixing of races over previous generations. Monteforte Toledo, *Guatemala: Monografía sociológica*, 90.

35. "La CCI y AGA opinan sobre el conflicto de la UFCO," *El Imparcial*, February 22, 1949, 16.

36. "Informe de la delegación USTPB," February 4, 1952, box 58, folder: 2/52, GDC, MD, LC.

37. Ernesto Juárez and Pedro Rossi, report of United Fruit workers' union joint meeting, November 10, 1951, box 30, folder: 11/51, GDC, MD, LC.

38. The CGTG was officially founded in 1951, after the CTG (founded in 1944) was renamed to reflect the new confederation's broader structure. See Robert J. Alexander, *A History of Organized Labor in Panama and Central America* (Westport, CT: Praeger, 2008), ch. 9; and Mario López Larrave, *Breve historia.*

39. Víctor Manuel Gutiérrez, "Informe a conferencia de los trabajadores de la UFCO-CAG y IRCA," n.d., box 18, folder: CGTG Reserve, GDC, MD, LC.

40. Piero Gleijeses, "The Agrarian Reform of Jacobo Arbenz," *Journal of Latin American Studies* 21, no. 3 (October 1989): 454; Robert Wasserstrom, "Revolution in Guatemala: Peasants and Politics under the Arbenz Government," *Comparative Studies in Society and History* 17, no. 4 (October 1975): 353–354.

41. Gleijeses, "The Agrarian Reform of Jacobo Arbenz." For earlier labor declarations about the land problem, see "CTG a los trabajadores de la ciudad y del campo," October 1946, Item 606, TFC, Benson-UTA; and "El problema del campesino: Materiales del Congreso General de la CTG," April 1950, box 14, folder: Background of Agrarian Reform, GDC, MD, LC.

42. Jim Handy's observations on the contentious and sometimes chaotic nature of the land reform is supported by the work of J. T. Way and his analysis of other state-centered infrastructure projects in Guatemala City during the reform period. See Jim Handy, *Revolution in the Countryside: Rural Conflict and Agrarian Reform in Guatemala, 1944–1954* (Chapel Hill: University of North Carolina Press, 1994); and J. T. Way, *The Mayan in the Mall: Globalization, Development, and the Making of Modern Guatemala* (Durham, NC: Duke University Press, 2012).

43. Dirección General de Estadística, *Censo agropecuario 1950,* vol. 1:95.

44. Much of the data on United Fruit land in Izabal is usually combined with its holdings on the Pacific coast. For a study that disaggregates some of the statistics on the reform for United Fruit expropriations, see José Luis Paredes Moreira, *Reforma agraria: Una experiencia en Guatemala* (Guatemala City: Imprenta Universitaria, 1963), 70–71.

45. *Octubre,* May 8 and 15, 1952. See also *Octubre,* June 26, 1952.

46. Folders "Quiriguá" and "No tiene nombre," Index 31, INTA-Decreto 900 Collection, AGCA, Guatemala City; "Campesinos de Izabal luchan por conquistar sus tierras," *Octubre,* December 4, 1952, 4; Víctor Segundo Carrillo to Leonardo Castillo Flores, December 22, 1952, box 13, folder: CNCG and Political Organizations, GDC, MD, LC.

47. "Nómina de las Federaciones Campesinas," n.d., box 20, folder: Unions I, Campesinos; Florentín López, Unión Campesina de Quiriguá, to Leonardo Castillo Flores, April 4, 1952, box 39, folder: 4/52. Both in GDC, MD, LC.

48. "Uniones campesinas de Izabal," 1951, box 39, folder: 7-8/51; Leonardo Castillo Flores to Abel Ceballos, February 24, 1954, box 43, folder: 2/54 IV. All in GDC, MD, LC.

49. Leonardo Castillo Flores to Florentín López, July 7, 1951, folder: CGTG Influence, box 19, GDC, MD, LC.

50. Julio H. López Estevez, Junta Agraria Departamental, February 27, 1954, folder "Lote #3," Paquete No. 2, Expediente 3, Index No. 17, INTA-Decreto 900 Collection, AGCA, Guatemala City.

51. Dirección General de Estadística, *Censo agropecuario, 1950,* vol. 1 (Guatemala

City: Dirección General de Estadística, 1951), 95; Eduardo Antonio Velásquez Carrera, *La Revolución de Octubre: Diez años de lucha por la democracia en Guatemala, 1944–1954*, vol. 2 (Guatemala City: USAC, Centro de Estudios Urbanos y Regionales, 1994), 98.

52. Cindy Forster in *The Time of Freedom* has demonstrated that a similar process took place in the Pacific region. The most active sectors for land reform were those agricultural workers from Tiquisate (United Fruit Company) and San Marcos (coffee plantations) who had already been active in the labor movement but still conceived of themselves as campesinos.

53. Comité Cívico Nacional, "Juramento anticomunista," n.d., Item 1604. See also Comité Cívico Nacional, announcement about the "Anticomunista" newspaper, February 1, 1952, Item 1601; CEUAGE, "Comité de Estudiantes Universitarios Anticomunistas Guatemaltecos en el Exilio," December 1953, Item 1660; "Acción Católica de Guatemala," July 2, 1954, Item 1738. All in TFC, Benson-UTA.

54. "Meeting Between Carter and Alberto," March 23, 1954, Freedom of Information Act Electronic Reading Room (FOIA), Doc-0000916844, pg. 13, last accessed August 16, 2019, https://www.cia.gov/library/readingroom/docs/DOC_0000916844.pdf.

55. "Manifestación el viernes 5 de febrero," February 4, 1954, Item 1874, TFC, Benson-UTA.

56. Toriello Garrido, *La batalla de Guatemala*, 184; Francisco Villagrán Kramer, *Biografía política de Guatemala: Los pactos políticos de 1944–1970* (Guatemala City: FLACSO Guatemala, 1993), 164.

CHAPTER 2

The Coastal Laboratory

Milpa, Conservation, and Agrarian Reform

Patrick Chassé

On the eve of the revolution, many Guatemalans families were living on the edge of hunger, struggling to afford basic necessities such as corn and beans. Inclement weather in the early 1940s caused successive crop failures, which triggered a cycle of scarcity and speculation that undermined food security throughout the country for the next decade. According to government statistics, the prices of corn, beans, and other common foods doubled between 1938 and 1945.[1] Editors for the Ministry of Agriculture's periodical, *Revista Agrícola*, urged the new president Juan José Arévalo to curb the "terrible problem of scarcity" by investing in rural modernization and crop diversification.[2] They argued that Guatemalan elites had exploited the country's natural fertility—promoting Guatemala as a land of "eternal spring"—without investing in agriculture.[3] Proponents of agricultural modernization argued that this exploitation caused widespread deforestation and soil erosion that left Guatemala very vulnerable to natural disaster and food shortages.

Between 1944 and 1954, Guatemalan policymakers embraced agrarian modernization—new hybridized crops, mechanization, and chemical fertilizers—as a solution to the environmental and food production problems that threatened to destabilize the revolution. The state's approach to rural development evolved rapidly during this period, shaped by indigenous organizing, national politics, and the environment. During President Arévalo's term (1945–1951), the state favored incremental agricultural reforms that ameliorated rural poverty without addressing the unequal distribution of land and capital. As Jim Handy has argued, Arévalo was reticent to antagonize large landowners because the national budget depended heavily on coffee exports.[4] Policymakers focused narrowly on technical assistance and education as a means to improving productivity. The Ministry of Agriculture dispatched agronomists throughout the country to teach campesinos about the benefits of conservation and modern agriculture. By the end of the 1940s, many agents openly questioned the viability of a rural development strategy that did not address inequality. Agents who worked closely with indigenous communities were impressed by their willingness to experiment with new crops and surprised by their persistent demands for new tools, seed, and fertilizers. By lobbying the Ministry of Agriculture and local officials, indigenous communities forced the state to rethink and expand its rural modernization efforts to address the unequal distribution of land and capital.

After President Jacobo Arbenz was elected in 1951, the government responded to peasant feedback with a package of agrarian reforms that combined land and capital reforms with new agricultural technologies. Policymakers repurposed the discourse of conservation and disaster to legitimize the contentious changes to land tenure introduced in the 1952 Agrarian Reform Law. The government argued that redistributing territory to campesinos—especially on the Pacific coast—benefited the nation because it put underutilized land into production and relieved pressure on highland forests. The use of conservation as a justification for the agrarian reform was effective, but it also demonstrated the unresolved race and class tensions that accompanied agrarian modernization. Throughout the revolution, state officials cited highland deforestation as proof that indigenous agriculture was inefficient—even destructive—but clearing trees on the coast was celebrated as an act of colonization because it opened up Guatemala's fertile coastal frontier.

There are still few environmental histories about Guatemala, and most focus on either the rise of coffee production in the nineteenth century or the expansion of industrial agriculture after the 1970s.[5] As a result, there is a historiographical gap between the 1930s and the 1960s during which the Pacific coast—the country's most important agroexport zone—was transformed by the expansion of industrial agriculture. This was a formative moment for Guatemalan agriculture, when modernizers introduced many of the most important technologies and techniques of the nascent "Green Revolution," including hybridized seeds, mechanization, and chemical fertilizers and pesticides.[6] This acknowledgment adds nuance to previous work by David Carey that attributes the popularization of fertilizers throughout the highlands to heavy promotion by United States Agency for International Development (USAID) technicians in the late 1950s and 1960s.

This article demonstrates how Guatemalan policymakers used the language of conservation to justify agrarian modernization and eventually land reform. It connects Guatemala to a wider international literature on forest and soil conservation, but emphasizes the national political and environmental dynamics that made the application of conservation in Guatemala distinctive.[7] The activism of indigenous communities forced the state to experiment with a more holistic model of agricultural development that tried to balance productivity, environmental health, and social well-being. This experimentation culminated in the 1952 Agrarian Reform Law, which redistributed land to thousands of campesinos, who quickly cleared their parcels and planted them with a wide variety of crops including maize, beans, and cotton. Guatemala's agrarian reform was cut short by the 1954 coup, but in just two years the Arbenz government demonstrated how an agrarian reform that empowered campesinos could quickly reduce inequality, improve productivity, and stabilize environmental problems.

Maize as Monoculture

At the beginning of the revolution, policymakers and agronomists used a conservation discourse that linked rural poverty, traditional agriculture, and deforestation to diagnose Guatemala's productivity problems. In their influential report on the state of agriculture, *Guatemala: Paradise Lost,* modernizers Leopoldo Zeissig and Angel Núñez Aguilar argued that chronic food shortages and deforestation were caused by the marginalization of "intelligent and vigorous" Mayans. They believed that the new government could correct "the gravest error of our history" by creating a rural extension program that demonstrated the benefits of new technologies to campesinos. Prior to the revolution, state support for new crops was limited to commercial cultivars grown on large plantations such as bananas, cotton, and rubber. The Ubico regime tried to stabilize corn prices by forcing campesinos to produce maize, but they did not support communities with technical support, loans, or tools.[8] After 1944, a new wave of modernizers such as Zeissig and Núñez Aguilar argued that the place of government agents was "at the side of the Indian, in front of our fertile fields."[9]

In their search for heightened productivity, modernizers routinely underestimated the intelligence of campesinos, who coaxed remarkable yields out of their small parcels of land. Government officials who sympathized with impoverished indigenous communities remained convinced that stubborn campesinos had to be shown the benefits of new—and largely unproven—crops and technologies by enlightened technicians. "Their ears will close," wrote the editors of the *Revista Agrícola*, "to any preaching and all insinuation that is not accompanied by a palpable demonstration: the campesino hears with his eyes."[10] The director general of agriculture, Hector Sierra, reiterated this point in an international collection about corn in Central America. He warned scholars that sudden changes to land tenure or agriculture would be rejected by indigenous communities. The "Guatemalan Indian does not even bother about where or how he plants his corn, his chief object being to have corn planted that he can take care of as tenderly as a father cares for his children."[11] Sierra's emphasis on education represented a significant policy shift for the Guatemalan government, which had for decades ignored or actively worked to undermine indigenous communities. However, this renewed attention came at a cost. The government became fixated on transforming the Maya into sedentary, market-oriented farmers, and government officials believed that corn was the main obstacle to rural modernization.

Government officials argued that indigenous cornfields produced low yields and caused deforestation and soil erosion. The Department of Forestry attributed 80 percent of deforestation to forest fires that occurred when campesinos used fire to open up new maize fields. This cultivation technique allegedly left "behind a cemetery of burned trees and soils prepared for the invasion of the destructive action of erosion."[12] The Soil Conservation Division acknowledged that maize was the "only wealth" of most campesinos, but they characterized "rudimentary" maize production as a monoculture that "degrades our soils."[13] Policymakers leveraged the power of the state—legislation, enumeration, and aerial surveillance—to regulate traditional agriculture. As James Scott notes, modern states governed by simplifying the countryside into legible categories that served as "a convenient, if partly fictional, shorthand" that the state turned into an imperfect reality using laws and other methods of coercion.[14] In Guatemala, modernizers focused narrowly on the biological characteristics of maize. They calculated ideal yields based on mechanized farms in the United States. This reductive approach ignored the complex intercropping and long-term fallowing cycles that Mayan farmers used to cultivate maize. Corn was never grown by itself, but rather it was the hub of an incredibly dense and resilient agricultural system called *milpa*. Campesinos cultivated corn alongside bean, squash, and a wide variety of trees, plants, vegetables, and edible weeds. This approach prioritized system resiliency over high yields, though it could also achieve the latter because campesinos farmed their small parcels of land intensively, and carefully recycled nutrients back into the system.[15]

In the 1940s, researchers showed that Mayan milpa agriculture was innately focused on conservation, prioritizing long-term productivity over larger crop yields. The anthropologist Raymond Stadelman demonstrated that indigenous milpa fields were part of a complex long-fallow system and that the deforestation observed by critics was only temporary. He found that forests in Huehuetenango were "continually being cleared and planted" to support communities.[16] Fields were opened with controlled burns and planted for several years until the soil was depleted. At this point, the land was allowed to return to forest, and the cycle was repeated again fifteen to twenty years later.[17] Stadelman noted that fire was a useful tool for clearing land and suppressing pests, but repeated burning could result in soil erosion and nutrient leeching because newly cleared land was exposed to intense rainfall.[18] Campesinos mitigated these issues by using contour furrows and carefully fertilizing fields with livestock manure.[19] Stadelman reported that in Todos Santos Cuchumatán, fertilization was "recognized by Indians as the salvation of the soil, without which the highlands would soon become useless for maize production."[20] This was a carefully constructed agroecosystem that required a large amount of land to function properly. By the mid-twentieth century, 88 percent of the population occupied just 14 percent of the country's farmland, meaning that most Guatemalans subsisted on less than two *manzanas*.[21] Inequality coupled with rapid population growth throughout the twentieth century limited campesino access to land, and many compensated by shortening their fallows or renting new land for milpa cultivation.[22] Over time, this forced intensification lowered yields and created some of the environmental problems that modernizers observed.

Government officials were not receptive to this nuanced analysis of indigenous agriculture because it challenged their efforts to create a sedentary agricultural population that was engaged in monoculture. Guatemalan modernizers were engaged with an international conservation movement that portrayed farmers and peasants as the cause of rural deforestation and soil erosion. Throughout the early twentieth century, scholars often used the Maya as an example of a civilization that was destroyed because the people failed to conserve scarce soils. In 1919, Orator F. Cook, an agronomist with the United States Department of Agriculture, argued that the Maya had engineered their own collapse by overworking delicate tropical soils until they were exhausted.[23] He noted that "milpa cultivation" was still a major cause of rural deforestation because campesinos frequently lost control of the fires they set to clear new maize fields.[24] Cook concluded that repeated burnings permanently destroyed soil fertility, transforming once lush regions such as the valley of Salamá, in the department of Baja Verapaz, into "artificial deserts cleared by human agency."[25] This misleading narrative fixed the Maya in time—suggesting that indigenous communities remained fundamentally the same over hundreds of years—and so ignored how poverty, unequal access to land, and rapid population growth forced Mayan communities to artificially intensify maize production.[26] Cook's observations, couched in technical language, contributed to an international discourse that characterized indigenous agriculture as inefficient and even destructive.

The potential link between environmental decay, overpopulation, and poverty was popularized by the American William Vogt, chief of the Conservation Section for the Pan American Union.[27] He argued that rapid population growth throughout Latin America was causing an untenable intensification of agriculture that would eventually lead to famine and war.[28] Vogt was heavily influenced by his work in Central America, and his conversation with a Mayan campesino was used as the closing vignette in three different publications. Vogt wrote: "A Guatemalan Indian—a literate one—summed up the problem well. I had been showing him, for the first time, the meaning of gullies through the corn and wheat fields, the chocolate color of the river that flowed by. He watched me for a long time, standing with me in the rain; then he said, 'Why my country is a New Atlantis. It is disappearing beneath the ocean.'"[29] The story, almost certainly apocryphal, captured Vogt's belief that patient education and leadership by technicians could stem soil erosion and deforestation. He advised Latin American countries to foster rural conservation with rural extension programs that combined technical outreach with adult education strategies.[30] Foreign experts such as Cook and Vogt cultivated a misleading but influential image of Central American forests in disarray and decay, threatened by the careless cultivation habits of uneducated campesinos.

Educate or Relocate

From the outset of the revolution, there was tension between proponents of slow reform through education—including the former educator President Arévalo—and those who endorsed more radical solutions, including colonization and relocation. This second group included the director general for agriculture, Hector Sierra, and Angel Núñez Aguilar, the coauthor of *Guatemala: Paradise Lost* and future head of the country's rural development agency, Instituto de Fomento de la Producción (Institute for the Development of Production; INFOP). They wanted to couple education to structural reforms that would help Guatemala create a rationalized agrarian landscape with export-oriented industrial farms on the coast and smaller, market-oriented farms throughout the highlands. This tension was evident in negotiations over a new forest law drafted by the Ministry of Agriculture in 1945, which was supposed to protect forests along major watersheds and on slopes with a grade over 15 percent. When the Ministry of Agriculture published the proposed law in June 1945, Article 24 firmly prohibited the use of fire to clear new land, a practice that was closely identified with subsistence corn production. To "eradicate this practice," the draft law gave the state the authority to resettle "reluctant cores" to areas that were less prone to soil erosion.[31] This language was eliminated from the final law, which protected forests along major watersheds and on slopes with an incline over 15 percent. Instead, the government made a commitment to convince farmers of the value of forests through education and demonstration.[32]

The Arévalo administration chose the path of least resistance and focused on education and technical outreach, avoiding the thorny land tenure problems that were the root cause of environmental problems throughout the highlands. Guatemala's rural extension and conservation campaign was inspired by the US New Deal, which was unsurprising given President Arévalo's admiration for Franklin D. Roosevelt.[33] The Guatemalan government emulated the Roosevelt administration's soil conservation strategy, combining rural extension work in rural communities with a media campaign that linked milpa production with deforestation, soil erosion, and disaster. Experts visited communities to present films and workshops exploring these themes, but they also published lengthy articles and photo essays that demonstrated the efficiency and productivity of modern agricultural practices.[34] These discussions appeared regularly in government publications such as *Revista Agrícola*, which tried to cultivate a shared sense of mission among literate farmers and community leaders. Policymakers hoped that agricultural experts could create abundance by teaching Guatemalans how to make wise use of scarce forest and soil resources, preventing potential disasters such as the dust storms that swept across the United States during the 1930s.[35]

In 1946, *Revista Agrícola* published a special issue focused on Guatemalan forests that featured aerial photography from the Pacific coast and the highlands. The government's Aerial Forest Service argued that photos taken from the air were powerful tools for education, and they asked farmers to learn to "read the land" in order to become, as they put it, "our best collaborator." This simple request was laden with ideological meaning:

reading the land correctly meant accepting the division of Guatemala's landscapes into an untapped lowland frontier and the overworked highlands. Photos of the Pacific coast emphasized the vast expanses that had yet to be planted with lucrative exports such as sugarcane and bananas. Only photos of farms close to Retalhuleu and the United Fruit Company (UFCO)–owned plantation of Tiquisate reversed the equation by showcasing large planted fields.[36] These images of orderly and productive fields were supposed to highlight the benefits of private initiative on the Pacific coast, which created productive fields out of lowland forests.

Viewing agrarian landscapes from afar enabled policymakers to identify agricultural practices they deemed wasteful and justify resettlement initiatives for communities that did not fit into their vision for a rationalized agrarian landscape.[37] The special issue featured aerial imagery of deforestation and soil erosion that was used to justify the state's efforts to impose conservation on Mayan campesinos. Photos from the Tecpán region showed how indigenous communities cultivated recently cleared land "that belongs to the forest" without taking precautions against soil erosion. "Meagre harvests," the authors wrote, "and the constant specter of desolation is the punishment of the man who destroys the forest, his best friend and firm ally."[38] Aerial photography gave experts an unrivaled ability to observe peasant activity but was often unable to capture the benefits of different types of traditional agriculture in situ. As James Scott argues, this simplification facilitated governance by reducing the natural world to a handful of key variables.[39]

The ministry also used advertisements to convince readers that inaction would lead to forest fires, soil erosion, and chronic food shortages. Some ads emphasized the immediate risk of forest fires, in an attempt to dissuade indigenous farmers from using fire to clear land. An ad published in late 1945 showed a frantic indigenous woman, her son, and their livestock fleeing a fire consuming their homestead. The text explained that these tragedies occurred frequently during the dry period and urged Guatemalans to collaborate with the Ministry of Agriculture's national forest campaign to minimize the risk of wildfires.[40] An ad on the opposite page featured an imposing hand in the top corner of the image, pointing at a campesino climbing a large tree to cut lower limbs for firewood. The Department of Forestry warned that this traditional means of gathering firewood robbed the soil of important nutrients and eventually killed the tree, leading to soil erosion.[41] The government encouraged all Guatemalans to cooperate with the revolutionary government, arguing that good citizens were also stewards of scarce forest resources.[42] This message was explicit in another advertisement that pictured a campesino and a forest ranger shaking hands in a symbolic bridging of the class and cultural gap that divided rangers—and government experts—from the communities they patrolled.[43]

The Ministry of Agriculture used the picturesque tourist town of Panajachel to raise awareness about the risks of deforestation. The town straddled the edge of Lago Atitlán, and the surrounding slopes were steep and susceptible to erosion. Intense tropical rains between May and October created rills and gullies on exposed land, which swept valuable soil downhill and into the lake. Often the most intense storms came late in the season, when the ground was saturated with water, and this heightened the risk of landslides and flooding.[44] The Ministry of Agriculture published images of fields in the region with a 75 percent slope "swept by the axe as it could not have been by a cyclone: no signs of the forest remain." The caption blamed uneducated peasants who preferred to "employ triple the effort in cultivating maize, where the natural laws are shouting their dissatisfaction. . . . Man is cultivating his own ruin."[45] The following page featured a drawing of treeless slopes, riddled with gullies and surrounding a raging river, and urged readers not to repeat the mistakes of Panajachel.[46] The government began a reforestation campaign around the town, and officials continued to attack traditional maize cultivation. An article profiling the success of the campaign warned that the axe and the "eagerness to harvest cobs on steep slopes" had destroyed the pine and cypress forest, exposing the ground to the rains that "write in the naked earth signs of death and desolation."[47] These warnings were prescient, as Panajachel was one of the main victims of devastating floods and landslides in 1949 that wrought tremendous damage across the south coast.

In 1946, the Ministry of Agriculture intensified its campaign to reform campesino agriculture by creating a national network of extension agents. Their charter called them "apostles of this crusade for the defense of the soil, the water, the tree" and urged agents to educate farmers by teaching them techniques that would lessen soil erosion and encourage them to see farming as an "economic enterprise."[48] Between 1946 and 1948, these extension agents traveled throughout the country introducing new agricultural techniques to small and medium farmers. They repeatedly emphasized "the necessity of abandoning [corn] monoculture" and adopting hybridized corn and alternative crops such as henequen, wheat, and cotton.[49] To their surprise, peasants and small farmers were eager to organize and diversify their crops.

Agents helped organize Committees for Agriculture, Livestock and Rural Industry, which became important political instruments for the state to exercise influence in the countryside. Across the country, committees quickly transcended their initial purpose and became popular vehicles for political organizing that enabled rural communities to communicate directly with the state. Their popularity anticipated the success of other community-level organizations during the revolution, including the Local Agrarian Committees who initiated the expropriations process during agrarian reform. The campesinos who participated in committees used their privileged access to the state to bypass local authorities and make appeals directly to the agents and the minister of agriculture. They emphasized their commitment to modernization and claimed that mechanization, new seeds, and fertilizers would help them escape poverty and improve productivity.[50]

The reports filed by extension agents and the letters from committees offer detailed insights into the complex financial and political problems restricting agricultural growth, at least from the perspective of government agents. Although the government promoted mechanization, there was a chronic shortage of tractors, and the Ministry of Agriculture's tractors were concentrated in Quetzaltenango and on the Pacific coast.[51] Mechanization was a popular theme in letters to the ministry, but most communities focused on the urgent need for farming tools. The agent for Alta Verapaz concluded his September report by noting the "unspeakable insistence" with which the "working poor" of Quiché, Baja Verapaz, and the Petén asked him for machetes and hoes in anticipation of the next planting season.[52] Although agents were often able to meet these individual demands, the shortage of tools was a sign of widespread poverty. More tools did not change the fact that 2 percent of the population controlled 70 percent of the country's arable land. Agents promoted the high yields secured through modern agriculture, but campesinos needed more land and better access to capital in order to expand production. Substantive rural change was impossible without an agrarian reform that enabled campesinos to access fertile land.

In December 1946, the Committee for Agriculture for Asunción Mita, Jutiapa, appealed to the minister of agriculture to intervene in a local land conflict. The committee wanted landowners to rent quality land to campesinos at a reasonable cost, stating that "life tends to get more expensive everyday mainly in these areas where there are no other means of subsistence."[53] The Section of Colonization and Lands worried that ministerial intervention would encourage campesinos to bypass administrative hierarchies. They urged the committee to look for a local power broker to deal with the issue.[54] Alcalde Don Maximiliano Ramírez tried to broker a meeting to discuss land problems between campesinos and local landowners, but the latter refused to attend.[55] The government finally dispatched the agricultural agent for Jutiapa, Isaías Benedicto Hernández, to investigate the land conflict. He found that over six hundred campesinos had no access to land because local landowners refused to rent to them.[56] The *alcalde* refused to call another meeting because local elites told him privately that they had already picked campesinos to rent their land.[57] Over fifty landless peasants met with the Committee for Agriculture and Benedicto to voice their concerns that they were "victims of the unjustified hatred of the landowners" who denied them land after they voted for President Arévalo. Instead, they selectively distributed land to more conservative campesinos.[58] For centuries elites had used their control over land to successfully discourage political organizing, which helped them maintain a status quo that was profitable for large landowners but detrimental to national productivity. During the revolution, campesinos began to openly challenge this arrangement, by lobbying extension agents and the Ministry of Agriculture to intervene on their behalf against powerful landowners. In his letter to the Ministry of Agriculture, Benedicto concluded that the state had to resettle campesinos before growing enmity between both parties led to "fatal consequences."[59] The General Section of Colonization and Lands agreed and identified nearly two hundred *caballerías* of land in the government-owned Colonia Montúfar that was available for campesinos.[60] This relocation defused a simmering rural conflict, but this was a temporary solution to a systemic problem: rural inequality.

Communities actively pushed the state to fulfill its rhetoric about the benefits of modernization, citing the productivity costs of rural inequality including a shortage of land, capital, and tools. In 1948, the Committee of Agriculture from Santa Cruz Naranjo, Santa Rosa, asked the government to help resolve a local corn shortage that caused artificially high grain prices in the region.[61] The committee wanted to be relocated to the National Farm Cerro Redondo, where better land would allow them to produce more food and avoid, as they put it, "the calamities that we are now suffering with the shortages of corn."[62] The administrator for Cerro Redondo declined the committee's request for resettlement, citing a lack of space. The administrator noted that there were already a considerable number of renters from the Santa Cruz Naranjo who picked coffee in return for access to land. To accept more would undermine their efforts to ensure that resident campesinos, or *colonos*, "live[d] contentedly and in the best way possible."[63] Although their efforts to secure new land failed, their agent tried with limited success to lobby local farmers to increase the amount of corn they were cultivating so that future shortages could be averted. "It's not reasonable," he wrote, "that Guatemala, being a country of farmers, has to import CORN from other countries."[64] While the government struggled to find suitable land for campesinos, food production suffered and rural inequality deepened.

The government passed two pieces of legislation during the 1940s that were supposed to ameliorate the demand for land: the Agricultural Emergency Law (1946) and the Laws of Forced Rental, passed in 1949 and updated in 1951. These laws enabled campesinos to rent unused land from large landowners in exchange for a percentage of their harvest. Some highland peasants successfully used the law to access new corn land on the coast, but landowners opposed the legislation and it benefited only a handful of campesinos.[65] Agricultural agents extolled the virtues of seed selection and fertilizers, but without land and adequate capital most campesinos were unable to realize the productivity promised by modernizers. At best, these technical fixes temporarily staved off rural demands for land by increasing the productivity of the small plots of land that campesinos tended. Too often the technical solutions were misguided and led to little or no improvement in production. Over the long term, this intensification on marginal land worsened the environmental problems the government wanted to solve, and government inaction undermined their support among campesinos.[66] This impasse eventually led to the creation of a new, semiautonomous rural development organization in 1948: the Institute for the Development of Production (INFOP).[67]

The motto of INFOP was simple but transformative in its emphasis on production as the means to redress inequality: "Produce more to live better." The institute stimulated modernization with targeted loans and a strong focus on technical assistance for famers, large and small. It also laid the groundwork for the 1952 agrarian reform by demonstrating the viability of the Pacific coast as a new agricultural frontier. It funded agricultural research that defined and quantified a poorly understood agrarian region that was dominated by undercapitalized plantations. INFOP also experimented with new crops and forms of land tenure on experimental farms. These controlled spaces were utilized to demonstrate the productive potential of modernization on the Pacific coast and the viability of a mixed farming landscape. It was, however, INFOP's decisive action after a natural disaster that earned the organization respect and gave it the leverage to promote coastal colonization as a systemic solution to food production problems.

Agrarian Reform as Conservation

In October 1949, Guatemala was subjected to a month of intense rainstorms that caused destructive floods and landslides throughout the countryside. Almost thirty inches of rain fell in the capital during the first fifteen days of October. The final deluge came in a rainstorm that raged for seventy-two hours, inundating communities around Lake Atitlán and Amatitlán. Surging rivers destroyed over fifty bridges and wrecked an estimated twelve hundred miles of highways. The Guatemalan government reported that at least fifty villages had been swept away by water or buried under landslides triggered by the storm.[68] "As each additional report arrives," President Juan José Arevalo explained to international media on October 19, "the disaster assumes greater proportions."[69] The disaster killed upwards of four thousand people and displaced seventy thousand.[70] Campesinos already living in poverty were devastated by the loss of their homes, their crops, and their livestock.[71] The storms destroyed many plantations and grain stores across the south coast, causing food shortages that plagued Guatemala for years.

Although large swathes of the Guatemalan countryside had been affected by the storms, two regions received special attention in early reports: the Motagua valley and Panajachel. On October 14, after 5 days of hurricane-like rain, the Motagua River burst its banks in the middle of the night and swept through towns and villages, carrying away homes, people, and livestock. Valley residents estimated that the river rose twenty-eight feet, and when the waters receded fertile fields were destroyed, and often buried by mud and debris. One elder remarked that he had never seen the like after eighty years living in the area.[72] In Panajachel, the ferocious river dragged huge boulders and ancient trees down from the mountains, sweeping aside the houses of the humble and leaving luxury hotels flooded. Locals coped with the devastation by remembering how the city had rebuilt after previous catastrophes. Elders cited an epic flood on October 4, 1881, that matched the ferocity of the recent disaster, though in the wake of that event most of the population left Panajachel for the south coast. Braulio Mayén, a longtime resident, sought meaning in the disaster by suggesting it was punishment for human misuse of nature: "The same Nature repentant for the gift given to us, jealous, unleashed her implacable fury against human works, to highlight more her own charms."[73]

Supporters of agricultural modernization saw the disaster as proof that milpa agriculture in the highlands was a threat to Guatemala's economic prosperity. The editors of *El Imparcial*, for example, dismissed metaphysical explanations and placed the blame squarely on human actions.

In an editorial titled "Neglect, Ignorance, and Ruin," they cited "incessant deforestation" and poor cultivation practices of highland farmers as the aggravating factor that allowed a destructive storm to become a catastrophe. Like others, *El Imparcial*'s writers sought to contextualize the storm by reminding readers of devastating storms in 1924, 1926, and 1931. They did so not to minimize its importance, but rather to emphasize that this storm was exponentially more destructive. Guatemala's best agrarian lands had been buried by landslides and scrubbed clean by floods. The damage was measurably worse, noted *El Imparcial*, where tree cover had been removed by deforestation. It reminded readers that though national defense was often thought of in terms of military arms alone, Guatemalans needed to initiate a new campaign to prevent the destruction of the nation's soils. This "national imperative" had to check the daily attacks on soils by Guatemalans who "only think about today and not tomorrow, in their immediate gain and in the least effort." The editorial rejected traditional agriculture in favor of modern cultivation practices. It warned that if Guatemalans failed to conserve soils, they risked a future where the country became an "immense desert whose fruit will be dust storms, floods in the winter, desolation and poverty forever."[74]

Policymakers looked to the lightly populated Pacific coast as fertile ground for modernization and resettlement schemes that could induce campesinos to abandon their community-managed milpas for more conventional single-family farms. The International Bank of Reconstruction and Development (IBRD) urged the Guatemalan government to relocate campesinos to new villages in "regions better adapted to progressive agriculture" such as the Pacific coast. In these managed spaces, the state could quickly treat tropical diseases and manage the transformation of indigenous peasants into industrious market farmers.[75] The Institute for the Development of Production, with the support of the IBRD, led coastal development efforts.[76] The organization had already garnered goodwill by acting quickly after the disaster to support the state and small farmers in need. It freely distributed hybrid corn seeds to farmers and extended a generous line of credit to the Arévalo administration, which bought food "to stave off the scarcity of subsistence goods that threatened inhabitants."[77] The disaster relief work undertaken by INFOP dovetailed with the institution's efforts to promote modern agriculture and encourage coastal colonization as a solution for Guatemala's environmental and food production problems.

Planners from INFOP worried that overpopulation throughout the highlands amplified deforestation, leading to more frequent and intense flooding throughout the lowlands. They used their experimental farms to demonstrate the productivity of modern agriculture and experiment with new forms of land tenure such as "usufruct," a form of long-term rental. The institution claimed that farmers who focused on conservation produced "more and better food" for the "continuous well-being of Man, last usufructuary of natural resources."[78] The institute's "conservationist doctrine" reconceptualized the farmer as a steward of natural resources instead of as an owner. Stewardship benefited the majority of Guatemalans over time, instead of a select few who benefited immediately and shared little of their wealth. Farmers could prosper if they collaborated with scientists to "not only increase the production of the earth but also maintain its fertility."[79] Farmers who adopted this stewardship model surrendered a measure of control to technicians, who became the arbiters of best practices regarding land use.

The institute justified this loss of local autonomy by emphasizing the benefits it could offer campesinos, including higher yields and better access to domestic markets. In a lengthy memorandum written in 1951, Juan Fernández Mendía, of INFOP's Cotton Division, proposed a new plan to distribute cottonseeds to campesinos on Guatemala's Pacific coast. He promised that this initiative would allow Guatemala's "huge, unproductive masses" to create "new communities of wealth" in a hitherto abandoned and unproductive region. Fernández Mendía estimated that upward of six thousand manzanas could be put into production if roughly ten thousand indigenous peasants and small farmers planted ten *cuerdas* each.[80] This would create a large supply of domestic cotton for Guatemala's textile industry and would offer small farmers a new revenue stream that would improve their quality of life.[81] The *Monitor del INFOP* argued that mixed land tenure encouraged crop diversity and increased the economic resiliency of an agrarian landscape. "[We] must mark," they wrote, "the path of progress in the productive labor of the peasant."[82] As a semiautonomous government agency, INFOP was able to freely experiment with alternative models of land tenure. Its experimental farms demonstrated how mixed land use could improve productivity and contribute to forest and soil conservation by relocating farmers to less environmentally sensitive regions. The institute established an important precedent for the Arbenz administration (1951–1954), which sought to diversify land tenure through agrarian reform.

The 1949 disaster caused widespread crop losses and destabilized food production across Guatemala, resulting in scarcity and speculation. By May 1951, the Guatemalan government reported that the cost of food in the capital was 21.5 percent higher than the year before. To mitigate public concern, the newly elected president Jacobo Arbenz took to the radio on May 1 to announce that he had submitted a study on Guatemala's food problem to the National Economic Council. Two days later, the president told the press that without major reforms, food shortages and inflation would continue to plague rural Guatemala. Arbenz blamed the food crisis on antiquated farming practices employed by the rural elite and highland peasants. He argued that shortages were the outward manifestations of a dysfunctional economic system that wasted Guatemala's natural wealth.[83] The disaster demonstrated the fragility of Guatemalan agriculture and gave Arbenz—who experienced serious crop losses on his own farm, El Cajón—the political justification for a sweeping agrarian reform.[84]

After a year of careful negotiation and planning, the Arbenz administration passed the Agrarian Reform Law (Decree 900) in June of 1952. The law was moderate and was implemented efficiently, notwithstanding opposition from large landowners and frustration from campesinos who wanted it to move faster. By 1954, the government had expropriated and redistributed an estimated 917,659 acres of land to 87,589 people, who received roughly ten acres each, though this varied depending on the quality of land.[85] Campesinos who received previously worked land were given between 8.5 and 17, whereas beneficiaries who received undeveloped land were given between 26 and 33 acres.[86] The majority of land distributed to campesinos was given out in lifelong usufruct. Decree 900 stipulated that usufruct could be revoked if campesinos did not plant the crops mandated by the government. This was justified as a means to maintain the production of crops that were important to the national economy—including coffee—but it also indicated the government's preference for state-led economic development. The usufruct model advocated by INFOP and instituted during the agrarian reform gave the state extra leverage to guide campesino production.[87]

Throughout the agrarian reform, experts struggled to balance conservation with efforts to diversify crops and increase food production. The government protected key resources from expropriation by embedding conservation in the spirit and the letter of the Agrarian Reform Law. Decree 900 had special clauses that protected land on slopes over 30 percent or those bordering watersheds from expropriation.[88] These regulations were sometimes ignored in the rush to distribute land to campesinos, but their presence indicates that the government saw conservation as a means to sustain the productivity of Guatemala's best farmland. Like their North

American counterparts, Guatemalan technicians and policymakers saw conservation as a way to extend the bounties of nature so that economic growth could be sustained over time.[89] However, the government's use of conservation as a justification for agrarian reform also exposed contradictions in their modernization agenda. State officials attacked highland deforestation as proof of the peasantry's rejection of modernity, but clearing trees on the coast was celebrated as an act of colonization that opened up Guatemala's fertile frontier. In the eyes of the government, a tree felled in the highlands destroyed the fabric of the nation, but a tree felled on the coast was the precursor to national development.

The government's preference for saving the highlands at the expense of lowland ecoregions reflected entrenched cultural ideals about the best kind of nature and the right kind of development. Modernizers emphasized the productivity benefits of modern agriculture that required large investments in chemicals, machines, and specialized seeds. They could not see the benefits of more flexible systems such as milpa agriculture, which could be easily established on new land and prioritized sustainability over raw productivity.[90] The Ministry of Agriculture's Soil Conservation Division warned Guatemalan officials in 1953 that production still lagged behind population growth, and they supported efforts to move campesinos out of the highlands. The division concluded that 12.4 *quintales* of corn per manzana was just enough to feed the population in 1949–1950, but they anticipated that rapid population growth and diminishing yields would result in serious shortages by 1956.[91] The division argued that with technical assistance campesinos could double their yields in less than a year without expanding the amount of land under cultivation. "If we make good use of our natural resources," wrote the division head, "we will get more crops to live better."[92]

The Arbenz administration hoped that the agrarian reform would hasten the transformation of indigenous campesinos into small yeoman farmers. Promotional material produced by the Ministry of Agriculture idealized the family farm that Decree 900 recipients would inhabit, featuring mixed-land use on rationalized and nucleated settlements.[93] For Arbenz and his fellow modernizers, the agrarian reform was the first step in a larger economic transformation that would transform Guatemala into a modern nation with a strong industrial sector. Carlos Manuel Pellecer, an influential labor organizer, argued, "Without an agrarian reform we can't speak about industrialization in Guatemala." According to Pellecer, beneficiaries of the agrarian reform would establish small farms that would increase food production and rapidly lower food costs. This would enable the majority of Guatemala's campesinos to abandon subsistence agriculture and become wage laborers on plantations or in factories.[94] The freedom to become wage laborers or establish lowland farms came with the implied cost of abandoning subsistence agriculture and the aspects of indigenous culture perceived as antithetical to modernity. As Marx observed, losing control of the means of production was capitalism's way of ensuring that workers were "free and unfree": free to sell their labor or crops, but wholly dependent on the market for their social reproduction.[95]

Although campesinos experimented with new farming techniques, crops, and forms of land tenure, the farms they created did not wholly correspond to the idealized models promoted by the state. Instead, Decree 900 beneficiaries subtly shaped the division of land to reestablish the basic structures that historically enabled indigenous communities to collectively control land and resources. For example, when Union Campesina members from Santa María Cauqué received land in Santiago Sacatepéquez, the Comité Agrario Local (Local Agrarian Committee; CAL) worked with Soil Conservation officer Virgilio Recinos to parcel out land. He used an ox-drawn plow to divide thirty-six manzanas of land into fifty-four parcels. Peasants were awarded land through a raffle system, but they set aside six parcels that they planned to farm together for the benefit of the community. After land was distributed, the Soil Conservation Division began leveling land to minimize soil erosion, and the peasants agreed to follow technical advice when planting and cultivating crops. This distribution of land struck a balance between conservation and community needs.[96]

Decree 900 beneficiaries subverted expectations about peasant agriculture by eagerly embracing new agrarian technologies and techniques that could improve productivity on newly cleared land. In April of 1953, the CAL of Puerto San José wrote to the minister of agriculture directly, requesting rice seeds of the "blue bonnet" variety that had recently been featured in the newspaper *Nuestro Diario*. The Ministry of Agriculture approved the CAL of Puerto San José's request for seeds in just two weeks, a rapid response considering the provision of seeds was technically the responsibility of the Departamento Agrario Nacional (National Agrarian Department; DAN). In lieu of payment, they asked the committee to return an equal amount of seeds to the ministry so that they could continue propagating seed stock.[97] Another letter, sent by the CAL of Pueblo Nuevo Viñas in April 1953, reported on the success of education efforts and urged the ministry to quickly send more pamphlets about modern agriculture.

They ended their letter with a pledge of support for Decree 900, "whatever it costs, so that we have a new Guatemala" under the government of Jacobo Arbenz.[98] Decree 900 beneficiaries deftly invoked the rhetoric of the administration to ensure that their demands were heard and acted upon quickly by officials in Guatemala City.

Many beneficiaries used their membership in the Confederación Nacional Campesina de Guatemala (National Peasant Confederation of Guatemala; CNCG) to request seeds, tractors, pesticides, and more from the state. The secretary general of the CNCG was Leonard Castillo Flores, and beneficiaries of the agrarian reform sent complaints, petitions, and requests to him, which he presented to the pertinent ministry.[99] Although campesinos did not abandon maize, they did incorporate modern techniques and technologies into the maize field. During this process, agronomists often gained the trust of communities and became important intermediaries between the state and the peasantry. In June of 1953, Castillo Flores asked the Ministry of Agriculture to immediately cancel the transfer of agronomist Alfonso Castañeda to a major pest control initiative. Castillo warned that his transfer would cripple Jalapa's efforts to combat erosion.[100] The ministry quickly cancelled Castañeda's transfer, a move that demonstrated the sway campesinos could exert over the state when they spoke in the language of conservation.[101]

Of course, peasants who received land during the agrarian reform sometimes found that agronomists used conservation to limit their access to land. Landowners often complained that peasants invaded their property without permission or settled on land that was not eligible for expropriation. The Arbenz administration tried to balance the growing opposition of landowners with the concerns of peasants, who were anxious that land was not being expropriated fast enough.[102] As these property conflicts unfolded, landowners tried to use the government's evident concern about conservation to force the government to intervene in their favor. For example, in February 1953 the United Fruit Company (UFCO) complained to the forest inspector for the Eastern Department of Izabal that peasants were illicitly occupying their land. The UFCO framed its concerns in the language of conservation, warning that peasants were clearing valuable forests close to the water source used by the town of Morales and its plantation, Bananera.[103] As Ingrid Sierakowski writes in chapter 1, Izabal's unique racialized politics created a particular challenge to both the UFCO and the revolutionary governments' plans.

The forest inspector launched an investigation and concluded that the local CAL had subdivided five caballerías of UFCO land, which contained precious lumber that was protected under Decree 900. Although he sympathized with the CAL's claim to lumber, he insisted that their settlement threatened an important watershed and encouraged relocation to nearby land. The inspector argued that the law protected peasant and landowner both by conserving land that might otherwise be destroyed by shortsighted speculation. "It is our obligation," he wrote, "to avoid by all means a destruction which will cause in time irreparable damages for the same peasants who forget precaution for tomorrow."[104] His evenhanded approach to the case did little to quell peasant grievances, because it appeared to favor the United Fruit Company. The local CAL accused the inspector of collusion with the UFCO and asked for his immediate dismissal.[105] The Ministry of Agriculture investigated and exonerated the inspector, who was surprised by the allegations.[106] Peasants who did not demonstrate their devotion to conservation—as defined by the state—lost valuable political capital, which harmed their efforts to obtain the financial and technical assistance necessary to develop their new land.[107]

Guatemala's agrarian reform was ambitious, but financial shortfalls and administrative issues often caused frustration among beneficiaries, who wanted to improve their land but lacked the means to buy tools, seeds, and inputs. Campesinos who did not use the language of modernization or conservation in their letters often found that their demands for assistance went unheard. In June 1954, just weeks before the US-backed coup, peasants from the highland town of Panimaquip, Totonicapán, desperately needed funds to help them collect the corn they had planted on Decree 900 land. They wrote to Castillo Flores to help them secure loans from the National Agrarian Bank so that they could continue tending their beans and corn. The peasants wrote that "now is the time of our poverty," referring to the hungry period right before the harvest when campesinos had exhausted their corn stores and bought corn from the market for inflated prices. They traveled to visit the bank manager in the coastal city of Mazatenango, and he assured them that an inspector would come to see their land. After fifteen days passed without a visit, they pleaded with Castillo Flores of the CNCG to intervene with the bank on their behalf. Eventually they gave up hope and left their land to go work for others. "Today," they wrote, "we are going with other compañeros to earn corn to sustain the family; because here we suffer with[out] maize because our harvest is yearly." Their harvest depended on receiving timely financial aid from the bank so they could hire help to clean the fields and guarantee a good crop. "Without cleaning in our land," they concluded somberly, "the crop will be ruined and we will lose everything."[108]

Under President Arbenz, the Guatemalan state attempted to fuse conservation with agrarian reform. By redistributing land, modernizers hoped to both relieve pressure on highland forests and create a pathway for Mayan campesinos to become farmers producing for the market. However, the case of Panimaquip demonstrates the limitations of the 1952 agrarian reform. The rapid transfer of land overextended the state, which lacked the financial and technical capacity to fulfill its commitments to Decree 900 beneficiaries. Many campesinos used their affiliation with the CNCG to leverage government assistance, but the success of their appeals depended on their persistence and their ability to use the language of conservation and productivity. Modernizers were more apt to help campesinos who demonstrated their commitment to new crops and technologies, while those who planted milpa had trouble getting financial and technical assistance from the government. The paradox of Guatemala's agrarian reform was that many campesinos obtained land, but some still lacked the means to establish the modern farms envisioned by Arbenz and other modernizers. Desperate campesinos often had to leave their new land, traveling to nearby plantations, where they sold the only possession they had: their labor.

Conclusion

Reflecting on the agrarian reform, María Vilanova de Arbenz emphasized its importance as a "type of experimental laboratory, of crops and technical innovations that gave a great push to the modernization of agriculture."[109] Her evaluation highlights the unexpected longevity of the agrarian reform during the revolution, which popularized modern agricultural technologies and techniques throughout rural Guatemala. The Agrarian Reform Law enabled the state to redistribute 17 percent of the country's farmland to over 100,000 families. This unprecedented transition of land created a new agrarian landscape that realized, briefly and imperfectly, the substantive changes to Guatemala agriculture that Arbenz promised in 1951. Beneficiaries eagerly experimented with new crops and fertilizers, but they also continued to cultivate milpa, tend small gardens, and keep livestock. By 1953, Guatemalan agriculture was thriving: coffee production increased, and there was an 11.8 percent increase in corn production compared to 1950.[110] Whereas previous efforts to transform the countryside had involved imposing new crops and technologies on campesinos, Decree 900 created a political space in which campesinos, technicians, and policymakers worked together to build a more diverse, equitable, and sustainable agrarian landscape.

The agrarian reform also established the importance of agricultural modernization and conservation, which became key ideas in the rural development discourse long after the revolution. Even under Arbenz, campesinos who wanted state support had the best results when they framed their demands in terms of conservation or productivity. These were fluid concepts that could be readily turned against communities by experts and politicians. Large landowners, for example, did not share Arbenz's belief that improving the peasantry's quality of life would bring collective prosperity. Where Arbenz and his followers saw a growing web of small producers becoming citizens, landowners saw nightmarish invaders ready to avenge themselves on the elite who had exploited them for generations.[111] The agrarian reform threatened the power of large landowners because it undermined the competitive advantages of Guatemalan plantations: cheap indigenous labor and abundant land.[112] After the 1954 coup, large landowners adeptly used the language of conservation and productivity to reclaim their lost land.

Large landowners—supported by experts—claimed that Decree 900 beneficiaries deforested protected land to plant milpa. Although they invoked conservation to reclaim their land, most eschewed reforestation and replaced small cornfields with lucrative exports. Agrarian modernization, divorced from concerns about equality and sustainability, helped Guatemalan elites produce fantastic yields, but the costs of production were borne by the indigenous population and the environment. After the coup, deforestation, soil erosion, and food scarcity intensified, but elites were convinced that these were cultural problems: symptoms of indigenous traditionalism that could be solved by imposing science, private property, and the market on the countryside. The legacy of this approach to rural development is evident in modern Guatemala, which has one of the highest rates of chronic malnutrition in the Americas and faces significant food production problems because of deforestation, soil erosion, and climate change. The 1952 agrarian reform remains relevant because it demonstrated that collaboration between campesinos and the state could create meaningful solutions for the food production and environmental problems facing Guatemala.

Notes

1. Leopoldo Zeissig, *Guatemala, paraíso perdido* (Guatemala City: Imprenta Hispania, 1946), 29–30.

2. Dirección General de Agricultura, "Perspectivas Incalculables para la Agricultura en Guatemala," *Revista Agrícola*, January 1945, 99; "Sección Editorial: Terreno abonado para obra constructiva agrícola," *Revista Agrícola*, February 1945, 184.

3. Dirección General de Agricultura, "Perspectivas incalculables para la agricultura en Guatemala," 99.

4. Jim Handy, *Revolution in the Countryside: Rural Conflict and Agrarian Reform in Guatemala, 1944–1954* (Chapel Hill: University of North Carolina Press, 1994), 27.

5. Examples include Stefania Gallini, *Una historia ambiental del café en Guatemala: La Costa Cuca entre 1830 y 1902* (Guatemala City: Asociación para el Avance de las Ciencias Sociales en Guatemala, 2009); Liza Grandia, *Enclosed: Conservation, Cattle, and Commerce among the Q'eqchi' Maya Lowlanders* (Seattle: University of Washington Press, 2012); and recent work on extractive industries by Luis Solano, "Development and/as Dispossession: Elite Networks and Extractive Industry in the Franja Transversal del Norte," in *War by Other Means: Aftermath in Post-Genocide Guatemala*, ed. Diane Nelson and Carlota McAllister, 119–142 (Durham, NC: Duke University, 2013).

6. David Carey Jr., "Guatemala's Green Revolution: Synthetic Fertilizer, Public Health, and Economic Autonomy in the Mayan Highland," *Agricultural History* 83, no. 3 (2009): 295.

7. Christopher R. Boyer, *Political Landscapes: Conservation, Forests, and Community in Mexico* (Durham, NC: Duke University Press, 2015); Sterling Evans, *The Green Republic: A Conservation History of Costa Rica* (Austin: University of Texas Press, 1999).

8. Kenneth J. Grieb, *Guatemalan Caudillo, the Regime of Jorge Ubico: Guatemala, 1931–1944* (Athens: Ohio University Press, 1979), 143–144 and 154; David McCreery, "Wage Labor, Free Labor, and Vagrancy Laws: The Transition to Capitalism in Guatemala, 1920–1945," in *Coffee, Society and Power in Latin America*, ed. William Roseberry, Lowell Gudmundson, and Mario Samper, 206–231 (Baltimore: Johns Hopkins University Press, 1995), 223.

9. Zeissig, *Guatemala, paraíso perdido*, 6 and 22.

10. "Valor teórico y real de los campos experimentales," *Revista Agrícola*, January 1945, 101–102.

11. H. M. Sierra, "Corn in Guatemala," *Plant Research in the Tropics: Research Bulletin 371*, ed. I. E. Melhus, 509–512 (Ames: Agricultural Experiment Station, Iowa State College, 1949), 509, 512.

12. Dirección General Forestal, "Guatemala Forestalmente," n.d., Min. Ag., leg. 421, Archivo General de Centro América (hereafter AGCA), Guatemala City.

13. "División de Conservación de Suelos," "República de Guatemala: Métodos de organización, para sus trabajos de conservación de suelos," July 2, 1949, Min. Ag., leg. 421, AGCA, Guatemala City.

14. James Scott, *Seeing Like a State: How Certain Schemes to Improve the Human Condition Have Failed* (New Haven, CT: Yale University Press, 1998), 24.

15. Miguel Altieri, "Agroecology: The Science of Natural Resource Management for Poor Farmers in Marginal Environments," *Agriculture, Ecosystems and Environment* 93 (2002): 3.

16. For a similar observation, see also Felix McBryde, *Cultural and Historical*

Geography of Southwest Guatemala (Washington, DC: US Government Printing Office, 1947), 19.

17. Raymond Stadelman, "Maize Cultivation in Northwestern Guatemala," in *Contributions to American Anthropology and History* 6, no. 33:83–263 (Washington, DC: Carnegie Institution of Washington, 1940), 117.

18. Ibid., 109–110.

19. Stadelman, "Maize Cultivation in Northwestern Guatemala," 101, 117; McBryde, *Cultural and Historical Geography of Southwest Guatemala*, 17.

20. Stadelman, "Maize Cultivation in Northwestern Guatemala," 104.

21. One manzana is roughly 1.73 acres. Handy, *Revolution in the Countryside*, 82.

22. Charles Wagley, "Economics of a Guatemala Village," *Memoirs of the American Anthropological Association* 43, no. 3 (1941): 31–44.

23. Orator F. Cook, "Vegetation Affected by Agriculture in Central America," *Department of Agriculture, Bureau of Plant Industry—Bulletin*, no. 145 (Washington, DC: Government Printing Office, 1909), 23; Cook, "Milpa Agriculture: A Primitive Tropical System," *Annual Report of the Smithsonian Institution for 1919* (Washington, DC: Smithsonian Institution, 1921), 326.

24. Cook, "Milpa Agriculture," 308 and 324–325.

25. Cook, "Vegetation Affected by Agriculture in Central America," 8, 10–12, and 15–16.

26. Charles Simmons, José Manuel Taranto T., and José Humberto Pino, *Clasificación de reconocimiento de los suelos de la República de Guatemala*, trans. Pedro Tirado-Sulsona (La Aurora, Guatemala: Ministerio de Agricultura, Instituto Agropecuario Nacional, Servicio Cooperativo Inter-Americano de Agricultura, 1959), 487 and 513.

27. Gregory T. Cushman notes the intellectual links between William Vogt and a leading American environmentalist, Aldo Leopold, in *Guano and the Opening of the Pacific World: A Global Ecological History* (Cambridge: Cambridge University Press, 2013), 246, 255–261, and 263.

28. William Vogt, "Hunger at the Peace Table," *Saturday Evening Post*, May 12, 1945, 109–110.

29. Vogt, "Hunger at the Peace Table," 110; William Vogt, "A Continent Slides to Ruin," *Harper's Magazine*, June 1948, 489. William Vogt, *Road to Survival* (New York: W. Sloane Associates, 1948), 192.

30. William Vogt, *The Population of El Salvador and Its Natural Resources* (Washington, DC: Pan American Union, 1946), 29.

31. Roberto Guirola, "Sección Forestal: El Ministro de Agricultura, Don Roberto Guirola, se dirige al Congreso de la Nación," *Revista Agrícola*, June–July 1945, 491.

32. "Aprobada la Nueva Ley Forestal," *Revista Agrícola*, August-September 1945, 555–563; Todo bosque por pequeño que sea . . . ," *Revista Agrícola*, July-December 1946, 361.

33. Jim Handy, *Gift of the Devil* (Boston: South End, 1984), 107.

34. División de Conservación de Suelos, "República de Guatemala: Métodos de organización, para sus trabajos de conservación de suelos," July 2, 1949, Min. Ag., leg. 421, AGCA, Guatemala City; Neil M. Maher, *Nature's New Deal: The Civilian Conservation Corps and the Roots of the American Environmental Movement* (Oxford: Oxford University Press, 2008).

35. Article 23 "Reglamento de los Agentes Generales de Agricultura," n/d, Min Ag., leg. 1887, AGCA, Guatemala City.

36. "Servicio Aéreo Forestal," *Revista Agrícola*, July-December 1946, 279.

37. David Biggs, "Aerial Photography and Its Role in Shifting Colonial Discourse on Peasants and Land Management in Late-Colonial Indochina 1930–1945," in *Cultivating the Colony: Colonial States and Their Environmental Legacies*, ed. Karen Oslund, Niels Brimnes, Christina Folke Ax, and Niklas Thode Jensen, 109–132 (Athens: Ohio University Press), 110 and 129; Biggs, *Quagmire: Nation-Building and Nature in the Mekong Delta* (Seattle: University of Washington Press, 2010), 12–13.

38. "Servicio Aéreo Forestal," 279.

39. Scott, *Seeing Like a State*, 24.

40. "¡Alerta Guatemaltecos! ¡Cuidado con los incendios!" *Revista Agrícola*, October-December 1945, 770.

41. "La censurable costumbre que existe hace muchos años," *Revista Agrícola*, July–December 1946, 360.

42. "Campaña forestal," *Revista Agrícola*, October–December 1945, 785.

43. Untitled Advertisement, *Revista Agrícola*, October–December 1945, 781.

44. United States Geological Service, "Landslide Types and Processes," accessed February 1, 2017, http://pubs.usgs.gov/fs/2004/3072/fs-2004–3072.html.

45. "Sección de Forestación y Conservación de Suelos: Erosión y deforestación en Panajachel, Medidas para Contrarrestarlas," *Revista Agrícola*, August–September 1945, 500.

46. "Campaña Forestal," *Revista Agrícola*, October–December 1945, 805–806.

47. "Reforestación en Panajachel" *Revista Agrícola*, October–December 1945, 781.

48. "Reglamento de los Agentes Generales de Agricultura," n.d., Min Ag., leg. 1887, AGCA, Guatemala City.

49. See, e.g., "Informe de Actividades del Departamento de Extensión y Fomento Agrícola: Primera quincena," November, 1946, Min. Ag., leg. 1887, AGCA, Guatemala City.

50. See Minutes of Comité de Agricultura Meeting, San Rafael Las Flores, Santa Rosa, September 28, 1947, Min. Ag., leg. 1886, AGCA, Guatemala City.

51. Miguel Reyes to minister of agriculture, March 19, 1948, Min. Ag., leg. 1887, AGCA, Guatemala City.

52. J. A Toruño to minister of agriculture, September 30, 1946, AGCA, Guatemala City.

53. Isaías Benedicto Hernández, general agent of agriculture for Jutiapa to minister of agriculture, February 8, 1947, Min. Ag., leg. 1886, AGCA, Guatemala City.

54. Sección General de Colonización y Tierras to Sección de Proyectos, December 27, 1946, Min Ag., leg. 1886, AGCA, Guatemala City.

55. Minutes of Committee of Agriculture from Asunción Mita, December 12, 1946, Min. Ag., leg. 1886, AGCA, Guatemala City.

56. Isaías Benedicto Hernández, agent for Jutiapa, to subsecretary of agriculture, January 27, 1947, Min. Ag., leg. 1886, AGCA, Guatemala City.

57. Isaías Benedicto Hernández, agent for Jutiapa, to minister of agriculture, February 8, 1947, Min. Ag., leg. 1886, AGCA, Guatemala City.

58. Isaías Benedicto Hernández, agent for Jutiapa, to subsecretary of agriculture, January 27, 1947, Min. Ag., leg. 1886, AGCA, Guatemala City.

59. Isaías Benedicto Hernández, agent for Jutiapa, to minister of agriculture, February 8, 1947, Min. Ag., leg. 1886, AGCA, Guatemala City.

60. One *caballería* is equal to roughly 110 acres. Enclosed in Miguel Angel Reyes

to minister of agriculture, March 19, 1948, Min. Ag., leg. 1887, AGCA, Guatemala City.

61. Committee for Agriculture for Santa Cruz Naranjo, Santa Rosa, to minister of agriculture, February 2, 1948, Min. Ag., leg. 1886, AGCA, Guatemala City.

62. Committee from Santa Cruz Naranjo to agent of agriculture for Santa Rosa, February 8, 1948, Min. Ag., leg. 1886, AGCA, Guatemala City.

63. R. Ferraté, inspector, to Departamento de Fincas Rústicas Nacionales, February 24, 1948, Min. Ag., leg. 1886, AGCA, Guatemala.

64. Infrascrito agente general de Agricultura del Departamento de Santa Rosa, n/d, Min. Ag., leg. 1886, AGCA, Guatemala City.

65. Handy, *Revolution in the Countryside*, 26, 81.

66. Isaías Benedicto Hernández, agent for Jutiapa, to J. Antonio Toruño, August 1, 1947, Min. Ag., leg. 1887, AGCA, Guatemala City.

67. John H. Adler, Eugene R. Schlesinger, and Ernest C. Olson, *Public Finance and Economic Development in Guatemala* (Stanford, CA: University Press, 1952), 264; Kalman Silvert, *Guatemala: National and Local Government Since 1944* (New Orleans: Middle American Research Institute, Tulane University, 1954), 37.

68. "Guatemalan Flood Toll is 4,000; Damage Is Placed at $40,000,000," *New York Times*, Oct 20, 1949, ProQuest Historical Newspapers: The New York Times (1851–2009), p. 1.

69. "Death Toll at 4000 in Guatemala Flood," *Washington Post*, October 20, 1949, ProQuest Historical Newspapers: The Washington Post (1877–1997), p. 18.

70. Official estimates were up to four thousand, but more conservative estimates by the Red Cross were five hundred. "Guatemala Flood Dead Put at 1000," *Washington Post*, October 19, 1949, ProQuest Historical Newspapers: The Washington Post (1877–1997), p. 3.

71. "55, 000 familias sin rancho: Fincas en ruina en la Costa Grande; parcelas de cafetal están perdidas; problema humano exige pronto atención," *El Imparcial*, October 22, 1949.

72. "El Motagua enfurecido se desborda sembrado el estrago en las Vegas," *El Imparcial*, October 20, 1949.

73. "Panajachel temblaba bajo el impacto de la inundación: Piedras enormes arrastradas como nuez," *El Imparcial*, October 22, 1949.

74. "Incuria, ignorancia y ruina," *El Imparcial*, October 24, 1949.

75. Economic Survey Mission to Guatemala, *The Economic Development of Guatemala* (Washington, DC: International Bank for Reconstruction and Development, 1951), 26–27, 82–84.

76. Economic Survey Mission to Guatemala, *The Economic Development of Guatemala*, vii, 29–30, 248.

77. "El INFOP y el fomento de la producción agrícola e industrial de alimentos básicos," *Monitor del INFOP* 2, no. 5 (1951): 10.

78. "La doctrina Conservanista de los recursos naturales en un Plan de Explotación de la Hacienda Cuyuta," *Monitor del INFOP* 1, nos. 1–2 (1950): 19, 21.

79. Ibid.

80. The smallest properties were measured in cuerdas, where one cuerda was equal to 0.3 acre. As mentioned earlier, a manzana was equal to 1.73 acres.

81. Memorandum to Dr. Gabriel Orellana H., Gerente del Dept. de Fomento from Juan Fernández Mendía, March 20, 1951, Sección de Algodón, p. 7, Min. Ag., leg. 1940, AGCA, Guatemala City.

82. "Misión y sentido del INFOP," *Monitor del INFOP* 2, no. 7 (1951): 1.

83. "Síntesis económica: Financiera de 1951 en Guatemala," *Monitor del INFOP* 2, no. 7 (1951): 28.

84. Patrick Chassé, "'Produce More to Live Better': Corn, Cotton and Agrarian Modernization" (PhD diss., University of Saskatchewan, 2017), 143–150.

85. Handy, *Gift of the Devil*, 128–129.

86. Richard H. Immerman, *The CIA in Guatemala: The Foreign Policy of Intervention* (Austin: University of Texas Press, 1988), 65.

87. *Ley de Reforma Agraría*, Decreto 900, 1952, Article 23, 38.

88. *Ley de Reforma Agraría*, Decreto 900, 1952, Article 11.

89. For a North American discussion of "wise use" and the management of water systems, see Matthew Evenden, *Fish versus Power: An Environmental History of the Fraser River* (Cambridge: Cambridge University Press, 2004).

90. For other Latin American conservation efforts, see Evans, *The Green Republic*; Emily Wakild, *Revolutionary Parks: Conservation, Social Justice, and Mexico's Natural Parks, 1910–1940* (Tucson: Arizona University Press, 2011).

91. In Guatemala, one quintal is 100 pounds or 46 kilograms.

92. Máximo L. Godinez M., "Plan General de la División de Conservación de Suelos, para los Trabajos Efectuarse durante el Año Fiscal de 1952/1953," n.d., Min. Ag., leg. 421, AGCA, Guatemala City.

93. "Reforma Agraría," *Revista Agrícola* vol 1, no. 2 (1953): n.p.

94. Carlos Manuel Pellecer, "Por la prosperidad de nuestra patria," *Octubre,* October 18, 1951.

95. Karl Marx, *Capital*, vol. 1, trans. Ben Fowkes (London: Penguin Classics, 1990), 272–273.

96. Acta No. 6 in "Minister of Agriculture, Nicolás Brol to Señor Gabino Alvarez y Compañeros c/o Comité Agrario Local de Santa María Cauqué, Sacatepéquez," April 26, 1953, Min. Ag., leg. 1940, AGCA, Guatemala City.

97. Comité Agrario Local del Puerto San José to minister of Agriculture, April 1953, Min. Ag., leg. 1940, AGCA, Guatemala City.

98. "Comité Agrario Local de Pueblo Nuevo Viñas to Minister of Agriculture," April 21, 1953, Min. Ag., leg. 1940, AGCA, Guatemala City.

99. Handy, *Revolution in the Countryside*, 96–97; Piero Gleijeses, *Shattered Hope: The Guatemalan Revolution and the United States, 1944–1954* (Princeton, NJ: Princeton University Press, 1991), 172–173.

100. Castañeda worked for the Soil Conservation Department, but also served as secretary general of the CNCG for Jalapa and was member of the Comité Agrario Departamental (Departmental Agrarian Committee; CAD). Castillo Flores to the minister of Agriculture, June 18, 1953, Min. Ag., leg. 1940, AGCA, Guatemala City.

101. Minister of agriculture to Castillo Flores, June 19, 1953, Min. Ag., leg. 1940, AGCA, Guatemala City.

102. Handy, *Revolution in the Countryside*, 105–110.

103. UFCO to Señor Guardia Forestal de Morales, February 18, 1953, Min. Ag., Leg 1940, AGCA, Guatemala City.

104. Letter to director General Forestal from Isidro Juárez Orellana, guarda forestal de Morales, February 21, 1953, Min. Ag., leg. 1940, AGCA, Guatemala City.

105. (8756) Memorandum of la Confederación Nacional Campesina de Guatemala to Señor Ministro de Agricultura, May 18, 1953, Min. Ag., leg. 1940, AGCA, Guatemala City.

106. Virgilio H. Alvarado, inspector de Bosques, Zona #3 to Director General Forestal, July 20, 1953, Min. Ag., leg. 1940, AGCA, Guatemala City.

107. Boyer, *Political Landscapes*, 4–5, 10, 12, and 123.

108. GuateDoc 8050P Mss 11, 555 Reel No. 50. Feet 101, Description: Correspondence of the Confederación Nacional Campesina de Guatemala (Reels 50–52).

109. María Vilanova de Arbenz, "El Soldado del Pueblo," p. 97, Serie Borradores de Libros, Arbenz Papers. For more on Vilanova see Piero Gleijeses, *Shattered Hope*, 134–136.

110. Handy, *Revolution in the Countryside*, 95; Handy, *Gift of the Devil*, 129.

111. This fear often resulted in the brutal suppression of indigenous communities who tried to organize. Jeffrey L. Gould and Aldo A. Lauria-Santiago, *To Rise in Darkness: Revolution, Repression, and Memory in El Salvador, 1920–1932* (Durham, NC: Duke University, 2008).

112. Jim Handy, "'A Sea of Indians': Ethnic Conflict and the Guatemalan Revolution, 1944–1952," *The Americas* 46, no. 2 (1989): 190–192, 199, and 204; Severo Martínez Peláez, *La Patria del Criollo: An Interpretation of Colonial Guatemala*, trans. Susan M. Neve and W. George Lovell (shortened from original), ed. W. George Lovell and Christopher H. Lutz (Durham, NC: Duke University Press, 2009), 81.

CHAPTER 3

Arévalo's Tomorrowland

The Revolutionary Crusade to Build and Defend the New Guatemala on the Petén Frontier

Anthony Andersson

> This is how President Arévalo has fulfilled his promises to the Nation. This is how the collaborators of the President have demonstrated the constructive force of Arevalismo.
>
> Promotional booklet for the First National Agricultural Colony at Poptún, 1950

The forests of the Petén frontier held a special significance for Guatemala's first democratically elected president. Juan José Arévalo, like most of his peers, imagined an "inexhaustible source" of precious wood and fertile soil lying idle under the jungle canopy.[1] Although no one had actually surveyed those woods when Arévalo took office, estimates of mahogany stocks worth more than Guatemala's entire gross domestic product circulated among the literate classes.[2] Scientists at the United Fruit Company (UFCO) believed that the Petén's exuberant vegetation indicated exceptionally rich soils, and therefore high agricultural potential—one of the company's head researchers confidently asserted in an influential article that "the utilization of science in the Petén" had opened the possibility of a "well-populated, prosperous community" in its "apparently fertile land."[3] More than natural resources beckoned the Arevalistas, however. In the minds of many revolutionaries, the Petén was innocent of Guatemala's history of caudillismo and "feudal" social relations. Its soil was virgin in a historical, as well as agrarian, sense, a "promised land" where the nation could be born again and its people redeemed. Accordingly, Arévalo launched a "national crusade" to "reconquer" and colonize the northern frontier, which his nationalist supporters described in millenarian terms. Arévalo's "sacred cause" in the Petén quickly became the costliest endeavor of his administration, which he called "the most significant event" for the future of the Guatemalan Revolution.[4] While the crusade failed to achieve its objectives and was abandoned by Arévalo's successor, its ambitious plans to remake the country on the frontier belie Arévalo's reputation as a cautious reformer. The revolutionary crusade to build the "New Guatemala" in the Petén embodied the ideals and contradictions of Arevalismo, and it cast long shadows over the political conflicts of the latter twentieth century.

To lead his crusade, Arévalo built a parallel state in the Petén, administered from a military research colony in the Poptún Valley, which he called "the axis of the reconquest." There, a militaristic ethic crystallized that fused woodland management with military governance, a union that endured even as it transformed from the agent of a democratic revolution into the servant of authoritarian repression. Arévalo's colony sponsored the first major scientific studies of the Petén's tropical forests, laying the foundations for the military reserves that were later converted into the Maya Biosphere Reserve and Tikal National Park. For all its grandiose economic dreams, Arévalo's rain forest crusade was an eminently political project, and political decisions determined its fate. In 1952, the revolution turned away from the Tomorrowland on the frontier in favor of land reform in the heartland of the here and now. In the 1960s, the military revived Arévalo's colony at Poptún as the core of an autonomous military command and resource management agency called La Empresa Nacional Fomento y Desarrollo de El Petén (The National Petén Development Company; FYDEP)—an institutional pillar of the counterinsurgent state, a springboard for the rise of independent military power, and wellspring of the violent conservation landscapes that dominate the Petén today.[5] Arévalo's colony has been largely forgotten, but it nonetheless weighed heavily on those who followed in its wake.

This chapter situates the Petén frontier amidst the national political currents and international scientific networks of the 1940s that created the institutions that later determined its fate. It briefly summarizes how the Petén became an isolated hinterland and how its forests came to figure prominently in Arévalo's particular brand of revolutionary political praxis. The heart of the chapter discusses events on the ground in the Petén, elaborating the rise and fall of the colony at Poptún, and how anxieties about indigenous peasants mixed with agronomy and forest science to shape the plans for the New Guatemala. I conclude with a discussion of the buried legacies of Arévalo's colony in the institution of the military, its principal benefactor.

Fabricating a Wild Frontier

The anthropologist Norman Schwartz described the Petén as the quintessential frontier.[6] In the Guatemalan popular imagination, the Petén is akin to the Amazon in Brazil: a geographically distinct region of vast lowland tropical forests, a remnant of a premodern wilderness. After the Spanish subjugated the local population in 1697, they showed no more interest in the place, and postindependence elites maintained this neglect. The Petén constitutes about a third of Guatemalan territory, and yet in the 1940s no more than five thousand people called it home.[7] Until 1964, no roads connected the Petén directly with the rest of the country—just a few mule trails used by Q'eqchi' merchants and forest workers from Alta Verapaz. To the west and north the department is bordered by the Mexican states of Chiapas, Campeche, and Quintana Roo. Belize (known from 1862 to 1981 as British Honduras) sits in a narrow strip of land between the Petén and the Caribbean Sea. Today the Petén is sold to tourists as a land lost to time. Yet not only are those "wild" forests full of history; they are a very modern artifact of human action.

The Petén forests have never existed free of human influence. The earliest Americans were already living there when the last Ice Age ended and the isthmus acquired a tropical climate. Their descendants sculpted the landscape to suit their needs over the millennia that followed.[8] The seat of the late classic Ancient Maya Empire rested in the Petén, with millions of souls making a living in the immensely productive mosaic landscape of what Anabel Ford and Ronald Nigh call the "Maya forest garden."[9] In the tenth century, a decades-long drought correlating with global climate changes destabilized the Maya polity and led many to migrate northward into the Yucatán, but the Maya "collapse" was more myth than reality. Many people continued to live in the Petén, though they left less monumental architecture.[10] When Hernán Cortés crossed the Petén in the sixteenth century, his army of some three thousand soldiers was hosted and fed by the locals without much apparent burden. Old World epidemics subsequently decimated the local population, but at least tens of thousands of people remained through 1697, when the Spanish conquered Tayasal, the last of the Maya kingdoms to fall, on the shores of lake Petén Itzá. The population further declined through the eighteenth and nineteenth centuries from a combination of disease, conflict, and outmigration. As the population thinned, the garden forests went progressively fallow, growing into dense woods that outsiders had difficulty seeing as anything other than a timeless jungle.[11]

Wood for global markets has been harvested in the Petén since the eighteenth century. Logging accelerated in the nineteenth century, when British loggers and their slaves traveled up the navigable rivers from the Belizean coast looking for mahogany.[12] They were soon joined by North American and Mexican firms, who logged the tributaries of the Usumacinta River, especially the Pasión and San Pedro in western Petén. By the 1920s, loggers had removed most of the accessible mahogany along the coasts and were moving aggressively into the Petén. Most of the mahogany exported from Belize and Mexico in the early twentieth century probably originated in the Petén, according to the US forester Bruce Lamb. Harvesting at that time was inefficient: for every mahogany log exported, another was lost in transport and countless other trees with no market value were felled along the way, simply left to rot. The effects of logging altered the distribution of tree species in the Petén such that scientists in the latter twentieth century were able to determine where logging had occurred based on the composition of the forests.[13]

Logging left its mark on the political landscape as well. In 1862, the British used their colonial-era logging concession to claim Belize as sovereign territory of the Imperial Commonwealth, dubbing it British Honduras. Guatemala never recognized British claims, but elites in the highlands had no interest in their northern frontier and never seriously confronted the "occupation." Arévalo's crusade suddenly made the "Belize Question" a pressing concern and a jingoistic lightning rod: without direct access to seaports and with no roads, the products of the Petén were subject to the tolls of British gatekeepers.[14] The nationalist icon Virgilio Rodríguez Beteta characterized British Honduras as a "blockade" of "seven seals," likening the opening of Guatemala's northern frontier to the second coming of Christ.[15] To turn the Petén into the promised land, Arevalistas argued, the "reconquest" of the northern frontier depended on the repatriation of the "lost territory" in Belize. To make matters worse, Mexico had shown an appetite for lands that Guatemalan elites did not care for. The sale of Soconusco and Chiapas to Mexico in the nineteenth century hung like specters over the Petén. Reasserting sovereign authority over the Petén (and Belize) was therefore a signal to Mexico as much as the British.

The Forests of Arévalo's Dreams

In the Petén, Arévalo aspired to combine his domestic and foreign policy into the "highest expression" of the New Guatemala. On the northern frontier, an array of nationalist causes were distilled into a neatly defined problem with a straightforward solution: a crusade to "recover and better defend forgotten Guatemalan lands." The reconquest of the Petén promised to stoke economic development, reassert the nation's sovereignty, bring the military into Arévalo's political coalition, and level Guatemalan society without resorting to land reform. It was Arevalismo in praxis.

Arévalo's forest policies were pulled in contradictory directions by the progressive ideals of the revolution and a deep-seated suspicion of peasant agriculture by scientists and political leaders alike (as Patrick Chassé outlines in chapter 2). Bruce Lamb, who directed Guatemala's first national forest inventory in 1950, lamented the "limited point of view" of Indian peasants, for whom valuable timber was "of no significance whatsoever" because they were too preoccupied with feeding their numerous children.[16] However, he supported the unionization of forest workers (many of whom were Maya), which his profession tended to see as integral to the rational management of the land.[17] The 1945 Forest Law included protections for forest workers, preceding and complementing the 1948 labor code legalizing unionization. That, plus the relatively favorable treatment of small farmers in the Forest Law—and Indian communities in particular, whose common lands were singled out for special protections—reflected a socially progressive interpretation of development that contrasted sharply with orthodox economic models, much like its "revolutionary forestry" cousins in Mexico and Chile.[18] Yet the Forest Service was first and foremost a police agency, charged with finding and punishing criminals. The practical goal of that coercive power was the conversion of "wasteful" woods with many undesirable trees into "sanitized" and scientifically "rationalized" timber farms of one or two commercially useful species.

Arévalo and his advisors expected that exploiting the "unused" resources in the Petén would spark industrial development, while much of the empty land could be filled with small farmers, "reliev[ing] the overcrowding" in the "overpopulated and exhausted" sierra.[19] A modern forest industry would generate high-wage jobs, accelerating the conversion of peasants to workers. Advisors counseled that the wise use of timber could pay for colonization investments, with surpluses padding the treasury once sawmills and infrastructure were in place.[20] National redemption was a lot to expect from idle woodlands, but European and North American technical advisors were exceedingly optimistic. Foresters at the time drew direct connections between forest management and national prosperity: healthy forests supported agriculture by regulating the climate, provisioned industry with raw materials, and drove social progress.[21] Olindo Secondini, an Italian chemist specializing in wood derivatives who was hired to advise

Arévalo's office of industrial development, said that Guatemala's extensive forest cover gave it the potential to become "the Switzerland of America."[22]

The Petén forests presented Arevalistas with challenges and opportunities distinct from the rest of the country, so they built a parallel state to lead the reconquest and administer the woods there. The parastate in the Petén rested on two institutional pillars: science and security. Half of the nation's woodland lay in the Petén, but no one knew much about it. Led by a corps of foresters, agronomists, and engineers, the crusade would "cleanse" the "vice" of underdevelopment from the land.[23] Whatever they contained, those forests were exceptionally vulnerable to foreign depredations; once a road was built into them, the Guatemalan peasantry would add a new, internal threat. Proclamations about inexhaustible resources aside, planners feared that "irrational" colonization would destroy the "hen that lays the golden eggs" and with it the country's best chance to change the course of Guatemalan history.[24] Only the strictest adherence to scientific counsel, enforced with military discipline, could prevent a national tragedy unleashed by a flood of peasant settlers, timber poachers, and foreign avarice. Arévalo named a military governor, consolidated local police under the Petén Forest Guard, and subjected the whole department to martial law.[25] Although its ends may have been progressive, the "New Guatemala" was thoroughly militarized.

Arévalo accepted the support of the US government and multinational companies for his nationalist project in order to accomplish as much as possible as fast as possible. His associate Virgilio Rodríguez Beteta expressed that the administration wanted to retake the Petén "purely on our own," but the government lacked the resources to go it alone. Most of the equipment came, directly or indirectly, from the US government, especially army surplus. The US State Department arranged for fertilizers, pesticides, clinical equipment, and some heavy equipment purchases from private parties in the United States. Doctors at the Primera Colonia Agrícola Nacional (First National Agricultural Colony; PCAN) enjoyed some of the most sophisticated labs in Central America at the time, thanks to a deal brokered with US Army medical units in the Panama Canal Zone.[26] Rodríguez Beteta conveyed the sense of urgency driving the decision to accept aid wherever it was available: "Let us rush . . . with energy, without vacillations, but at the same time expertly and scientifically, as the job demands, to advance the great national enterprise of the resurrection of the Petén."[27]

Revolutionary Reconquest

The focal point of the reconquest was a military base, research complex, and planned city collectively dubbed the PCAN. The complex was nestled in a valley of the Maya Mountains near the tiny village of Poptún, in the southeast of the department. At an average elevation about four hundred meters higher than the rest of the department, the "cool climate" in Poptún was misleadingly reputed to resemble Guatemala City more than the torrid lowlands that surrounded it.[28] It was a mosaic landscape of dense pine woods blending into grasslands and ringed by hot broadleaf rainforest. Scouts chose the site in October 1945, and the army flew in the first contingent of workers to set up what amounted to a logging camp, like dozens of others scattered across the department. With nothing but hand tools, workers cut and milled hundreds of trees, using the lumber to build a rustic kitchen, dining hall, dormitory, laundry, garage, and shed for an electrical generator. Colonel Ernesto Álvarez, the governor general, set a furious pace of work. Once parts for a sawmill arrived, construction accelerated and workers raised the first buildings of the colony proper, including more comfortable dorms, cafeterias, administrative offices, residential duplexes, warehouses, commissaries, a hospital, an airstrip and hangar, barracks, a post office, and an herb garden. Every building had electric lighting, and all residences boasted indoor plumbing. By the middle of November, hundreds of men and women lived and worked at the colony, surveying the environs, felling trees, building shelters, planting crops, spraying DDT, and conducting patrols. Agronomists began studies on crops, soil, wood, and pasture grasses.[29] In less than two months, the sleepy hamlet of Poptún had become a busy frontier town, which visiting US journalists described as the most modern anywhere in the Guatemalan countryside.[30]

In the five years that followed, workers expanded the facilities at the PCAN with more housing, a jail, and a state-of-the-art hospital. Anticipating the arrival of large numbers of colonists, they cleared and leveled eighteen acres for a planned city adjacent to the military base, patriotically named Tecún Umán after the slain Maya warrior king and martyr of resistance to the Iberian conquistadors. Arévalo helped to select an urban plan for the new city from submissions received through an international competition. Its wide central avenues and small side streets marked out a grid—divided, rationally enough, into civic, commercial, industrial, recreational, and residential districts.[31]

Apart from the colony, a separate "mission" focused on cutting a road through the jungle, which the army dubbed the Ruta Militar, to connect the PCAN to a port on the Sarstún River. From there, ferries ran the short distance downriver and along the Caribbean coast to Guatemala's main Atlantic terminal at Puerto Barrios. Thousands of Q'eqchi' Maya peasants, mostly from Alta Verapaz, were recruited to risk injury and illness building the Ruta Militar.[32] In terms of both labor and material, the Ruta Militar was by far the costliest piece of the colonization effort. Despite the relative flatness of the Petén compared to the Guatemalan highlands, its "broken" karstic landscape was cut through with river and arroyos, sinkholes, and abrupt limestone outcroppings—all covered in dense vegetation and drowned in mud during the six months of the rainy season. Engineers used a lot of dynamite and heavy machinery, but of necessity most of the work clearing and grading the land was done by hand.[33] Unsatisfied with early progress, Governor Álvarez recalled an "expeditionary force" that had been sent to open a logging camp in "the bush" on lake Petén Itzá, in the center of the department, to bolster the ranks on the Ruta Militar. He also created a "Reincorporation Office," led by the army lieutenant and civil engineer Oliverio Casasola, to more effectively oversee the project that advisors deemed the "backbone of colonization."[34]

Arévalo's crusade was about the *projection* of power as much as anything, and in this regard proximity to Belize played into the choice of the PCAN's location. The PCAN was called "the focal center for political operations irradiating toward Belize."[35] From Poptún, mule trails (the presumed routes for future roads) fanned out from Poptún to the rest of the department and into Belize. The southern terminus of the Ruta Militar, not coincidentally, sat within sight of Belizean territory. Once complete, the road would allow the deployment of large numbers of ground troops to the Petén for the first time. Together, the colony and road cut off many of the smuggling routes through Belize. Furthermore, smuggling trails could be turned against the British by using them to deploy Guatemalan troops. Arévalo's lieutenants also assumed an aggressive posture toward Mexico. The Petén Forest Guard and the army set up outposts at the airstrips of derelict logging camps on the San Pedro and Pasión Rivers, the department's principal western outlets, and troops at Poptún were kept ready for aerial deployment to confront any "incursion."[36] Income from new forest industries and farming might eventually support a robust security apparatus in the Petén, but Arevalistas were prepared to heavily subsidize the project for years to come. As one advisor put it, profitable or not, the PCAN and Ruta Militar were "a mandatory corollary to the Guatemalan aspiration to recover its territory of Belize."[37]

FIGURE 3.1. *The axis of Arévalo's "Reconquest."*

A dispute at the Belizean border in 1948 illustrated the preeminence of political considerations regarding Belize over economic motivations. Guatemalan troop movements had provoked the British into sending a battalion of Royal Marines from Jamaica to Belize City and a strike force to intercept what they perceived as an imminent invasion. Diplomats negotiated a stand-down on both sides, but Arévalo responded spitefully by closing the border, cutting off virtually all exports from the Petén.[38] Timber that had already been cut piled up in warehouses, rotting. The two US lumber companies with concessions in the Petén shut down their operations entirely, abandoning some of the world's first mahogany plantations outside of the US Forest Service's research station in Puerto Rico. Bruce Lamb called out the saber rattling for turning science and rational management into a casualty of politics.[39]

Rationalization and Racial Anxiety

Arévalo and his advisors believed that the success of the colony hinged on scientists' power to control the jungle landscape. The chief scientific advisor to the PCAN, a Colombian agronomist named Juan Pablo Duque, envisioned an initial "experimental phase" of colonization, during which technical experts would decipher the local ecology and determine the most appropriate methods for achieving the government's objectives before large numbers of settlers arrived. Only then would colonists be allowed in to live in planned towns, subject to strict supervision. Given five years to work without the distraction of neighbors, Duque predicted, the colony's technicians would learn all they needed to direct the full-scale colonization on the sturdy foundation of science.[40]

At the outset, the scientists at the PCAN foresaw few natural obstacles standing in their way, but Guatemala's racial composition made them anxious. Duque believed that landscapes were a product of cultural values, which he understood primarily through the framework of race.[41] In fact, Duque explicitly ignored nature in his initial report, contending that scientists would quickly overcome any ecological challenges they encountered. He instead chose to focus on how to Europeanize settler communities. Agronomists arrived with the conviction that large pre-Colombian populations indicated high soil fertility; however, they also believed that the "nomadic" system of slash-and-burn agriculture used by the peasantry was a remnant of the very practices that had led the Ancient Maya to ruin. Foresters had a more nuanced view of forest soils, but they agreed that "shifting agriculture" was the greatest threat to Latin America's timber reserves.[42] For Duque, the large number of Indian workers at the colony and the Ruta Militar was a potential time bomb: if not supervised and cared for, their "irrational" instincts would inevitably lead them to cut and burn the forest to plant milpa, while poaching timber and archaeological artifacts for cash. For development to proceed along scientific, rational lines, he argued, the workforce had to be closely policed and unauthorized immigration prohibited.[43]

Demography aside, the first step in rationalizing the rainforest environment was to "sanitize" it from malaria, gastrointestinal infections, yellow fever, and a host of other endemic diseases that afflicted nearly everyone who lived there. More than a dozen doctors and nurses at the PCAN dedicated themselves to injecting vaccines and treating sick patients, while "mobile medical units" visited remote villages, bringing medicine to those who could not make the trip to the colony. Sanitation teams sprayed thousands of pounds of "the new insecticide DDT" and oiled every swamp they could find in a war to eradicate mosquitoes.[44]

The "inexhaustible spring of wealth" would generate prosperity only if scientists determined the most efficient crops and cultivation methods to feed the workforce (and hopefully generate new revenue streams). Agronomists at the PCAN cleared thousands of acres of forest and savannah for experimental crops and "improved" pasture grasses. Led by an advisory team from Ohio State University's School of Agriculture, researchers borrowed techniques from around the world to see what worked and what did not, including industrial chemical inputs, the *taungya* organic farming system from British India, and mechanical irrigation.[45] The UFCO sold the colony cuttings and seeds of hemp and African oil palm from its experimental plantations in Izabal, and even paid for shipping costs at the urging of US diplomats.[46] Growing crops locally would, of course, make colonization easier and more profitable, but the principal horticultural preoccupation of the Arévalo administration in the Petén involved trees, which were expected not only to finance the investments in infrastructure and research, but to swell the national treasury.

The capstone of the "experimental phase" of colonization was a forest survey and management plan, carried out by two US foresters under the auspices of INFOP in 1950. Leslie Holdridge (the same person who invented the Holdridge Life Zones rubric still in use today) and Bruce Lamb were hired to survey all of Guatemala's forests, but time and funding constraints, plus the difficulties of travel in the countryside, led them to narrow the study to focus on the Petén, which they and Arévalo deemed the highest priority. They adapted the best practices of their profession to the limitations imposed by local conditions, using old aerial photos from Shell Oil Company prospectors and spot checks in a handful of locations believed to be most representative of the area's known vegetation "types." Holdridge and Lamb stressed that such a study was only a "preliminary examination," but it nonetheless stood as the most complete scientific assessment of those woods for two decades.[47] The full-scale maps produced by their team were kept out of the public domain, being distributed exclusively to the military, indicating the national security significance of the forest survey.[48]

Holdridge and Lamb's study, shortcomings notwithstanding, definitively confirmed that the legendary timber resources in the Petén were no myth. Lamb wrote that Guatemala had more "reserves of standing mahogany" than any country besides Brazil, with the possible exception of Mexico.[49] The Petén alone could satisfy half of global demand for mahogany, according to his estimates, and that was only one of dozens of species with market potential in Europe and North America. Using "secondary" species would be especially important during the first few years, he argued, because "the composition of the forest is so complex" that using as many trees as possible would be necessary to reach production levels sufficient to "cover the costs of logging" in such a difficult and remote environment. Once operations were up and running, however, timber could easily outstrip bananas as Guatemala's second-most-valuable export. Further down the line, once the forests had been rationalized and the first generation of

FIGURE 3.2. *Millworkers somewhere in the Petén prepare logs for the sawmill, 1940s.*

managed trees had matured, production would skyrocket, making timber the cornerstone of a new industrial economy.[50]

The two North American foresters designed an ambitious plan to rationalize, conserve, and exploit the Petén forests as part of an integrated project of agricultural colonization and forestry. They divided the land into six "management blocks" based mostly on vegetation types, with some allowances for the locations of rivers, trails, and settlements. Each block comprised a roughly homogenous microclimate and distribution of dominant tree species, with its own outlet for logs. To contain wildfires, they suggested chopping the entire surface area of the department into a grid of geometric plots between 120 and 200 hectares in size, separated by firebreaks 100 meters wide. Lamb suggested that the firebreaks could then be used for crop farming, putting tens of thousands of hectares of land to use growing food without harm to the forest itself. From the air, the sea of green would look like an irregular checkerboard of various states of mature,

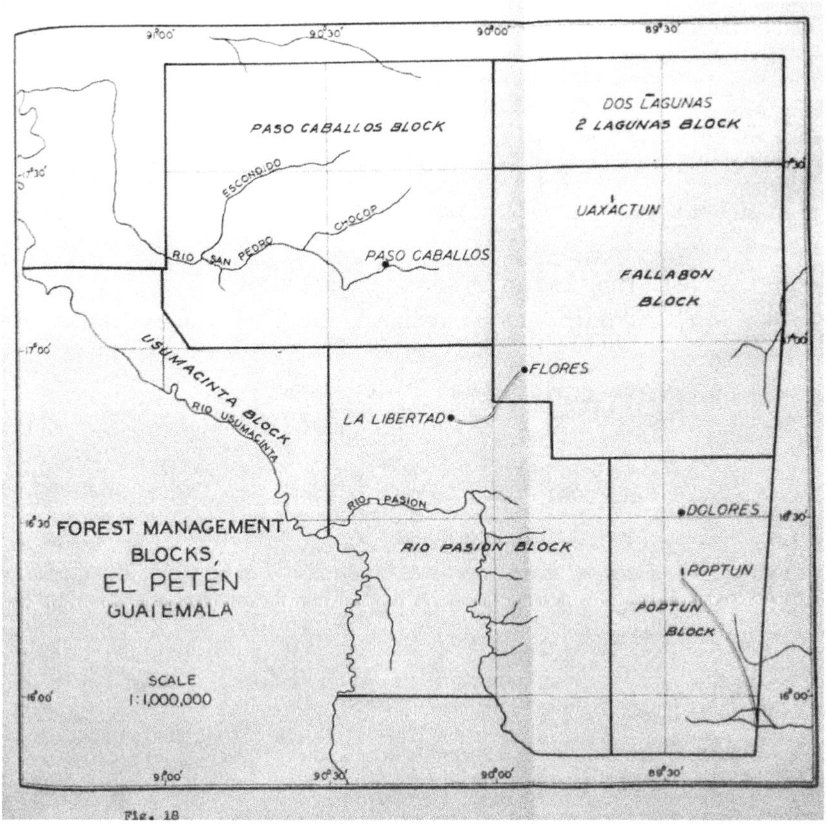

FIGURE 3.3. *Lamb's proposed forest management blocks.*

cutover, and regrown woods. Lamb did not seem to think the Guatemalan government was likely to follow through with this suggestion, but he insisted that the low labor costs in the country made the idea feasible.[51]

Lamb wrote up a detailed management plan for the Poptún block, which, due to the presence of the PCAN, deserved "special attention" in order to "serve as a basis for designing similar plans for the other parcels."[52] Lamb subdivided the Poptún block into forty plots with approximately two thousand mahogany trees in each. One plot per year would be selectively harvested for forty years, along with clearing of unwanted or sick trees and replanting with healthy young trees from nurseries at the PCAN. In the forty-first year, the cycle would start over in the "improved" plots, yielding considerably higher volumes than the first cut. Both Lamb and Holdridge had extensive experience in Caribbean forests and were aware of monoculture plantations' susceptibility to pests in the tropics. They therefore recommended multispecies plantations on ecological, as well as economic, grounds. Lamb recommended supplementing the sawmill at the PCAN with another, larger facility where the Ruta Militar met the Sarstún River. The riverside location allowed cut logs to be sunk and stored underwater to minimize warping and splitting, while processed lumber could be loaded directly onto ships bound for New Orleans.[53] Echoing Duque, he cautioned against letting Indian peasants into the woods, because he did not believe they could be trusted to understand the value of conserving timber.

Retreat and Buried Legacies

1950 was a banner year for Arévalo's crusade, marking the end of the PCAN's experimental phase. The forest survey was generating excitement, while workers finished the first residential neighborhood at Ciudad Tecún Umán and the first families had moved in. Agronomists were successfully growing all manner of crops around Poptún, and Arévalo hosted a large delegation to inaugurate the Ruta Militar. Lieutenant Casasola was singled out for praise for his thrift and the quality of the road. However, it soon became clear that the experimental phase of the revolutionary colony would be its last.

When Colonel Jacobo Arbenz succeeded Arévalo in 1951, the PCAN lost its most ardent booster. The critics, from conservative columnists to multilateral development agencies, lambasted the colony as a poorly conceived money pit. The World Bank did, in passing, admit that Guatemala had "almost unlimited" forestry potential, but it was a moot point. Arbenz's embrace of the World Bank and, in turn, its focus on lenders' concerns meant that the Petén was too risky—bankers preferred a cautious, pay-as-you-go approach to development by increasing coffee exports. Without Arévalo to defend the costs of maintaining the PCAN, Arbenz and legislators began redirecting funds, shutting down research, laying off workers, and absorbing what remained into the Ministries of Agriculture and Public Works. By June 1952, the colony had effectively ceased to function. In October, it was formally liquidated and its facilities transferred to the Departamento Agrario Nacional (National Agrarian Department; DAN), under the Ministry of Defense. Supporters and state officials penned mournful and sometimes scolding obituaries to the crusade, lamenting that the revolution had abandoned rationality in favor of economic fantasies and agrarian radicalism.[54]

Yet the First National Agricultural Colony was not primarily a victim of a prodigal administration, as most commenters argued. It was indeed expensive but was not jeopardizing the national budget, which high coffee prices were padding anyway. The Ruta Militar was completed, eliminating the largest line item, as was the infrastructural work at Ciudad Tecún Umán. International aid from US agencies and universities was funding most of the research, with more expected through the Department of Agriculture's Point Four Program.[55] Politics, not economics, determined the colony's fate, when Decree 900 shattered the assumptions about justice and development that had given the project its raison d'être. Arbenz's land reform was exactly the kind of radical, immediate, and risky restructuring of Guatemalan society that Arévalo's colony had meant to avoid.

Arbenz's retreat from the frontier did not signify the end of the forest crusade's influence. The Ruta Militar channeled the focus of development in the Petén for the next twenty-five years, narrowing many possibilities for routes in and out of the Petén down to a few that incorporated its length into their own. The most viable alternative—from Cobán, in Alta Verapaz, to Sayaxché, on the Pasión River, no matter its hypothetically preferable route through existing population centers—would be far more expensive than linking Cobán and Puerto Barrios to the southern stretch of the Ruta Militar.[56] With the Ruta Militar in place, the gaze of the state and its development activities were concentrated in the Southeast, rather than in the river basins in the Southwest, where most of the land suitable for mechanized agriculture was located.[57] The road also guided the flow of spontaneous settlement in later decades and encouraged larger numbers of unauthorized colonists than would otherwise have braved the woods, as refugees from state terror in the highlands and Pacific coast sought safety and liberty in the northern forests.[58]

By 1954, Arévalo's colony was all but forgotten, but it had not disappeared. A few colonists had remained, tending their gardens as the forest reclaimed those of their erstwhile neighbors. Reporters from *El Imparcial* described a landscape eerily reminiscent of the Maya ruins: once glorious buildings, temples of progress, now lost under a shroud of vegetation.[59] That image of the colony in ruins was deceptive, or at best incomplete. The PCAN ceased to be a colony, but it remained an active military base. Soldiers continued to run the sawmill, survey routes for new roads, conduct patrols, and tend the fields of maize and sugarcane, plus their own kitchen gardens. In Ciudad Tecún Umán, officers moved into the empty houses.[60] The revolution had left the Petén, but the army was there to stay.

The colony's greatest legacy resided in the institution of the army. At the PCAN, a bond was forged between the forests and the military that survived decades of political upheaval and civil war: in various guises, from

1945 until 1990, the de facto or de jure government in the Petén was the Ministry of Defense. The lieutenant in charge of the Ruta Militar, Oliverio Casasola, had only begun his career when the colony closed. He eventually became the longest-serving director of FYDEP, the parastatal military command that governed the Petén from 1960 until 1990, and in the popular imagination he is virtually synonymous with it.[61] The principal instrument of counterinsurgency in the Petén, FYDEP had Arévalo's colony as its institutional foundation. It was FYDEP that established the forest reserves that later became the Maya Biosphere Reserve. By the 1970s, the officer corps at the base in Poptún had produced some of Guatemala's first "entrepreneurial" military leaders, who extracted personal fortunes from the forests, eventually accumulating power and wealth to rival the traditional oligarchs.[62]

The authoritarian regimes that wanted to claim Arévalo's Petén legacy for themselves tried to erase it from history—for two decades, Casasola did not talk publicly about his early career during the revolution, except in vague terms.[63] In 1955, the Guatemalan Army (by then under the command of counterrevolutionary officers) took credit for miraculously transforming Poptún into a flourishing self-sufficient farm, but it was in fact occupying the fields of the PCAN; it simultaneously claimed to have built a road through the jungle, which was in fact the Ruta Militar, which had been continuously and diligently maintained.[64] All of the development projects after 1954 depended directly on the infrastructure, facilities, institutions, and experience gained through Arévalo's revolutionary crusade. Although few on either side of Guatemala's civil war have admitted so, the philosophy and practice of "counterinsurgent environmentalism" that emerged in the Petén during that conflict was, to a great extent, a contradictory legacy of the revolution itself.

Notes

1. Quotation from Arévalo's first speech to the National Assembly. "Primer Informe al Congreso Nacional," March, 1, 1946, in *Arévalo: Discursos desde una Guatemala inconclusa* (Guatemala City: Catafixia Editorial, 2014), 96.

2. See editorial by Virgilio Rodríguez Macal in *El Imparcial*, May 29, 1952. The values cited by Rodríguez Macal are based on some generous assumptions and are taken out of context of management, market conditions, and transportation costs.

3. Atherton Lee, "Guatemala's Intriguing Petén Problem," *Bulletin of the Pan American Union* 80, no. 4 (April 1946): 181–186. The article was translated into Spanish soon after its English publication and was discussed at length by Virgilio Rodríguez Beteta in his two-volume *El libro de Guatemala Grande: Petén-Belice* (Guatemala City: Tipografía Nacional, 1951).

4. Arévalo's quote comes from "Primer Informe," 96. The most prominent civilian voice of millenarian nationalist discourse with regard to the Petén can be found in Rodríguez Beteta, *Guatemala Grande.*

5. This is the subject of my dissertation, "Environmentalists with Guns: Conservation, Revolution, and Counterinsurgency in the Petén, Guatemala, 1944–1996" (PhD diss., New York University, 2018).

6. Norman Schwartz, *Forest Society: A Social History of Petén, Guatemala* (Philadelphia: University of Pennsylvania Press, 1990), esp. the introduction and ch. 1.

7. How many people actually have and do live there is a politically charged matter subject to debate. See Liza Grandia, "Cuantas personas quiere que vivan en el Petén?," in *Nuevas perspectivas del desarrollo sostenible del Petén*, 137–156 (Guatemala City: FLACSO, 2000).

8. See Charles Mann, *1491: New Revelations of the Americas before Columbus* (New York: Knopf, 2005), esp. ch. 8, "Made in America."

9. On February 1, 2018, researchers using Lidar technology announced the discovery of evidence of far more extensive urban construction and earthworks in the Petén than had previously been recognized, indicating much larger and denser pre-Colombian populations than prevailing estimates. Based on the new findings, researchers working with the PACUNAM Foundation, which sponsored the study in cooperation with National Geographic, claim there could have been ten to fifteen million people living in the Maya lowlands, whereas earlier population estimates had ranged from one to five million. See Tom Clynes, "Exclusive: Laser Scans Reveal Maya 'Megalopolis' below Guatemalan Jungle," *National Geographic*, February 1, 2018, https://news.nationalgeographic.com/2018/02/maya-laser-lidar-guatemala-pacunam/; and Jacey Fortin, "Lasers Reveal a Maya Civilization So Dense It Blew Experts' Minds," *New York Times*, February 3, 2018, https://www.nytimes.com/2018/02/03/world/americas/mayan-city-discovery-laser.html. Ironically, the new estimates correlate with those of Sylvanus Morley, which had been widely dismissed since the 1970s.

10. Anabel Ford and Ronald Nigh, *The Maya Forest Garden: Eight Millennia of Sustainable Cultivation of the Tropical Woodlands* (New York: Routledge, 2015).

11. Schwartz, *Forest Society*; Ford and Nigh, *The Maya Forest Garden*. See also Inga Clendinnen, *Ambivalent Conquests: Maya and Spaniard in the Yucatán, 1517–1570* (Cambridge: Cambridge University Press, 2003).

12. Jennifer Anderson, *Mahogany: The Costs of Luxury in Early America* (Cambridge, MA: Harvard University Press, 2012).

13. Leslie Holdridge and Bruce Lamb, *Los bosques de Guatemala* (INFOP, Guatemala City: 1950), 97–99.

14. John Patrick Bell, "Proyecto Arevaliano," *Anuario de Estudios Centroamericanos*, 19, no. 1 (1993): 23–35.

15. Rodríguez Beteta, *Guatemala Grande*, preface to vol. 1.

16. Bruce Lamb, "Utilization, Distribution, and Management of Tropical American Mahogany" (PhD diss., University of Michigan, 1953), 201.

17. See F. A. Silcox, "Forestry and Labor," *Journal of Forestry*, no. 4 (1920): 317; and Burt P. Kirkland, "Effects of Destructive Lumbering on Labor," ibid., 318–320.

18. Thomas Klubock, *La Frontera: Forests and Ecological Conflict in Chile's Frontier Territory* (Durham, NC: Duke University Press, 2014); Christopher Boyer, *Political Landscapes: Forests, Conservation, and Community in Mexico* (Durham, NC: Duke

University Press, 2015); Emily Wakild, *Revolutionary Parks: Conservation, Social Justice, and Mexico's National Parks, 1910–1940* (Tucson: University of Arizona Press, 2011).

19. "Primera Colonia Agrícola Nacional Poptún," promotional booklet published by Arévalo's public relations office in 1950, AGCA, Hemeroteca Nacional de Guatemala, Guatemala City (hereafter, AGCA, Hemeroteca).

20. Probably first elaborated by Holdridge and Lamb in *Los bosques de Guatemala* (1950). The claim appears throughout Rodríguez Beteta's *Guatemala Grande*, published in 1951, and reappears after the colony's closing. See Leopoldo Zeissig's articles in *El Imparcial*, June 8, 9, 11, 12, and 19, 1953; and Virgilio Rodríguez Macal's editorials in the same paper, May 29 and 30, 1952.

21. On the flip side, mismanaged woodlands led to desertification, chaos, and savagery. See the discussion of Raphael Zon's "Forest and Human Progress," *Journal of Forestry* 20, no. 1 (1921): 58–64.

22. Olindo Secondini B., *La foresta en Guatemala: Fuente de trabajo y de riqueza-desarrollo económico y cultural del país* (Guatemala City: INFOP, 1951).

23. Rodríguez Beteta, *Guatemala Grande*, iv.

24. See "Revalorización de la tierra: Pan para hoy, hambre para mañana," *El Imparcial*, December 6–7, 1948. Leopoldo Zeissig makes the same point in *El Imparcial*, June 19, 1953.

25. Acuerdo Gubernativo, June 20, 1945, and "Reglamento para el funcionamiento de la Guardia Forestal en el departamento del Petén," July 20, 1945, AGCA, Hemeroteca.

26. Information on the provisioning of the colony can be found in the correspondence between colony officials, US diplomats, and private suppliers in AGCA, leg. 1247, Guatemala City.

27. Rodríguez Beteta, *Guatemala Grande*, 2:213, 220.

28. The likely origin of this belief is José Víctor Mejía, *Datos Geográficos* (Guatemala City: Tipografía Nacional, 1904). The father-son team of Virgilio Rodríguez Beteta and Virgilio Rodríguez Macal are the two most-read authors on the Petén, and both describe Poptún in Edenic terms. See the father's *Guatemala Grande* and the son's novel *Carazamba* (Guatemala City: Piedra Santa, 1953). Scientists from the United States were less persuaded by the myth and found the place oppressively hot. See Cyrus Longworth Lundell, *The Vegetation of the Petén* (Washington, DC: Carnegie Institution of Washington, 1936); Lamb and Holdridge, *Los bosques de Guatemala*; and Charles S. Simmons, José Manuel Tárano T., and José Humberto Pinto Z., *Reconocimiento de los suelos de la República de Guatemala*, trans. Pedro Tirado-Sulsona (Guatemala City: SCIDA, 1959).

29. For information on the first months of work at the colony and on the Ruta Militar, see "Primer Informe," 96. Decree 217, n.d., leg. 1259, AGCA, Guatemala City, which retroactively authorized funding for the work; and Acuerdo Gubermental, July 1, 1946, leg. 1247, AGCA, Guatemala City, which established the governing regulations of the PCAN.

30. *Cedar Rapids Gazette*, October 27, 1946. Mentioned in the correspondence of colony administrators in leg. 1248, AGCA, Guatemala City.

31. Blueprints for the planned city and photographs of the first (and only) neighborhood built appear in the promotion booklet "Primera Colonia."

32. At least some of the roadworkers were prisoners captured during failed coup

attempts against Arévalo. See "Anticomunista narra el terror a que fue sometido en Poptún," *El Imparcial*, October 4, 1954.

33. See "Memoria de la Primera Colonia Agrícola Nacional en Poptún, correspondiente al Año 1946," leg. 1263, AGCA, Guatemala City; "Memoria de los trabajos efectuados en la Primera Colonia Agrícola de 'Poptún,' correspondiente al Año de 1947," leg. 1248, AGCA, Guatemala City; "Memoria de los trabajos realizados en la 'Primera Colonia Agrícola Nacional de Poptún,' departamento del Petén, del 1º de Enero al 30 de Noviembre de mil novecientos cincuenta," leg. 1263, AGCA, Guatemala City.

34. Francisco Boburg, *Los caminos del Petén*, 31–32, a self-published memoir of a retired (now deceased) officer that is sometimes found in the bookstores around Flores. The backbone quote comes from Duque, "Informe Preliminar," leg. 1247, AGCA, Guatemala City.

35. José Aybar de Soto, *Dependency and Intervention: The Case of Guatemala in 1954* (Boulder, CO: Westview Press, 1978), 129; Bell, "Proyecto Arevaliano"; Rodríguez Beteta, *Guatemala Grande*, 137.

36. See *Reglamento para la Guardia Forestal del Petén*, July 20, 1945; Acuerdo Gubernativo, April 23, 1948. Both in AGCA, Hemeroteca.

37. Juan Pablo Duque, "Plan Ganadero," leg. 1247m AGCA, Guatemala City.

38. *El Imparcial*, December 27, 1948.

39. Holdridge and Lamb, *Los bosques de Guatemala*, 99; see also Lamb, *Mahogany of Tropical America* (Ann Arbor: University of Michigan Press, 1966), 158–159.

40. "Plan Ganadero," leg. 1247, AGCA, Guatemala City.

41. On racial ideology and ideas of "ladinoization" in Guatemala, see Arturo Taracena Arriola, "Estado guatemalteco e identidad nacional indigenismo, integración y desarrollo (1944–1965)," in *Etnica, estado y nación*, vol. 2 (1944–1985), ed. Arturo Taracena Arriola, 29–88 (Antigua, Guatemala: Centro de Investigaciones Regionales de Mesoamérica, 2004), 29–88.

42. See, e.g., Lamb's argument in *Mahogany of Tropical America*, 43.

43. "Plan Ganadero," leg. 1247, AGCA, Guatemala City. This prejudice among scientists working in the Petén spanned otherwise yawning political divisions and influenced scientific production through the rest of the century. See Norman Schwartz, "Colonization of Northern Guatemala: The Petén," *Journal of Anthropological Research* 43, no. 2 (1987): 170–171; and chapters 4, 5, and 6 of my dissertation, "Environmentalists with Guns."

44. See annual memorias in leg. 1247, 1248, and 1263, AGCA, Guatemala City; Duque "Plan Ganadero," leg. 1247, AGCA, Guatemala City; and the 1950 "Primera Colonia" promotional booklet.

45. The dean of that school, Dr. Cunningham, and at least one of his graduate students, Charles F. Simmons (later dean of Auburn's agronomy school), worked at the PCAN. They are listed and photographed in the promotion booklet "Primera Colonia."

46. See correspondence on provisions in leg. 1247, AGCA.

47. Leslie Holdridge and Bruce Lamb, *Los bosques de Guatemala*.

48. See letter from Hugo Cerezo D., chair of the History and Anthropology Institute, to Governor General Álvarez, February 23, 1949, leg. 1248, AGCA, Guatemala City.

49. He made this claim some years later, based on research done for the forest survey. See Lamb, *Mahogany of Tropical America*.

50. Holdridge and Lamb, *Los bosques de Guatemala*, 168, 186, and 189–190.

51. Ibid., 167–199.

52. Ibid., 169–172.

53. Ibid., 191.

54. See Virgilio Rodríguez Macal, *El Imparcial*, May 29 and 30, 1952; César Augusto Padilla, *El Imparcial*, June 19, 1952; Leopoldo Zeissig, *El Imparcial*, June 8, 9, 11, 12, and 19, 1953; Ramón Blanco, *El Imparcial*, May 22, 1953; and Pedro Pérez Valenzuela, *El Imparcial*, April 12–21, 1954.

55. See preface to *Guatemala Grande* and *El Imparcial*, December 4, 1948, for expectations of continued US research assistance.

56. The World Bank favored the Cobán-Sayaxché route, which had been begun and then abandoned by Ubico and which followed an old and well-trafficked mule trail frequented by Q'eqchi' merchants and *chicleros* (the latex tappers emblematic of the rugged frontiersman in the Petén).

57. Simmons, Tárano T., and Pinto Z., *Reconocimiento de los suelos de la República de Guatemala*, 571–584.

58. Schwartz, *Forest Society*; Richard Newbold Adams, *Migraciones internas en Guatemala: Expansión agraria de los indígenas kekchíes hacia El Petén* (Guatemala City: Centro Editorial José de Pineda Ibarra y Ministerio de Educación, 1965); Mario Eduardo Váldez Gordillo, *Territorio y geopolítica: Insurgencia y desmovilización en el Petén* (Tuxtla Gutiérrez, Mexico: Universidad de Ciencias e Artes de Chiapas, 2014).

59. *El Imparcial*, August 31 and October 4, 1954.

60. "Colonia Poptúm [*sic*] pasa al DAN," *El Imparcial*, December 19, 1952.

61. A bust of Casasola greets visitors on the causeway to the Petén's island capital, Flores (though few likely notice it behind the large hotel and beer advertisements). An inscription on its pedestal credits Casasola for leading the nation's efforts to open and reincorporate the Petén. See also the eulogy to his passing in *El Imparcial*, May 23, 1979.

62. This is discussed in chapters 3 through 5 of my dissertation, "Environmentalists with Guns." The Lucas Brothers, in particular, used FYDEP to launch their political careers before taking control of the national government in the late 1970s and initiating the bloodiest phase of the counterinsurgency. Events in the Petén were closely associated with the better-studied military development and counterinsurgency initiatives in the Franja Transversal del Norte (Northern Transversal Strip; FTN), immediately to the south of the Petén. See Luis Solano, "Development and/as Dispossession: Elite Networks and Extractive Industry in the Franja Transversal del Norte," in *War by Other Means: Aftermath in Post-Genocide Guatemala*, ed. Carlota MacAllister and Diane M. Nelson, 119–142 (Durham, NC: Duke University Press, 2013).

63. Although he did bring it up after the center-Left Revolutionary Party won the 1966 elections, in an attempt to co-opt the party's political rhetoric by staking his work at FYDEP as the natural heir to Arévalo's legacy. See the coverage of his speech "Grandezas y Miserias del Petén," *El Imparcial*, October 3, November 18, and 20 November, 1967.

64. *El Imparcial*, June 20, 1955.

PART II

New Frames

CHAPTER 4

The "Indigenous Problem," Cold War US Anthropology, and Revolutionary Nationalism

New Approaches to Racial Thinking and Indigeneity in Guatemala

Jorge Ramón González Ponciano

The governments of Juan José Arévalo (1945–1951) and Jacobo Arbenz (1951–1954) attacked the "indigenous problem" by eliminating debt peonage; promoting literacy, bilingual education, the protection of labor rights, and public health; combatting alcoholism; revalorizing indigenous crafts; and, most important, implementing agrarian reform. They bet on turning indigenous people into mestizos or ladinos, in order to establish, with anthropology's help, a "homogeneous nationality" of consumers and literate citizens receptive to urban progress and liberal democracy. Notwithstanding their rather moderate scope and focus on capitalist modernization, such measures were immediately stigmatized as communist. Although Guatemalan anticommunism has roots prior to the start of the Cold War, the mobilization of the fear of communists and indigenous people promoted by the 1954 counterrevolution was decisive in interrupting the reformist experiment. Democratic advances resulting from the confluence of Guatemalan and North American scholars were almost totally reversed, and, in their place, it was suggested that the "indigenous problem" would be resolved by applying the social sciences to social integration, transculturation, and community development. In a few years, the country went from the nation building and Pan-American *indigenismo* of revolutionary nationalism to the nation destroying of regressive modernization and anticommunist paranoia. Both in Guatemala and in the United States, fear of the red menace grew to mass proportions, which eliminated critical voices and forced academia's ideological alignment with the defense of the Christian, white, and civilized West's values. The counterinsurgent state resorted to genocide to stem social rebellion, and after the signing of the peace accords, the "indigenous problem" was joined by the "shumo problem" and the exacerbation of antiplebeian racism, which continues the genocidal praxis by justifying the extermination of poor and marginalized youths considered expendable.

Background of the "Indigenous Problem"

The origin of the so-called indigenous problem in Guatemala goes back to the colonial debate over the humanity of indigenous people and their potential for conversion to Christianity. In the construction of the "problem," the creation of stereotypes about savage, idolatrous, bloodthirsty, indolent, dirty, and drunk indigenous people took over, which remain present in the contemporary racist mentality. Another crucial space for this construction was the debate over the best method to "civilize the Indians" at the end of the eighteenth century, which, according to Matías de Córdoba,[1] could be accomplished by promoting the "creation of wants and needs." Almost a hundred years later, Antonio Batres Jáuregui reiterated the civilizing effectiveness of the "creation of wants and needs" and recommended suppressing linguistic diversity and communal land ownership.[2] The agroexport elite was not interested in the "creation of wants and needs" and resorted to the discourse of laziness to justify forced labor as a civilizing option. In the name of the war against idleness, the coffee-grower dictatorships enacted vagrancy laws that guaranteed abundant labor for work on the plantations and in public works. Newspapers and official documents spread the stereotype of austere and frugal workers who do not require much salary to survive and who, because of their illiteracy, are not capable of enjoying the status of citizens. Also emphasized was the narrative of the "pure Indian," characterized as a docile and industrious worker, not ladinoized, traditionalist, observant of his customs, and uncorrupted by ladinos, who voluntarily welcomes the patron's tutelage and readily assumes his place in the socioracial hierarchy. The press supported foreign immigration, which solidified the moral leadership of whiteness among the ladinos that the Liberal Reform legally defined as nonindigenous, who adopted the anti-indigenous and antiblack sentiment of the white elite, though it considered them racially inferior to the "pure Indian." During the 1920s, the most conservative intellectuals were inclined to restore the status of indigenous people as colonial servants, while the most progressive ones, influenced by the agrarianism of the Mexican Revolution and European and South American eugenic thought, spoke out in favor of the educability of indigenous people, agrarian distribution, and public-health programs that sought to combat alcoholism and regulate marriage.[3]

General Ubico and the First Indigenista Group

After assuming the presidency in 1931, General Jorge Ubico eliminated universities' autonomy and decided that the university should "work for the Indian's incorporation into modern civilization."[4] Ubico rejected the influence of the Mexican Revolution and Mexican president Lázaro Cárdenas's socialist indigenismo, and during his tours in Guatemala's interior, Ubico attacked literate indigenous people, managers of their communities' affairs and accused of being communists, with particular spite merely because they knew how to read and write.[5] The dictator decided that an indigenous problem did not exist in Guatemala, since it was already being resolved through military service and teaching literacy in the barracks. However, he was pressured by the North American authorities to implement the recommendations contained in the *Acta de Pátzcuaro*, which was signed in May 1940, and, with it, US-sponsored *indigenista* Pan-Americanism was inaugurated. For the purposes of making room for that commitment and following the visit of the Office of Indian Affairs commissioner, Emil J. Sady, to Guatemala, the First Indigenista Group was formed in the Guatemalan capital in December 1941, proposing to carry out ethnographic studies "to try to preserve the indigenous customs and ideas that are currently useful, and to modify or replace whichever ones work against their normal economic and cultural evolution."[6] Its members—lawyers and men of letters who shared an interest in indigenous culture—later became prominent officials, diplomats, writers, and university professors. David Vela, a well-known writer and journalist, chaired the group. He was assisted by two secretaries, Alfonso Orantes and the then high school graduate Manuel Galich. Seven sections were established under the responsibility of a director supported by three members and a secretary: Jorge Luis Arriola, for the Educational Section; Mario Monteforte Toledo, for the Economic and Statistical Section; Epaminondas Quintana, for the Biological Section; José Castañeda, for the Artistic Section, Flavio Herrera, for the Legal Section; Flavio Rodas, for the Linguistic Section; and José Joaquín Pardo, for the Bibliographic, Reporting, and Propaganda Section. Vela was named a member of the executive committee of the Instituto Indigenista Interamericano (Inter-American Indigenous Institute; III) and, thanks to Robert Redfield's support, took a three-month-long tour of the United States, which included visits to indigenous reservations and conversations with John Collier, the director of the National Indian Institute of the United States. In the following decades, Vela held positions on the executive directorates of numerous indigenista initiatives and took under his wing Antonio Goubaud Carrera, an aide-de-camp and disciple of Redfield and Sol Tax in Chicago; Goubaud was later named the first director of the Indigenista Institute and after that the Guatemalan ambassador in Washington, DC.

As late as 1943, at a meeting of the isthmus's ministers of public education in Panama, dictatorship officials reaffirmed that the situation of Guatemalan indigenous people did not have the proportions or characteristics of a problem. Nevertheless, Ubico tolerated the First Group's activities and had important allies among the leading members of the III. One of them was the Guatemalan Carlos Antonio Girón Cerna, whose positions on the dictator's labor policies reflect the contradictions of wanting to make the forced compulsion to work compatible with directed cultural change. Girón Cerna was the secretary-general of the III's provisional executive committee and the first editor of the journal *América Indígena* and the *Boletín Indigenista*, and temporary head of the III after Moisés Sáenz's death. After General Ubico canceled peons' debts to their bosses by decree, Girón Cerna wrote: "To prevent the Indian, now without obligations, from abandoning work on the plantations, which would have caused enormous damage to our economy, the Vagrancy Law was enacted, which forces peasants who do not have their own crops to produce on the plantation or plantations that they choose for a minimum of 100 workdays per year." Removed from the III directorate upon the arrival of the Mexican Manuel Gamio, Girón Cerna argued that "the program of studies on the Indian recommended at Pátzcuaro turns out to be bad and full of gaps" and proposed establishing measures to take advantage of the unoccupied time of indigenous people devoted to agriculture. He recommended using the teachings of applied anthropology and establishing anthropology schools or departments to train experts in indigenous affairs, as well as integration brigades, with a preference for indigenous staff, for "overcoming the natural mistrust of the Indians against the white's civilizing ways."[7]

Manuel Gamio, Central America, and Pan-American Indigenismo

Gamio replaced Girón Cerna and was named the director of the III in 1942. A disciple of Franz Boas and a supporter of eugenic *mestizaje*, he was always attentive to the development of indigenismo in Central America, and in July 1943, he visited Guatemala, Honduras, and El Salvador, accompanying Ernest Maes, the secretary of the National Indian Institute. Concerned about the antidictatorial spirit that prevailed in Central America, Maes warned in his letter to Redfield: "It is essential to avoid that said [*indigenista*] institutes become centers of political debate in which Indianists, with well-intentioned but futile purposes, only devote themselves to making revolutionary speeches about the Indian, rather than developing effective methods for confronting the indigenous problem."[8] Maes was probably worried about individuals such as Manuel Galich, Vela's assistant in the First Indigenista Group and an anti-Ubico student leader at the University of San Carlos (USAC) Law School, who demanded the restoration of university autonomy and the creation of an Indigenista Sciences Institute. Maes later became the director of the Servicio Cooperativo Interamericano de Educación (Inter-American Cooperative Education Service; SCIDE), and Galich became the new revolutionary government's minister of education in 1945.

Redfield's Lecture and the Inauguration of the National Indigenista Institute

In 1944, Ubico was toppled and Juan José Arévalo was elected president. In the face of a scarcity of Guatemalan professional cadres, North American experts, primarily anthropologists and linguists, were responsible for advising, among other things, the literacy and bilingual education programs of the Arévalo and then Arbenz governments. Among them, one can mention Mark Hanna Watkins, Norman McQuown, William Griffith, Benjamin Paul, Richard N. Adams, and the linguists from the Summer Linguistic Institute. In June 1945, when the Second World War was about to end, Redfield delivered the lecture "Ethnic Groups and the Creation of a Homogeneous National Identity in Guatemala" at the Paraninfo of the University of San Carlos's Medical School, one of the oldest and most venerable buildings for Sancarlistas. Despite the lecture's applicability to the history of anthropology, modernization, and directed cultural change in Guatemala, it is little known in the English-speaking academic world.

At the Paraninfo, Redfield insisted that the Guatemalan "problem" "was not just rural, but indigenous" and could be solved, as in many areas of the world, through "education" and "economic modernization." He warned that both had caused the "demoralization and even the disappearance" of many indigenous groups in Africa, North America, and the South Pacific islands, but that in Guatemala, such measures would not be so difficult because the "Indians" were willing to become ladinos and racial prejudice did not exist in the country. Moreover, the "Indians" were already accustomed to the use of money, the free market, and economic transactions based on individual responsibility. To illustrate the case, Redfield gave the example of an indigenous woman who regretted getting married, and who, with the goal of giving back the money that the groom had paid during the proposal, went to the capital to work as a servant. Redfield argued that cultural change aimed at "the formation of a Guatemalan nationality" and advised by "locally-trained anthropologists" would be based on three premises: (1) the Indians would have to become ladinos to be able to exercise their rights as citizens; (2) education, understood as learning to read and write in Spanish, was a requirement for exercising those rights; and (3) the individualist character that the Indians displayed on a daily basis in their personal interactions would help the entire process. "Guatemala's problem," Redfield argued, was to try to make the country's ethnic groups become "a complete nationality," and to reach that goal, traditional institutions would have to be eliminated through education. "One has to think," he added, "that educating is, frequently and regrettably, equivalent to disintegrating." He referred to the usefulness of anthropology and "the current Guatemalan anthropologists and those who are educated in the future" in "forging a nationality," produced by the "change or transmutation" of many ethnic groups, which "form the heart of Guatemala" and which "are now ready to receive the impulses of modern civilization."[9]

Weeks later, on September 26, at the same hall, the Instituto Indigenista Nacional (the National Indigenista Institute; IIN) was inaugurated. Manuel Galich, minister of education and member of the First Indigenista Group, said in his speech that of all the national problems, "the Indian is the most severe among them," and he reiterated the importance of "truly scientific research" of the "fundamental Guatemalan problem." Galich promised that with "slow effort, based on science, to proceed afterward with methodical action," the objectives of the recently inaugurated IIN would be achieved. For his part, Antonio Goubaud Carrera, the first director, asserted that indigenismo, "without a doubt, is the manifestation, the symptom of a particular social malaise. Where there are no indigenous people, there is no *indigenismo*." And he reinforced the civilizing premise noted by Galich: "The problem of ethnic diversity is our fundamental problem." "How many Guatemalans will there be," Goubaud wondered, who, "speaking languages foreign to the national language, dressing in costumes that point them out to the rest of the population, plagued by beliefs that moderate enlightenment eliminates, tied to technologies that date back thousands of years—how many, one might wonder—will think that Guatemala is not just what frames the mountains bordering their social community?" "To confront this problem, the government founded the IIN," Goubaud concluded.[10] Once in office, he combined administration and academia to confront the "problem," and he gave himself time to write a paper on the criteria for defining the ethnic group, which, in the style of Matías de Córdoba, defended the "creation of wants and needs," salary and consumption. In a letter to John Collier, for example, he insisted that the IIN should foment greater indigenous participation in the economic structure. "With it," Goubaud asserted, "indigenous people will come to have a better economic position that will allow them to increase their purchasing power, raise their standard of living, and contribute broadly to national life, both in reference to the country itself as well as what concerns the entire American hemisphere."[11]

Arevalista and Arbencista Indigenismo

President Arévalo aspired to a Central American unionism based on the abolition of the feudal regime, a new organization of the proletariat, and the education of indigenous people. Upon taking office, he announced: "We will bring schools to the small villages and some of those schools will have wheels to climb the mountains and get into the forests."[12] During his government, the National Department of Literacy, Misiones Ambulantes de Cultura Inicial (Mobile Missions of Basic Culture), Núcleos Escolares Campesinos (Clustered Schools for Peasants), the Popular University, Night Schools, Rural Normal Schools, and IIN-sponsored bilingual teacher-training centers were created. At the end of his term, Luis Cardoza y Aragón wrote: "Our government, with different names for its departments, is in reality an indigenous affairs department or, better, it should be."[13] To measure the magnitude of the "indigenous problem," the Ministry of Education organized a convention of indigenous teachers in June 1945 in Alta Verapaz, which recommended creating a normal school for rural teachers and night schools for adults. In January 1946, the school census revealed that four-fifths of the rural student population remained without schools. Then, the most extensive program of rural education and literacy that can be remembered in all of Guatemalan history was undertaken.

Thanks to an agreement signed between the US State Department, the National Indian Institute, and the IIN, Mark Hanna Watkins, the first Afro-descendant graduate of the University of Chicago's Department of Anthropology, arrived to study the distribution of Guatemala's indigenous dialects and languages. This African American linguist's presence in Guatemala at this important moment in its history has been practically erased from the national memory of indigenismo.[14] At the request of William J. Griffith, a representative from the Inter-American Education Foundation, Inc., Watkins led the team that selected Chimaltenango as the most suitable site for setting up a Regional Rural Normal School, in the very heart of the Cakchiquel region. In 1946, Norman McQuown, also from Chicago, arrived to establish the fundamental phonemes of K'iche', Q'eqchi', Kanjobal, Tz'utujil, and Xinca and to carry out a special study of Mam. His work, together with that of Watkins, allowed for developing the alphabets and phonetical, morphological, and syntactic bases of Cakchiquel for the primers that would be used in the literacy campaign that began in 1948.

In November 1949, the first Conference of Linguists was held, at the end of which were developed the alphabets for writing Cakchiquel, Mam, K'iche', Tz'utujil, Kanjobal, Jacalteco, Aguacateco, Chuj, Q'eqchi', Pocomchí, Chortí, and eastern and central Pocomam. The conference acknowledged the contributions of Watkins and McQuown, and in August 1950, the government formalized the alphabets of the four majority languages: K'iche', Cakchiquel, Mam, and Q'eqchi'. A census of bilingual rural teachers and a survey of the four major linguistic regions were conducted to select the places with the best conditions to begin the literacy campaign. The IIN, in cooperation with the National Literacy Committee and under the advisement of the Summer Linguistic Institute, chose the Q'eqchi' region, the one with the highest monolingualism in the entire country.

The accomplishments were so evident that in Paris, during a UNESCO meeting in 1951, it was emphasized that "after Mexico, Guatemala is the most advanced country in the development of a policy for the revalorization of the indigenous people." Previously, in 1950 in Montevideo, the Ibero-American Congress of Education recommended that all the continent's educational institutions build federation-type schools similar to those in Guatemala.[15] The IIN translated ads and educational programs for the radio, electoral propaganda, public health and agricultural guidance manuals, and Decree 900, the Agrarian Reform Law, which made Jacobo Arbenz go down in history as a progressive military man different from the rest of the officers who betrayed the revolution's ideals and tore apart Guatemalan society.[16]

Indigenista Studies

In its first ten years, the IIN carried out more than one hundred socioeconomic studies and monographs. It continued the study on nutrition that the Carnegie Institute had started in 1942 and in which Goubaud, Juan de Dios Rosales, and Agustín Pop participated. The work conditions in indigenous industries, annual distribution of time, rates of productivity, and uses of free time were researched. Benjamin Paul, a professor at Harvard University, advisor at the Chimaltenango Normal School, and member of the SCIDE, developed, with Goubaud's help, a sociological research guide on the ecology, housing, furniture, dress, agriculture, industries, occupations, social organization, structure, and individual lifecycles in indigenous communities. As Sarah Foss discusses in greater detail in chapter 7 of this volume, a survey in 311 markets and a questionnaire to research the ethnic criteria in each municipality were also conducted. A rural credit system was developed for textile production as a domestic and artisanal industry with a fixed consumer market and potential to grow. Laws were issued to protect textiles and their producers, which sought to eliminate customs barriers and to provide credit facilities. The SCIDE supported the training of field technicians for the Núcleos Escolares Campesinos and the Misiones Ambulantes de Cultura Inicial (Clustered Schools for Peasants and the Mobile Missions of Basic Culture), made up of a certified teacher, an army officer, a final-year medical student, and an agricultural expert, with an express prohibition on including more employees, except for indigenous interpreters. In the most remote corners of the republic, these misiones would spread the "cult of patriotic symbols and the historical values of the nation in addition to explaining to the peasants their civic responsibilities and civil rights, initiating them in the knowledge of minimal military notions and inciting them to knowledge about the October Revolution's moral origin and social meaning, decrying the political vices of past regimes and the new political mentality."[17]

Despite the overlap between revolutionary nationalism's educational goals and the SCIDE's purposes, diplomatic stumbles were not lacking. The agreement with the SCIDE was canceled because of complaints against that organization's officials, who, "taking advantage of the possibilities that education offers, began to undermine the foundations of Guatemalan nationality, arousing in the learners an exaggerated sense of gratitude and admiration toward the country that was offering that cooperation."[18] President Arévalo said in his 1950 report to Congress that the service was ended due to fiscal reasons, but he left a record of the many requests that the government do so because of the belief that elements among the teachers were disturbing the unity and nationalist spirit surrounding education. The SCIDE's work shows the limits to the optimism awoken after the end of World War II vis-à-vis closer US–Latin American relations, given that the North

American strategy prioritized Europe's reconstruction and the only area for continental cooperation was the Inter-American Treaty of Reciprocal Assistance, invoked to attack Guatemalan revolutionary nationalism.[19]

The Indigenista Debacle

The incorporation of agrarian reform into the indigenismo of Arbenz's government precipitated mercenary intervention, and once installed in power, Colonel Carlos Castillo Armas suspended the IIN's activity and then incorporated it into the recently created General Directorate of Rural Socio-Educational Development. Labor unions were suppressed, and agrarian struggles and political dissent were criminalized. In 1955, one of the IIN's tasks was to translate a lesson dedicated to Guatemalan peasants into K'iche' for the National Committee of Defense against Communism. Four months after the counterrevolution started, this committee had 72,000 persons accused of being communists recorded in its files and expected to reach 200,000, a figure tragically close to the result of the extermination programs that the state executed in the following decades.[20]

In order to not touch the *latifundia* and to dodge the structural need for agrarian reform, the United States established a model of anticommunist developmentalism in Guatemala that included applying the social sciences to "social integration." Castillo Armas traveled to the United States in November 1955 to receive honorary doctorates from both Columbia University and Fordham University and a certificate of recognition from the University of Houston. The Pan-American Society also gave him a medal during a dinner at the Waldorf Astoria Hotel in New York, where, as at the universities, he was congratulated for having extirpated the communist threat in the hemisphere and overthrown a government opposed to Christian principles. With these actions, Rooseveltian Pan-Americanism was buried and the national security doctrine, with the disastrous consequences that we know, gained space. On the eve of his return, Castillo Armas announced that his government had decided to organize "a conference of eminent university professors and students, particularly from the United States, who have been studying the anthropological, social, ethnic, psychological and economic problems," he said "of my country."[21] This conference took place from June 17 to 23, 1956, in Guatemala City, and from it, the Seminario de Integración Social Guatemalteca(Guatemalan Seminar for Social Integration; SISG) emerged; it was recognized as "the first experiment on social integration" carried out in the world, consisting of applying the social sciences to the transculturation and formation of Guatemalan citizenship. This was a very different transculturation from the one conceptualized by Fernando Ortiz for the Caribbean and defined instead as synonymous with acculturation and directed cultural change. David Vela and Jorge Luis Arriola reappeared on the SISG Advisory Council; Arriola, who had been a member of the First Indigenista Group and later the director of the IIN, acted as the general secretary of the SISG and later as the executive secretary of the Fourth Inter-American Indigenista Conference, scheduled to take place in Guatemala in 1957, but held in 1959 because of the assassination of Castillo Armas. By acclamation, Vela was elected executive chairman of that Fourth conference, which, in the end, gave the SISG a vote of confidence and issued resolutions in honor of Tecún Umán, Goubaud Carrera, and Moisés Sáenz.[22]

Already turned into a lower-level organization, the IIN was put in charge of creating the Museum of the Guatemalan Indian and supporting the establishment of the Day of the Indian. Despite its decline, a "Comprehensive Plan for the Improvement of an Indigenous Community" (1956/1960) praised the institute's experience in resolving "Guatemala's fundamental social problem" and decried that "the natives continue putting up a passive defense in the face of the benefits that cultural changes offer them."[23] Another useful document for evaluating the ethnographic and indigenista work that the IIN, the SISG, and other authorities from Guatemala and the United States implemented in the 1950s and '60s is Calvin P. Blair's study about the North American staff and social science research in Guatemala, which identifies three priorities of academic work during the 1950–1967 period: communism, business opportunities, and tourism. Since 1950, Blair wrote, the presence of the United States has become ubiquitous, with a mix of North American officials, academics, religious people, and military men, praying, spying, or trying to help. Perhaps no other Latin American country in recent times has experienced such penetrating and evident influence from a foreign power. And surely no small country, with the exception of Panama, has felt so much influence from the United States in relation to its size and global importance.[24]

In the 1970s, the government promoted first community development and then cooperativism; although both of these were anticommunist in character, they were replaced by the army's civic action programs. Instead of indigenismo and the ethnographic studies carried out from the more or less benevolent and conservative perspective of the North American and Guatemalan academy, the indigenous population remained subject to the brutalities of a militarized state that, presumably, would have to protect it from communist aggression. The IIN and SISG were extinguished and with them the positivistic scientism that was expected to achieve the creation of a "homogeneous nationality." After the erasure of that legacy, the restoration of moral leadership of whiteness, and the human and institutional destruction that still endures, became more conspicuous, and it is largely the result of the oligarchy's political backwardness and the anticommunist paranoia that guided the foreign policy of the United States.

The "Indigenous Problem" and the New Plebeian Indigeneity

The history of the Guatemalan "indigenous problem" cannot be restricted to the scope of the indigenous-ladino dichotomy, without any connection to international history and the geopolitics of global capitalism. The perception of indigenous people as a "problem" in Guatemala and in many of the continent's countries is linked to the US "Indian Problem," aggravated by the conquest of the West after the dispossession of Mexico in 1848 and to other problems that are part of civilizing modernity thought from the perspective of white supremacy, such as the "Mexican Problem," the "Black Problem," the "Yellow Problem," the "Irish Problem," the "Jewish Problem," the "Brown Problem," and the "Muslim Problem." The discourses around these "problems"—supported by scientific racism, eugenics, whiteness, and social Darwinism—were key to the ideological advance of Manifest Destiny and the Monroe Doctrine, which guided the imperial expansion of the United States and were an important part of the indigenista Pan-Americanism or Inter-Americanism of the first half of the twentieth century.

In Guatemala, the failure of the "homogeneous nationality" that sought to make indigenous people citizens did not only obey the constraints of indigenista Pan-Americanism and the racist and eugenic thought of ladinos and creoles. North Americans and Guatemalans coincided in favorably considering the symbolic superiority of mestizoization and ladinoization as a substitute form of eugenic mestizaje. From 1954, revolutionary nationalism was stigmatized as communist, and capitalism was naturalized as an inevitable destiny, which Guatemalans, like other peoples around the world, would have to go through to achieve the long-desired democratic development as opposed to the socialist and communist model. This naturalization of capitalism and the dichotomization of society into indigenous people and ladinos gave rise to the exoticized reinvention of the country as a living museum, a cultural laboratory that would permit observing the surviving folk cultures, irremediably condemned to disappear. The anti-Marxist purge of the Cold War facilitated the emergence of a tutelary defense of Mayan indigeneity, which reduced indigenous oppression to the acts of ladino power and erased the articulation of local racism via whiteness and global capitalism. Indigenous peoples were represented as passive, timeless, and homogeneous victims, outside the meritocracy and the spectrum of political positions that go from the most radical to the most conservative.

It was not considered important to examine the ethnogenesis of castes and the mestizo world or to review the ethnographic contradictions that decades earlier had moved Redfield and Tax to maintain that the ladinos were nothing but redressed indigenous people. The "ladinophobia" of some anthropologists made the Western world synonymous with the ladino world. They ignored the overlaps between being white for Guatemalan creoles and Euro–North Americans, and being white for ladinos, who consider themselves white but who are considered inferior by the elite. In recent years, in order to support the cause of indigenous culturalism, the ethnic dichotomy was reracialized, presenting indigenous people and ladinos as two different and conflicting "races." Against the warning formulated by Brubaker and Cooper in regard to the undifferentiated use of "categories of practice" and "categories of analysis,"[25] it is assumed that because a "racial" self-identification exists on the part of individuals and groups, that implies the actual existence of groups identifiable as "races."

The study of indigeneity has to leave the ethnicized and racialized realm in which it has been encapsulated and critique the exoticized construction of the Maya that serves the naturalization of the place of everyone within the national and international hierarchies of capitalism and whiteness. From the perspective that establishes indigeneity as starting from the existence of the European colonist and a situation of internal colonialism, the ladino has never been recognized as "native." To the contrary, trends and historical reality have put the ladino in the place of the colonizer and oppressor. Hence the conceptual stumbles of Carlos Guzmán Böckler and Jean Loup Herbert,[26] who, despite their outstanding ethnographic contribution to the study of racism and decolonization, classified ladinos as a dominant and homogeneous social class and ignored the presence and historical power of the creole and Euro–North American oligarchy.

Although abandoning the ladino as a label of self-identification is not as frequent in Guatemala as it is in neighboring Chiapas, the representation of the ladino as a closed space, homogeneous and radically opposed to the indigenous world, does not leave any room to visualize the processes of fluidity and transculturality that have been the norm for centuries. Nor does it allow for the complex multicultural interaction that occurred during the armed rebellion, which bet on decolonization and the dismantling of the structures of economic oppression and political exclusion. The critique of exoticized indigeneity would help to see intercultural anticapitalism and the different types of countercultural and antidictatorial, cross-class, and transnational insurgency that go beyond the narrow space of the indigenous-ladino dichotomy and are part of the history of struggles for social justice in Guatemala. However, academic conservativism continues to represent the social insurgency against the oligarchic order as an initiative of ladino and creole leftists, inside which indigenous peoples were passive companions, or populations "between two fires."

In approaching the history of political violence, the Mayan genocide is strongly emphasized, leaving aside the "anti-Communist genocide,"[27] a policy that was part of the counterinsurgent state's multiple strategies. Likewise, in the study of ethnicity, inequality, and political conflicts, the role of the creole oligarchy's heterodox sectors, "traitors" to their "race" and their class—Antonio Goubaud Carrera, María Cristina Vilanova, Aura Marina Arriola, Marta Elena Casaús Arzú, Arturo Taracena Arriola, María Concepción Sáenz, Mario Tejada Bouscayrol, and many others who were victims of state repression—has not been incorporated. On the other hand, one cannot lose sight of the conceptual and generational inertia of figures on the "sympathetic [solidario] Left" such as Edelberto Torres Rivas, the dean of social sciences in Central America, criticized by the K'iche' historian María Aguilar for his opinions on the lack of political thought in Guatemala.[28] Torres Rivas, interviewed by Méndez Salinas, argued that the current political thought in Guatemala is not "capable of explaining some of the most important things, like the so-called 'indigenous problem'" and how "colonial features are maintained, how they can be overcome, and which measures must be taken for indigenous citizens to indeed be citizens and indigenous people."[29]

But on top of that, it is necessary to research and make visible the historical consequences of the oligarchy's political backwardness, characterized by its opposition to contributing fiscally to the state and its militant rejection of *igualamiento* (equalization) as the product of social mobility and the development of citizenship for all. In the second half of the twentieth century, while in the Western world Keynesianism inclined to public spending, consumption, and the creation of a middle-class society was gaining popularity, in Guatemala the most rancid of oligarchic thought founded Francisco Marroquín University in 1971 to promote neoliberalism and push the savage modernization of capitalism. Another source of international pride for this racist and elitist conservatism was the recognition that in the 1970s some of its most radical representatives gained acceptance into the top ranks of the World Anti-Communist League, at the same level as the most reactionary elites from Taiwan, South Korea, and the Latin American Southern Cone, especially for their decision to create death squads within their political organizations.[30]

Although it is the primary historic beneficiary of the semislave or poorly paid labor of several generations of indigenous and ladino workers, the Guatemalan oligarchy lacks a sense of social or moral obligation to the least-privileged members of society. The high concentration of land in a few hands is a structural hindrance to the creation of jobs, and the refusal to pay taxes and fair wages is responsible for the "social death" of the nonwhite majority, a fact that can be conceptualized as genocide according to international law and reflected in the human development indices. As in any situation of internal colonialism, the oligarchy and the subservient bourgeoisie that accompanies it—in which the military, corrupt officials, and now drug traffickers stand out—behave like an occupier that does not recognize the natives as citizens, and resorts to brute force to maintain a de facto apartheid and crush any sign of popular dissent. Its obsessions with purity of blood and "pure races" make it vehemently reject the "ladinoized Indian." The oligarchy controls part of the cultural capital associated with the hoarding of Mayan archeological items and actively participates in the commercialization of cultural difference, whether through the privatization of patrimony and colonial and pre-Columbian archeological research, or through environmental conservation with a Neo-Malthusian orientation, which has turned the latifundia into protected areas.

The oligarchy rejects the equalization of not only indigenous people who want to pass for ladinos but also the mongrel rabble of working-class ladinos, stigmatized as *chancles*, *aguacateros*, *cachimbiros*, *choleros*, or *shumos*, all labels that allude to the plebeian, dark-skinned masses, perceived as a threat to decency and good manners. Like the indigenous majority, these nonwhite masses suffer the consequences of the absence of an inclusive national project, and from a broader perspective on indigeneity in Guatemala, they should be conceptualized as native actors marginalized by national and foreign white supremacy's acts of power. An area in which these acts of power are manifested in extremely harsh ways, and that should be incorporated into studies about the genocide, is the continuum between "ethnic cleansing," anticommunist genocide, and contemporary "social cleansing," focused on the extermination of people considered expendable, mostly youths of scarce resources, marginalized and criminalized by the neoliberal state.

In my research, I explore the historical existence of an indigeneity that redefines the plebeian ladino as nonwhite and the moral leadership of whiteness, which conceives the "shumo problem" as a continuation of the "indigenous problem." The indigeneity of the "shumo problem" does not merit the attention of cultural anthropologists, for whom plebeian mestizos lack the primordial traditions or cultural traits trafficable on the market of identities. Despite its visibility, the antiplebeian racism of the "shumo problem" remains absent from studies on racism in Guatemala, generally focused on ladino society's anti-indigenous sentiment. This antiplebeian racism, in which the anti-indigenous sentiment and antiblack sentiment of colonial origin converge, responds in part to changes in status markers resulting from indigenous and mestizo migration to the United States, which now allows many Guatemalans and their families to access goods that until recently were considered the exclusive patrimony of the elite, such as speaking English and other languages, and having access to vehicles and cutting-edge household goods and technologies, as well as living the experience of civility and the application of law in a postindustrial society. The narratives of this antiplebeian racism have transnationalized to such a degree that Los Angeles, the US city with the most Guatemalans, is "The Shumo Mecca," unlike Miami, Houston, or New York, which continue to be places for "shopping" and temporary residences for the elite.[31] A new debate on indigeneity in Guatemala has to incorporate anti-shumo sentiment, antiplebeian racism, and the ways in which the rejection of *igualamiento* and the unwritten norms that indicate which place each person or group should occupy in society hinder the development of citizenship for all, at the national and global levels.

In Guatemala, as in other countries, neoliberalism made the world elitist, impoverished the middle sectors, pauperized the working class, sharpened the racialization of inequality, and revived social Darwinism, which narrows social mobility and full citizenship. The continuing contemporary rejection of the indigenous, the Afro-descendant, and the plebian, and their perception as "problems," infringes upon everyone's right to have access to the state, public money, fair salaries, and, consequently, the experience of freedom, preached by more conservative liberals. Thus, in Mexico, for example, after three decades of neoliberalism, the Movimiento de Regeneración Nacional (Movement for National Regeneration; MORENA) emerged, mockingly re-christened by racist supremacy as *morenaco* ("mob of darkies and Indians"), alluding to the combination of *morenos*, people with dark skin, and *nacos*, a derogatory label for referring to mestizoized indigenous people. Similar cases are the antiplebeian hysteria that motivates a good deal of the anti-Chávez propaganda within and outside Venezuela, and the Brazilian elite's racist reaction to the presence of Afro-descendants in the universities and the increase in their buying power as a result of the social programs of Lula da Silva and Dilma Rousseff. In that context, the indigeneity of the shumo is an expression of the rejection of igualamiento on the part of the elites, who have maintained since colonial times that citizenship is only for whites, the learned, and property owners; and that the masters and the "decent people" should not share the same space with the servants and the "ordinary people."

Notes

1. Matías de Córdoba, *Utilidades de que todos los indios y ladinos se vistan y calcen a la española, y medios de conseguirlo sin violencia, coacción, ni mandato: memoria premiada por la Real Sociedad Económica de Guatemala en 13 de diciembre de 1797* (Guatemala City: Imprenta de D. Ignacio Beteta, 1798).

2. Antonio Batres Jáuregui, *Los indios: Su historia y su civilización* (Guatemala City: Tipografía La Unión, 1894).

3. Marta Casaús Arzú, "De la incógnita del indio al indio como sombra: El debate de la antropología guatemalteca en torno al indio y la nación, 1921–1938," *Revista de Indias* 65, no. 234 (2005): 375–404.

4. Beatriz Palomo de Lewin, "La Universidad en la década de 1920–30 y durante el régimen de Jorge Ubico (1931–1944)," *Estudios* 6 (1975): 207.

5. Federico Hernández de León, *Viajes presidenciales*, vol. 1 (Guatemala City: Tipografía Nacional de Guatemala, 1940), 49, 159, 326, and 327.

6. *Boletín Indigenista* 2, no. 1 (March 1942): 7–9.

7. Carlos A. Girón Cerna, "La Nueva Paz del Indio," *Revista de la Universidad de San Carlos*, October–December, 69, 70, and 79.

8. *Boletín Indigenista* 3, no. 4 (December 1943): 210.

9. *Boletín Indigenista* 5, no. 3 (September 1943): 41–45.

10. *Boletín Indigenista* 4, no. 4 (December 1995): 362–364.

11. *Boletín del Instituto Indigenista Nacional* 2, nos. 2–3 (March–June 1946): 86–87.

12. Juan José Arévalo, *Escritos políticos* (Guatemala City: Tipografía Nacional de Guatemala, 1945), 143, 144.

13. Luis Cardoza y Aragón, "El gobierno del presidente Juan José Arévalo, apuntes para un balance," *Revista de Guatemala* 1, no. 1 (April–June 1951): 32.

14. Margaret Wade-Lewis, "Mark Hanna Watkins: African American Linguistic Anthropologist," *Histories of Anthropology Annual* 1 (2005): 181–218.

15. Alberto Ordóñez Arguello, *Arévalo visto por América* (Guatemala City: Ministerio de Educación Pública, 1951), 46.

16. See Roberto García Ferreira, "La revolución guatemalteca y el legado del presidente Arbenz," *Anuario de Estudios Centroamericanos* 38 (2012): 41–78; Piero

Gleijeses, *Shattered Hope: The Guatemalan Revolution and the United States, 1944–1945* (Princeton, NJ: Princeton University Press, 1991); Greg Grandin, *The Last Colonial Massacre: Latin America in the Cold War* (Chicago: University of Chicago Press, 2004).

17. "Instituto Indigenista Nacional: 1947," *Boletín Indigenista* 3, no. 1 (March 1948): 40.

18. Carlos González Orellana, *Historia de la educación en Guatemala* (Guatemala City: Editorial José de Pineda Ibarra, 1970), 58.

19. See Jorge Ramón González Ponciano, *Diez años de indigenismo en Guatemala: La primera época del Instituto Indigenista Nacional (1944–1954)* (México, DF: Escuela Nacional de Antropología e Historia, 1988).

20. Stephen Schlesinger and Stephen Kinzer, *Bitter Fruit: The Untold Story of the American Coup in Guatemala* (Garden City, NY: Anchor, 1982), 221.

21. Edith Evans Asbury, "Guatemala Chief Gets Two Degrees: Columbia and Fordham Cite Castillo, Who Also Is Feted by Pan American Society," *New York Times*, November 6, 1955.

22. "El Seminario de Integración Social Guatemalteca," *Boletín Indigenista* 16, nos. 2–3 (August 1956): 164.

23. Instituto Indigenista Nacional, "Plan de mejoramiento integral de una comunidad indígena," *Boletín del Instituto Indigenista Nacional* 2, nos. 1–4 (1960 [1956]): n.p.

24. Calvin P. Blair, Richard P. Schaedel, and James H. Street, *Responsibilities of the Foreign Scholar to the Local Scholarly Community: Studies of U.S. Research in Guatemala, Chile and Paraguay* (Washington, DC: Council on Educational Cooperation with Latin America, Education and World Affairs; and the Latin American Studies Association, Library of Congress, 1969), 16, 17, and 11–43.

25. Rogers Brubaker and Frederick Cooper, "Beyond 'Identity,'" *Theory and Society*, 29, no. 1 (2000): 1–47.

26. Carlos Guzmán Böckler and Jean Loup-Herbert, *Guatemala: Una interpretación histórico-social* (México, DF: Siglo XXI Editores, 1970).

27. Norman Naimark, *Genocide: A World History* (New York: Oxford University Press, 2017), 104–123.

28. Translations mine. "Somos el 'problema indio,'" *El Periódico*, August 15, 2016, https://elperiodico.com.gt/opinion/2016/08/15/somos-el-problema-indio/.

29. Luis Méndez Salinas, "Edelberto Torres Rivas: Más vale cínico que pesimista," *Nómada*, July 13, 2016, accessed July 16, 2016, https://nomada.gt/edelberto-torres-rivas-mas-vale-cinico-que-pesimista/.

30. Scott Anderson and Jon Lee Anderson, *Inside the League: The Shocking Exposé of How Terrorists, Nazis, and Latin American Death Squads Have Infiltrated the World Anti-Communist League* (New York: Dodd, Mead, 1986).

31. See Jorge Ramón González Ponciano, "The *Shumo* Challenge: White Class Privilege and the Post-Race, Post-Genocide Alliances of Cosmopolitanism from Below," in *War by Other Means: Aftermath in Post-Genocide Guatemala*, ed. Carlota McAllister and Diane M. Nelson, 307–329 (Durham, NC: Duke University Press, 2013).

CHAPTER 5

Youths and Juan José Arévalo's Democratic Government in Guatemala, 1945–1951

Arturo Taracena Arriola

The collective behavior of young urban Guatemalans in the postwar period would have important effects on culture, values, the search for identity, and the struggle for social reforms. In a way, it assumed countercultural forms and discourses in opposition to what was then Guatemala's official culture, which was under the hegemony of the liberalism introduced by the 1871 Revolution, and which Ubiquismo—the regime in which they grew up—had brought to its highest glory. Undoubtedly, such behavior was favored not only by the ideas of the October 1944 Revolution, but also by the social, political, and economic measures undertaken in an earlier presidency (1945–1951), by Juan José Arévalo's government.

This chapter presents the role played by three youth organizations, which initially defined themselves as Arévalo's supporters but who would soon radicalize to the point that their leaders were among the young people who came together to found the Partido Comunista de Guatemala (Guatemalan Communist Party; PCG) in secrecy in September 1949.

These organizations were the Grupo Saker-ti de Artistas y Escritores Jóvenes (Saker-ti Group of Young Artists and Writers), a cultural organization founded at the start of 1946; the Asociación Socialista (Socialist Association), formed at the beginning of 1947 by University of San Carlos Law School students, with an eye to promoting Marxist thought; and the Alianza de la Juventud Democrática Guatemalteca (Guatemalan Alliance of Democratic Youth), a sectarian organization that was founded in the middle of the same year.

In the framework of the so-called Cold War, these organizations expressed the ideological concerns of some urban youth sectors, made up of university students, teachers, artists, and workers, which would at length decide the fate of the so-called Guatemalan Spring and, along with it, the fate of these organizations.

This radicalization in Guatemalan social thought is usually explained by different external and internal factors. The range of external factors includes the growing influence of the Soviet Union after World War II; the arrival of Communist exiles from different Latin American countries (Cuba, the Dominican Republic, Chile, and El Salvador), as well as Spanish refugees, in Guatemala; and the opening to circulate Marxist literature from Argentine, Chilean, and Mexican publishing houses. Among the internal factors cited are the return of Guatemalan exiles trained as Marxists in Mexico (e.g., Ernesto Capuano and Alfonso Solórzano) and the intellectual leadership of Guatemalan politicians such as José Manuel Fortuny Arana (b. Santa Rosa, 1916). But what Mario Monteforte Toledo (b. Guatemala City, 1911) has emphasized as "his [Arevalo's] attitude toward the Communists" has seldom been explored.[1]

That is to say, with the ambivalence with which President Arévalo faced the start of the Cold War, he sought to quickly draw a parallel between fascism and communism, ideologies that in his judgment represented poles that were equidistant from the "spiritual socialism" that he encouraged as a philosophy for reforming democracy. In practice, what occurred was the modern start of the closing of political spaces for ideological reasons—in this case, because of an anticommunist stance. However, in analyzing the impact that such a position had, one must note that this stance found fertile ground in the anticommunist postures that the Catholic hierarchy and the Guatemalan bourgeoisie had held since the 1930s, as a result of the peasant insurrection in El Salvador. This discourse had penetrated deeply into important sectors of Guatemalan society, in both urban and rural areas.

Arévalo's anticommunist thought is well known, and its concrete manifestations have usually been mentioned in works that study the period known as Guatemala's "democratic spring," but at the same time, it has not been analyzed as a whole for two reasons: first, the oversized role of communists in democratic Guatemala, especially during Jacobo Arbenz Guzmán's government; and second, the tendency to reduce anticommunist thought to just the role of the Catholic Church and antirevolutionary political groups.

Thus, the impact of Arévalo's anticommunism, along with that of a good number of his supporters, on post-Ubiquista-dictatorship Guatemalan youth—above all, among his young supporters—has not been analyzed. Some took it up as a rallying cry, especially in the bosom of the Frente

Popular Libertador (Popular Liberation Front; FPL) and Renovación Nacional (National Renovation; RN) parties, while others came to question such an ideological position and ended up adhering to communism from the ranks of the Partido de Acción Revolucionaria (Revolutionary Action Party; PAR).

This historical reductionism (*reducción histórica*) can be seen below, summarized in Bernardo Arévalo de León's account of anticommunist activity during Arévalo's presidency:

> The country was divided and lived through a turbulent reality. The polarization came to be fixed around a dichotomy between communism and anticommunism, facilitated by the growing influence of members of the Communist Party in the Government, but the reality is that anticommunist preaching had begun a long time before the Communists appeared on the political scene as central figures. In the 1930s, anticommunism had been an obsession and justification for Ubico; in 1945, the Catholic Church was already warning that the red "ghost" roamed the streets, and in 1947, at the Bogotá Conference, the opposition distributed satirical materials [*pasquines*] denouncing Arévalo's *communist* dictatorship and its designs on *continental expansion*.[2]

Another way of seeing this type of historiographical absence can be noted in sociologist John Holger Petersen's dissertation entitled "The Political Role of University Students in Guatemala: 1944–1968." In it, beyond failing to consider any of the youth organizations, or any of their leaders, he only begins to talk about the existence of any anticommunist policy in Guatemala in 1951, that is, after Arbenz took power and the public appearance of the Communist Party.[3] This tendency to set the anticommunist watershed in the midst of Guatemalan youth starting with the 1950–1951 conjuncture can also be seen in other doctoral dissertations that have examined the subject of the student movement during the revolutionary decade, effectively ensuring that the Arévalo government remains excluded as a promoter of anticommunism.[4]

Undoubtedly, in the Guatemalan anticommunist discourse of the 1940s, there existed a dichotomy of, on the one hand, seeing Arévalo as a "Communist" because of the social and economic reforms that his government promoted and, on the other hand, the perspective of the leader and his closest supporters, who applied that epithet to those who really were, or whom they believed to be, Communists. The latter was a way to point out stigma and, at the same time, minimize the political impact of their activities at times when the elites were opposed to the social and economic reforms that the government was promoting. By 1947, the elites had coalesced around the opposition's work of reversing or restraining the course that the Revolution of 1944 had taken. Their strongman was colonel Francisco Javier Arana, chief of the Armed Forces.

Since he had assumed the presidency in 1945, Arévalo saw those who professed Marxist ideas as harmful to democracy. Thus, in January 1946, he would close the "Claridad" School, which had been founded in July of the previous year, because he believed that it served to disguise Marxist theses as teacher education and because it was supported by Salvadoran Communists;[5] moreover, in September 1947, he would include Communism and the Soviet Union as elements subversive to democracy in his speech, "About a Conspiracy." In it, he boasted that "luckily, until now, the Guatemalan Communists who reside in Guatemala are no more than a dozen among Guatemalans, Salvadorans, and Hondurans."[6]

In this way, the field of ideological dispute was set so that the influence of the few existing Communists would grow among a certain sector of young middle- and working-class Guatemalans, eager for structural social reforms and an openness to the world, in a context in which the erstwhile allies, the United States and the Soviet Union, grew apart and paved the way for the Cold War to emerge.

As Alfredo Guerra Borges, one of the radicalized students, has pointed out: "An objective fact is that the Communists did not insert themselves into the [October] revolutionary movement, but rather had formed a part of it since before they made their ideological choice, since the days of 1944, and they were not a foreign body in the group of center-left democratic parties, because they had been active in its ranks since 1944."[7] That is, the university youth had stood out in the struggle against *ubiquismo*, and it would be in the bosom of this group that the ideological dispute discussed here would play out, to the extent that "many students jumped from university halls to seats in Congress and to high posts in the government."[8]

For that reason, I will focus on describing the processes of founding and radicalizing in three student groups (the Saker-ti Group of Young Artists and Writers, Socialist Association, and Guatemalan Alliance of Democratic Youth) and their growing confrontation with President Arévalo. Although they did not propose toppling him—as the Guatemalan Right and, therefore, a group of university students headed by Mario Méndez

Montenegro, wished to do—these three organizations had to create the political conditions to replace Arévalo with a more radical president in the November 1950 elections. Colonel Arbenz would be the chosen candidate.

Thus, in the context of the confrontation created by the Cold War, from the perspective of both camps of university youths and workers, one of its most contradictory consequences was Colonel Arana's assassination and the subsequent outburst of the most important of the plots against the Arévalo government, in June 1949. This time, the attempted coup d'état against the state had come from the Aranistas, and it was neutralized after several days of combat in Guatemala City. Immediately, pressures on the Arevalista government from the United States made it shift to the right vis-à-vis the political-diplomatic ideas outlined by the minister of foreign affairs, Enrique Muñoz Meany (b. Guatemala City, 1907): a frontal battle against fascism, Latin American dictatorships, and colonialism.[9] The new minister of foreign affairs, Ismael González Arévalo (b. Santa Rosa, 1909), the president's cousin, would strengthen the anticommunist discourse as a display of drawing closer to Washington, making many students and workers who had been seduced by Communist ideas, given their position as leaders, opt to form a party that was independent of the existing political forces.

The Social Thought of the Saker-ti Group of Young Artists and Writers

The Grupo Saker-ti de Artistas y Escritores Jóvenes emerged in the middle of 1946 as a cultural organization, founded at the initiative of teacher Huberto Alvarado Arellano (b. Quetzaltenango, 1927), who became its secretary-general. Between 1947 and 1949, he focused on carrying out artistic exhibits in the provinces (Quetzaltenango, Sololá, Guatemala, Baja Verapaz, Chiquimula, Zacapa, Escuintla), and likewise successfully brought the magazine *Saker-ti* to light, reproducing texts and illustrations by its members as well as Latin American and European intellectuals. Meanwhile, he supported his mentor, Luis Cardoza y Aragón (b. Antigua Guatemala, 1902), in editing *Revista de Guatemala* (Guatemala's Magazine) and in the operation of the Casa de Cultura (Cultural House) until 1954.

The cultural dimension of the Sakertianos' endeavor was not limited to contemporary art or the rescue of pre-Hispanic heritage but extended to the debates over social reality in three areas: the situation in which indigenous Guatemalans found themselves and their culture; the need to confront the agrarian question in a country of great economic inequalities, and with a major presence of imperialist interests; and the need to produce "realist" art, which would raise social awareness.

In his essay "Notes on Imperialism," which appeared in *Saker-ti* magazine's 5–6 edition, Alvarado Arellano touched on the subject of the indigenous question, proposing that economic rather than social reasons were keeping indigenous people in Guatemala in a state of social subordination and misery. Likewise, reflecting on the subject "Guatemala as Problem," he indicated that the majority of Guatemalans' problems were explained by an economic situation that, while indeed of colonial origins, was now conditioned by the presence of US imperialism. Given that Guatemala is an agrarian country, eminently oriented to agroexport, and subject to a regime of servitude that weighed on the majority of its population, formed by indigenous people, it must be understood, he wrote, that "as long as a solution is not sought for the indigenous problem, it will not be possible to begin economic efforts toward liberation. GUATEMALA. INDIGENOUS COUNTRY. Undeniable truth." Moreover, it was not acceptable to speak of ignorance and alcoholism causing the misery of indigenous people as the official discourse of the Instituto Indigenista (Indigenista Institute) maintained, since "THE INDIAN PROBLEM IS LINKED TO THE LAND PROBLEM, or really, it is one and the same. Resolving the fair distribution of land, the Indian will be liberated economically and will have the possibility of overcoming his current human condition."[10] For that reason, only by means of "A DEMOCRATIC AGRARIAN REFORM will the liberation of the Indian be achieved."

As can be seen, the agrarian question, which President Arbenz's government would take up again later, has long roots in the thought of the Guatemalan Left and youths, influenced in large measure by the writings of the Salvadoran Communist leader Max Ricardo Cuenca. In an article in the newspaper *Mediodía* in 1946, entitled "Guatemala's National Problem," he pointed out that Guatemala had two immediate challenges of historical importance: the first was to resolve the "agrarian problem," in order to put an end to the concentration of land in only a few hands and to the persistence of the "feudal forms of production and exploitation of land." The second was to solve the "national problem [that] has generally been called the 'indigenous problem.'" However, the "first is conditioned by the second; that is, if it manages to resolve the agrarian problem, the national problem will have an easy solution."[11]

Although at that moment it was strategic to focus on the solution to the agrarian question, one had to trace the necessary guidelines for correctly resolving the national question in a country composed of "approximately,

85% of Indians who do not speak Spanish; who speak their own languages and dialects, who live in regions that are very separate from each other, who have very different customs, and this indigenous majority exists in these conditions, which is what gives the Guatemalan national question such importance."[12] In conclusion, according to Cuenca, Arévalo's government could serve as an example for the continent by "eliminating feudal servitude by means of Democratic Agrarian reform" and by "creating a new nationality based on self-determination and joining together the nationalities and Indian national minorities, now oppressed and exploited."

However, the Guatemalan president's agenda did not consider it, because he believed that the agrarian struggle would be a source of tension with the propertied class and with the transnational interests of the United Fruit Company. Hence, his program would focus on promoting the Labor Code, establishing social welfare, developing the public education system, respecting university autonomy, promoting bank reform and industrial development, and fostering political and union organization, but not on the mostly indigenous Guatemalan countryside. On the last point Arévalo argued the importance of avoiding its radicalization, aware that on the one hand, postwar inflation had affected the agricultural peace because of the existing low salaries and, on the other, pressure from the Association of Guatemalan Farmers would have a political effect. Thus, he made the army take control of strikebreaking in the countryside in December 1946 and January and April 1947.[13]

At the end of 1948, the Saker-ti Group published a declaration of principles under the title "Siete afirmaciones" (Seven Assertions), the fourth of which maintained that "art can fulfill its function when it reflects real situations of social life."[14] Although it had still not embraced socialist realism, as it would do starting in 1951, the cultural organization already pointed toward the adoption of socialist ideas, yet without maintaining Marxist thought per se. This was what Huberto Alvarado himself revealed when he published an a posteriori critique of what he believed to have been the Sakertianos' idealistic thought.

He noted that the aforementioned founding manifesto had been based on a petit bourgeois humanism, a reflection of the social composition of its members at the time, which was in turn based on a concept of freedom that was confused because it stemmed from an ethics that did not define freedom as a political exercise; rather, it was based on a notion of creative freedom.[15]

Already by then, this was a veiled critique of the position that Luis

Cardoza y Aragón, the intellectual godfather of the sakertianos, had held from 1930 to 1952; at this point, he was confronted by the Mexican Communists, especially Juan de la Cabada, with whom he had argued in 1934 about the freedom of creation and the danger of making militant art.[16] By then, the Saker-ti Group had already adopted the ideology of socialist realism that was so repugnant to its old mentor.

The Socialist Association and Marxism

The student-run Asociación Socialista (Socialist Association; AS) was founded at the beginning of 1947 by students from the Law School at University of San Carlos de Guatemala, under the leadership of Bernardo Alvarado Monzón (b. Guatemala City, 1925) and with the participation of Carlos René Valle y Valle (b. Guatemala City, 1925) and Carlos Alvarado Jerez (b. Ciudad de Guatemala City, 1923). Alvarado Jerez and Alvarado Monzón were half-brothers by the same father, Bernardo Alvarado Tello, the famous attorney and liberal politician, a leader in Guatemalan masonry, and the former rector of the National University.[17]

Although we do not have writings from the AS because of its short-lived existence, one can see from its name that the organization was branded by publicly taking on an ideology that not only assumed class antagonisms with the idea that society is conditioned by the relations of production, but also advocated for the need to transform the structure of the Guatemalan state. However, the organization soon disbanded when its leaders went on to participate in the PAR's radical version, and to inspire the founding of the Guatemalan Alliance of Democratic Youth in that same year, 1947, coinciding with the enlistment in the alliance of some of the Saker-ti Group's students and artists.

Guatemalan Alliance of Democratic Youth and Its Program and Platform

The Alianza de la Juventud Democrática Guatemalteca (Alliance of Democratic Youth of Guatemala; AJDG) was founded in mid-1947; its first general secretary was the teacher Rafael Díaz Gómez, who in November 1948 was succeeded in the position by the Salvadoran journalist José H. Zamora Corletto. The AJDG began to organize on the initiative of several university students, led by Bernardo Alvarado Monzón, who was the brother-in-law of the aforementioend Zamora Corletto. According to the AJDG's June 1949 "National Report," the organization had managed to come to fruition through an agreement among the Socialist Group (with twelve members), the Saker-ti Group (with twenty-two members), and the representatives of working-class youth from the Confederación General de Trabajadores de Guatemala (Guatemalan General Labor Confederation; CGTG), for which the number of members is not specified but was possibly fewer than that of the other groups.[18]

In November 1947, the coordinating committee, headed by Alvarado Monzón, issued the Manifiesto a la Juventud Guatemalteca (Manifesto to Guatemalan Youth), which established the need to create a youth organization that had as its goals the defense of Guatemalan democracy, the maintenance of world peace, the defeat of fascism, and the battle against racial discrimination and imperialism. To that end, the organization proposed a conference of the country's Democratic Youths, to take place the following month at the offices of the Instituto Nacional de Señoritas Belén (Belén National Institute for Young Women) in Guatemala City. Besides him, the signatories were José H. Zamora Corletto himself, the worker Flaminio Bonilla J.,[19] the sculptor Adalberto de León Soto (b. Quetzaltenango, 1919), and Manuel de Jesús Alvarez.[20]

This initiative was framed by the idea of forming a Guatemalan branch of the Worldwide Federation of Democratic Youth, established in London in 1945, immediately after the Worldwide Youth Conference had concluded. However, the vast majority of organizations from Western countries left the federation at the start of the Cold War in 1947, with the effect that in November of that year, the organization was relaunched with the Socialist bloc's clear influence. On December 2, the Guatemalan conference's coordinating committee circulated the AJDG's Programa de Principios (Program of Principles), underscoring the inalienable rights of Guatemalan youth to food, work, health, education, and places for recreation, at the primary as well as secondary and university levels.

Additionally, in its programmatic platform, it committed to defending the October 20 Revolution's political conquests; achieving an effective democracy to end misery and exploitation; and demanding that the different "indigenous nationalities" leave their semifeudal condition and fully enter into the national setting, until then represented by the ladino minorities. Finally, the federation espoused clear support for national liberation struggles at the global level and thus the rejection of colonialism and fascist dictatorships, alluding to the political-diplomatic program developed by Muñoz Meany for the 1944 Guatemalan Revolutionary Junta.[21] All these were principles that the Guatemalan youth leaders indicated had been included in the Atlantic Charter signed by Franklin Delano Roosevelt and Winston Churchill in 1941 and incorporated into the January 1, 1942, United Nations Declaration.[22] These ideas were confirmed in the ADJG's constitutional conference on December 21, 1947.

In an interesting section, "The Youth and Indigenous Nationalities," the AJDG's *Program of Principles* noted that the solution to the "indigenous majorities problem" in Guatemala should be considered a priority, and for that reason "concrete ways of freeing them from the backwardness and contempt in which they find themselves" must be presented. Such an initiative was

> immediately recognizing all their rights, attributable to their condition as humans and in their capacity as citizens; bringing them [Western] culture, using their own languages as a vehicle for this purpose; raising their deplorable social condition, creating needs and adjusting these needs to an individual, just economy. . . . In this regard, the youth will fight for appropriate legislation [. . .] so that, applied efficiently and quickly, they will take our indigenous nationalities out of the inhuman condition in which they are mired: semi-slavery.[23]

One can see the influence of reading Joseph Stalin's *Marxism and the National Question* (1913), characterizing the different Guatemalan ethnicities as nations within the framework of the state, as well as that of the *indigenista* thought embodied in the October Revolution and influenced by Mexican *indigenismo*. This indigenismo was based on assimilating indigenous persons through education, citizenship, and economic participation, albeit while respecting their culture through the preservation of the language; that is, it spoke out against *la castellanización forzada* (forcing them to speak Spanish). This approach, while novel for the era, did not refrain from endorsing the historic possibility of the *ladinización* (ladinization) of indigenous persons, this time pushed as much by the Revolutionary Junta as by Arévalo's administration.[24]

As a result of this first conference, Rafael Díaz Gómez,[25] a teacher, was elected as the alliance's secretary-general, with Bonilla and Zamora keeping their positions. For his part, Alvarado Monzón faded into the background, since he was already personally interested in founding a Guatemalan Communist Party and acting publicly as a cadre for the PAR.

Meanwhile, in December 1947, the AJDG confirmed its participation in the Continental Federation of Democratic Youth Conference, which would take place in Mexico during April 1948. Poet Otto Raúl González (b. Guatemala City, 1921) was responsible for representing the AJDG at the conference, and in his speech he reaffirmed the alliance's will to struggle for the "conquest and development of advanced social and political principles, within the healthy democratic experiment that we have been living since 1945, with Doctor Juan José Arévalo's Government." Subsequently, he went on to decry that Guatemala was already being assigned the red epithet and accused of maintaining "close relations with the U.S.S.R." For that reason, he considered it appropriate for the ADJG to endorse the "wealth of principles that provide concrete solutions for the better development of democratic ideas on the entire Continent."[26]

During September 1948, Carlos Manuel Pellecer Durán (b. Antigua Guatemala, 1920), who was in Paris as the Guatemalan Embassy's chargé d'affaires, was transferred to Warsaw, Poland, to represent the AJDG at the Worldwide Youth Conference, the first of those conferences at which the Guatemalan youth association was present through 1954.[27] Later, Pellecer Durán returned to Guatemala, coinciding with several of the young students in the PGT's founding.

Nevertheless, the AJDG's activity report, entitled "On the First Year of Struggle,"[28] recognized that at the end of 1948, the alliance still had not taken off organizationally, with other youth groups assuming more importance and activity, as was the case with the Saker-ti Group. The growth strategy would be to accentuate organizing not only students, but also workers, taking advantage of the typographer Octavio Reyes Ortiz's presence in the organization.

Starting at the end of 1949, the AJDG left the banner of apoliticism behind to establish itself as a left-wing democratic organization, and in 1950 it came to be under the influence of the PCG, of which—as we will see—its main leaders were founders. According to Schneider, at that time, it already had thirty-five hundred student and worker members. Its new secretaries-general would be Huberto Alvarado Arellano for 1949–1951 and Edelberto Torres Rivas (b. Guatemala City, 1930) for 1952–1954, with Carlos René Valle y Valle named as the organization's secretary.[29]

Within the framework of drawing closer to the Communists, the AJDC not only contributed to organizing the first PCG Conference, which took place in Guatemala City during March 1951, but also sent an important delegation to the Third Conference of the Worldwide Federation of Democratic Youth, organized in Berlin, East Germany. The delegation comprised Huberto Alvarado Arellano, Edelberto Torres Rivas,

Hugo Barrios Klee (b. Guatemala City, 1929), Oscar Edmundo Palma (b. Guatemala City, 1930), Octavio Reyes Ortiz, and Elena Chávez Castillo (b. Huehuetenango, 1922).

The Youths and the Temptation of Partisan Militancy

The first student attempt to establish a Communist party in Guatemala occurred in May 1947, when the AS started talks with representatives from the Vanguardia Socialista (Socialist Vanguard; VS), an organization composed mainly of journalists and headed by Alfredo Guerra Borges (b. Guatemala City, 1925) and with the participation of the Salvadoran writer Pedro Geoffroy Rivas, who had been a member of the Salvadoran Communist Party and the Mexican Communist Party in the 1930s.[30] Guerra Borges, as a member of Vanguardia Nacional (National Vanguard; VN), a party founded in July 1944, had traveled in 1946 on a scholarship to Chile, where he became a Communist and started relationships with members of that country's Communist Party. Upon his return to Guatemala, he got in touch with the Spanish biologist and Communist Rafael de Buen y Lozano, who had been a refugee in Central America since 1941, and put him in contact with workers from the dissolved CGTG. In and of itself, having named their group Socialist Vanguard indicated a Leninist-influenced approach to the extent that a Communist Party must be the vanguard of the country's working class, having the essential task of incorporating Marxist knowledge into the labor movement to be able to lead the anticapitalist struggle and take power. Both Guerra Borges and Geoffroy Rivas participated in the radio broadcast *La Voz de Guatemala* (The Voice of Guatemala) and worked at the *Diario de Centro América*; the former would become its editor.

This meeting could not take place because of a betrayal on the part of the president. The consequence of this betrayal was that, using the constant anti-Communist conspiracies it faced as an excuse, the Arevalista government suspended constitutional guarantees, resulting in postponement in talks between the AS and VS.[31] Guerra Borges told me that within the Socialist Vanguard it was always thought that this treachery had come from journalist Eduardo Martínez Arenas, who had been the editor of the official newspaper *Mediodía*, as well as his colleague, the Salvadoran Communist and writer Matilde Elena López, both of whom worked at the Department of Propaganda at the Office of the President of the Republic.[32]

In this maneuver, the declaration of the break of the FPL with the PAR on May 31, 1947, had been decisive. In his memoirs, President Arévalo notes that the FPL had revived its "anti-Communist stance," and to illustrate it, he reproduces the points of divergence, which were essentially ideological in nature: "a) disagreements over different ways of interpreting the Revolutionary Action Party's ideology; b) the impossibility of getting any difference between the P.A.R.'s higher leadership and its newspaper [*órgano periodístico*]; c) the assumption that there were elements within the P.A.R. that were allied with 'international Communism' or totalitarian tendencies."[33] The main signatories of such an anti-Communist position were Mario Méndez Montenegro (b. Guatemala City, 1910), Mario Monteforte Toledo (b. Guatemala City, 1911), Víctor H. Giordani Huertas (b. Quetzaltenango, 1912), Manuel Galich López (b. Guatemala City, 1913), Julio César Méndez Montenegro (b. Guatemala City, 1915), David Guerra Guzmán (b. Chiquimula, 1917), Alfonso Bauer Paiz (b. Guatemala City, 1918), and Oscar de León Aragón (b. Guatemala City, 1921), which, in general, meant the political and academic generation prior to that of the youths from Saker-ti Group, the Socialist Association, and the Guatemalan Association of Democratic Youth.

Marco Antonio Villamar Contreras (b. Guatemala City, 1927), the youngest of Mario Méndez Montenegro's followers, noted that aside from age, the youths were different from the others because they had not really been leaders in the 1944 revolutionary process and because they had opted ideologically for Communism: "The process [*sic*] well under way, the Cultural House [Casa de la Cultura] was founded and the Saker-ti Group emerged, with writers and artists from a younger generation, politically engaged with the popular classes."[34] Three months after the split between the FPL and the PAR, Arévalo delivered the speech "On a Conspiracy," in which he included Communism and the Soviet Union in his analysis of the elements that were disruptive to Guatemalan democracy. This official anti-Communist position came to reinforce and modernize the one that had existed since the 1930s, now framing it within the context of the Cold War, so that the PAR could still try to include some popular demands in order to capture the participation of the masses. This made dealing with the disputes of the peasants and workers, prime electoral clients of the day, one of the Arevalista parties' main activities.

In his memoirs, Bauer Paiz noted that "Mario Méndez planned the re-founding of the FPL, and the spirit and consciousness of the university group that linked us lasted until the point that those of us who opposed that measure were defeated, that fundamentally it consisted in accusing the party and the labor movement of being penetrated by international extremists, and that there was the danger of the revolution falling into the hands of communism, with which we were obviously offering a service to imperialism."[35]

For the purposes of this argument, it is interesting that it was the assertion of generational university camaraderie that prompted the signatories to take the step of separating from the PAR in order to decry the Communist influence in their midst. Indeed, this camaraderie existed among those students who had entered the University of San Carlos at the end of the 1930s and the beginning of the 1940s and had played an important role in the October 20, 1944, revolution. That is to say, it is a reflection of the sociological dimension of the intergenerational struggle over the direction of the political project that emerged from the Guatemalan October Revolution, beyond the anti-Communist attacks on the parties and the student organizations that openly defined themselves as such.

It was under these conditions, already in a context of secrecy and in the face of the Arevalista government's decision to prevent the founding of a Communist party, that some of the individuals who had been involved in the SV, SA, Guatemalan Alliance of Democratic Youth, and PAR formed the group the Vanguardia Democrática Guatemalteca (Guatemalan Democratic Vanguard; VDG) on September 28, 1947, with the intention of creating a Communist Party within a "reasonable time," that is, when the anti-Communist climate of the Arévalo government became less intense. Fortuny Arana became the secretary-general at the start of 1948 at the same time that he continued to act publicly as one in the PAR.[36] Among those involved in the party, besides Fortuny Arana, were the aforementioned Bernardo Alvarado Monzón, Carlos René Valle y Valle, Alfredo Guerra Borges, and Carlos Manuel Pellecer. Also joining them as members of the party were the youths Víctor Manuel Gutiérrez (b. Guatemala City, 1922), a teacher and the leader of the Sindicato de Trabajadores de la Educación de Guatemala (Guatemalan Education Workers' Union; STEG); José Luis Ramos, of working-class origins; and Mario Silva Jonama (b. Antigua Guatemala, 1925), a teacher and member of the STEG.

As Gleijeses points out:

> Together they tried to move the PAR toward Marxist positions. Their growing radicalism put them in the party's minority; they increasingly clashed with the anti-Communist factions led by [Augusto] Charnaud McDonald [b. Guatemala City, 1914] and Humberto González Juárez [b. Jutiapa, 1913]. At the PAR

convention in March 1949 they were defeated— "They slaughtered us"—382 votes to 120. In the name of party unity, they were given positions, but they could no longer expect to change the PAR's course. Knowing that a Communist Party could work freely once Arbenz assumed the presidency, they created the PCG at the end of 1949.[37]

The Youths and the Founding of the Guatemalan Communist Party

The reasonable time that the Democratic Vanguard gave itself lasted exactly two years to the day, since on September 28, 1949, forty-three men and women, most of them in their twenties, met to found the Guatemalan Communist Party at a school located in Colonia "Eden" in the capital's zone 5, separated from Matamoros Fort by a ravine and directed by teacher Gabriel Alvarado.

The meeting was presided over by the saddler Pedro Fernández, who had been working for the creation of a Communist Party since 1946 and who had been in contact with the Spanish exile Rafael de Buen y Lozano since 1945. Guatemala was going through a delicate situation, since—as has already been mentioned—in June of that year, 1949, a coup d'état led by supporters of Colonel Arana, who had been killed at the hands of men directed by the minister of defense, had failed. Muñoz Meany believed that banishing those involved would affect the government's image; for that reason, he confronted President Arévalo, which led to Muñoz's resignation. The outcome was the naming of Ismael González Arévalo (b. Taxisco, Santa Rosa, 1906) as his successor in the position of minister for foreign relations, and González Arévalo shifted Guatemalan foreign policy to the Right.[38] Given this situation, the Communists had to continue working underground; they were already convinced that it was necessary to establish their own party, which they did two months after Muñoz Meany's resignation and self-exile in Canada.

Most of the PCG's founders came from the Democratic Vanguard, but some had previously been involved in youth-related organizations. Lacking a complete list, one can conclude initially that 4 were members of the Socialist Association (Bernardo Alvarado Monzón, Carlos Alvarado Jerez, Carlos René Valle y Valle, and Marco Antonio Chávez); 2 were from the Saker-ti Group (Humberto Alvarado Arellano and Jacobo Rodríguez Padilla [b. Guatemala City, 1922]); 1 was from the Socialist Vanguard (Alfredo Guerra Borges); and 3 were from the Guatemalan Alliance of

Democratic Youth (Flaminio Bonilla, José H. Zamora Corletto, and Octavio Reyes Ortiz). This total of 10 accounts for 23 percent of the PCG's founders. I am sure that this percentage will increase when one can confirm other youths' participation in these three organizations, and even more so if we could specify who of those present formed part of the youth section of the CGTG, which helped establish the AJDG.

In that way, from the start, the political culture of young Guatemalan Communists was dictated by clandestine behavior, which stemmed from a type of sui generis "entryism,"[39] by remaining PAR members between 1947 and 1950, while at the same time being members of the VDG and, subsequently, of the PCG. Only on May 20, 1950, did Fortuny Arana, Alvarado Monzón, Valle y Valle, and Guerra Borges—along with Silva Jonama, Ramos, and other members of that party—present their irreversible resignation from the PAR and make their intention of creating "a vanguard party, a proletarian party, based on Marxist-Leninism" clear. A month later, on June 21, they founded the newspaper *Octubre*, edited by Fortuny and Guerra Borges, as a platform for the PCG's legalization, and on September 8, they established the "Jacobo Sánchez" Cadre Schools.[40]

Arévalo soon made them pay for such a political challenge. On September 13, 1950, his government shut down *Octubre*, and the "Jacobo Sánchez" School two weeks later. The president believed that "the Communists had the right to express their opinions in private, but not to proselytize."[41] The newspaper reappeared in November 1950, after Arbenz's overwhelming electoral victory, but the cadre school was closed for two years. Bringing anticommunism into the legal arena did not spare Arévalo criticism from his own supporters.

Mario Monteforte Toledo—then a fervent anticommunist—wrote about the subject in the prestigious journal *Cuadernos Americanos* (American notebooks):

> The number of Communists in Guatemala, both bashful and open ones, is very limited. Those who oppose their programs and their doctrines—that is, the overwhelming majority of Guatemalans—have fought them hard in the ideological field; but when they have tried to outlaw them or violently repress their activities, even the ultramontane Right has opposed it, as happened some months again when the entire Congress [*Congreso en pleno*] censured the Executive for having shut down a Marxist training school and a newspaper that one of the Stalinist groups edited.

> In a country that is creating norms and practices with respect to man, it would be incongruous to persecute these minority groups whose sole effectiveness resides in agitation, since the tactics that their leaders advise for America at the current moment inhibit them from giving positive solutions for the needs of our peoples.[42]

In turn, with respect to Arbenz's performance as president-elect, he predicted: "He takes the Communist label that his opponents placed on him during the electoral contest badly; regardless, one of the major problems of his government will be to maintain its position of tolerance toward the Communists who supported him without alienating the army's trust and capital's cooperation."[43]

For his part, researcher Piero Gleijeses points out that the first public documents signed by the PCG appeared in April 1951, a month after Arbenz's inauguration. Then, on June 21, PCG members celebrated the first anniversary of *Octubre*. By then, the party had a hundred members and it was still illegal. Its legalization came in December 1952, in the setting of its second Congress. In it, they changed the name to the Partido Guatemalteco del Trabajo (Guatemalan Labor Party; PGT), taking into account the difficulty that they had borne, as Communists, in reaching the "masses,[44] above all in the face of the Guatemalan political class. Less than two years later, the PGT was once again banned, starting at the end of June 1954, a situation that lasted until the December 1996 Peace Accords. The then-young Communists had the alternatives of exile, resignation, or going underground once more. For his part, Arévalo was consistent with his anticommunist stance for the rest of his life.[45]

Notes

1. Mario Monteforte Toledo, *Guatemala: Monografía sociológica* (México, DF: UNAM Instituto de Investigaciones Sociales, 1959), 311.

2. César Bernardo Arévalo de León, "Del estado violento al ejército político: Violencia, formación estatal y ejército en Guatemala, 1500–1963" (PhD diss., University of Utrecht, 2015), 222.

3. John Holger Petersen, "The Political Role of University Students in Guatemala: 1944–1968" (PhD diss., University of Pittsburgh, 1969).

4. See Virgilio Álvarez, *Conventos, aulas y trincheras: Universidad y movimiento estudiantil en Guatemala*, 2 vols. (Guatemala City: FLACSO/USAC, 2002); and Heather A. Vrana, "'Do Not Tempt Us': The Guatemalan University in Protest, Memory, and Political Change, 1944–Present" (PhD diss., Indiana University, 2013).

5. Piero Gleijeses, *La esperanza rota: La revolución guatemalteca y Estados Unidos, 1944–1954* (Guatemala City: Editorial Universitaria, 2005), 99.

6. Francisco Villagrán Kramer, *Biografía política de Guatemala: Los pactos políticos de 1944–1970* (Guatemala City: FLACSO, 2009), 74–75.

7. Alfredo Guerra Borges, "Apuntes para una interpretación de la revolución guatemalteca y su derrota en 1954," *Política y Sociedad*, no. 42 (2004): 138.

8. Huberto Alvarado Arellano, "En torno a las clases sociales en la revolución de Octubre" *Alero* 8, 3rd ser. (September–October 1974): 3.

9. Arturo Taracena Arriola et al., eds. *El placer de corresponder: Correspondencia entre Muñoz Meany, Cardoza y Aragón y Arriola (1945–1952)* (Guatemala City: Editorial Universitaria de la Universidad de San Carlos, 2004).

10. Huberto Alvarado Arellano, "Apuntes sobre el imperialismo," *Saker-ti* 5–6 (May–August 1948): 21–24.

11. Max Ricardo Cuenca, "El problema nacional en Guatemala," *Mediodía* 2 (December 1, 1946): 1–2 and 9–10.

12. Cuenca, "El problema nacional en Guatemala."

13. Jim Handy, "National Policy, Agrarian Reform, and the Corporate Community during the Guatemalan Revolution, 1944–1954," *Comparative Studies in Society and History* 30, no. 4 (October 1988): 698–724.

14. Grupo Saker-ti, *Siete afirmaciones* (Guatemala City: Tipografía San José, 1948).

15. Huberto Alvarado, *Preocupaciones* (Guatemala City: Ediciones Vanguardia, 1967), 131–148.

16. Huberto Alvarado, "Memoria y revolución: Una polémica en la LEAR. Luis Cardoza y Aragón, Juan de la Cabada, El Machete," *Memoria* 38 (México, DF: CEMOS, 1992), 41–47.

17. "Los dirigentes del P.G.T. desaparecidos por Arana están en la lucha popular," *Correo de Guatemala*, no. 24 (October–December 1972): 6–7; Augusto Cazali Avila, *Historia de Guatemala, siglo XX: Los militares en el poder. El gobierno de Carlos Arana Osorio, 1970–1974* (Guatemala City: Universidad de San Carlos de Guatemala, Dirección General de Investigación, 2002), 74.

18. Cazali Ávila, *Historia de Guatemala,* 62.

19. Zamora Corletto was a journalist of Salvadoran origins, and Bonilla was a leader in the CGTG.

20. Alianza de la Juventud Democrática Guatemalteca (AJDG), *Alianza de sectores de la juventud guatemalteca en la lucha nacional por la democracia, la libertad y la paz mundial* (Guatemala City: Tipografía Nacional, 1949), 9–10.

21. AJDG, "*Alianza de sectores,*" 17–20.

22. Ibid., 11–16.

23. Ibid., 18.

24. Ibid.

25. Díaz Gómez was member of the STEG and a member of the union's Board of Directors in the department of Guatemala in 1949, and chief of the Literacy division in Arbenz's government in 1952. See Simona Violetta Yagenova, *Los maestros y la Revolución de Octubre (1944–1954): Una recuperación de la memoria histórica del Sindicato de Trabajadores de la Educación de Guatemala* (Guatemala City: Editorial de Ciencias Sociales, 2006), 118 and 208.

26. Huberto Alvarado Arellano, "Apuntes sobre el imperialismo," *Saker-ti* 5–6 (May–August): 29–30.

27. Ronald M. Schneider, *Communism in Guatemala 1944–1954*, with a forward by Arthur P. Whitaker (New York: Frederick A. Praeger, 1959), 259.

28. AJDG, *Alianza de sectores*, 41–44.

29. Schneider, *Communism in Guatemala 1944–1954*, 260.

30. Alfredo Guerra Borges, interview, Mexico City, October 25, 2013.

31. José Luis Balcárcel, "Recuperación del socialismo en Guatemala," *Dialéctica* 11, no. 18 (1986): 115.

32. Alfredo Guerra Borges, interview, Mexico City, October 25, 2013.

33. Juan José Arévalo, *Despacho presidencial* (Guatemala City: Editorial Oscar de León Palacios, 2008), 255–256.

34. Marco Antonio Villamar Contreras, *Significado de la década 1944–1954 conocida como la Revolución guatemalteca de octubre* (Guatemala City: Artes Gráficas, Impresos de Integración S. A., 1993), 58.

35. Alfonso Bauer Paiz and Iván Carpio Alfaro, *Memorias de Alfonso Bauer Paiz: Historia no oficial de Guatemala* (Guatemala City: Rusticatio Ediciones, 1996), 104.

36. United States State Department, *Intervention of International Communism in Guatemala* (Washington, DC: Department of State Publications), 50–51; Alfredo Guerra Borges, interview, Mexico City, October 25, 2013.

37. Gleijeses, *La esperanza rota*, 102.

38. José Alberto Cardoza, interview, Mexico City, January 17, 1985; Alfredo Guerra Borges, interview, Mexico City, October 25, 2013.

39. A political tactic of Trotskyite origin, which involves secretly participating in the bosom of a labor union or political party, without publicly saying that one is a member of the Fourth International.

40. Gleijeses, *La esperanza rota*, 97, 103.

41. Ibid., 97.

42. Mario Monteforte Toledo, "Guatemala 1951: Isla de esperanza" *Cuadernos Americanos* 60, no. 1 (January–February 1951): 34–35.

43. Ibid.

44. Gleijeses, *La esperanza rota*, 253–254.

45. See Julio Pinto Soria, Arturo Taracena Arriola, and Arely Mendoza, eds. *Correspondencia en el exilio: Luis Cardoza y Aragón, Juan José Arévalo, 1950–1967* (Guatemala: Editorial Universitaria / Universidad de San Carlos de Guatemala, 2011).

CHAPTER 6

Rethinking Representation and Periodization in Guatemala's Democratic Experiment

David Carey Jr.

> All the [indigenous] men took their machetes because the ladinos wanted to finish us off. "Ladinos felt that they deserved everything even the poor man's crops," my dad said. My dad had been in the military. . . . They wanted to finish us off. Then Zaragozanos came, fired on us, and killed our people indiscriminately. Many poor people were born to the Word of God and the earth was filled up with them. The people all left their houses and then we experienced a terrible famine. I was only seven. I could barely lift myself up and I would get tired. My grandmother told me we must move on and look for weeds in Chwako'ok. . . . That is how we suffered from famine. You might be lucky to throw a few seeds, or you might find some money, but you owned nothing and you had no corn.
>
> Ixtoya, Kaqchikel-Maya (henceforth Kaqchikel), elder from Patzicía

On October 22, 1944, just two days after Federico Ponce Vaides, General Jorge Ubico's (1931–1944) hand-picked successor, abdicated the Liberal dictatorship under pressure from a widespread popular movement, fighting broke out between Kaqchikel and ladinos in the town of Patzicía. Ixtoya's description of the massacre captures its genocidal horror and reverberations thereafter as survivors scattered and scavenged for food. The events were an early indication of how devastating the arrival of the revolution was for some rural *indígenas*. For others, the failure of the Juan José Arévalo administration (1945–1951) to improve education and eradicate forced labor signaled a revolution that began with unfulfilled promises.

Led by Lieutenant Trinidad Esquit Morales, about twenty-five Kaqchikel men armed with machetes, stones, and axes gathered in Patzicía to support Ponce (who had promised them land) and protest ladino domination of local resources, particularly land. Intent on quashing the uprising, twenty-two ladinos armed with guns arrived from the nearby ladino town of Zaragoza. Responding to a machete fight with firearms gave them a lethal advantage. With more ladinos arriving from other towns, the assailants rounded up and killed Kaqchikel men. As the carnage multiplied, many Kaqchikel fled to the surrounding hills, canyons, and towns. When the civic guard from Antigua and the national army from Guatemala City finally restored order a few days later, between twelve and fourteen ladinos and between fifty and nine hundred indígenas had been killed. The disproportionate victimization of indígenas continued in the subsequent court proceedings, in which thirty-three Kaqchikel men were arrested, about a dozen of whom were put to death; the others served out lengthy prison sentences. In contrast, no ladinos were ever tried, let alone convicted.

In light of the massacre, capital punishment, imprisonment, and famine that marked the initiation of democracy, the early years of the Ten Years of Spring (1944–1954) were anything but for the survivors and other indígenas in the area. Ubico's regime was totalitarian and ruthless with those suspected of dissension. Yet even as strong-armed rule restricted liberties, many indígenas appreciated the clarity with which Ubico articulated and enforced the rules of the game. With its promise of participation and liberty, democracy introduced capricious and unpredictable governance in the eyes of some rural Guatemalans. They experienced the Arévalo administration very differently from urban working- and middle-class ladinos, many of whom supported and some of whom instigated the revolution. As news of the killings spread throughout the country, a macabre hue settled on the new democratic government.[1] A few months after the massacre, one man explained that his grandmother "was suffering from symptoms of mental disorder due to her advanced age and the impression the wretched events in Patzicía on October 22 made on her spirit."[2] Suggesting that hers was not the only case of post-traumatic stress disorder, Kaqchikel oral histories vividly reconstruct images of bloodshed, persecution, displacement, and terror.[3]

Lingering memories of the Patzicía massacre help to explain the seemingly contradictory arguments that the revolution unleashed disorder and insecurity in some indigenous communities while little changed in others. Suggesting the limits of reform during the Arévalo years, such dramatically different experiences and recollections speak to the many manifestations of the revolution and the diversity of its effects. While survivors of the massacre, their descendants, and others frame the revolution as a cautionary tale, those with geographical or temporal distance from the massacre pushed the revolution to go further (as indigenous parents who demanded a better education evince). Between those two perceptions of the revolution, a broad spectrum emerges that ranges from staid continuity to radical change.

While Patzicianos experienced the new government as a harsh rupture from the past, some indígenas benefited from Ubico's demise. The transition from dictatorial to democratic rule was a complex process that played out slowly and differently across place and time. During this protracted period, national politicians and institutions struggled to communicate their ideas to rural residents and, in turn, to incorporate local perspectives into national agendas.

Since many promises of the revolution remained unfulfilled and some reforms did not go far enough, 1944 was hardly a watershed moment for many rural indígenas. Two areas of promised reform suggest the limits of the early revolution: the elimination of forced labor and the improvement of educational opportunities. During the Arévalo administration, the benefits from those initiatives were negligible at best for many rural peoples. When measured by the yardsticks of free labor and better education, the differences between dictatorship and democracy were difficult to discern for many rural indígenas.[4]

I draw upon *jefe político* (governor) papers, municipal archives, and oral histories conducted between 1997 and 2001 to reconsider Arévalo's administration as a dramatic break with past politics. Penned during his rule, documents from rural towns in Sacatepéquez, a province adjacent to Guatemala City, demonstrate that forced labor mechanisms so prevalent during Ubico's reign persisted despite democratic promises of their elimination. To "expand cultivation to the extent possible," the new government enforced vagrancy laws.[5] In turn, community members pressed into municipal service appealed to the governor for exemptions.[6] Diminished but not eliminated, forced labor continued to mark the lives of rural Guatemalans during Arévalo's reign. Those tasked with enforcing it could be intimidating and corrupt. "The authority in my pueblo is partial and threatening," complained one forty-year-old agriculturist from San Antonio Aguascalientes (henceforth, Aguascalientes) a few months after Ubico's ouster.[7] For indigenous leaders from Santa Lucía Utatalán, the Ubico and Arévalo regimes were equally bad.[8]

By shifting the focus from individual political ruptures to wider political conjunctures and processes across time, this chapter builds on a recent historiographical trend of rethinking periodization to disrupt accepted chronologies and to shed new light on rural realities.[9] Like other contributors in this volume, most notably Patrick Chassé, in chapter 2; Jim Handy, in the foreword; Heather Vrana and Julie Gibbings, in the introduction; and Anthony Andersson, in chapter 3, I examine peripheral places to flesh out the complexities of the revolution that was anything but monolithic.

Another upsetting feature of the new Arévalo government concerned the nature of its proposed reforms. Many reforms were all but imperceptible in rural areas; others contradicted indigenous values and upset delicate patron-client relations. The revolutionary state's slow response to the Patzicía massacre initiated that perception. Whereas the relatively predictable manner by which Ubico ruled helped to check the power of local economic and political elites, the democratic regime's failure to clearly articulate its agenda and governing procedures led many rural indígenas to understand the revolutionary state's intervention to be less benign than that of its dictatorial predecessor. Without clear communication, the Arévalo administration's effort to ensure basic literacy for rural people seemed rife with ulterior motives when viewed from below. Looking back on the Arévalo government through the lens of the civil war and genocide, many Kaqchikels today criticize reforms for jeopardizing the entrenchment of a fragile democratic experiment.[10] Rather than channel unrest, the narrative goes, the revolution unleashed it. The Arévalo government often appeared complicit with local exploiters.

Although popular resistance slowed democratic reforms, some popular demands sought their acceleration or fulfillment as residents challenged local and national authorities who responded slowly and often inadequately in the eyes of progenitors. If the archival record from Sacatepéquez is any indication, indígenas could accept, reject, challenge, or propel the revolution in ways that directly affected their lives. With that agency, students' parents, conscripted laborers, farmers, and other locals influenced the course of the revolution. Intent on increasing the production of domestic agriculture, revolutionary officials provided financing and advice for small-scale farmers, who in turn shaped the course of agricultural production.[11] When agricultural mandates were ill informed, indigenous farmers defied them and thereby maintained the most effective practices. On December 11, 1945, two literate farmers complained that the *intendente* (mayor) insisted they plow their sweet potato fields horizontally instead of vertically. For "many years" they had been working with vertical furrows because horizontal sowing did not yield a good harvest. To compromise, "they offered to use vertical furrows on land that was not level, but the intendente would not accept it."[12] When the governor's inspector sided with the intendente, farmers from Aguascalientes and Santa Catarina Barahona (hereafter Barahona) refused to cultivate their land even though they already had tilled it. "That prohibition does us grave harm because we will lose our work and the means to support our families," they explained.[13] Reconsidering his initial decision, the governor asked the Barahona mayor to form a commission to investigate the situation. Noting that farmers in the area had been growing sweet potato "for about 100 years . . . and experience has advised them to do it that way," commission members suggested adhering to that wisdom.[14] Conceding local expertise, the governor concurred. By rejecting counterproductive agricultural mandates even as they accessed government financing, indigenous farmers propelled the revolution forward. By 1949, efforts to stimulate domestic-use agriculture were bearing fruit—that sector grew by 3.6 percent from 1944 to 1949.[15]

Even before the revolution, indigenous elites, entrepreneurs, and peasants in places such as Quetzaltenango had organized and advanced their agendas. Such indigenous mobilization continued throughout the early years of the revolution, both supporting and opposing it. Almost immediately, rural indígenas petitioned the new government for access to forest and other communal land for grazing and planting. As the revolution increasingly advocated for laborers, small-scale entrepreneurs and other members of the middle class pivoted against the Jacobo Arbenz Guzmán government (1951–1954). To protect their own interests and distinguish themselves from their poor and working-class counterparts, local indigenous individuals and other elites pushed back against popular demands.[16] Greedy and corrupt officials also precipitated problems. One Sacatepéquez forest inspector would consider people's requests only if they paid him 1.5 quetzals and provided lunch and transportation. Too poor to pay for such expenses, farmers complained on May 15, 1946, that they could not prepare their fields for planting without the forest inspector's consent.[17] As denunciations mounted, he was reassigned.[18] Indicating that he had tempered his behavior, by the time he had returned to his post in November, he granted a man and his mother-in-law permission to cut four trees on her Aguascalientes property. They reported no improprieties in their exchanges with him.[19] Active petitioners could curb unscrupulous officials.

In addition to land claims that energized poor and working-class residents during the revolution, other concerns motivated indigenous participation. Indigenous leaders recognized education as a crucial component to their children's success.[20] In the process of providing education and literacy, schools encouraged assimilation and nationalism—crucial components of the revolution's agenda. Yet, as we will see, complaints from rural parents about tardy or absent teachers, hollow pedagogy, and female students' labor suggest that incompetent, racist, and sexist teachers undermined the government's goals. Unlike in neighboring Mexico, where schools served as sites of negotiation between rural inhabitants and authorities over citizenship and national identity, in rural Guatemala, schools largely failed to advance a cultural revolution. Whereas those exchanges helped to cement the Mexican Revolution in the 1930s and 1940s, albeit unevenly and intermittently, such discussions seldom took place in rural Guatemalan schools.[21] If Archivo General de Centroamérica (General Archive of Central America; AGCA) records from Sacatepéquez are any indication, instead of engaging rural residents in conversations about citizenship, nationalism, and other unifying forces, teachers and administrators could not get past daily problems that arose with their job performance and inability to deliver an education that rural indigenous parents recognized as legitimate. Far from passive recipients of the new government's goals, indigenous people demanded the fulfillment of democratic educational promises. Local authorities' failure to quickly and effectively address those demands eclipsed the potential to engage in broader discussions about how to advance the revolution.

Transitional Growing Pains and Gains

As a microcosm of what was happening throughout the country, Sacatepéquez residents experienced a broad array of aspects of the revolution, ranging from beneficial and calm to detrimental and disorderly. Some municipal workers were particularly adept at advancing their agendas through the transition. Perhaps in an effort to shore up political loyalty, the waning dictatorial government responded favorably to the request by municipal employees of San Miguel Milpas Dueñas (hereafter Dueñas) for a raise: their salaries increased by 15 percent in August 1944.[22] Fewer than six months later, the new democratic government gave them another raise.[23]

As the new democracy unfolded, political parties propagated and upset local rule. By 1946, each municipal election had at least one political party candidate (mostly from the Frente Popular Liberator [Popular Liberation Front; FPL]). Local leaders had not navigated political parties since the 1920s. When two men wanted to hold a rally with marimba music for the Político Renovación Party in 1946, the Dueñas mayor was convinced it would cause unrest and thus encouraged the governor to deny the request. Accustomed to Ubico's rule, during which political rallies were forbidden, the mayor feared the worst. Should the governor grant the license to hold the festivity, the mayor insisted that the Civil Guard be sent to maintain order.[24]

Although Político Renovación was not very large in 1946 (by 1952 it would become the Renovación Nacional [National Renovation; RN] Socialist Party and unite with the Partido de Acción Revolucionaria [Revolutionary Action Party; PAR] to advocate for indigenous rights and improve local conditions), some political rallies turned violent. Moreover, adversarial relationships among (and within) political parties and between them and the government were not uncommon. Among other issues, parties fought over the compulsory labor required for municipal work and who should provide it.[25] When a 1948 struggle between FPL and PAR left the FPL incumbent alcalde dead, *El Imparcial* claimed: "Blood runs almost to the point of becoming a river; . . . rare are the communities in which the elections were conducted with tranquility and where the people are satisfied with the results."[26] Portraying the democratic transition as unruly and residents as disgruntled, the journalist's hyperbole suggests a broader sentiment about the potential for unrest with political participation, particularly if indigenous people gained ground. If the Patzicía uprising was any indication, according to ladino journalists, indígenas could hardly be afforded full citizenship in a democracy.[27]

In an effort to prevent unrest during the transition to a new government, democratic authorities patrolled the streets for vagrants.[28] Local administrators informed national officials about the identities, ages, *cédula* (identification card) numbers, and residency of men conscripted into service.[29] The same month that Arévalo took office, fifty-four people were arrested for vagrancy in Antigua.[30] By April, public order and "peace helped everyone to fulfill their various labors," according to local representatives. Amidst coercive efforts to maintain social order, officials distinguished participatory from authoritarian rule by stressing democracy's freedoms: Holy Week was marked with "the greatest liveliness and liberty."[31]

Yet democracy did not necessarily bring out the best in everyone. Less than a year into the new administration's rule, government employees' tardiness was so regularly "unfavorably commented upon by the public" that Arévalo implored officials to ensure that workers in their departments "attend their respective offices with all punctuality during the regulated hours, eight am on the dot."[32] Lest they fail to heed his admonition, he warned, "It would be lamentable to have to return to the systems of control used by past administrations."[33] Such exchanges speak to the challenges of transitioning from a dictatorial to democratic government and the temptation to employ authoritarian measures to undergird democracy. Responding to public outrage again less than two weeks later, the administration chastised employees because of the "immoderate use of telegraph services in government offices, for things that could have been sent by mail." This "excessive" use caused long delays of paid messages at telegraph offices, which in turn led to "public distrust and protests."[34] The swath of the Guatemalan 'public' protesting bureaucratic abuses from the very government charged with improving people's lives was sufficiently large and that the Arévalo administration felt compelled to address its concerns.

Many indígenas associated the revolution with unrest and disorder. As was true in the K'iche town of Cantel, Quetzaltenango, democratic municipal elections regularly usurped traditional civil-religious leaders' influence and thereby buttressed changes in local governance that began in the 1930s, when Ubico replaced locally selected mayors and other community leaders with (ladino) intendentes loyal to him.[35] Even when indigenous leaders maximized their power and authority, poor and working-class indígenas were more likely to benefit from their rule than that of intendentes who "spoke no Kaqchikel." Since intendentes had no relationship with people in the towns they governed, they "would not pay attention or address your problem," explains one Kaqchikel elder.[36] Compounding many local leaders' sense of disenfranchisement and marginalization in the 1930s, the proliferation of political parties and municipal elections beginning in 1945 further challenged the authority of indigenous patriarchs, who, as a result, labeled democracy disorder.

Fearful of power shifts should indigenous masses participate in democracy, journalists, politicians, and intellectuals also portrayed democracy as disorder. In a manifestation of reservations about democracy in a predominantly indigenous nation, the 1945 Constitution tasked teachers with promoting civil and moral formation through ethnic improvement. Indígenas in particular were not quite fit for self-government according to that document's framers. The editors of *El Estudiantil* were especially concerned about "constitutional order" on the day the constitution went into effect.[37]

For different reasons, many poor and working-class Kaqchikels equated good governance with order. Looking back through the lens of the civil war at a revolution born in violence, political change was perilous. Disorder begot hostility.[38] Although their calculus differed from that of elites, they too associated democracy with unrest and insecurity.

Despite these perceptions, indigenous leaders' national participation became increasingly organized and vibrant over time. By 1948, most elections fielded more than one candidate, and many PAR indigenous candidates won mayoral seats. As uncharted territory for many Guatemalans, such democratic processes were unsettling for local leaders obsessed with maintaining social order. As local affiliates of political parties, unions, and peasant leagues increasingly opposed the state, the Arévalo administration struggled to understand and respond to dissent. Interpreting the process as chaos, many Kaqchikel elders understood that the democratic transition would be challenging. "Democracy is disorder. You need some time to develop it," explained B'eleje' K'at.[39]

Even as people anticipated transitional challenges, keeping indígenas in their place was paramount to both dictatorial and democratic governments. In light of ladino fears that indígenas wanted to rectify perceived historical injustices, democracy may have exacerbated racial tensions by its tendency to give rural, lower-class indígenas increased voice and political clout.[40] Some local ladino officials considered indigenous people threats to social order. For instance, when Marcelino Morales stabbed Señor Alfonzo Vásquez García in a Dueñas cantina on a May evening in 1948, Mayor Jorge Fernández attributed it to racial tension: "Badly directed by a certain element, the indigenous population in this town hates ladinos simply because they have been led to believe that the land the ladinos possess belongs to the municipality and they live always with the evil intention of harming ladinos. . . . Morales is one of those who holds that belief, of having a right to ladino properties."[41] According to Fernández, simple-minded indigenous people were duped into believing that ladinos controlled municipal resources. Whether or not Vásquez acquired his land by expropriating indigenous landholdings is unclear, but Morales's animosity likely was informed by a long history of ladinos usurping the land, labor, and other resources of indigenous people. Deep-rooted racial tension persisted through regime change.

In addition to the indígenas and other marginalized Guatemalans who benefited from the democratic experiment, women enjoyed increased recognition for their contributions. Whereas documentation from the first months of the Arévalo administration demonstrates how democratic officials generally continued to narrowly define women's work as "feminine trades or others," by the late 1940s women's labor came into sharper focus.[42] A 1948 document listed domestic worker, (manual) laborer, office worker, professional, and other as potential career options for women.[43] Suggesting a softening of the sexual division of labor, the same document identified the last four categories as possibilities for men's career options along with farmer, merchant, and agricultural day laborer. Despite the masculinization of agricultural labor, women too engaged in it.[44] Even if women's agricultural contributions escaped the attention of public officials, their labor was more broadly conceived and (as a result) valued during the democratic regime. That recognition did not supersede their exalted positions and responsibility as mothers, however. Pregnant teachers, for example, were afforded maternity leave.[45] Motherhood remained the pinnacle of femininity during the revolution.

Perhaps associating the new regime with visions of spring cleaning, some revolutionary officials no longer considered relevant the patron-client networks that Ubico had sustained. Following the example of conservation maintained during the Ubico dictatorship, the Aguascalientes mayor Federico Santos López summoned the Forest Inspectors when community members wanted to prune trees that were creating too much shade. Much to his dismay, one inspector arrived completely drunk, yelling "obscene words . . . [and] making all kinds of excuses not to go" to the site. After they relented, the inspectors insisted petitioners cut down "the young trees and not the [older] ones with signs that they would soon die."[46] The combination of the inspectors' vulgar behavior and ignorance of their trade prompted Santos to observe that at least one inspector was a "servant of the past Regime, he did not behave with decency, now if that man did it because everyone here is indigenous, he should not think [that way], we are in an era of Democracy and not with our hands tied as past Administrations have had us."[47] Like the multiple ways people experienced the revolution, officials, bureaucrats, and other state agents differed on how the new government should operate and progress. These competing voices and contradictory actions—particularly around patron-client relations—contributed to perceptions of democracy's disorder.

With their proximity to the capital, abundant natural resources, and agricultural fecundity, Aguascalientes residents and leaders were accustomed to government interventions. Armed with the knowledge that standing water bred mosquitoes, which in turn spread malaria, Guatemalan president Lázaro Chacón's administration (1926–1930) collaborated with Aguascalientes in 1927 to drain a lake that propagated mosquitoes.

Although municipal leaders did not deny the public health threat posed by the lake, much was at stake for community members who relied on it for the provision of resources (fish, water, and reeds). As this engineering endeavor unfolded, national authorities and local community members negotiated over working conditions, distribution of lake-bed lands, and conservation. Indigenous leaders and residents did not accept this invasive campaign without criticism.[48] Nor were they willing to endure abusive and incompetent authorities some twenty years later.

The kinder, gentler, more progressive democratic rule may have encouraged some employees to take risks that harsh physical punishment during Ubico's administration may have deterred. Concerned that the municipal treasurer had been gone for seven days after he asked for a day off to retrieve clothes in Guatemala City, the Barahona mayor invited a National Treasury agent to inspect the municipal treasury box. Opened by a carpenter, the box was short $134.95 quetzals. The authorities suspected "premeditated embezzlement."[49] They immediately ordered Valenzuela's capture so he could be tried in court. Even as the judicial system functioned during dictatorial rule, some thieves and other transgressors were subject to harsh corporeal punishment.[50] B'eleje' Kawoq, a sixty-year-old Kaqchikel day keeper, explains: "Ubico . . . was a strict man who eliminated thieves. You could leave your tools and belongings in the street and they were there when you returned. I once saw when a man stole money from the municipality. They made an example of him by burning his hands. . . . Ubico did not miss anything."[51] Whether or not Ubico's harsh rule deterred criminals is difficult to discern, but many rural Kaqchikels I interviewed perceived his reign to be more safe and secure than the subsequent democratic regimes.[52]

As historians such as Jennie Purnell and Miguel de la Serna have demonstrated, past experiences with resource control and political relationships influence how communities respond to change and revolution.[53] Although the archival record is less forthcoming in the case of rural Guatemala, the Patzicía and Aguascalientes cases suggest that local leaders' and residents' approaches to the revolution were similarly informed by past experiences of racist violence, capricious authorities, and expropriated resources (principally land).

Continuities and Shifts in Forced Labor

One of the legacies of Ubico's regime (and those prior to it) was the discourse of laziness. As a result, people feared being labeled lazy or becoming lazy. Conveniently espousing stereotypes that fueled forced labor mechanisms, many ladino labor brokers, *finqueros* (large-landed estate owners), and elites considered laziness indigenous people's "natural inclination."[54] Like many of his contemporaries, Ubico's minister of agriculture insisted the vagrancy law precipitated the "resurgence of a new type of aborigine . . . and one can say without exaggeration that this new rural man has abandoned vices like laziness and alcoholism."[55] Manifested in obligatory road service and the *boletos* men had to carry to prove they had completed the requisite number of days of manual (primarily farm) work, *trabajos de vialidad* (forced labor) was one of the dictator's oppressions that the democratic regime promised to eradicate. Yet the 1945 Constitution, which made labor obligatory and laid the groundwork for vagrancy legislation, reveals that framers of democracy were influenced by prerevolutionary discourse that associated indígenas with indolence.

Even as he disassembled some compulsory labor, Arévalo reinforced municipal service obligations. Within a few months of taking office, he was approving nominations to municipal posts.[56] Most apparent in the resignation letters citing illness or penury as excuses for noncompliance, such mandates were onerous. Leaving municipal drafts of labor intact, the new Constitution's muted vagrancy law was intended to prevent *finca* owners from enriching themselves through low wages enforced by labor legislation.[57] Arévalo worked with local authorities and military forces to prevent rural labor organization and ensure a sufficient labor supply for harvests (and elsewhere as needed). Reluctant to relinquish power to the new president, the head of the three-man junta that oversaw the immediate transition to democracy (October 20, 1944–March 15, 1945), Colonel Francisco Javier Arana, insisted on tight control over labor. Threatening to overthrow Arévalo in 1949, Arana was shot to death on July 18, 1949. Even though Arévalo loosened labor policies in the countryside and afforded labor organizations more freedom thereafter, his suspicion of rural organizing and political constraints limited the revolution's early actions.[58]

Indicating constitutional changes worked in many ways, some rural residents considered the new vagrancy law radical. "Now we are free. We are equal to Ladinos. . . . No one can force us to work on a coffee plantation far away against our will. We will go only if we want to," noted some indígenas.[59] Even if persistent unequal relations betrayed the romanticism of such observations, the way rural residents remember the past contributes to their perceptions of Arévalo as much as any act that can be attributed to him does. "Arévalo made a major change. He ended slavery and terminated the work mandates. Everyone worked from their own volition, and that has continued to today," insisted an elder Kaqchikel farmer from Barahona.[60] By strategically curtailing rather than eliminating forced labor, Arévalo elevated his position among many rural indígenas. Such idealized memories attest to his success as a populist who promised radical change and delivered limited reform.

The cessation of certain types of forced labor but not others led some to perceive qualitative as well as quantitative differences between compulsory labor during the two regimes. Some appreciated the way work, even forced labor, provided structure and security. "Ubico was the best president for us. We, as indigenous people, like to work. We look for work and we do it well, so the *vialidad* and mandates were good for our lives. It was honorable," explained B'eleje' Kawoq.[61] Even as B'eleje' Kawoq's assertion challenged racist discourse that depicted indígenas as lazy, other indigenous raconteurs surmised that revolutionary liberties induced some to stray from law and order. One group of Kaqchikel men recalled, "When Arévalo became president, he gave freedom. There was no pressure so that is when laziness began. If you did not want to work, then you did not, but with Ubico all had to work or they were punished. Laziness increased and then came the time of violence."[62] Looking back through the lens of the civil war, some Kaqchikel men associated the laziness they attributed to labor freedoms with violence. Of course, neither new labor legislation nor muted vagrancy laws encouraged laziness; rather, they afforded highland residents greater freedom in determining for whom they would work and when. Allusions to laziness in Kaqchikel oral histories about the revolution can be likened to other tropes that demonize certain class, racial, and often gendered groups.[63]

Even though corvée labor and a vagrancy law persisted during the revolution, workers enjoyed more freedoms than they had during the Ubico dictatorship. According to many Kaqchikels reflecting on the past, those freedoms increased incidences of sloth, public intoxication, theft, and murder. While such observations lent credence to their assertion that a growing number of people turned to vices and crime, they were not alone in their perceptions.[64] In his capacity as the chief of medicine at the Asilo de Alienados, Dr. Miguel F. Molina noticed that by late February 1945, "about eight months ago more or less, the hospitalization [*ingreso*] of alcoholics at the Insane Asylum [Asilo de Alienados] has increased in an alarming manner, as a phenomenon with a certain parallel relationship with the liberty that the nation's inhabitants enjoy."[65] Even if his math did not quite align with the October revolution, his association of increased inebriation with democracy was clear.

Kaqchikel elders did not necessarily blame Arévalo for this fate, though. A former San Juan Comalapa mayor insisted, "Arévalo was the best president. He gave us rights, but then it fell apart. Too many thieves took advantage of it all."[66] To his mind, rolling back restrictions in favor of rights created an opportunity for corruption that the Ubico administration kept at bay with harsh punishments. Other raconteurs attributed increased disorder and crime to abrupt political change rather than to individuals.[67]

Whether or not individuals accused of theft were guilty is difficult to ascertain from the criminal record, but local authorities strove to maintain order by holding workers accountable for their actions. During his turn as the mail carrier, twenty-year-old bachelor and farmer Pedro Ordóñez was provisioned by the municipality with an oilcloth cape for the winter rains. At some point during the week of May 12–18, 1946, he hung it in the Barahona municipal building, only to find it missing when he returned to retrieve it. Convinced he was robbed, Ordóñez considered the mayor's insistence that he pay for it unfair: "I am poor. . . . I am a man who earns only enough for my daily sustenance . . . I cannot yield a single cent . . . with which to pay."[68] Threatened with incarceration, he begged the governor to consider his "state of poverty [and] not obligate him to pay for the cape."[69] Less than a year old, the cape was the only one the municipality had. Maintaining that those who are entrusted with such a valuable accoutrement should be responsible for taking care of it, the mayor insisted that Ordóñez pay seven quetzals to replace it. Perhaps his unequivocal stance was informed by his knowledge of a scandal in neighboring communities the previous year whereby some postal carriers collected their salary and then denied doing so to solicit payment from municipalities. Some postal "employees can be unscrupulous."[70] As much as Ordóñez' behavior may have enraged the mayor, the mayor denied threatening to jail him: "That is a lie, that is not how people are treated in my office."[71] Reluctant to become embroiled in a local dispute, the governor asked the mayor to resolve it.[72] The mayor drew a sharp contrast between Arévalo's and Ubico's rule by underscoring his measured rather than punitive approach.

Education and Popular Demands

A professor of philosophy, Arévalo made educational reform a cornerstone of his administration. While recognizing the shortcomings of that campaign, historians generally have cast his efforts to improve access to and the quality of education in a positive light. Although some parents remained reluctant to send their daughters to school, the Arévalo government acted on its promise to expand and improve education, particularly in rural areas. In practice, the emphasis was on infrastructure, though staffing also increased.[73] When informed that two schools in Aguascalientes were in disrepair in 1947, he appropriated 513.34 quetzals to fix them.[74] Although the slow bureaucratic pace frustrated local officials, that same year the president earmarked funding for school repairs in neighboring Barahona.[75] In 1947, education appropriations bested those of the military for the first time, as the new administration nearly doubled what its predecessor had allotted to education.[76] Expenditures on education increased 707 percent, from 1,330,000 quetzals in 1944 to 10,735,572 quetzals in 1954.[77] Given that no new schools had been constructed since 1920, the 89 percent increase in the number of new schools from 1944 to 1954 is remarkable.[78]

As was true during the Ubico years, school attendance was mandatory during the Arévalo and Arbenz regimes. Teachers were tasked with ensuring parents sent their children to school.[79] At times, their efficacy created problems. In response to the Sacatepéquez governor's 1945 circular, Dueñas authorities compelled parents to send their children to school. With ninety male and sixty-seven female students, "but only two professors, [it was] completely impossible that they could give classes."[80] As attendance increased, providing adequate staffing was crucial.[81] In his 1945 annual report on education, the mayor explained that even though school attendance was irregular, half the children in school had to stand because they did not have enough benches. One professor had to teach two grades. The government regularly resolved such challenges. When the Barahona mayor reported that the increased enrollment necessitated a parallel increase in teachers in 1945, a new professor was appointed almost immediately.[82]

In areas that lacked schools, officials pressured wealthy landowners to build them. Dependent on year-round resident laborers, some of whom insisted that their children be educated and afforded economic privileges by the state, haciendas and plantations in other parts of Latin America provided an education for the children who lived on them.[83] Offering insight into power relations between the government and business interests, the Dueñas mayor notified national education officials that Salvador Falla Aris and his family had failed to build a school even though thirty-one children lived on the family finca; the closest school was seven kilometers away.[84] Although slow to address the issue, by May 1946, the minister of public education informed Falla that he needed to open a school, which would be inspected by the government.[85] A little more than two weeks later, Falla had dedicated four *cuerdas* (4,810 square yards) to build Club Agrícola

Escolar and asked for barbed wire to demarcate the property.[86] Compelling finqueros to provide schools or at least access to them for children on their estates was one of the Arévalo administration's defining characteristics.

Geography, more than interest, conspired to undermine the revolution's education goals. Even with an "army of unemployed teachers" in cities (75 percent of teachers worked in the capital), leaders of the Sindicato de Trabajadores de Educación Guatemaltecos (Guatemalan Education Workers Syndicate; STEG) struggled to convince teachers to accept rural posts.[87] To attract people to the profession, Arévalo increased the monthly salary from the six to thirty quetzals.[88] He also founded the Escuela Rural Normal to train teachers, who would develop functional community-centered rural schools.[89] Not surprisingly, STEG considered teachers "the nerves, the antennae, and the spirit of the working class and the people" and crucial to the success of the revolution.[90] Yet, even as teachers established twenty *núcleos escolares campesinos* (campesino schoolchildren centers) in Chimaltenango and other Kaqchikel-speaking regions, the endeavors had "little success or impact."[91] Grounded in paternalism and steeped in racism, those educational institutions fell short of the revolution's rhetoric of emancipation.

As the growing corps of teachers sought to transform what many of them considered retrograde campesinos into citizen-farmers, the state's increased presence in rural communities created tensions. At the intersection of racism and classism, one teacher kicked ladino and indigenous students out of school, demanding they return properly dressed.[92] Many ladino teachers thought educating indígenas was futile because of the "innate ignorance of Indians."[93] Such perceptions often led to prejudicial and even violent exchanges in school. "I only went to school for two years, because the teachers hit you and yelled at you. They were all ladinos so I hated it," recounted one Kaqchikel woman.[94] A number of Kaqchikel elders remembered how teachers singled out indígenas for humiliation and punishment.[95] "They used to hit girls with *traje* [indigenous clothing] in school," recalled a seventy-two-year-old woman.[96] Another female elder captured the trepidation of many indigenous students: "I did not want to go to school. I was afraid because only ladinos were the teachers—that was fright!"[97]

Far from resisting reforms, rural peoples often pushed the democratic government to fulfill its promises. If denunciations about teacher truancy are any indication, parents cared deeply about their children's education. Teachers who missed school prompted parental complaints that compelled local officials to investigate teacher truancy and find replacements even when such absences were attributed to medically verified illnesses or maternity leave.[98] Throughout the Ten Years of Spring, teacher truancy was a problem. In their campaign to enforce punctuality, local officials regularly enlisted governors.[99] Recognizing that many teachers neglected their jobs and often were absent from them, STEG spent much of the decade trying to balance democratic processes within the union with the need to discipline wayward teachers.[100] Intent on being involved in the schools, many rural residents eagerly embraced education. Resonating with Elsie Rockwell's findings in Mexico, highland Guatemala schools were socially constructed through the daily process of conflict and contestation.[101]

STEG's failure to address the shortcomings of teachers undermined the efficacy of their participation in community politics that the union insisted was part of their job. When that work interfered with teachers' school responsibilities, rural residents surmised that teachers were not prioritizing students. Those tensions speak to a broader phenomenon of national organizations struggling to square national goals with local realities.

The aforementioned narratives regarding indigenous laziness likely informed parents' efforts to improve education. Many Kaqchikel parents refused to allow their daughters to attend school, convinced it would only make them lazy. An evangelical woman recalled, "I did not attend school. . . . My mother and father did not want us to go, and they did not give us permission to go. . . . Boys went, but they said girls would be lazy if they went. I almost cried and I still do. I lament it because I do not know anything. I cannot read. . . . No school, no knowledge."[102] Another Kaqchikel elder pointed out that families' need for female labor informed the discourse of indolence. "I never went to school—we just worked in the house. I wanted to go, but they said there are only laziness and thieves in the school. Only men went; women did not attend school—they just wove."[103] A 1948 study of Aguascalientes noted that parents needed their children's labor "to support the family."[104] As much as girls regretted the lost opportunity, teacher truancy and languor reinforced notions that girls had little to gain from attending classes. Some teachers assigned female students domestic chores instead of lessons. That parents pressed local authorities to hold teachers accountable suggests they believed a state-sponsored education could be valuable.

In communities where illiteracy rates were high, parents had a keen sense of the challenges that people without a formal education faced. Among the generation of parents whose children were attending school in Aguascalientes and Barahona in the 1940s, between 70 and 78 percent of women and between 46 and 56 percent of men were illiterate.[105] High illiteracy rates notwithstanding, Aguascalientes enjoyed a rich tradition of education. By 1874, the community already had two schools at a time when many indigenous communities had none.[106] In the 1920s, evangelical missionaries established a school in Aguascalientes that earned such a fine reputation that evangelical families from other communities (as far away as Patzún) sent their children to study there.[107] With that history, a fervent passion for quality schools and teachers is not surprising among Aguascalientes indígenas. They were not so much resisting the revolution as compelling it to provide a better education.

For poor parents who struggled to send their daughters to school (some Aguascalientes' families could not afford to purchase school uniforms), however, reports that they were working instead of learning there must have been particularly frustrating.[108] Absent all week without giving any notice, Ofelia González, the director of the Barahona girls' school, had "completely abandoned her students and furthermore she employed the girls in the kitchen, three or four girls a day."[109] Motivated by the "many complaints from parents that their daughters were losing a lot of time" in their studies, the mayor asked that González be replaced.[110] In addition to cooking, female students often cleaned schools.[111] A pattern of girls working rather than studying in highland schools similarly emerges in Kaqchikel oral histories. "When I did go to school they [the teachers] made me grind corn and weave. I was just in the kitchen so there was nothing in my notebook. . . . There was no teaching, just suffering," noted an elder from a village near Tecpán.[112] For many indigenous parents whose daughters worked for rather than learned from teachers, the revolutionary government's educational reforms and rhetoric rang hollow. That they fought to have exploitative teachers replaced with competent ones suggests they still believed education was vital despite evidence and experiences to the contrary.

When superiors tried to hold teachers accountable, many fought back. Insisting they arrive to school on time, not leave early, and curtail field trips in favor of classroom pedagogy, the Barahona school director earned the ire of teachers who complained he was "their persecutor [*verdugo*] and in that oppressive manner they could not work with freedom."[113] Teachers often chafed at school directors' oversight. After explaining that teachers needed someone who would attend to their needs and procure materials for their classrooms instead of vigilantly observing them and undermining their control of students by affording them dispensations, Alejandro Lazaro accused the director of being a "little dictator."[114] Set against their call for "freedom," that moniker evoked a powerful image of what the revolution had sought to overcome.

In his defense, the thirty-two-year-old school director Joaquin Ordóñez López explained that he limited field trips because teachers planned so many that students' studies suffered; instead of attending to students on the trips, teachers simply hung out. Because "it was the only way to ensure that teachers attended to their work punctually,"[115] he arrived at the municipal office early and visited individual schools to observe teaching and tidiness. Although the governor's response is lost, given the regular complaints he received about truant and exploitative teachers, he likely favored the zealous director.[116] A few months later, on October 29, the Barahona mayor Luis Saqche' reported that students were receiving a "bad education" and wasting time with teachers who failed to show up at school, let alone fulfill their teaching obligations.[117] If the frequency of such disparaging reports is any indication, learning under Arévalo's rule was hardly an improvement from what took place under his predecessor.

Refusing to endure counterproductive teachers, parents leveraged their power vis-à-vis national and local authorities and established their sway in rural schools. The mayor's dismissal of the Barahona school director Ofelia González demonstrates how parents went through local political channels to remove problematic personnel. They also appealed to regional authorities. Dissatisfied with the Aguascalientes primary school teacher Natividad Méndez, parents petitioned to have her transferred to another school in 1945. The governor recognized that their claims that she was "incapable of performing her duties, of an advanced age, and other things in that manner" were intended "to hide the truth." But he conceded that even though "she worked with dedication and possessed the necessary preparation . . . , she always irritated the disgruntled neighbors and that was detrimental to the good progress" of the school.[118] Despite his evaluation that the teacher was both committed and talented, the governor granted the parents' wish—an indication that local indígenas enjoyed considerable influence.

Complaints about Méndez and González speak to the challenge of hiring teachers. While training and teaching talent were readily discernible, *honradez* (integrity) proved far more difficult to judge.[119] After repeatedly insisting she was broke, Zoila Blanca de Coronado fled Aguascalientes, where she taught in the girls' school. Her absence was problematic for both her students and her landlord, to whom she owed two months' rent by June 1946.[120]

While vocal parents could run a teacher out of town, their participation was not always forthcoming. Given that his suggestion to move the overcrowded Dueñas school to a new location had elicited no response, the mayor concluded that community members had "little interest in the education of their children."[121] The archival record suggests that such indifference was the exception, not the rule.

With good reason, parents were vigilant about their children's teachers, whose responsibilities were closely related to the state's interests in "defending physical health, civic and moral formation, the instruction and initiation of activities of practical order [and] . . . reorganiz[ing] rural schools with an eye toward the country's social problems."[122] When the Arévalo administration abolished military conscription, it looked to education to acculturate indigenous people. Decreed on March 8, 1945, the National Literacy Law revealed officials' preferred means of assimilation and legislators' low estimation of indigenous and poor ladino lifestyles: "The Guatemalan alphabet is an urgent step to canceling the cultural debt existing in large sectors of the country."[123] If education was a source of national transformation, teachers were the boot soldiers who molded young minds, bodies, and souls. Like STEG, the Confederación de Trabajadores Guatemaltecos (Confederation of Guatemalan Workers; CTG) recognized that teachers were particularly crucial for organizing people in rural areas. In many towns, teachers headed local union and political party affiliates. In some cases, teachers were the mayors.[124] That influence was more than many parents wanted for their children.

Given the revolutionary curriculum and Arévalo's determination to assimilate indigenous people, parents were rightly concerned about acculturation.[125] Founded on La Alameda Finca in Chimaltenango to facilitate learning Kaqchikel, the Escuela Rural Normal had a curriculum that was based not only on math, reading, and writing but also on health, hygiene, agriculture, and the rural home industries of the region. In addition to teaching, trainees became social workers in rural communities. Even though indigenous language acquisition was elusive—of the thirty-two students who graduated in February 1948, only three spoke Kaqchikel; the rest had studied English—the school produced quality teachers who were sensitive to the challenges of rural life. In truth, they learned about rural realities to facilitate students' civic and moral formation through practical activities.[126] Even with an indigenous teacher, parents in Santa Lucía Utatlán perceived the school as a ladino institution bent on changing indigenous society by acculturating their children. Despite efforts to offer a curriculum based on rural lives, indigenous parents saw education as a form of external regulation, rather than a manifestation of local tradition or knowledge.[127]

In Mexico, schools sought to provide venues where rural residents, teachers, and authorities negotiated over the meanings of citizenship, nationalism, rights, and expectations. At times such idealistic efforts (and the schools themselves) failed. In rural Guatemala, discussions and negotiations were so dominated by such issues as teacher truancy, incompetence, and exploitation of female students that national inclusive overtures had little time to emerge. Like many of their counterparts in Mexico, teachers in rural Guatemala often could not get past practical problems to have discussions about citizenship and national identity, even as STEG leaders encouraged teachers to devote more time and energy to politics than to teaching.[128] Although some rural indigenous parents resisted education for their daughters, many demanded that school be worthwhile, respectful, and inclusive. Failing to advance a cultural revolution via the schools, problematic teachers constrained the democratic administration's ability to cement its programs and to attract further popular support. Although teachers generally supported the revolution, a lack of broader middle-class (including many indigenous elites) support thwarted the revolution's ability to withstand the 1954 coup.

Conclusion

Like most revolutions, tensions between continuity and change marked the Arévalo administration. Many Ubico-period laws and regulations continued during Arévalo's government: forced labor, mandatory school attendance, compulsory office holding. The persistence of such laws and regulations suggests democratic rule did not introduce significant change in many rural indígenas' lives. For most Kaqchikels, the regime's continuities with its predecessor mitigated the impact of revolutionary reforms. While shifts in economic policies resulted in less intervention in marketplaces, for example, daily sanitation and other public health inspections there ensured that the state's presence continued to be felt. In light of the limited change that marked the Arévalo administration's efforts to contain the power of workers, landowners, and even officials, perceptions of continuity are not surprising. Nor are recollections of unrest surprising given that structural reforms (however incremental) and democratic elections undermined elite power and transformed local political and economic relations. The irreconcilable tensions inherent in challenging those hierarchies caused uncertainty and insecurity. Taken as a whole, these seemingly contradictory perspectives—that the revolution introduced disorder and that continuity rather than rupture characterized it—capture well the complexity of rural Guatemalans' experiences of their nation's democratic experiment. Oral history and archival evidence suggest rural indígenas experienced the revolution in ways that ranged from noticing little change to either benefiting from or being marginalized by the transition to democracy in a particular moment (often of violence) or in protracted, incremental changes.

The most dramatic break with the past was experienced by survivors of the Patzicía massacre, for whom terror would forever taint the revolutionary government. As I have argued in the first section of this chapter, the dominance and pervasiveness of Kaqchikel memories of the Patzicía massacre suggest that moments of violence eclipsed policy adoption in rural areas, a process that, given infrastructural and personnel limitations, was already slow and partial.

Without regular visits to rural communities, Arévalo was less accessible (and less of a populist) than Ubico. Rather than arriving to deploy his own brand of justice or challenge local ladino powerbrokers, at times his revolutionary rule seemed to accommodate elites. The 1944 Patzicía massacre was the most egregious manifestation of that favoritism. Instead of prosecuting ladino perpetrators, authorities and the media vilified indígenas as thugs bent, supposedly, on raping ladino women. When corrupt ladino officials such as the forest guards exploited indigenous communities without substantive sanctions, the administration perpetuated an image of ethnic allegiance that jeopardized indigenous livelihoods and security. Such exploitation also informed many rural residents' sense that democracy unleashed disorder.

Reconsidering the primacy of the Ten Years of Spring does not discount the significance of shifting from authoritarian to democratic rule or the ascendency enjoyed by the winners— reformist-minded junior military officers, students, middle-class activists, urban workers and their subsequent political representatives, and a few indigenous elites. It merely suggests that in a nation as diverse and polarized as Guatemala, perceptions of the past and experiences of events can be radically different. A large and growing body of scholarship on Latin American revolutions suggests that to be the nature of revolutions.[129] A multiplicity of historical narratives enriches the study of the past; affording each fair consideration and creating the conditions whereby multiple historical narratives can coexist contribute to a more just, democratic nation.

Notes

I wish to thank Jim Handy, Heather Vrana, Julie Gibbings, Adele Perry, and Patrick Chassé, whose critical comments on earlier versions of this essay vastly improved it.

1. Richard N. Adams, "Ethnic Images and Strategies in 1944," in *Guatemalan Indians and the State, 1540–1988*, ed. Carol Smith, 144–145 (Austin: University of Texas Press, 1990).

2. December 8, 1944, packet 126, Archivo Municipal de Patzicía.

3. David Carey Jr., "A Democracy Born in Violence: Maya Perceptions of the 1944 Patzicía Massacre and the 1954 Coup," in *After the Coup: An Ethnographic Reframing of Guatemala 1954*, ed. Timothy J. Smith and Abigail E. Adams, 73–98 (Urbana: University of Illinois Press, 2011).

4. Report to Ministerio de Agricultura y Minería de Ernesto Ramírez, August 11, 1945, box 31, Agricultura, Loyola-Notre Dame Library, Special Collections (hereafter LNDLSC), Guatemala Collection (hereafter GC).

5. Ibid.

6. Letter to gobernador from Inspector de Guardia de Hacienda, Antigua, March 22, 1947, box 3, Informes, LNDLSC, GC.

7. Petition from Tomás Pen Guachin, San Antonio Aguas Calientes (hereafter Aguascalientes), January 24, 1945, box 15, Economía, LNDLSC, GC.

8. Leo Suslow, *Aspects of Social Reform in Guatemala, 1944–1949: Problems of Social Change in an Underdeveloped Country* (Hamilton, NY: Colgate University, 1949), 123.

9. Claudio Javier Barrientos, "Texturas, políticas y fisuras de memorias campesinas: Fragmentos para una contraescritura de la historia reciente en Chile," *Revista de Estudios Latinoamericanos* 1 (2009): 44, 46, and 48–49; Dagmar Herzog, *Sex after Fascism: Memory and Morality in Twentieth-Century Germany* (Princeton, NJ: Princeton University Press, 2005), 1.

10. David Carey Jr., *Our Elders Teach Us: Maya-Kaqchikel Historical Perspectives. Xkib'ij kan qate' qatata'* (Tuscaloosa: University of Alabama Press, 2001).

11. Victor Bulmer-Thomas, *The Economic History of Latin America since 1920* (Cambridge: Cambridge University Press, 1987), 114.

12. December 11, 1945, box 31, Agricultura, Audiencia, LNDLSC, GC.

13. Letter to Gobernador Civil Departamental de Luis Saqche' et. al, December 13, 1945, box 31, Agricultura, LNDLSC, GC.

14. Intendencia Municipal: SCB, December 19, 1945, box 31, Agricultura, LNDLSC, GC.

15. Bulmer-Thomas, *The Economic History of Latin America since 1920*, 115.

16. Greg Grandin, *The Blood of Guatemala: A History of Race and Nation* (Durham, NC: Duke University Press, 2000), 202–207, 209–219.

17. Letter to Gobernador de Luis Saqche', alcalde de Santa Catarina Barahona (hereafter Barahona), May 15, 1946, box 19, Terrenos, LNDLSC, GC.

18. Distribución de las Zonas Forestales, Antigua, October 18, 1946, box 19, Terrenos, LNDLSC, GC.

19. Jefatura Guardia Forestal, Antigua, November 25, 1946, box 19, Terrenos, LNDLSC, GC.

20. Edgar Esquit, *Otros poderes, nuevos desafíos: Relaciones interétnicas en Tecpán y su entorno departamental (1871–1935)* (Guatemala City: Magna Terra Editores, 2002); Edgar Esquit, *La superación del indígena: La política de la modernización entre las élites indígenas de Comalapa, siglo XX* (Guatemala City: Instituto de Estudios Interétnicos, Universidad de San Carlos, 2010); Grandin, *The Blood of Guatemala*.

21. Mary Kay Vaughn, *Cultural Politics in Revolution: Teachers, Peasants, and Schools in Mexico, 1930–1940* (Tucson: University of Arizona Press, 1997).

22. Letter to Intendente Municipal, San Miguel Milpas Dueñas (hereafter Dueñas), August 4, 1944, box 22, Economía, LNDLSC, GC.

23. Letter to Jefe Político de Sacatepéquez, Dueñas, January 24, 1945, box 22, Economía, LNDLSC, GC.

24. Letter to the Governador de Dueñas alcalde, 1946, box 23, Festividades, LNDLSC, GC.

25. Jim Handy, *Revolution in the Countryside: Rural Conflict and Agrarian Reform in Guatemala, 1944–1954* (Chapel Hill: University of North Carolina Press, 1994), 24, 43–44, 52, and 131; Rubén E. Reina, "Chinautla: A Guatemalan Indian Community," in *Community Culture and National Change*, ed. Richard Adams, publication 24, 55–130 (New Orleans: Middle American Research Institute, Tulane University, 1972); Grandin, *The Blood of Guatemala*, 206, 214; Richard Newbold Adams, *Crucifixion by Power: Essays on Guatemalan National Social Structure, 1944–1966* (Austin: University of Texas Press, 1970), 187 and 189; Jim Handy, "National Policy, Agrarian Reform, and the Corporate Community during the Guatemalan Revolution, 1944–54," *Comparative Studies in Society and History* 30, no. 4 (October 1988): 703 and 706; Jim Handy, *Gift of the Devil: A History of Guatemala* (Boston: South End, 1984), 167–171; J. T. Way, *The Mayan in the Mall: Globalization, Development, and the Making of Modern Guatemala* (Durham, NC: Duke University Press, 2012), 55.

26. *El Imparcial*, January 8, 1948.

27. For other journalistic accounts that exaggerated indigenous depravity to discount indígenas as citizens who could participate in democracy, see *Nuestro Diario*, October 24 and 30, 1944; *El Imparcial*, October 24, November 7, 18, and 30 1944; *Impacto*, October 23, 1977; Handy, *Revolution in the Countryside*, 55; Forester, *The Time of Freedom: Campesino Workers in Guatemala's October Revolution* (Pittsburgh: University of Pittsburgh Press, 2001), 92–93; Richard N. Adams, "Las masacres de Patzicía de 1944," *Revista Winak Boletín Intercultural* 7, nos. 1–4 (June 1992): 3–40; Heather Vrana, *This City Belongs to You: A History of Student Activism in Guatemala, 1944–1996* (Oakland: University of California Press 2017), 48.

28. Aguascalientes, May 2 and June 2, 1946, box 13, Informes, LNDLSC, GC.

29. Departamento de Sacatepéquez, Ciudad Vieja, 1948, December 29, 1944, box 6, Estadística, LNDLSC, GC.

30. Antigua, March 1945, box 2, Fomento, LNDLSC, GC.

31. Antigua, April 11, 1945, box 2, Fomento, LNDLSC, GC.

32. Dirección General de Asistencia Social, Guatemala City, January 21, 1946, circular #6, leg. 23259, Archivo General de Centroamérica (hereafter AGCA).

33. Ibid.

34. Dirección General Asistencia Social, Guatemala City, January 31, 1946, leg. 23259, AGCA.

35. Carey, *Our Elders Teach Us*, 212–216; David McCreery, *Rural Guatemala 1760–1940* (Stanford, CA: Stanford University Press, 1994), 311, 319.

36. Oral history interview, conducted by the author with Kab'lajuj Ajpu', San

Juan Comalapa, May 5, 1998. Hereafter, I simply list the interviewee's name and the place and date of interview. Due to the continued political volatility of Guatemala and recurrent human rights abuses, I have preserved the anonymity of oral history interviewees for their safety by using pseudonyms. Unless otherwise noted parenthetically, I conducted all oral history interviews, which were done in Kaqchikel. All translations from Kaqchikel to English are my own. Like archival documents, oral histories are subjective sources with historical trajectories. Unlike archival sources, oral histories change over time depending on the past they are describing and the contemporary circumstances (particularly the audience and storytellers' motives) in which they are recounted. In highland Guatemala, events such as the nation's civil war (1960–1996) are ever-present lenses through which elder Mayas recount the past. See David Carey Jr., *Oral History in Latin America: Unlocking the Spoken Archive* (New York: Routledge, 2017).

37. Vrana, *This City Belongs to You*, 23, 30, and 74 (quote).

38. Manning Nash, *Machine Age Maya: The Industrialization of a Guatemalan Community* (Chicago: Phoenix Press, University of Chicago Press, 1967); Paul McDowell, "Political and Religious Change in a Guatemalan Community" (PhD diss., University of British Colombia, 1974); June Nash, "Recovering the Truth of the 1954 Coup: Restoring Peace with Justice," in *After the Coup: An Ethnographic Reframing of Guatemala 1954*, ed. Timothy J. Smith and Abigail E. Adams, 49–72 (Urbana: University of Illinois Press, 2011).

39. B'eleje' K'at, Comalapa, November 5, 1997.

40. Report to Gobernador de Dueñas, September 5, 1949, box 20, Informes, LNDLSC, GC.

41. Letter to Gobernador de Dueñas, May 28, 1948, box 20, Informes, LNDLSC, GC.

42. Letter to Intendente Municipal de Aguascalientes from Florencio Mazariegos López, Director General de Estadística, February 23, 1945, box 16, Estadística, LNDLSC, GC.

43. Dirección General de Estadística, Estadística de Faltas, Aguascalientes, March 1948, box 16, Estadística, LNDLSC, GC.

44. David Carey Jr., *Engendering Mayan History: Kaqchikel Women as Agents and Conduits of the Past, 1875–1970* (New York: Routledge, 2006).

45. Letter to Gobernador de Luis Saqche', Barahona, October 29, 1946; letter to Ministerio de Educación Inspection, November 11, 1946. Both in box 32, Economía, LNDLSC, GC.

46. Letter to Gobernador de Federico Santos López, alcalde de Aguas Calientes, Antigua, May 11, 1946, box 19, Terrenos, LNDLSC, GC.

47. Ibid.

48. David Carey Jr., "Malaria Miasmas: Labor, Health, and Land in a Lake Draining Project, 1920–1948" (paper New England Council of Latin American Studies Annual Meeting, Norton, MA, November 9, 2013).

49. Report from Barahona, June 19, 1948, box 32, Economía, LNDLSC, GC.

50. David Carey Jr., *I Ask for Justice: Maya Women, Dictators, and Crime in Guatemala, 1898–1944* (Austin: University of Texas Press, 2013).

51. B'eleje' Kawoq, Tecpán, June 9, 1998.

52. Carey, *Our Elders Teach Us*, 195–219.

53. Jennie Purnell, *Popular Movements and State Formation in Revolutionary Mexico* (Durham, NC: Duke University Press, 1999); Miguel La Serna, *The Corner of*

the Living: Ayacucho on the Eve of the Shining Path Insurgency (Chapel Hill: University of North Carolina Press, 2012), 9 and 16–17.

54. *Diario de Centro América*, December 4, 1936.

55. *Memoria del Ministerio de Agricultura 1939* (Guatemala City: Tipografía Nacional, 1940), 28.

56. Gobernación de Sacatepéquez, June 12, 1945, box 15, Economía, LNDLSC, GC.

57. Handy, *Revolution in the Countryside*, 24 and 52–53.

58. Handy, *Revolution in the Countryside*, 30, 35, 64, 66, and 182–183; Jim Handy, "The Violence of Dispossession: Guatemala in the Nineteenth and Twentieth Centuries," in *Politics and History of Violence and Crime in Central America*, ed. Sebastian Huhn and Hannes Warnecke-Berger, 281–323 (New York: Palgrave Macmillan, 2017), 291–293.

59. Handy, *Gift of the Devil*, 124; Skinner-Klée, *Legislación indigenista de Guatemala* (Guatemala: Instituto Indigenista Interamericano, 1995), 121–122; Handy, *Revolution in the Countryside*, 24; Adams, *Crucifixion by Power*, 185.

60. Wuqu' Ajpu' (Jun Tojil interview), Barahona, 1998.

61. B'eleje' Kawoq, Tecpán, June 9, 1998.

62. B'eleje' Tz'i', Junlajuj B'atz, and Junlajuj Toj, Xetonox, Comalapa, May 20, 1998.

63. Laura Briggs, *Reproducing Empire: Race, Sex, Science, and U.S. Imperialism in Puerto Rico* (Berkeley: University of California Press, 2002), 192.

64. Waqi' Imox, Tecpán, May 3, 1998; Wuqu' Kame (Jun Tojil interview), Barahona, ca. 1998.

65. Asilo de Alienados, Guatemala, Dr. Miguel F. Molina, Médico Jefe del Asilo de Alienados, February 21, 1945, leg. 23259, AGCA.

66. Waqi' Iq', Comalapa, December 12, 1997.

67. B'eleje' K'at, Comalapa, November 5, 1997.

68. Letter to the gobernador de Pedro Ordóñez, May 20, 1946, box 33, Quejas, LNDLSC, GC.

69. Ibid.

70. Letter of Servicio de Comunicaciones, Dirección y Auditoria de Correos to Gobernador, Guatemala City, October 23, 1945, box 7, Quejas, LNDLSC, GC.

71. Letter to the gobernador de alcaldía de Barahona, May 24, 1946, box 33, Quejas, LNDLSC, GC.

72. Gobernación de Sacatepéquez, May 27, 1946, box 33, Quejas, LNDLSC, GC.

73. Dueñas, April 26, 1945, box 22, Economía, LNDLSC, GC.

74. Letter to the Alcalde de Aguascalientes, April 23, 1946, box 15, Economía, LNDLSC, GC.

75. Barahona, April 17, 1945, June 14, 1945, and June 20, 1945, box 32, Economía, LNDLSC, GC.

76. Handy, *Revolution in the Countryside*, 51; Suslow, *Aspects of Social Reform*, 24; Handy, *Gift of the Devil*, 107–108.

77. Carlos González Orellana, *Historia de la educación en Guatemala* (México, DF: Colección Científico Pedagógica, 1960), 336, 354.

78. *El Imparcial*, March 18, 1948; González Orellana, *Historia de la educación en Guatemala*, 336 and 354.

79. Santiago Zamora, 1948, box 27, Educación, LNDLSC, GC.

80. Dueñas, May 18, 1945, box 15, Educación, LNDLSC, GC.

81. González Orellana, *Historia de la educación en Guatemala*, 336, 354; John Gillen, "San Luis Jilotepeque: 1942–55," in *Community Culture and National Change*, ed. Richard Adams, 23–27 (New Orleans: Middle American Research Institute, Tulane University, Publication #24, 1972), 26.

82. Barahona, May 16, 1945, box 32, Economía, LNDLSC, GC.

83. Hacienda San Vicente, October 4, 1946, Jefe Departamento de haciendas de Junta Asistencia Pública, Quito, Museo de Medicina, Quito, Ecuador, Asistencia Publica (AP) 1188; dirección de educación Pichincha, November 10, 1947, Hacienda Moyurto, AP 1102; Junta Central de AP, contesta oficio (de escuela), Quito, November 25, 1947, AP 1102.

84. Ministro de Educación Pública de Dueñas, May 29, 1946, box 15, Educación, LNDLSC, GC.

85. Antigua, May 30, 1946, box 15, Educación, LNDLSC, GC.

86. Letter to the alcalde de Dueñas, June 17, 1946, box 15, Educación, LNDLSC, GC.

87. Handy, *Revolution in the Countryside*, 71.

88. *El Imparcial*, March 22, 1948; Suslow, *Aspects of Social Reform*, 26–27.

89. González Orellana, *Historia de la educación en Guatemala*, 354–357; Suslow, *Aspects of Social Reform*, 30–32.

90. Handy, *Revolution in the Countryside*, 28.

91. Way, *The Mayan in the Mall*, 64.

92. Handy, *Revolution in the Countryside*, 71–72.

93. Rubén Reina, *The Law of the Saints: A Pokomam Pueblo and Its Community Culture* (New York: Bobbs-Merrill Company, 1966), 267.

94. Ixpim, Comalapa, July 7, 2001.

95. Carey, *Engendering Mayan History*, 200–202.

96. Ixq'anil, Comalapa, June 25, 1998.

97. Ixchipix, (Ixk'at), Paquixic, Comalapa, June 29, 2001.

98. Barahona, June 9, 1946, box 32, Economía, LNDLSC, GC.

99. Letter to the Gobernador de Ciudad Vieja, June 9, 1945, box 29, Economía, LNDLSC, GC; Handy, *Revolution in the Countryside*, 71–72.

100. Handy, *Revolution in the Countryside*, 71–72.

101. Elsie Rockwell, "Schools of the Revolution: Enacting and Contesting State Forms in Tlaxcala, 1910–1930," in *Everyday Forms of State Formation: Revolution and Integration of Rule in Modern Mexico*, ed. Gilbert M. Joseph and Daniel Nugent, 170–208 (Durham, NC: Duke University Press, 1994).

102. Ixchikoj, Comalapa, July 3, 2001.

103. Ixmay, Comalapa, June 2, 2001.

104. Instituto Indigenista Nacional, Ministerio de Educación Pública (Antonio Goubaud Carrera, Director), Publicaciones Especiales del Instituto Indigenísta Nacional, no. 6, *San Antonio Aguas Calientes: Síntesis socio-económica de una comunidad indígena Guatemalteca* (Guatemala City: Instituto Indigenista Nacional, 1948), 47.

105. Carey, *Engendering Mayan History*, 188–189.

106. Sheldon Annis, *God and Production in a Guatemalan Town* (Austin: University of Texas Press, 1987), 27.

107. Carey, *Engendering Mayan History*, 195.

108. Instituto Indigenista Nacional, *San Antonio Aguas Calientes*, 47.

109. Letter to the Inspector Técnica de Barahona, October 17, 1946, box 32, Economía, LNDLSC, GC.

110. Letter to the Inspector Técnica de Barahona, October 17, 1946, box 32, Economía, LNDLSC, GC. Even today, teacher truancy is a major problem in developing nations such as Guatemala; see Nicolas Kristoff, "Malada's Fight Continues," *New York Times*, September 27, 2015.

111. Directora de Escuela Mixta, Ceballos, 1948, box 28, Educación, LNDLSC, GC.

112. Ix'ajmaq, Tecpán, June 2, 1998.

113. Letter to the Gobernador de profesores de Barahona, August 14, 1946, box 32, Economía, LNDLSC, GC.

114. Barahona, August 19, 1946, box 32, Economía, LNDLSC, GC.

115. Antigua, August 22, 1946, box 32, Economía, LNDLSC, GC.

116. Barahona, Ezequiel Baeza Porras a gobernador, May 31, 1945, box 33, Quejas, LNDLSC, GC.

117. Barahona alcalde to gobernador, October 29, 1946, box 32, Economía, LNDLSC, GC.

118. Letter to the Director de Escuelas Primarias, de Ernesto Ramírez, October 10, 1945, box 15, Educación, LNDLSC, GC.

119. Barahona, June 9, 1946, box 32, Economía, LNDLSC, GC.

120. Barahona, June 3, 1946, box 33, Quejas, LNDLSC, GC.

121. Dueñas, December 12, 1945, box 15, Educación, LNDLSC, GC.

122. Letter to the Inspector Técnico de Educación, November 28, 1946, box 15, Educación, LNDLSC, GC.

123. González Orellana, *Historia de la educación en Guatemala*, 338.

124. Handy, *Revolution in the Countryside*, 69 and 72.

125. Carey, *Engendering Mayan History*, 177–206.

126. González Orellana, *Historia de la educación en Guatemala*, 354–360; Suslow, *Aspects of Social Reform*, 30–32.

127. Suslow, *Aspects of Social Reform*, 27.

128. Vaughn, *Cultural Politics in Revolution*.

129. See, e.g., Gil M. Joseph and Greg Grandin, eds., *A Century of Revolution: Insurgent and Counterinsurgent Violence during Latin America's Long Cold War* (Durham, NC: Duke University Press, 2010).

PART III

New Actors

CHAPTER 7

"A pack of cigarettes or some soap"

"Race," Security, International Public Health, and Human Medical Experimentation during Guatemala's October Revolution

Abigail E. Adams and Laura Giraudo

"A pack of cigarettes or some soap" was the compensation the US Public Health Service (PHS) offered "Indian" men prisoners for blood draws during STD experiments in Guatemala, 1946–1948.[1] The historian Susan Reverby unearthed the study's archive in 2010 and identified its direct connection with the Tuskegee Syphilis Experiment (1932–1972). Unlike the infamous Tuskegee study, US researchers intentionally, secretly, and often brutally infected Guatemalans with sexually transmitted diseases.

The news shook up historical memories in both countries. US president Barack Obama apologized to the people of Guatemala on October 1, 2010. He ordered the Presidential Commission for the Study of Bioethical Issues (PCSBI) to investigate the newly international scope of the shameful decades metonymically referred to as the Tuskegee studies.[2] Guatemalan president Álvaro Colom commissioned the official report *Consentir el daño*. Both reports, the PCSBI's "*Ethically Impossible*" and Guatemala's *Consentir el daño*, make clear that the study's ethics violated the contemporary research standards and public norms of the United States and Guatemala; in Guatemala, furthermore, intentionally infecting someone with an STD was illegal.

The Guatemalan report authors highlighted the dissonance evoked by the news of the 1940s STD experiments: "It would have been logical to point to the despotic, authoritarian, freedom-suppressing government of the tyrant Jorge Ubico. But, to the contrary, the news was about the democratic administration of the humanist Dr. Juan José Arévalo."[3]

Arévalo knew about and sanctioned the research.[4] Guatemala did not request the study, but it continued years after the two countries broke diplomatic relations.[5] How could this atrocity have occurred under Arévalo—the democratically elected leader who ended decades of dictatorships and brutal forced labor; the anti-imperialist champion and nationalist who challenged the United States' support for contemptible dictators; the high-minded "spiritual socialist" who promoted civil liberties, participation, inclusion, and human rights?

The authors of "*Ethically Impossible*" located no materials about Guatemala's motivations for supporting the STD experiments, and they leave that question aside.[6] They note the initial connection: a Guatemalan doctor on a US PHS fellowship pointed out that prostitution was legal in his country, and might be useful in US PHS STD research.[7] The Guatemalan report turns to the context: Guatemala's political and material dependence on the United States; the subaltern status of its medical community members to their US colleagues; and Guatemala's continued structures of exclusion, marginalization, racism, and discrimination. The authors also describe Arévalo's inexperience, arrogance, and genuine admiration for the Roosevelt administration.[8] Others note that the STD study provided US funding "to upgrade Guatemala's inadequate public-health infrastructure, to import scientific expertise," and to obtain STD treatment for its troops.[9]

In this chapter, we address the question, "How could this have happened?" with contributions drawn from our historical memory work on a disease now classed as a "neglected tropical disease" by the World Health Organization: onchocerciasis. Also known as "river blindness" and "Robles disease," onchocerciasis was a hot inter-American topic into the 1940s and Arévalo's administration. Our work reveals that what appears merely as a coincidence—a Guatemalan doctor in the right place (those US PHS research labs) at the right postwar time—was one strand of dense networks resulting from decades-deep Guatemalan-US public health diplomacy, research, campaigns, and networks. The work on onchocerciasis, in particular, created collegialities, reciprocities, and international biomedical prestige for Guatemala, which directly and indirectly informed the Arévalo administration's handling of the STD human experimentation. For example, this chapter's opening quote about the meager and unhealthy compensation offered to the Guatemalan human subjects reflects the advice of US PHS official Joseph Spoto, who participated in the Guatemalan onchocerciasis campaigns.

Our research shows that the Guatemalan-US STD human medical

experimentation emerged from those networks and transactional opportunistic dependencies, in a complex, dynamic, international public health context in which the aspirations of the Guatemalan October Revolution overlapped with the promise of the postwar era (including major wartime medical advances, e.g., in typhus and infection control), the persistence of prewar "racial positivism" (the ideology that Modern Progress would whiten populations), and the realities of the incipient Cold War.

It is no news to historians that the October Revolution overthrew a dictator, but not Guatemala's legacies of racism, oppression, and compromise, despite the revolutionaries' desire for a clean break. Julie Gibbings and Heather Vrana (see the introduction in this volume), among others, note that Arévalo's "revolutionary" approach was actually gradualist social reform, such as improved public health care, rather than structural change, such as agrarian reform. Many marginalized Guatemalans experienced little relief; the chaos and disorganization after 1944 made life more difficult and dangerous (see Carey Jr., chapter 6 in this volume).[10] This volume makes clear that ongoing municipal forced-labor drafts and prohibitions on much rural labor organizing, even after Arévalo's labor code became law, were due not to lack of resources, disorganization, or inattention but rather to Arévalo's strategic choices and priorities as he set his modernist agenda (see chapter 6 in this volume).[11]

Arévalo established health care as one of his administration's priorities, along with education and labor reform.[12] He acknowledged health and medical care as human rights, established by Article 25 of the 1945 Universal Declaration of Human Rights, which his administration translated into several Mayan languages, printed, and distributed widely.[13] Improving health care was also necessary to advance other priorities such as opening the Petén (see Andersson, chapter 3 in this volume) and obtaining international prestige. So while Arévalo deployed the era's progressive rhetoric, colored (or confused) by his own "spiritual socialism," he also showed instrumental disregard toward achieving what he could in public health.

The arena of public health is also where Arévalo's postwar faith in rationalist governance and science melded with the policies of social assimilation that Arévalo and his officials continued, as well as the long-standing "positivist" language of social hygiene and racial *degeneración*.[14] These policies occurred even while his administration's newly relevant *indigenistas* combated the pseudoscience of biological racing/inborn (tempera)mentalities; Sarah Foss and Patrick Chassé (chapters 2 and 8 in this volume) show how Arévalo's regime focused intensely on Indian embodiment.

El Imparcial
diario independiente
centavos 5 ejemplar
Director: ALEJANDRO CORDOVA. Casa editora: UNION TIPOGRAFICA.
AÑO XXII. — GUATEMALA, C. A., VIERNES 9 DE JULIO DE 1943.

Educación por Medio de los Cuarteles

Es Inminente la Lucha Decisiva Por la Base Nipona de Munda

Cortada Quedó la Línea de Bairoko

A Sólo 2 Millas del Puerto Están los Americanos

Mapa demostrativo de las operaciones que las fuerzas norteamericanas están desarrollando en las islas Salomón para ganar el control del puerto estratégico de Munda.

Procesión de Convoyes Aliados Amontonan la Tormenta Invasora

Mientras las Bases de Sicilia son Sometidas a una Tempestad Ininterrumpida de Bombardeos

Los Contadores Van a Sesionar el Once

Instalada la Central Contra la Onchocerca

Organízanse las Dependencias y el Personal; Pláticas de Técnicos

Desfilarán Equipos de Estudiantes

Programa de Juegos Universitarios

Primer Ensayo Orquestal de Peruchío

Participación del Coro Guatemala

Practicantes Para el Hospital General y Otros Acuerdos

Encuéntrase en la Capital el Señor Philip Raine

Celebrará Reunión el Domingo la Sociedad del Niño

FIGURE 7.1. *"Instalada la central contra la Onchocerca," Publicación de el diario* El Imparcial, *9 de julio de 1943, portada. Archivo Histórico de CIRMA (The War and Onchocerciasis Loom,* El Imparcial *front page July 9, 1943, CIRMA Historical Archive).*

Other public health actors, including the indigenistas and US researchers, framed STDs and onchocerciasis by racialized discourses of blame, positivist hierarchies, speculative vectors, transmissions, and immunities concerning "Indians," "whites" and "*negros*," who in both countries were increasingly organized and mobile (see Ingrid Sierakowski, chapter 1 in this volume). These public health networks, agencies, and players first took shape in the early twentieth century, when the emblematic tropical diseases of yellow fever and malaria threatened international US commerce with "drastic quarantines."[15] United States officials, academics, medical practitioners, and philanthropists such as those gilded-era globalists the Rockefellers[16] coordinated with or joined inter-American public health campaigns, particularly through the US PHS-staffed Pan American Sanitary Bureau (PASB), founded in 1902.

By Guatemala's October Revolution, the entwined commercial and public health networks morphed further into important tools of foreign, military, and economic policy, influenced by new institutional actors and emphases on modernization.[17] The postwar, incipient Cold War national security ideology heightened the threat of both onchocerciasis (because of its presence in the path of the Pan-American Highway) and STDs (because of the impact on soldiers).

The cigarettes and soap of our title—the shockingly inadequate compensation for human medical research subjects—perfectly capture the era's racialized and securitized context, its urgency and entrenchment. Cigarettes are the emblematic reward to soldiers in war,[18] the treat exchanged between comrades, in these cases, the war against disease; the bar of soap, a meme of so-called social hygiene, was once again "forci-voluntarily" imposed on the "Indians."

The Impact of Robles's Discovery: Fame and Frustration

The Guatemalan and US roles in inter-American campaigns against onchocerciasis illustrate how early public health diplomacy and programs prioritized commercial and then security interests and created cultures of collaboration, as well as participation in science, progress, and modernization for Guatemala. Guatemala's work on onchocerciasis resulted in international prestige. The campaigns also illustrate the blurry line between medical experimentation and attempted treatment.

Onchocerciasis, or "Robles disease," is a nonfatal skin and eye disease that remains a major cause of blindness worldwide and is caused by a parasitic filarial (threadlike) worm, *Onchocerca volvulus*, which is transmitted by blackflies. In Africa, both the illness (known as "craw-craw") and its connection to the filarial worm had been documented and studied since the 1870s.[19] Onchocerciasis was first discovered and treated in the Americas in 1915 by the public health–minded Guatemalan doctor Rodolfo Robles Valverde. Dr. Robles's contribution to onchocerciasis research was threefold: he documented onchocerciasis in the Americas, identified the blackfly as the vector, and connected the worm to both the known skin pathologies and the potentially blinding eye infections.[20]

Robles's discoveries led to other advances by Guatemalan researchers, including Dr. Rafael Pacheco Luna, who in February 1918 published the still-classic study of the onchocerciasis eye lesions.[21] Because of Robles's work, researchers were able to identify onchocerciasis in Oaxaca and Chiapas, Mexico (1925 both reports), recognize the ocular impact in Africa, and ascertain that the African and American worms were one and the same.[22] To date, Robles's accomplishments are noted in most scientific articles about onchocerciasis, often with laudatory statements, such as "His insight was remarkable."[23] Guatemala's highest medical award is named in his honor, as is an ophthalmological hospital in that country's capital city.[24]

Robles's experience fits with the turn-of-the-century admiration and collegiality proffered by European colleagues to Latin American scientists and medical doctors, as described by Cueto and Palmer. The era of bacteriology had opened, and with it, the creation of heroic "microbe hunters." Robles is among several Latin Americans whose accomplishments are memorialized in the diseases named for them, such as Brazilian physician Carlos Chagas. Many Latin Americans trained in European institutions, particularly France, where "Paris medicine" was held in the highest esteem.[25] Robles, who was born in Quetzaltenango in 1878, graduated in 1904 from the medical school of the Sorbonne, Paris, where he studied "colonial medicine,"[26] and later (1922) earned his doctorate at the University of Paris, specializing in malariology, public health, and mycology. His efforts to establish a Pasteur Institute in Guatemala demonstrate his allegiance to these cosmopolitan medical circles centered in Paris.[27] Reciprocally, France awarded Robles with the Legion of Honor.

Robles's education led him to make the connection to African onchocerciasis one day in 1915, when an eight-year-old boy was brought to his clinic by his mother, the owner of a nearby coffee plantation. The child had skin lesions and a small tumor on his forehead that Robles removed. When the physician dissected the tumor, he found the larval stage of the filarial worm and realized that a previous patient, a small girl from the neighborhood with similar skin problems, might be hosting the same parasite. He was able to confirm his hunch and treat her as well.[28]

Now identified, onchocerciasis posed a concern for Guatemala's critical coffee interests. The areas affected by the illness (between 500 and 1,500 meters above sea level, on the Pacific coast slopes of the Sierra Madre range) coincided with coffee plantations and the peak of blackfly activity (January and February mornings) with coffee harvests. In 1927, Dr. Richard Pearson Strong, the founder of Harvard's School of Tropical Medicine, headed an onchocerciasis expedition with the collaboration of Dr. M. Ochoa, of the Dirección General de Sanidad Pública (Guatemalan Board of Health;

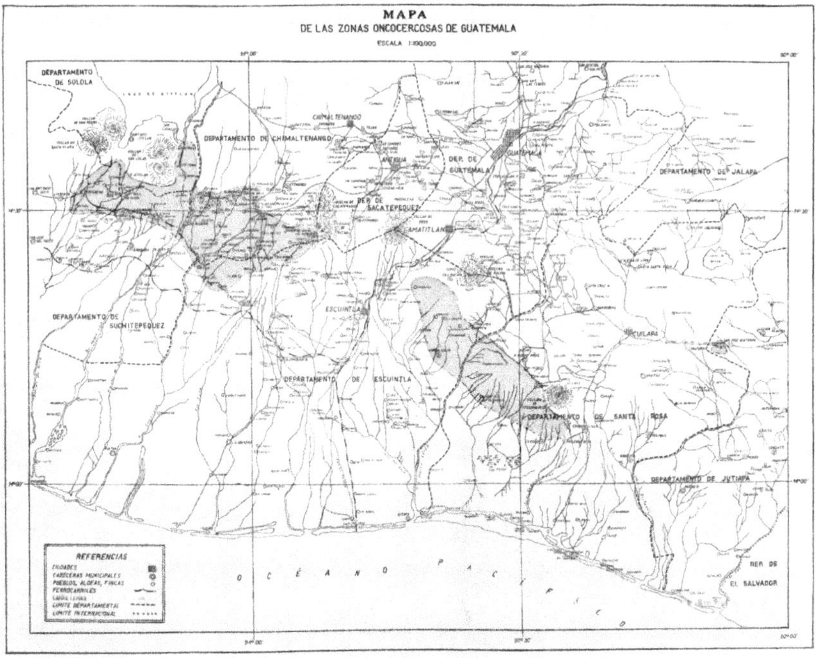

FIGURE 7.2. *"Mapa de las zonas oncocercosas de Guatemala," s/f, Fondo I.I.I., Archivo Histórico, PUIC-UNAM. (Map of Endemic Onchocerciasis Infection, Guatemala, c. 1942, Inter American Indian Institute Archives, Historical Archive, PUIC-UNAM).*

DGSP), inaugurating transnational collaboration in clinical field studies.[29] In 1932, the DGSP created a dedicated commission to onchocerciasis.[30]

In contrast to the considerable glory gained for Guatemala by its onchocerciasis researchers, progress in treating the disease was unforthcoming. There were no triumphant eradication announcements such as those yielded by earlier inter-American yellow fever and malaria campaigns. Treatments were painful, heavy on side effects, and largely unhelpful. For decades, the main treatment was nodulectomy, the surgical removal of the cysts or nodules formed by the worms' larvae, with limited success and too often secondary infections. Later (1930s–1940s), health professionals turned to nonsurgical treatments, including forced quarantine and relocation; the testing of several oral, injectable, and caustic topical drugs directly on patients; and environmental eradication of the blackflies. All efforts to interrupt transmission, eliminate the disease's vectors, or treat patients proved frustrating to public health officials, damaging to most patients, and unrewarding to all.[31]

Frustration with onchocerciasis had mounted by the 1940s, when in less than a decade researchers reported rapid increases in the numbers of infected Guatemalans. A 1934 survey documented over ten thousand infected people, 29 percent of the population, within an area of one thousand square kilometers. That number doubled to twenty thousand by 1940, along with the appearance of new affected (although highly endemic and isolated) areas.[32] The areas of infestation lay directly in the path of Pan-American Highway construction and threatened not only commerce but also Guatemala's modernity and national and international security.

"Racing" against the Tide of Onchocerciasis, the 1930s and 1940s

In the 1930s and 1940s, racialized discussions concerning onchocerciasis proliferated in scientific, national press, and indigenista publications. The discussion revolved around "responsibility" for harboring and transmitting the disease ("los negros"), from which race to which race it spread, whether the disease was an "indigenous disease" or "pathology," and whether "white" people were at risk.

These discussions contrast sharply with the first two decades of writing about "Robles disease." In general, the tone of the earlier publications is clinical, descriptive, and evidence based. Researchers firmly dismissed "race" as a factor. In 1925, the Mexican doctor Miguel Bustamante stated explicitly that race had no effect on protection from or transmission of the illness.[33]

In fact, the first two recorded cases of onchocerciasis, the much-circulated story of Robles's discovery, concerned the legitimate children of coffee plantation owners, people not identified as "negro" or "indígena." The eight-year-old boy, the son of the coffee finqueros of "San Francisco Miramar" in Suchitepéquez, was Alberto Ruiz Aguilar, who grew up to be a capital city lawyer.[34] The other case, the little girl, was the boy's cousin.[35]

This is not to assert that Robles and his contemporaries were free from racist ideologies. Robles was a proponent of social hygienics; the term emphasizes individual and urban cleanliness to maintain health and protect national economies and well-being. Hygiene movements descend directly from Latin American positivism and political ideologies of "order and progress."[36] Robles worked in Tecpán on a health commission during the Spanish Influenza epidemic of 1918–1919, and he publicly criticized nurses and doctors for neglecting the town's indigenous ill. But, along with the majority of ladinos and elites of the time, he attributed the high death toll "solely to the deplorable hygienic conditions" and alleged penchant for moonshine of the Maya.[37]

Beginning in 1931, the first year of Guatemala's Ubico dictatorship, the issue of race ricochets through medical and nonmedical publications about onchocerciasis. These include bizarre assertions, including by biologists, that "whites" were immune to onchocerciasis,[38] despite continuing documentation of the disease's impact on all peoples and "all nationalities."[39] Moreover, African-descended people were blamed for propagating "Robles disease" in the Americas.[40] Still others described the illness as an "indigenous disease" and "endemic," in other words, rooted in a certain "bounded" population and place.[41] Overwhelmingly, writers blamed the frustrating lack of effective treatment on the victims, the affected indigenous peoples. The public intellectual, president of Guatemala's Sociedad de Geografía e Historia, and by then theosophist and advocate of indigenous peoples and rights Fernando Juárez Muñoz listed onchocerciasis among the "terrible" diseases he described in a paragraph subtitled "El *indio* es sucio" ("The indio is filthy"). His concluding advice: the daily use of soap.[42]

Ironically, the full amplitude of this racialist ricocheting—and the bizarre assertions—about onchocerciasis was displayed by a new inter-American set of actors dedicated to the social and behavioral sciences, the indigenistas, at the First Inter-American Indian Conference held in Pátzcuaro, Mexico, in 1940. Writing from Pátzcuaro, Guatemala's vigorous indigenista David Vela regularly reported the proceedings to *El Imparcial*, the paper he edited, repeating claims that indigenous communities suffered from the 'indigenous' disease because of their 'lack of civilization' and their 'absurd' beliefs and resistance to public health officials. His solution, nine years into Ubico's control of the countryside: quarantines enforced by military brigades.[43]

Vela's reporting drew on the conference's final resolutions and on three of four presentations made by a public health official (Dr. Luis Figueroa), an entomologist (Dr. Alfonso Dampf), and the Mexican anthropologist Julio de la Fuente, all of whom spoke urgently about onchocerciasis as a growing "inter-American problem" and an "indigenous" disease.[44] They called for anthropological, historical, and social training for doctors and other health workers, but not before describing the obstacle of "ill-tempered Indian people" who resisted all public health efforts, including relocation, and clung to useless beliefs and legends. They blamed African-descended people for transmitting onchocerciasis: first to the Americas generally, when they arrived as enslaved captives, and then to Guatemalan coffee plantations, when they served as West Indian contract workers *acosando* (bothering) indigenous peoples. Dampf also sounded the alarm about the disease's impact on the construction of the Pan-American Highway—and the Pan-American Highway's potential for spreading the disease farther north. He amplified that alarm in 1942 and reasserted erroneously that onchocerciasis did not have an impact on the "white race."[45]

In stark contrast with the focus on "indigenous mentality," the fourth presentation, which Vela largely ignored, was by the Zapotec representative from Oaxaca, Taurino Santiago, who spoke about the structural exclusions suffered by his people. He listed demand after demand of services needed to fight against onchocerciasis: electricity, telephone service, schools, work, potable water, and the creation of more sanitary brigades.[46] His voice is that of the indigenistas described by Sarah Foss (chapter 8 in this volume), calling out governments for neglecting and oppressing their citizens.

The indigenistas drew on all the discourses and resources available in order to carve out a niche for themselves as the scientific experts on "indigenous diseases." And at Pátzcuaro, they often sounded like today's progressive medical anthropologists, when they proposed working with doctors and health workers in indigenous regions to collect local knowledge about diseases, treatments, and indigenous medicinal plants, when they urged doctors and health workers to "open their minds" with anthropological, historical, and sociological training.[47] That specific training and research, the indigenistas argued, was best provided by the Instituto Indigenista Interamericano (Inter-American Indian Institute; III).

However, the delegates at Pátzcuaro (as in Resolution XVIII on "Indigenous pathology") also urged the Inter-American Indian Institute to "investigate the influence of the Indian races and indigenous traditions on regional pathologies." Dampf, de la Fuente, and Vela blamed indigenous people's "difficult character" and lack of social hygiene.[48] Pátzcuaro's presentations and resolutions also struck a note that would reverberate into the Ten Years of Spring: the threats to national security and the military posed by both the disease and its indigenous afflicted, particularly with regard to the Pan-American Highway.

Inter-American efforts to combat the illness ramped up and expanded to include new actors, such as the III and the United States' new Office of the Coordinator of Inter-American Affairs (OCIAA); its coordinator for four years, Nelson Rockefeller; and its related Servicio Cooperativo Interamericano de Salud Pública (Inter-American Cooperative Health Service; SCISP), all out to "wage war" on disease.[49] In fact, in 1942, one of the III's first projects was to combat onchocerciasis and to introduce the OCIAA to the work as a funder. The project resulted directly from the initiative of Dr. Carlos Estévez, director of Guatemala's DGSP, who seized upon a 1941 visit to Guatemala by Emil J. Sady, a US anthropologist, an III representative, and a Bureau of Indian Affairs staffer. Estévez arranged for Sady to tour an onchocerciasis-afflicted community and provided him with a six-page DGSP report on onchocerciasis so he could obtain funding for creation of a transnational committee, formed by Guatemalan, Mexican, and US experts. The DGSP's report offered a brief summary of the discovery, investigation, and treatment of the disease, noting the need for research on "social, racial and economic conditions of the infected"; the military importance of the Pan-American highway route through Guatemala; and the threat posed by possible dispersal of various endemic diseases, including onchocerciasis.[50]

In review, except for some lonely voices, such as that of the Zapotec delegate to Pátzcuaro Taurino Santiago calling out the structural violence and government neglect of indigenous communities, these documents on onchocerciasis in the last years of the Ubico presidency present images of multiplying but hyperendemic "cysts" of "indigenous" infection and ignorance, quarantined naturally but unstably by race, and about to be lanced by the Pan-American Highway, possibly with national and international military security implications.

The racial anxiety evident at Pátzcuaro was punctuated by the bravado of modern biologists, who asserted in the face of decades of clear evidence to the contrary, that "whites" could not contract the illness.

In most indigenista and medical thought of the time, the indígena-ladino (white) "racing" is further destabilized by the "negros." The "negros" re-pose the earlier century's positivist and disturbing menace of race degeneration. For example, Vela, Dampf, and others depict entire indigenous villages struck blind, pushed toward the edge of the racial pit of the Belgian Congo they invoke, as did Asturias two decades earlier.[51] According to these men, both indígenas and African-descended people were to blame for the spread and intractability of the disease. They were both "resistant" and not "resistant" (immune) enough. The indígenas, they asserted, could not be made to move away from infected areas into quarantined communities of the infected; their stasis threatened modernity.

Meanwhile, these men lamented, the "negros" were increasingly mobile, organized, and "bothersome," spreading beyond the "quarantines" of the Jim Crow–informed Caribbean plantations of United Fruit Company (UFCO) to the newly opened Tiquisate venture, just down the Pacific slope from the onchocerciasitized coffee plantation "cysts."[52] With them and into national politics came their activism, against which coffee exporters sided with UFCO stakeholders (see Ingrid Sierakowski, chapter 1 in this volume).

"The more things change . . .": Public Health and Onchocerciasis in Guatemala's October Revolution

After the October Revolution, these anxious narratives and actors circulated in Guatemala amidst the themes of democracy, spiritual socialism, human rights, social security, education and health for all, and, soon, the global victory over fascist and racist atrocities. As an assimilationist, Arévalo aimed to integrate the indigenous majority, closed off in their *patrias chicas* ("little homelands"), into the new nation, the *patria grande* of democratic Guatemala. His rhetoric emphasized individual rights, participation, and inclusion; the state was to protect individuals as workers and provide education. The focus on education easily slipped into the "soft" neo-Lamarckian eugenics of race improvement through self-improvement and generational transmission,[53] as well as the soft essentialism of "culturalism" and indigenous mentality.[54] Arévalo used the positivist language of social hygiene, for example, in describing the 1947 typhus campaign "focusing on the indigenous race, because of the misery and lamentable hygiene in which they live."[55] He and his officials blamed Maya people as uncooperative and ignorant (see Patrick Chassé, chapter 2 in this volume, on the framing of subsistence corn farming), and they sanctioned force as a necessary means to achieve their top priority, such as the attempts by fieldworkers of the Instituto de Nutrición de Centroamérica y Panamá (Institute of Nutrition of Central America and Panama; INCAP) to draw blood from indigenous schoolchildren (see chapter 8 in this volume) or proposed forced relocation (see chapter 2 in this volume).

His public health efforts benefited from World War II's medical miracles and the advances that developed effective and fairly painless vaccines for typhus, as well as the use of DDT to control disease vectors. Penicillin was successfully mass-produced in 1941, and is credited with reducing the war's mortalities to one-eighteenth of those of World War I. Suddenly the tedious, painful, humiliating, and often ineffective treatments for many diseases and illnesses were over. But not for sufferers of onchocerciasis.

Arévalo depended on US public health projects and on relationships and resources maintained under Ubico,[56] including the construction of Guatemala's Roosevelt Hospital (finally completed after the 1954 coup). Under Ubico, Guatemala signed an agreement in 1943 with SCISP to continue cooperation from 1945 through 1949, which Arévalo honored.[57] Arévalo's administration, for example, received support from SCISP for the typhus campaign, starting almost immediately with a February 1945 conference and then exchange of experts.

Arévalo's 1947 typhus campaign was a biomedical success, and it essentially eradicated typhus in Guatemala. David Carey Jr.'s oral histories with Kaqchikel Maya in Sacatepéquez document how many people valued his successful campaign to eliminate typhus and admired how the new DDT killed other insects.[58] Arévalo is remembered for establishing health centers in their highland communities. Carey Jr.'s Kaqchikel interlocutors described how the president respectfully explained an upcoming vaccination campaign to allay fears and worked through local leaders, rather than forcibly imposing vaccinations. Some even "remembered" Arévalo going into people's homes himself.

But indigenous Guatemalans under Arévalo also remembered heavy-handed public health measures, such as being sprayed without their consent with DDT, during a campaign undertaken by the rural health brigades,[59] which were not particularly nuanced in terms of biopolitics.

Furthermore, Arévalo achieved no public health triumphs over onchocerciasis. The infection rates were grim. By January 1945, 30,000 of the 160,000 people living in the Guatemalan Pacific coast onchocerciasis zone were found to suffer from the disease. The month prior, December 1944, the director of the sanitary brigades, Dr. Díaz, located another infected area in Huehuetenango.[60] The news did not augur well for the completion of the Pan-American Highway or development of the Pacific coast (see Patrick Chassé, chapter 2 in this volume), both priorities for Arévalo.

Three texts about onchocerciasis—written by two Guatemalans and one US-American—span the Arévalo era's discursive spectrum of "racing" public health concerns, ranging from a call to end the state's participation in structural violence against indigenous peoples, to racist blame and shame.

In July 1944, the month when the overthrown Ubico fled Guatemala, Dr. Epaminondas Quintana presented a report on the sanitary conditions of Central America at the University of California, Berkeley.[61] Quintana was a physician, public health official, indigenista, columnist, and literary figure.[62] His report was a manifesto describing the terrible conditions suffered by Central America's marginalized and indigenous workers, who struggled to take care of themselves, their families, and their communities while their government invested more in the military and blamed them for their suffering—onchocerciasis, anemia, parasites, devastating rates of infant mortality, venereal diseases (which Quintana traced to the US military).

Quintana resonated with the voice of the Zapotec representative to Pátzcuaro and the rhetoric of the revolution. He exhorted officials to respect rural indigenous peoples, their contributions to public health, and their well-founded mistrust of outsiders, particularly government officials. Over his many decades of public health work, he followed his own advice. It was Quintana who took III official Emil Sady to the areas affected by "Robles disease" in 1941. His confidence in the capacity of Guatemala's Maya later shaped the *mística* (crusading spirit) of the 1950s post-coup malaria campaign, and he continually decried public health officials' treatment of the poor and indigenous through 1973.[63]

A second text exemplifies the continuing international prestige conferred on Guatemalan biomedical researchers, the 1946 article published by Pacheco Luna, author of the classic 1918 study of onchocerciasis's ocular impact. Pacheco Luna's overview of the disease, its treatment status, and growing infection rates made no mention of the Pan-American Highway or of national security interests. Pacheco Luna did not "race" the disease and merely noted the theory that it had arrived in sixteenth-century Guatemala with enslaved Africans brought by Spanish monks. He lamented the lack of effective treatment and the debilitation caused by the disease; he blamed no one.[64]

The third voice of the era's discursive spectrum is William Clark, one of the US PASB–funded researchers working during the Arévalo administration on the disease.[65] Clark's article—a thorough clinical examination of the environmental, entomological, and histological nature of onchocerciasis—is larded with constant commentary about racial categories, primitive nations, and backward people, as well as assurances that for "white persons . . . as already pointed out, the number of cases reported is still very small."[66]

The campaigns against onchocerciasis continued, directed by the DGSP and bolstered by the PASB and SCISP, which provided mobile health units to support "sanitary brigades."[67] In January 1945, the month of the bad news about the high Pacific coast infection rates, the US Army Institute of Pathology established an onchocerciasis laboratory in Guatemala supported by the OCIAA and SCISP.[68] The PASB and DGSP installed an experimental center in Yepocapa, Chimaltenango. The newly founded Instituto Indigenista Nacional de Guatemala (Guatemalan National Indian Institute; IING) distributed some materials on onchocerciasis through the *misiones ambulantes* (mobile missions) to indigenous communities.

And the line separating attempts to try new, often damaging and painful treatments and medical experimentation remained blurry. Public health officials had high hopes that DDT would reduce the disease's vectors, and, beginning in 1945, the DDT was experimentally used in Guatemala by the PASB, but with limited results.[69] In 1947, doctors tried creosote both topically and by injection (again painfully) into patients' cysts—without benefit. They introduced diethylcarbamazine, a treatment strategy that took many years and inflicted serious secondary effects on patients.[70] It would be decades before an effective, and mercifully painless, treatment would be developed for onchocerciasis: Ivermectin, an antiparasitic medication taken orally twice a year for several years, developed by Merck and Co. Merck has provided the drug free of charge worldwide since 1987. In July 2016, Guatemala became the fourth country in the world after Colombia (2013), Ecuador (2014), and Mexico (2015) to be verified free of onchocerciasis, 101 years after Robles's discovery.[71]

Those Cigarettes and Bars of Soap

The US-controlled inter-American public health networks in Guatemala that Arévalo depended upon, particularly the onchocerciasis campaigns, made possible the US STD study, but also the national security- and race-inflected ideologies of Arévalo's and the United States' public health interests. In terms of personnel, there was considerable overlap between the two diseases, including the OCIAA's Nelson Rockefeller and the PASB's director Fred L. Soper.[72] Dr. John C. Cutler, who led the STD study in Guatemala, cited the work of George C. Shattuck, the Harvard tropical medicine specialist who oversaw Strong's early work on onchocerciasis; conducted a medical survey of Guatemala, including of onchocerciasis in 1932; and focused on STDs.[73] John Murdock, a PASB subdirector, helped set up the first regional public health organizations, worked with Carlos Estévez and Francisco Díaz on the onchocerciasis campaigns, and arranged the transfer of the US PHS Venereal Disease Research Laboratory (VDRL) labs in Guatemala over to the Guatemalan government.[74] Luis Galich, Arévalo's DGSP director, directly oversaw the inter-American cooperation with the STD and onchocerciasis studies.[75]

The PASB's Caribbean sector chief based in Guatemala, Dr. Joseph Spoto, proved the most direct and influential connection. Spoto, a respected onchocerciasis researcher,[76] commissioned other onchocerciasis researchers (including William Clark and ethnographers).[77] From 1946 to 1948, he was the assistant chief of the US PHS Venereal Disease Division, serving in Guatemala and in the United States; he had worked previously on STD control at the US-Mexican border.

Cutler's supervisor, John F. Mahoney, asked Spoto to help arrange for the study, writing Cutler that he had "the highest regard for [Spoto's] judgement and ability."[78] Spoto introduced Cutler to Guatemalan officials in public health, the military, and interior ministry.[79] But his impact went far beyond introductions. He directly shaped the VDRL study's design regarding the various Guatemalan "races," informed consent, and choice of research subjects. When Cutler expressed his frustration with the "Indian" prisoners, writing, "The Indians had . . . very widespread prejudices against frequent withdrawals of blood. . . . uneducated and superstitious," Spoto advised Cutler not to confuse the "Indians" by providing them explanations. He recommended compensating prisoners with a pack of cigarettes, soap—or nothing.[80] Spoto identified other "Indian" subjects for the study, namely, those among the children of the Totonicapán orphanages.[81]

It is less clear how directly onchocerciasis affected the way Cutler and others "raced" the Guatemalan STD studies and how the "Indian" subjects were viewed, treated, and coerced by the STD researchers. Cutler, for example, accepted Spoto's advice about the compensation, though he had budgeted for much more compensation.[82] Cutler wanted to work with "pure" Indians; he hoped that the Carnegie Institute would arrange a highlands site for him (their is no indication that that happened). He asserted that the study subjects were "Indian" ("85% . . . with pure Indian features indicating no mixture [with other races]").[83] Did he use Guatemalan standards to assess Indian features? He apparently did not consult the IING.[84]

Both the Arévalo-era typhus and onchocerciasis campaigns demonstrate the ambivalent, contradictory, and contested racial discourses of Guatemala's public health space, which drew in multiple US and Guatemalan framings of deserving/menacing Maya and African-descended peoples. Guatemalans of the era, such as Quintana, challenged the racist ideas that onchocerciasis was an "indigenous" disease, that it did not affect "whites," that "uncooperative," "superstitious" "Indians" and African-descended people were to blame or be treated as objects.

Cutler himself both challenged and reinforced the ideology of biological race; he wanted to conduct "pure" science by working with "pure" Indians,[85] in part to overturn the theory of his boss, the US surgeon general, Thomas Parran. Parran, as well as Shattuck, held that syphilis was "biologically different" in "negros," Central American "Indians," and whites.[86] Cutler wrote in his 1955 Final Syphilis Report that there was no evidence of Indian "racial immunity" from syphilis.[87]

The inter-American scientific circles in that expansive postwar era were intimate and well networked with high-level officials and philanthropists. Borrowing Charlene Galarneau's observation of the VDRL researchers, these were small, coherent, professional networks, each with their own cultures.[88] The onchocerciasis campaigns, secretive US PHS studies, and indigenista networks were inter-American enclaves, rather like UFCO banana plantations, patrias chicas, perhaps even cysts, in which racisms and reciprocities entangled.

In these circles, Guatemalans such as Robles and Pacheco Luna entered the vanguard of international biomedical research. The vanguard was where Arévalo wanted to move Guatemala.

Arévalo's rhetoric on health care for all soared higher than his actual achievements. As he ended his term in 1951, the World Bank reported the atrocious state of Guatemalan public health, where "malaria, intestinal parasites, tuberculosis, filariasis [onchocerciasis], malnutrition and unsanitary dwellings are still sapping the energy of vast numbers of Guatemalans and reducing their capacity."[89] The PASB called out Guatemala for spending a mere 2 percent of its national budget on public health in comparison to the other Latin American countries, which spent from 4 percent to 12 percent.[90] Today, the "secret" STD experiments are remembered, rather than the successful eradication of typhus. No amount of soap will clean that stain.

The physical brutality endured by the STD Guatemalan research subjects resonates with the painful interventions inflicted on onchocerciasis sufferers for decades, known as therapeutic experimentation. The connection is speculative, but the horror inflicted by the Guatemalan studies is not: the dehumanizing voyeurism, cutting, abrasions, injections, blood draws, and repeated spinal taps. Penicillin was available as a painless, effective cure for STDs but withheld from most of the infected subjects, including the prostitutes.[91] As Diane M. Nelson observed regarding the end of "la violencia,"[92] Guatemala's 1944 democratic revolution was not a "single cut" to end the physical brutality exercised on Indian bodies, including that of medical experimentation and treatment.

Notes

This chapter is part of a larger comparative research project on the different socio-politico-medical framings, organizations, and handlings of onchocerciasis in Mexico and Guatemala, in which each country's indigenista and public health movements interacted with racialized nationalisms before and during the Cold War. This work is an outcome of the RE INTERINDI research project "The Other Sides of *Indigenismo*: A Socio-Historical Approach to Ethnic and Racial Categories and their Uses in Latin American Societies" (HAR2013-41596-P), financed by Spanish MINECO and directed by Dr. Giraudo, the founder of the INTERINDI Network (www.interindi.net). In researching the primary sources for this chapter, Dr. Giraudo consulted the archives of the Archivo Histórico del Instituto Indigenista Interamericano

(Inter-American Indian Institute; AHIII), now at the PUIC-UNAM's Centro de Documentación Manuel Gamio), and the Archivo Histórico de la Secretaría de Salubridad y Asistencia (Mexican Health Secretary; AHSSA), both located in Mexico City; Dr. Adams consulted the archives of the Centro de Investigaciones Regionales de Mesoamérica (Center of Mesoamerican Regional Research; CIRMA), located in Antigua Guatemala. We would like to thank Angélica Caal for her supporting work in the CIRMA and other Guatemalan archives.

1. PCSBI, *"Ethically Impossible": STD Research in Guatemala from 1946 to 1948* (Washington, DC: PCSBI, 2011), 54. The study's follow-up continued through 1953.

2. PCSBI, *"Ethically Impossible,"* 2–3; Susan M. Reverby, "'Normal Exposure' and Inoculation Syphilis: A PHS 'Tuskegee' Doctor in Guatemala, 1946–1948," *Journal of Policy History* 23, no. 1 (2011): 6–28. The time that elapsed before Reverby's work actually caught someone's attention is stunning. She first presented her findings at a January 2010 conference, but "no one took notice," according to Donald G. MacNeil Jr. ("Syphilis Tests in Guatemala," *New York Times*, October 1, 2010). Only when she sent an article about the findings in June 2010 to the *Journal of Policy History* did a review editor, a former Center for Disease Control and Prevention director, urge her to contact the US government.

3. Rafael Espada, *Consentir el daño: Experimentos médicos de Estados Unidos en Guatemala, 1946–1948* (Guatemala City: Comisión Presidencial para el Esclarecimiento de los Experimentos Practicados con Humanos en Guatemala, 2011), 41.

4. Espada, *Consentir el daño*, 12n2.

5. PCSBI, *"Ethically Impossible,"* 106; Espada, *Consentir el daño*, 41.

6. PCSBI, *"Ethically Impossible,"* 106.

7. Dr. Juan Funes, a Guatemalan physician and public health official directing Guatemala's STD programs, with the support of the Rockefeller Foundation. Funes was a fellow of the Office of the Coordinator of Inter-American Affairs (OCIAA) during 1945 at the US PHS Venereal Disease Research Laboratory (VDRL) in Staten Island. The VDRL, founded in 1927, carried out the Tuskegee Study. During World War II, funding by the US government for STD research expanded, as a matter of national security because of STDs' impact on soldiers (PCSBI, *"Ethically Impossible,"* 12). Researchers at the VDRL failed to actively infect human subjects between 1943 and 1944, at the US Penitentiary in Terre Haute, Indiana (ibid., 15–16). Funes suggested trying "normal exposure" through unprotected sexual intercourse with infected Guatemalan prostitutes. Working through the PASB and funded by the VDRL and NIH, Dr. John C. Cutler headed the study in Guatemala, from July 1946 to December 1948. The PASB built, supplied, and later donated an STD research laboratory in Guatemala City; paid for travel; and negotiated agreements for research work with Guatemalan officials and institutions. Guatemala's government funded some staff and supplied facilities such as public health STD treatment centers, government hospitals, military medical installations, orphanages, insane asylums, and the penal system. The studies "involved the intentional exposure to STDs of 1,308 research subjects from three populations: prisoners, soldiers, and psychiatric patients. . . . the researchers documented some form of treatment for 678 subjects. Commercial sex workers, in most cases also intentionally infected with STDs, were used to transmit disease. In addition, . . . the researchers conducted diagnostic testing of 5,128 subjects including soldiers, prisoners, psychiatric patients, children, leprosy patients,

and Air Force personnel at the US base in Guatemala. This diagnostic testing, which included blood draws as well as spinal punctures, continued through 1953" (PCSBI *"Ethically Impossible,"* 5–7).

8. Espada, *Consentir el daño*, 41–43.

9. Matthew Walter, "Human Experiments: First, Do Harm," *Nature* 482, no. 7384 (2012): 150.

10. J. T. Way, *The Mayan in the Mall: Globalization, Development, and the Making of Modern Guatemala* (Durham, NC: Duke University Press, 2012), 42.

11. Jim Handy, *Revolution in the Countryside: Rural Conflict and Agrarian Reform in Guatemala, 1944–1954* (Chapel Hill: University of North Carolina Press, 1994), 66.

12. *Juan José Arévalo*, "Inaugural Speech," in *Escritos políticos y discursos*, 15–20 (Havana: Cultural, 1953).

13. Adams, "Antonio Goubaud Carrera: Between the contradictions of the Generación de 1920, and American anthropology," in *After the Coup: An Ethnographic Reframing of Guatemala 1954*, ed. Timothy J. Smith and Abigail E. Adams, 17–48 (Urbana: University of Illinois Press, 2011).

14. Lydia Crafts, "Sanitizing Interventions: PHS VD Research in Guatemala and the Rise of International Health" (MA thesis, University of Texas at Austin, 2012); Lydia Crafts, "Experimenting on Guatemala," NACLA, August 15, 2016, https://nacla.org/news/2016/08/15/experimenting-guatemala.

15. Bolivar Lloyd, "The Pan American Sanitary Bureau," *American Journal of Public Health and the Nation's Health* 20, no. 9 (September 1930): 925–929; Marcos Cueto, *The Value of Health: A History of the Pan American Health Organization* (Washington, DC, 2006); Marcos Cueto and Steven Palmer, *Medicine and Public Health in Latin America: A History* (New York: Cambridge University Press, 2015), 77.

16. Marcos Cueto, *Missionaries of Science: Latin America and the Rockefeller Foundation* (Bloomington: Indiana University Press, 1994); John Farley, *To Cast Out Disease: A History of the International Health Division of the Rockefeller Foundation, 1913–1951* (Oxford: Oxford University Press, 2003); Stephen Palmer, *Launching Global Health: The Caribbean Odyssey of the Rockefeller Foundation* (Ann Arbor: University of Michigan Press, 2010); Gisela Cramer and Ursula Prutsch, eds., *¡Américas unidas! Nelson A. Rockefeller's Office of Inter-American Affairs (1940–46)* (Madrid: Iberoamericana, 2012).

17. Marcos Cueto, "International Health, the Early Cold War and Latin America," *Canadian Bulletin of Medical History* 25, no. 1 (2008): 17–41.

18. Robert N. Proctor, *Golden Holocaust: Origins of the Cigarette Catastrophe and the Case for Abolition* (Chicago: University of Chicago Press, 2011), 1.

19. J. O'Neill, "On the Presence of a Filaria in 'Crawcraw,'" *Lancet* 1 (1875): 265–266; Patrick Manson, "Filaria volvuloxus," in *Hygiene and Diseases of Warm Climates*, ed. A. H. Davidson, 1016 (London: Pentland, 1893).

20. Rodolfo Robles (through Dr. Eduardo Aguirre Velasquez), "Una nueva enfermedad ha sido diagnosticada en Guatemala," *La República*, December 29, 1916. Horacio Figueroa Marroquín, Robles's biographer, describes the newspaper article as the first scientific report by Dr. Robles to the medical community. See Horacio Figueroa Marroquín, "The Discovery of Robles Disease," *Tropical Medicine and Health* 43, supplement (2015): 7.

21. Rafael Pacheco Luna, "Disturbances of Vision in Patients Harbouring Certain Filaria Tumours," *American Journal of Ophthalmology* (February 1918): 122–125.

22. Miguel E. Bustamante, "Probable existencia de la Oncocercosis en Chiapas," *Gaceta Médica de México* 66 (1925); 496–501; José E. Larumbe, "La oncocercosis en Oaxaca," Academia Nacional de Medicina de México, December 1926 (republished in *Gaceta Médica de México* 58, no. 9 [1927]: 606–614).

23. Hiroyuki Takaoka, "Review of the Biology and Ecology of Adult Blackflies in Relation to the Transmission of Onchocerciasis in Guatemala," *Tropical Medicine and Health* (The Japanese Society of Tropical Medicine) 43, supplement (2015): 72.

24. Frank Richards Jr. et al., "One Hundred Years after Its Discovery in Guatemala by Rodolfo Robles, *Onchocerca volvulus* Transmission Has Been Eliminated from the Central Endemic Zone," *American Journal of Tropical Medicine and Hygiene* 93, no. 6 (2015): 1300.

25. Cueto and Palmer, *Medicine and Public Health*, 58–62.

26. Richards Jr. et al., "One Hundred Years After," 1300.

27. Cueto and Palmer, *Medicine and Public Health*, 81–82.

28. Robles, "Una nueva enfermedad." The patient, Ruiz Aguilar, confirmed the history of Robles's discovery: Figueroa, "The Discovery of Robles Disease," 10.

29. Richard P. Strong, "Onchocerciasis in Guatemala," *Science*, new ser., 73, no. 1900 (May 29, 1931): 593–594; Richard P. Strong et al., *Onchocerciasis: With Special Reference to the Central American Form of the Disease* (Cambridge, MA: Harvard University Press, 1934).

30. DGSP, Report sent by Dr. Ernesto Marroquín G., Dr. José N. Bernhard, and Dr. Julio Roberto Herrera S. (Filarial Section) to the Director Carlos Estévez, December 23, 1941, 2, Guatemala, Estévez, Archivo Histórico del Instituto Indigenista Interamericano (hereafter AHIII).

31. PASB, *Annual Report of the Director, 1951* (Washington, DC: PASB, 1952); William Clark, "Ocular Onchocerciasis in Guatemala: An Investigation of 1,215 Natives Infected with Onchocerca Volvulus," *Transactions of the American Ophthalmological Society* 45 (1947): 477; Jorge F. Méndez Galván and Olguín Bernal Héctor, "Oncocercosis: ¿La próxima enfermedad eliminable en México?," *Bol Med Hosp Infant Mex* 68, no. 2 (2011): 130–137.

32. DGSP, Report sent by Dr. Ernesto Marroquín G.; Francisco Peña Trejo, "Nota sobre la oncocercosis," *Boletín de la Oficina Sanitaria Panamericana* (July 1932): 711; Dampf, "La carretera Panamericana y el problema de la oncocercosis," *Boletín de la Oficina Sanitaria Panamericana* (August 1942): 757.

33. Miguel E. Bustamante, "Probable existencia de la Oncocercosis en Chiapas," *Gaceta Médica de México* 66 (1925): 501.

34. Horacio Figueroa Marroquín, "The Discovery of Robles Disease," 10.

35. Clark, "Ocular Onchocerciasis in Guatemala," 462.

36. Cueto and Palmer, *Medicine and Public Health*, 67–68.

37. David Carey Jr., *Our Elders Teach Us: Maya-Kaqchikel Historical Perspectives. Xkib'ij kan qate' qatata'* (Tuscaloosa: University of Alabama Press, 2001), 125.

38. Alfonso Dampf, "La oncocercosis como problema interamericano de los indígenas" (paper, biological section, First Conference of Indian Life [Primer Congreso Indigenista Interamericano], Pátzcuaro, Mexico, April 1940).

39. Herón Barragán Callejas, "La Oncocercosis en Chiapas" (BA thesis Universidad Nacional Autónoma, Facultad de Medicina, Mexico City, 1932).

40. Raphael Silva, "Ocular onchocerciasis," *Southern Medical Journal* 25, no. 2 (1932): 113–117.

41. Francisco Peña Trejo, "Nota sobre la oncocercosis," *Boletín de la Oficina Sanitaria Panamericana* (July 1932): 709–717.

42. Fernando Juárez Muñoz, *El indio guatemalteco: Ensayo de sociología nacionalista* (Guatemala City: Tipografía Latina, 1931), 143–144; Abigail E. Adams, "Antonio Goubaud Carrera."

43. David Vela, *El Imparcial*, May 1940.

44. Resolution XXI on the "Oncocercosis," "Acta Final del Primer Congreso Indigenista Interamericano. Pátzcuaro, Mich., México," in III, *Primer Congreso Indigenista Interamericano*, vol. 1 (Mexico City: III, 1940). Luis Figueroa Ortiz, "El aspecto social de la oncocercosis"; Dampf, "La oncocercosis"; Julio De la Fuente, "Creencias indígenas sobre la oncocercosis, al paludismo y otras enfermedades." The three papers were presented at the biological section, First Conference of Indian Life (Primer Congreso Indigenista Interamericano), and published in III, *Primer Congreso Indigenista Interamericano*, vol. 5 (Mexico City: III, 1940).

45. Dampf, "La carretera Panamericana y el problema de la oncocercosis," 757.

46. Santiago Taurino, "Pliego de peticiones," April 6, 1940, III, *Primer Congreso.*

47. Resolution XIX on "Indigenous beliefs about diseases," "Acta Final del Primer Congreso."

48. "Acta Final del Primer Congreso."

49. George C. Dunham, "The Cooperative Health Program of the American Republics," *American Journal of Public Health and the Nation's Health* 34, no. 8 (August 1944): 817–827.

50. DGSP, Report sent by Dr. Ernesto Marroquín G.; Carlos Estévez-Emil Sady correspondence, 1941–1942; Manuel Gamio-Carlos Estévez correspondence, 1942, Guatemala, Estévez, AHIII; Manuel Gamio-Donovan correspondence, 1943–1944, Guatemala, Donovan, AHIII.

51. Dampf, "La carretera Panamericana y el problema de la oncocercosis," 757; Vela, *El Imparcial*, May 1940; Miguel Angel Asturias, *Sociología guatemalteca: El problema social del indio* (MA thesis, Guatemala City: USAC, 1923).

52. Cindy Forster, *The Time of Freedom: Campesino Workers in Guatemala's October Revolution* (Pittsburgh: University of Pittsburgh Press, 2001), 16–20.

53. Nancy Leys Stepan, *"The Hour of Eugenics": Race, Gender, and Nation in Latin America* (Ithaca, NY: Cornell University Press, 1992).

54. Adams, "Antonio Goubaud Carrera."

55. Carey Jr., *Our Elders Teach Us*, 127.

56. Richard N. Adams, *Crucifixion by Power: Essays on Guatemalan National Social Structure, 1944–1966* (Austin: University of Texas Press, 1970), 185.

57. Espada, *Consentir el daño*, 11.

58. Carey Jr., *Our Elders Teach Us*, 127–129.

59. David Carey Jr., *Engendering Mayan History: Kaqchikel Women as Agents and Conduits of the Past, 1875–1970* (New York: Routledge, 2006), 45.

60. "Informe sobre el progreso de las investigaciones de la oncocercosis," December 1943 to January 1945, 43 pages, Exp. D-1-295, AHIII.

61. Epaminondas Quintana, "Estado sanitario de Centroamérica," Comité de Relaciones Internacionales, Sesión de verano de la Universidad de California, July 8, 1944, Guatemala, Quintana, AHIII. According to the letter Quintana sent (September 4, 1944) to Manuel Gamio, the III's director, together with the transcription, his speech was organized by "Inter-American Affairs," i.e., the Institute of

Inter-American Affairs (IIAA), specifically created as a OCIAA's subsidiary corporation in charge of the health and sanitation program. The document was later (March 1945) published by the *Boletín Indigenista*, the III's newsletter.

62. Dennis Casey, "Indigenismo: The Guatemalan Experience" (PhD diss., University of Kansas, 1979), 116.

63. Quoted in Diane M. Nelson, *Reckoning: The Ends of War in Guatemala* (Durham, NC: Duke University Press, 2009), 263.

64. Rafael Pacheco Luna, "Notes on Onchocerciasis in Guatemala," *British Journal of Ophthalmology* (1946): 234–237.

65. Including H. Elishewitz, 1944–1945, H. Dalmat, 1947–1953, and L. Gibson 1948–1952; cited in Takaoka, "Review of the Biology and Ecology," 72.

66. Clark, "Ocular Onchocerciasis in Guatemala," 500.

67. Pan American Sanitary Bureau (PASB), *Annual Report of the Director. Fiscal Year 1942–1943*, Pub No. 904 (Washington, DC: PASB, April 1944), 23.

68. "Informe sobre el progreso de las investigaciones de la oncocercosis," 1945, 24.

69. The Mexicans Dr. Bustamante and Dr. Mazzotti advised against the chemical's use in Mexico, considering the Guatemalan experience. Dr. Bustamante to health secretary, June 18, 1947, SSA, Sub-A, caja 4, exp. 2, 1945–1979, Archivo Histórico de la Secretaría de Salubridad y Asistencia (hereafter AHSSA).

70. PASB, "Annual Report of the Director, 1951," 1952.

71. In 1992, the Onchocerciasis Elimination Program for the Americas (OEPA) established a permanent program in Guatemala, supported by the government of Guatemala, the Pan American Health Organization, Merck and Co., the US Centers for Disease Control and Prevention, and the Carter Center. Richards et al., "One Hundred Years After."

72. Espada, *Consentir el daño*, 5.

73. George C. Shattuck, "Syphilis and Yaws in Guatemala," in *A Medical Survey of the Republic of Guatemala*, ed. G. C. Shattuck, 142 (Washington, DC: Carnegie Institution of Washington, 1938).

74. PCSBI, "*Ethically Impossible*," 71–72.

75. Report of Dr. Martínez Báez, April 11, 1949, Sub SyA, caja 27, exp. 10, 1948–1951, AHSSA.

76. PCSBI, *"Ethically Impossible,"* 74.

77. Clark, "Ocular Onchocerciasis in Guatemala," 467.

78. John Mahoney to John Cutler, November 18, 1946. Cited in PCSBI, *"Ethically Impossible,"* 32 and 175n233.

79. PCSBI, *"Ethically Impossible,"* 30.

80. Ibid., 54.

81. Ibid., 38–40.

82. Ibid., 54.

83. Ibid., 73–74.

84. Neither we nor Susan Reverby (p.c.) have found that the IING contributed to the STD study.

85. PCSBI, *"Ethically Impossible,"* 73–74.

86. Ibid., 72; George C. Shattuck in 1938, quoted in Reverby, "'Normal Exposure,'" 11n27.

87. PCSBI, *"Ethically Impossible,"* 73–74. The Tuskegee researchers, including Cutler, also later claimed they wanted to show scientifically that syphilis was as deadly

for African Americans as it was for Caucasians. James H. Jones and Nancy M. P. King, "*Bad Blood* Thirty Years Later: A Q&A with James H. Jones," *Journal of Law, Medicine and Ethics* 40, no. 4 (2012): 867–872.

88. Charlene Galarneau, "'Ever Vigilant' in 'Ethically Impossible': Structural Injustice and Responsibility in PHS Research in Guatemala," *Hastings Center Report* 43, no. 3 (May–June 2013): 41.

89. International Bank for Reconstruction and Development, *Economic Development of Guatemala (Economic Survey Mission)* (Baltimore, MD: Johns Hopkins University Press 1951), 121.

90. Stephen M. Streeter, *Managing the Counterrevolution* (Columbus: Ohio University Press, 2000), 161.

91. Galarneau, "'Ever Vigilant,'" 36–45; Susan Reverby, "Ethical Failures and History Lessons: The U.S. Public Health Service Research Studies in Tuskegee and Guatemala," *Public Health Reviews* 34, no. 1 (2012): 3.

92. Nelson, *Reckoning*, 74.

CHAPTER 8

"Una obra revolucionaria"

Indigenismo and the Guatemalan Revolution, 1944–1954

Sarah Foss

Francisco Rodríguez Rouanet was appalled when he saw the condition of the village's wells. Dead animals and trash contaminated the water that the community had collected in deep holes during the rainy season. For months, this stagnant water served as the drinking supply for the village, and every winter, when the rains returned, the supply was replenished. This village, located outside the municipal center of San Pedro Carchá, Alta Verapaz, lacked the money to purchase a pump to access safer groundwater, and as a result, community members suffered from a host of preventable illnesses.[1] Rodríguez encountered this all-too-common scene in his work for Guatemala's newly formed Instituto Indigenista Nacional de Guatemala (National Indigenist Institute; IING).

Founded in 1945 as one of the revolutionary government's first initiatives, the IING trained Guatemalans such as Rodríguez in ethnographic methods and sent them to conduct community surveys throughout the country. The data informed government ministries about rural conditions and identified "social problems" that confronted indigenous populations.[2] Ethnographers such as Rodríguez seemed to define what they termed "social problems" as failures of the state to provide for citizens' basic needs, for example, access to safe drinking water. Concerned that his reports fell on deaf ears, Rodríguez bottled a sample of the village's water and delivered it personally to the Ministry of Public Health. After examining the water and confirming its high level of contamination, the ministry financed and built a well with a pump in this village. From then on, the community had access to an adequate supply of potable water. When interviewed sixty years later, Rodríguez still proudly recalled the appreciation that the village had for his role in bringing attention to this critical issue.[3]

Through the IING, both the institutional staff and their host communities came to understand and participate in the 1944–1954 Revolution. The revolutionary mythos of this important institute held that the state should first carefully study and diagnose problems, then positively intervene in rural areas to improve the health and welfare of all Guatemalans. The IING effectively bridged centuries of distance as ethnographers produced reports about these locales in order to advise politicians based in Guatemala City on how to best implement the revolution's vision for the nation into these rural regions. The revolutionary government's efforts to study and classify the indigenous population reveal the tendency toward an ordering of society based not on local knowledge but rather on scientific, technocratic guidelines, the very definition of what James C. Scott has termed a "high modernist" ideology.[4]

This chapter explores how the IING helped revolutionary state-builders rethink their relationship to the indigenous population, as these ethnographers positioned themselves as representatives of indigenous communities and culture through the authority that the state granted to the IING. Their work was complex, as the ethnographers experienced meaningful work that they pursued at personal cost. At the same time, by using ladinos and indigenous elite as ethnographers, the IING reinforced existing social hierarchies. For the revolutionary leadership, what it called the "Indian Question" was part of the larger nation-building problem. Just as the state created new relationships with other actors, such as workers and students, it also reconstructed its relationship to indigenous citizens, positioning them as a vital part of the national imaginary and of national progress. Through the IING, the revolutionary government crafted programs in an imperfect, and at times highly problematic, attempt to create a more equitable, inclusive society. While the revolutionary government in some ways accomplished this vision, it also put in place a modernizing project that was top-down and centralized, giving little space to alternate ideas of modernity. The IING officially abandoned any biological understandings of race, but in positioning itself as the producers of expert knowledge about indigeneity, it reinforced the paternalism that the state had long expressed toward indigenous communities.

Until recently, little serious scholarly inquiry into the history of *indigenismo* existed, as many scholars simply dismissed it as a neocolonial and paternalistic project, taking the analysis no further than this oversimplified categorization. Recently, there have been efforts to revise this previously predominant interpretation of indigenismo, and while these efforts do not ignore its problems, they also consider it as an important idea within a specific historical context.[5] In the literature on Guatemala, scholars have often limited their discussion of indigenismo to the 1930s or only mention the contradictions in *indigenista* politics without centering it as the subject of their investigation.[6] Other scholarship, including González Ponciano, chapter 5, and Adams and Giraudo, chapter 7 in this volume, specifically examines Guatemalan indigenismo, making clear the important connection between indigenista discourse and the racialization of class, exploring public health initiatives, presenting fascinating histories of key indigenista figures such as Antonio Goubaud Carrera, or elucidating the neoimperialist interactions between Guatemalan and US anthropologists.[7] Yet no scholarship has focused on the IING or on the individual histories of IING staff, the very people positioned as the expert voice on Indian affairs. In analyzing these histories, this chapter reveals the personal lived experiences and interpretations of revolutionary indigenismo and the historical meanings that it acquired.

The IING hired both ladino and indigenous staff, and it was these low-level bureaucrats who put into practice the revolutionary ideas for the IING. Both written and oral archives indicate that these individuals did not frame their work as fitting within a high modernist agenda or as perpetuating forms of colonialism and cultural racism. Instead, these ethnographers proudly claimed that their work greatly assisted their fellow citizens. Rather than seek to prove one of these perspectives right, and the other wrong, I follow James Ferguson's lead by studying the social consequences of ideas and seeking to understand how the "dominant problematic work[s] in practice." For the purposes of this volume, I interrogate the historical significance of the idea of indigenismo within the context of the Guatemalan Revolution, working to understand the multiple and intersecting historical meanings attributed to this idea and the ways in which IING staff exercised their own agency in putting the revolution into practice.[8]

Inter-American Indigenismo and the Guatemalan Revolution

At the 1938 Pan-American Conference in Lima, Peru, delegates revealed their preoccupation with the hemisphere's Indians in their thirteenth resolution. Calling for a conference to explicitly address the social and economic problems facing the region's indigenous populations, and notably identifying these populations as full citizens, delegates from throughout the Americas suggested that an Inter-American Indian Institute (III) would be a valuable resource. Finally, an III conference took place in April 1940, in Pátzcuaro, Mexico.[9] Although Guatemala did not send an official delegation, two Guatemalans, the lawyer and journalist David Vela and the Guatemalan consul to Mexico Carlos Girón Cerna, unofficially attended the Pátzcuaro meeting.[10] The resulting acts that the delegates discussed and wrote reflected their nationalist tendencies to integrate their indigenous populations more fully into the nation with the goals of building cohesion and also drawing these populations more directly into the national economy. At the same time, delegates believed that the III would foster important Pan-American collaboration that would strengthen hemispheric security during World War II.[11]

For member nations of the III, and specifically in Mexico and Peru, indigenismo had been gaining prominence as an important tool of nation building and social engineering. In particular, two scholars highlight how the intellectual transitions illustrated at the Pátzcuaro meeting had been influencing national politics. Alexander Dawson argues that postrevolutionary Mexican indigenistas no longer viewed "backwardness" as determined by a biological understanding of race. Instead, they identified structural, socioeconomic factors as the reason for the poverty they saw in rural indigenous regions, cementing the relationship between indigenista discourse and state development projects. Thus, development served as a tidy solution, at once addressing these issues and furthering the nation-building agenda of the Lázaro Cárdenas government.[12] Marisol de la Cadena's work on identity politics in Cuzco, Peru, emphasizes a local variety of indigenismo that framed "backwardness" in cultural, not biological, terms and focused on the acquisition of decency as the solution to this "problem."[13] Clearly, various versions of indigenismo existed simultaneously, and the official version was often appropriated at the local level or at the individual level to take on very different, highly contextualized meanings. Yet this focus on the cultural politics of indigenismo relegates the unequal access to resources and opportunities that prevented this acquisition of symbolic capital to the background.

As in Peru and Mexico, in Guatemala the struggle to define "the Indian" was part of the struggle to conceptualize the good citizen, and in the process new categories of a racialized social identity emerged, ones that did not neatly fit within the preexisting *Indian-ladino* divide. Indigenismo worked to create certain kinds of citizens, creating what María Josefina Saldaña-Portillo calls the "two new manifest subjects . . . the modern, fully developed subject and its premodern, underdeveloped counterpart."[14] The IING employees were instrumental in helping the state categorize its citizens as modern or premodern Indians. Ethnographers studied this "premodern, underdeveloped" Indian and, based on their acquired knowledge, designed solutions to transform this population into "modern, fully developed" citizens. Like Dawson's historical subjects, they also identified state-sponsored development projects as solutions for socioeconomic issues, and like the *cusqueño* elite, their individual interpretations of indigenismo at times challenged the institutional definition, thus complicating how we understand the state's relationship to the indigenous population during the Revolution. Staff of the IING reframed what contemporaries termed the "Indian problem" in a way that cast it as a problem not with the presence of indigenous people but with how the state understood and interacted with these populations. While the staff remember their work as how they exercised their patriotic duties to bring equal access to resources and extend citizenship ties across Guatemala, their work reinforced neocolonial relationships that continued existing, even under the guise of democratic revolution.

"A teacher always had power there": Intellectual Networks in the IING

When Juan José Arévalo Bermejo was elected to the presidency in late 1944, Guatemalan anthropologist Antonio Goubaud Carrera returned to the capital from fieldwork and began petitioning the new president to create Guatemala's own Indian institute and join the Inter-American Indian Institute. Goubaud was well connected in this Inter-American indigenista network, as he had received a master's degree from the University of Chicago in 1943, where he studied under the US anthropologists Sol Tax and Robert Redfield.[15] In chapter 5 in this volume and elsewhere, González Ponciano details the preoccupation that Tax and Redfield had with folk cultures and development efforts, and he traces how Redfield's advocacy for modernization via applied anthropology reflected US foreign policy goals of bringing economic stability and security to the hemisphere.[16] However, Tax, although Redfield's colleague, did not share this optimism about applied anthropology, instead proposing an alternative that mandated agency for anthropological subjects. Tax did not coin the term until 1951, but his ten years of experience in Guatemala shaped his critique of applied anthropology and the distinction he made between it and action anthropology. For Tax, applied anthropology was a top-down project that reinforced state policies of assimilation, giving communities little to no voice. In contrast, action anthropology called for the creation of knowledge through active collaboration with communities, not the application of broad, abstract theories to specific locales.[17] Tax's philosophy shaped how Chicago-trained

Guatemalan anthropologists such as Goubaud would utilize development projects as part of their anthropological investigations and specifically in structuring the IING. Thus, while at Chicago, Goubaud would have been exposed to both of these philosophies of anthropology and likely brought elements from both tendencies to shape his own viewpoints about how the discipline could influence the Guatemalan Revolution.

Shortly after taking office, President Arévalo asked Goubaud to draft a resolution that would create a Guatemalan Bureau of Indian Affairs.[18] Goubaud did just that, and in early 1945 he wrote to his Chicago advisors that Arévalo had agreed to create an Indian Institute, even quoting the president as having stated, "Truly this department is of tremendous significance for Guatemala, and it will have to provide scientific data concerning the Indian population on all phases of government, education, the army, public health, economics, social organization."[19]

On August 28, 1945, by presidential decree, the Guatemalan government created the IING.[20] The IING's statutes confirmed that the institute would be a collaborative and technical institute with a central mission of "elevat[ing] the cultural, social, and economic levels of indigenous groups." To do so, the IING would conduct some studies that would be immediately applicable and others that would expand Guatemalans' knowledge of the country's indigenous population.[21] When Guatemala's minister of education, Manuel Galich, publicly announced the IING's creation at its inauguration, he stated that he did not "fear hyperbole" in referring to the institute's foundation as "una obra revolucionaria" (a revolutionary work) because the government was finally taking seriously the challenges confronting the majority of Guatemala's indigenous population.[22]

Unsurprisingly, Goubaud was named director, and Tax wrote that he and Redfield were "pleased as punch" and that the institute "will have one of the most important functions of any branch of government."[23] Goubaud and Rodríguez were two of the IING's first employees, where they met for the first time. Unlike Goubaud, Rodríguez had no prior training in ethnography or anthropology; prior to the revolution he had worked as a bartender at a restaurant on the Sexta Avenida in downtown Guatemala City. Through a familial connection with Galich, Rodríguez obtained a job in the fieldwork division of the IING.[24] Influenced by the suggestion of Redfield, Goubaud decided that hiring indigenous schoolteachers as ethnographers for the fieldwork division would help facilitate more effective research, as these men would have the language and cultural skills needed to communicate with host communities. Almost immediately,

Goubaud hired and trained Rosalio Saquic (hometown: Santa Lucía Utatlán and Nahualá, language: K'iche'), Luis Felipe Utrilla (San Bernardino Suchitepéquez: K'iche'), José Botzoc (San Juan Chamelco: Q'eqchi'), and Agustín Pop (San Pedro La Laguna: Tz'utujil). After completing approximately six weeks of training with Goubaud in Guatemala City, the men returned to their hometowns to practice interviewing informants, mapping communities, recording family census cards and genealogies, and keeping a fieldwork diary.[25] Soon after, the IING hired additional fieldwork staff, including Martín Ordóñez (Sololá, Kaqchikel), Hipólito Menchú (San Cristóbal Totonicapán, K'iche'), Ricardo Ixcol (San José Chacayá, K'iche'), and Pablo Morales Alonzo (San Juan Ostuncalco, Mam).[26] Finally, in 1951, Hélida Esther Cabrera, a bilingual *ladina* fluent in Spanish and Tz'utujil, became the first (and only) female ethnographer, and she was the one ethnographer besides Rodríguez who was not a schoolteacher. These individuals, with their own vested interests and perspectives, constituted the IING during the revolution.[27]

The ethnographers came from rural families, which made it easier for them to understand local rural conditions. For example, Ordóñez's mother raised pigs and sold sausages and other pork products, Saquic came from a family of farmers, and Pop's family worked as fishermen. Receiving a daily stipend of three quetzals while traveling outside of their home communities and an annual salary of eight hundred quetzals, these men and one woman received training and gradually learned how to conduct ethnographic research and write monographs. The ethnographers mainly worked in towns near their home that spoke the same language, attending meetings at the central office in Guatemala City only occasionally. They regularly sent reports to the office on a wide range of topics, including agriculture, religion, daily life, and social relations.[28] By 1946, the IING was fully functioning and working toward completing its mission of researching and producing knowledge about Guatemala's diverse population.

As schoolteachers, these men likely enjoyed a relatively elite position in their hometowns, as they had a salaried job, were bilingual in Spanish and a Mayan language, and had basic literacy skills. The IING recognized that all of these men, in the words of Rodríguez, "as teachers, had local leadership, at least within their community, for no matter how small the community was, a teacher always had power there." Thus, these ethnographers, with the exception of Cabrera and Rodríguez, would have been positioned as indigenous intermediary figures who were responsible for creating representations of indigenous towns and people.[29] Cabrera, on the other hand, came from a prominent ladino family in Santiago Atitlán, though the absence of her father made her family's economic situation more precarious than in past generations. Nevertheless, as a ladina from a formerly elite family, she still enjoyed a privileged status in her hometown. Rodríguez was from Guatemala City, and he quickly was promoted to fieldwork director, so he rarely conducted ethnographic research on his own. Thus for all the ethnographers, their work at the IING permitted them to guide the way in which the state would think about indigeneity and the problems confronting indigenous communities. They at once participated in the state's modernizing project in the countryside while also attempting to mitigate what they believed to be negative associations and actions directed at these populations.

While official institutional positions leave a deeper archival trace, it was individuals who shaped the work of the institute. Through their work, they held the power to shape policy, but they could also refuse to practice certain procedures or could half-heartedly implement aspects of IING programs that they found to be problematic. Analyzing the historical importance of the IING during Guatemala's Revolution from both an institutional and an individual perspective allows for moving beyond simplified explanations of the IING's efficacy. Instead, moving between these two scales of analysis permits an exploration of how the high modernist agenda of the IING had various individual interpretations, even among those tasked with implementing it throughout the countryside.

In 2015, the two living members of the IING from the revolutionary period, Rodríguez and Cabrera, shared their memories of their work with me. Both were ninety-four at the time, and both claim that their work with the IING was the most meaningful work in which they ever engaged. While sipping sweet coffee out of china cups that once belonged to Justo Rufino Barrios's wife, Rodríguez recounted that his career at the IING began in order to support his growing family, but that very quickly he realized the IING provided a means for him to make a positive contribution to his society. Rodríguez always maintained that the IING served as a liaison with the state, and through examples such as this chapter's opening anecdote, he explained how rural communities gained access to important resources via IING intermediation on their behalf.

Cabrera worked for the IING for only five years, yet she identifies this period as life defining. The IING position was Cabrera's first job and her opportunity to move from her home of Santiago Atitlán to the capital and gain economic independence from her family. Few women had the opportunity to work as equals alongside men and travel throughout the country, she explained, as she proudly told of befriending her informants and continuing to correspond with them long after her scheduled fieldwork visits. When I visited her in Santiago Atitlán in 2015, the few IING publications that she still owned were carefully guarded in an antique armoire. With tears in her eyes, she repeatedly lamented that her late husband burned all of her *diarios de campo* out of his jealousy over her having held a prestigious governmental posting. On one occasion, she angrily pointed to his framed photograph, which hung on the wall in her dining room and, addressing him directly, cried out that she could forgive his affairs, she could forgive his selfishness, but she could never forgive him for burning her fieldwork diaries. These diaries, for Cabrera, represented how she had made a positive contribution to her society and gave her a feeling of great importance and satisfaction in the work she had recorded within their pages.

Neither Rodríguez nor Cabrera interpreted their work as part of the state's modernization project, nor did they see any inherent racism or paternalism in their work. Rather, they occupied the position of trustee, concerned with the desire to improve the conditions under which their fellow citizens lived. Tania Murray Li defines the central goal of trusteeship, arguing that it "is not to dominate others—it is to enhance their capacity for action, and to direct it."[30] Benevolence motivated the IING members' action; personal sacrifice characterized their daily lives. Their experiences at the IING empowered them; for Rodríguez, the work gave him a sense of profession and a means to financially support his family, and for Cabrera the IING position allowed her to challenge gendered roles and patriarchal hierarchies.

While I do not deny their experiences or question their motivations, the very fact that they were directing the possible actions for indigenous populations to take, that they were categorizing these individuals and representing them to the central government, once again reinforces the same racial and class hierarchies in Guatemalan society. This intellectual network generated at the IING at once allowed employees to practice revolution by trying to help Guatemala's more marginalized populations. However, it failed to completely overturn paternalistic relationships that existed between Indians and ladinos and between indigenous communities and the state.

Diagnosing the "Indian Problem": IING Community Monographs

One of the most important ideas that the IING generated from its inception was a redefining of the "Indian question." Moving away from explanations that attributed contemporary problems confronting the indigenous population to the innate character of "the Indian," the IING instead identified the question as socioeconomic. Instead of blaming "the Indian" for what contemporaries termed "backwardness," the IING squarely placed the blame upon the state, arguing that the state had failed to provide for its citizens. Yet institutional policy also positioned its expert staff as the producers of knowledge regarding the Indian's wants and needs, only perpetuating the colonial relationship of the Indian subject to the king that nineteenth-century indigenous and ladino elite had maintained as they positioned themselves as civilizers of the indigenous population. Now, in the context of the revolution, this relationship was recast within a discourse about the relationship of the Indian citizen to the state. Clearly, the Arévalo government's end goal was the modernization of indigenous communities, often per the dictates of experts, not of communities themselves. Where this administration departed from previous governments in terms of state Indian policy was in recognizing people that it categorized as Indians as equally intelligent and fully capable of adopting aspects of modern life and in the process becoming important members of the nation. Absolutely paternalistic, and revealing the continued tendency to view indigenous populations as premodern, this shift in indigenista thought that the revolutionary state encompassed does demonstrate an important shift in official policy. This new approach positioned socioeconomic development, not continued exploitation or the introduction of foreign immigrants, as the solution to creating a more meaningful and more equitable relationship between these marginalized populations and the state. However, before the national government could design programs to alleviate socioeconomic problems, it first needed to become aware of local conditions, thus necessitating the need for numerous studies on all aspects of rural Indian life.

In the first year of the IING's existence, staff members dedicated themselves to creating knowledge about indigenous communities for primarily nonindigenous audiences. Using George Murdock's Cross-Cultural survey as a guide, ethnographers traveled throughout the highlands, stayed with host families, and eventually compiled their data into community monographs. Originally developed under the title "Outline of Cultural Materials," Yale University's Human Relations Area Files project used Murdock's survey to collect an abundance of cross-cultural data with the goal of standardizing the study of foreign cultures. The survey was very comprehensive; 557 questions spanned an array of topics, from religion, local political structures, childrearing, and sexuality to the acquisition of honor and respect.[31] But beyond the data that ethnographers collected, what is most important about this methodology is that it marks the professionalization of anthropological studies under the IING. In selecting the IING as the institute to scientifically collect information to guide state policies, Guatemalan policymakers revealed their profound trust in social science and in the role of experts. This decision also reinforced the coloniality of the very process of producing knowledge about Guatemalan indigenous populations. Ethnographers used this survey, created with very Western categories and from the perspective of a Western understanding of social organization, to neatly fit local indigenous cultures into this mold in order to make these populations legible to the revolutionary government and thus manageable.[32] Furthermore, allowing IING ethnographers to collect, categorize, and write reports cemented the problematic reality that the state received elite representations of indigenous populations, thus reinforcing existing hierarchies between indigenous intermediary elite figures and their towns and between ladinos and indigenous people.

However, Rodríguez and Cabrera did not view their work as further strengthening the colonial relationship that indigenous populations had with the state. Instead, they positioned themselves as learners who humbly traveled to distant communities where they sought to provide resources that, from their perspective, these communities desperately needed, again reflecting how the historical significance of the IING for the revolution was both one of empowerment and one of subjection. In each community they visited, they presented themselves to the municipal government, explaining that they were state representatives who had come to learn about local life and to inform the government of any problems the community wanted resolved. The mayor typically arranged housing for the visiting ethnographer, who usually resided in the locale for one week. Living conditions varied in each town; Cabrera recalled sleeping in corn troughs and on the floor of the municipal government or the local school, and even hanging her hammock in trees. As she related to me, "To tell you the truth, for me it was very exciting to sleep in the trees like Tarzan!"[33] Visiting various families in each town to get an array of perspectives and responses, Cabrera spent a few hours with each informant, casually covering the themes in the guide.[34]

After completing the surveys, the researcher compiled a report that not only contained ethnographic data based on the surveys but also made suggestions to various government ministries about what kinds of needs the community had. Rodríguez recalled reporting a lack of roads, high levels of disease, and the absence of drinking water, as described in the opening anecdote. The IING never formally published the majority of these reports, and when the archive was destroyed with the closing of the institute in 1986, this fascinating data was lost, for which Rodríguez "cries tears of blood." Thus it is impossible to know how many communities were surveyed; Rodríguez estimated that when he left the IING in 1975, he and his colleagues had surveyed over 150 communities.[35]

About ten community monographs were published in the IING's first decade, including one written by ethnographers Agustín Pop and Simón Otzoy. In December 1946, Pop, a Tz'utujil Maya from San Pedro La Laguna, and Otzoy, a Kaqchikel Maya from Tecpán, spent eight days in San Bartolomé Milpas Altas as IING ethnographers. This was not the first study or monograph that either man had written, and like the other studies in the series, the San Bartolomé monograph rigorously followed the standard format, touching upon many diverse subjects and carefully elaborating upon those that the IING deemed particularly important and necessary to report to government ministries. While the historical record does not reveal exactly how these monographs were used, the information regarding community centers, local resources, and social organizations did permit the Arévalo government to extend its gaze into these communities. Rodríguez recalled that employees from state ministries and members of the national university frequently visited the IING's library to consult these studies, gathering the information necessary to justify their projects and programs for the countryside.

Also notable is how these monographs were produced. As mentioned, the majority of the IING's ethnographers were Maya, and it was they who created this new knowledge about these communities. Yet in doing so, they fully relied on the information that their informants provided. Thus, informants could choose what to divulge about their communities, and this information was included or omitted, and categorized, according to the ethnographer's discretion. While the final monographs were intended to enhance and streamline governance in the countryside, and the design of the research was inherently colonial, the very process by which these monographs were produced did afford Maya informants and ethnographers the power to determine what to include and how to include it.

Pop and Otzoy's fifty-nine-page monograph opens with a detailed map of San Bartolomé Milpas Altas. The gridlike streets present a sense of order to the community, and a detailed key explains the numbers and abbreviations used to designate schools, governance buildings, churches, and stores. Emphasis is placed on roads and infrastructure with no attention given to natural geography or landmarks, demonstrating an understanding of space as man-made and relatively recently constructed. Without infrastructure, space appears blank on the white page, void of meaning and civilization.[36]

In the pages that follow, Pop and Otzoy explored several themes of San Bartolomé's community life, including local economy, infrastructure, political and religious hierarchies, and integration with the nation. In this predominantly Kaqchikel community of 1240 people, the ethnographers relied on nineteen informants' testimonies to shape their information. While the authors preserved the confidentiality of their informants' names to some extent, they did identify each person by initial and a series of characteristics, including age, ethnicity (indígena or ladino), marital status (single, married—with distinctions between common-law, civil, and/or ecclesiastical—and widowed), occupation, and literacy status. Of the nineteen informants, all were male, were indigenous, and were or had been married. Only three were illiterate, and the average age was 54.89 years.[37] Pop and Otzoy reported that the municipality's entire population was urban.[38] While possible, it is highly unlikely that the municipality did not have rural villages surrounding the municipal center. However, for the IING, what was important to analyze was life in the main urban community, and the monograph's authors do not mention anyone or anywhere outside this discrete urban space. It is impossible to know whether this was a reflection of Pop's and Otzoy's own positions as indigenous elites who were from municipal centers or was an institutional decision to exclude these regions. What we can infer, however, is that the IING's decision to structure the final versions of the monographs in this way informed the Arévalo government's understanding that it was this population who had the potential to rapidly modernize and become contributing members of society. It was the municipal centers, therefore, where the state should focus efforts in hygiene and literacy campaigns, nutrition studies, the expansion of rural markets, and eventually, during the Arbenz administration, the structuring of the agrarian reform. In prioritizing the municipal center, the IING thus neglected the more marginalized citizens in the surrounding villages.

In discussing local power structures, the ethnographers described the content of the three town meetings held in 1946. On all three occasions, the community leaders talked about local development initiatives, such as expansion of communal pasturelands, distribution of cement tubing for piped water, and bridge repair on the main road that connected the community with the departmental capital. By emphasizing these topics, Pop and Otzoy argued that local residents were indeed concerned with what the state would perceive to be modern development initiatives, and they also emphasized that residents were not "backward" or "uncivilized" by choice but rather were constrained by their socioeconomic status.

While Pop and Otzoy had to closely abide by the structure established by the Cross-Cultural Survey, they found several occasions to draw attention to the poverty confronting San Bartolomé's indigenous residents. For example, when noting the amount of land necessary to sustain a family of five, the authors stated that while most residents did own some land, few had a sufficient amount for subsistence and thus were forced to either rent land or work as day laborers for low wages.[39] Similarly, when describing the adobe houses common to the community, the authors wrote that "most indígenas prefer sleeping in beds but lack the money to buy them."[40] The town's few ladinos all wore shoes, while the majority of Indians did not own shoes for lack of financial resources.[41] Accompanying the text is also a detailed chart of the variety of agricultural products grown in the community, debunking the misconception that indigenous people only ate corn and beans. Farmers in San Bartolomé cultivated other crops such as cabbage, cauliflower, carrots, beets, and several kinds of fruit. However, in order to supplement familial income, farmers often had to sell these products at markets in nearby Guatemala City and Antigua.[42] Thus, the authors suggested that malnutrition and a diet based on a few agricultural staples were not due to an unwillingness to cultivate alternative crops, nor were they based on an ignorance of other types of foods. Rather, they were a direct result of local socioeconomic conditions. In including these examples in their monograph, Pop and Otzoy revised popular interpretations of indigeneity that had posited that alcoholism, indolence, and ignorance were explanations for the "underdevelopment" of rural, indigenous Guatemala. Instead, these ethnographers strongly refuted these assertions and offered an alternative understanding of local problems, problems they believed to emanate from the state's failure to address the economic exploitation and unequal access to resources that indigenous communities faced.

The IING Maya ethnographers, by producing these monographs, were instrumental in transforming indigenismo from an appreciation of pre-Columbian Maya culture to a program that actively sought to remedy the neglect that contemporary indigenous communities had experienced from their government. Through presenting local problems as issues of access to resources—notably land and money—and local leaders as agents of change who collectively sought development projects for their community, the IING ethnographers challenged prevailing notions of biological inferiority and helped to reshape how the social category of "the Indian" was understood in Guatemala. They revised the idea of the indolent Indian, instead presenting engaged citizens who only needed financial resources to "improve" their lives. Likewise, this reconceptualization placed the responsibility of providing the means for this improvement upon the state, not upon indigenous populations themselves, and served to justify the state's modernization program and design of indigenous citizenship. However, even though IING staff challenged existing racialized understandings of indigeneity, this transformation of the relationship between the indigenous citizen and the state that they expressed through their work also reinforced existing ideas about the utility of a citizen, as it still largely ignored populations living outside municipal centers, rendering them incapable of participating in the nation.

Indigenismo in Action: Knowledge Production and Nutrition Campaigns

The community monographs reveal how the IING combined its scientific approach to indigenismo with practical applications and policy suggestions. The IING's primary function was to serve as an anthropological research institution, yet IING staff put their studies into practice by collaborating with other governmental and international institutions to introduce tangible changes to the countryside. These partnerships demonstrate the revolutionary government's reliance on expert, not local, opinion to diagnose and cure social problems. Recognizing that productive citizens needed to be well nourished, one of the IING's first collaborations was with the Instituto de Nutrición de Centro América y Panamá (Nutrition Institute of Central America and Panama; INCAP). Founded in 1946 at the Third Inter-American Conference on Agriculture, the INCAP was headquartered in Guatemala City and generously funded by member nations and by the Kellogg Foundation.[43] Although newspaper accounts covering the INCAP's creation describe the institution in broad humanitarian terms, its work was inherently political as well. The individuals and outside foundations who supported the INCAP wanted to continue fostering the hemispheric solidarity and security initiatives that grew out of the interwar period and the United States' Good Neighbor Policy, initiatives appropriately criticized for their neoimperialist agendas. Particularly in the late 1940s, after the conclusion of World War II and in the advent of the Cold War, inter-American cooperation was a critical component of US foreign policy toward

Latin America, and institutions such as the INCAP helped to make these political agendas more palatable by recasting them in humanitarian terms.

In 1947, the INCAP began conducting fieldwork in rural areas, many of which were overwhelmingly indigenous. The goal of this fieldwork was to collect food samples, identify dietary patterns, and collect biological specimens to be analyzed in INCAP laboratories in Guatemala City. With this research, scientists could identify deficiencies in local diets and create supplements to combat the countryside's rampant malnutrition. Creating a healthy citizenry through a defined dietary plan was a key component of Arévalo's plan to modernize Guatemala, as he believed that healthier, more energized citizens would be better workers and more positively contribute to the national economy. Yet just as the monographs both supported and challenged the high modernist project to render indigenous society legible to Guatemala City's policymakers, so too did nutrition projects yield ambivalent results.

The staff of the INCAP began data collection and medical examinations in the predominantly Kaqchikel community of Magdalena Milpas Altas (hereafter Magdalena) in May 1950. The staff members Betty Pineda, Ana Díaz, and Dr. Roberto Síndara Lacapo attempted to collect blood and fecal samples and photograph children in the nude in order to study malnutrition. As one might imagine, these children's parents were not supportive of strangers taking nude photographs of their children, nor did they trust these outsiders to run tests and collect biological samples. Obtaining blood samples also met resistance because to *magdaleños*, blood was a sacred life force. One was believed to have a determined supply of blood; thus, it was considered dangerous and foolish to take one's blood out of one's body voluntarily.[44] When INCAP nutritionists attempted to collect blood samples for analysis, locals considered this a disrespectful and violent act. Similarly, magdaleños felt that their privacy was being violated with the request to take nude photographs of their children. Particularly for indigenous magdaleños, the state had long forced them to use their bodies to provide free labor, at times even forcing them to haul heavy loads on their backs as nothing more than beasts of burden. This request to photograph their children in the nude must have added humiliation and insult to this history, literally stripping their children down to be nothing more than an object of scientific scrutiny.

Another aspect of INCAP's nutrition program in Magdalena was the school lunch project. Students received soy milk, tortillas, and avocado on

Mondays; beans on Tuesday; a salad on Wednesday; avocados on Thursday; beans on Friday; and fruit and peanuts on Sunday. Additionally, these nutrition experts taught children about personal hygiene, washing clothes, and personal discipline, using films and sound recordings to present these lessons.[45] While some students and families did participate in these studies, many residents resisted INCAP's efforts. At times this resistance was outright, with families refusing to send their children to school. As one woman explained this refusal to Ana Díaz, the foreigners "are fattening up the children and they are going to take them away."[46] Other forms of resistance were less overt, and one common tactic was the refusal to eat the lunches. Pineda recounts how one Kaqchikel girl, Agripina, often cried and ran home during lunchtime, with the explanation that she had plenty of food at home. Another group of girls refused to eat because they said that the soy milk upset their stomachs. One boy, Alfonso, also refused to eat because of a stomachache. Finally, several children, particularly Kaqchikel children, did not come for their free lunch during the harvest season, as they left to work in the fields at 5 a.m. and did not return until late afternoon. Despite these forms of what James Scott calls everyday resistance, the INCAP maintained a strong presence in this community for the yearlong duration of the nutrition program, yet its presence caused debate about how magdaleños should interact with these potentially dangerous foreigners.[47]

Distrust of the INCAP's motivations was clear in the refusal of students and parents to participate in the project. Families feared that these nutritionists wanted to steal their children, and they feared that outside medicine and food would bring illness and other forms of bodily harm. To help understand these cultural beliefs, the INCAP collaborated with the IING to send anthropologists and indigenous ethnographers to Magdalena to study and then devise methods for navigating different cultural beliefs and practices regarding medicine, science, and the human body. The North American anthropologist Richard Adams; his Guatemalan ladina wife, Betty; and the IING K'iche' Maya ethnographer Rosalio Saquic analyzed nutritional habits and collected samples and data.[48] These anthropologists became important intermediaries between the INCAP and Magdalena, helping to communicate the nutrition program's goals and agendas to local leaders as well as educating medical staff on local beliefs regarding medicine, food, and the body. The Adamses and Saquic lived in Magdalena for several months, spending each day conversing with residents, networking and gaining the support of key local leaders, and participating in celebrations and events. They learned about local medical practices and beliefs and communicated these to INCAP nutritionists in order to redesign experiments or incorporate more information sessions and demonstrations prior to collecting actual samples. With the trust and rapport that they were able to achieve, INCAP programs were able to be more successful in the future, though never without resistance and controversy.

The collaboration that the IING lent to the INCAP for nutrition projects reflects the transition in indigenismo to emphasize anthropological studies with immediate practical application. For indigenistas, indigenous people were not physically inferior but rather lacked the resources and the knowledge to properly nourish their bodies. The Adamses and Saquic served as crucial intermediaries, utilizing ethnography to understand local consumption patterns and beliefs and then translating this knowledge into tangible projects. Seeking to curb rural malnutrition was certainly a noble cause. Saquic, although K'iche' Maya and not Kaqchikel Maya, would have been aware of broader shared belief systems regarding the body and blood, and he did help to communicate the misunderstandings that occurred in Magdalena between residents and INCAP medical staff. While there is no evidence that the INCAP or IING staff ever forced magdaleños to participate in this project, there is also no suggestion in the historical record that they asked permission to conduct their studies in Magdalena or any indication that they ever revised their program to incorporate the suggestions of local residents.

Once again, knowledge production, in this case regarding diet, rested in the hands of state employees and nonindigenous experts. The Adamses' and Saquic's presence certainly must have helped mitigate serious points of conflict, and while they may have been able to incorporate some of the values of action anthropology through collaborating with local leaders, they failed to attribute anything beyond very limited agency to magdaleños. Through the INCAP program, the revolutionary governments allowed for the state's exertion of power over the Indian's body. In constructing this malnourished, premodern ethnic subject in need of humanitarian aid, the state assumed the role of diagnosing and curing what it perceived to be a problem via these two institutions. The knowledge that the state valued resided with formally educated experts, not with local people who had gained knowledge through lived experience. Through nutrition programs, the formal ties between experts, development, and governance continued to solidify as an important trifecta in official Indian policy.

Conclusion

One of the first acts of the revolutionary government was to create the IING. Tasked with studying indigenous communities, informing the government about daily life in these villages, and collaborating on applied projects designed to improve the socioeconomic challenges facing indigenous citizens, the IING played a critical role in the revolutionary state-building process and in producing knowledge that often served to reinforce the state's modernizing development plan. Yet at the same time as the IING participated in this process, there are instances in which staff challenged what they perceived to be misperceptions about indigenous culture or held the state accountable for not fulfilling its responsibility to meet every Guatemalan's basic needs.

IING staff and indigenista intellectuals were often well intentioned, dedicating their lives to serving their country and helping those they perceived to be less fortunate citizens. One can hardly critique Rodriguez's efforts to draw the Ministry of Health's attention toward the lack of drinking water or Saquic's efforts to change INCAP blood-draw procedures. Oral histories and written sources reveal proud memories of this service and positive relationships with their host communities; as Cabrera explained, her work at the IING was not a job but rather a vocation, one that she was still practicing in 2015 in her home in Santiago Atitlán.[49] For many IING staff, the interactions that they had with indigenous communities transformed these ethnographers' view of their society and shaped their experience of the revolution.

At the same time, IING staff reinforced existing social hierarchies that were highly racialized in Guatemala. As sources also reveal, these dedicated individuals still held personal biases and on occasion revealed moments of less overt forms of cultural prejudice, as expressed with Pop and Otzoy's exclusion of villages from the map of San Bartolomé. Through ethnographic research, the IING, an institute comprising ladinos and indigenous elite, determined who was a modern, fully developed subject and who was not. They, as outside interlocutors, depicted rural indigenous life to state ministries and helped design interventionist projects intended to improve living conditions in rural regions. Yet while reinforcing existing social hierarchies that the revolution failed to change, these individuals still challenged some prevailing notions about indigeneity and thus complicate the historical meaning of the IING and of revolutionary indigenismo.

As this chapter demonstrates, rethinking revolutionary indigenismo allows for a broader historical analysis of the revolution's nation-building project. For ten years, the IING enjoyed prestige and was able to conduct studies that had tangible outcomes designed to improve rural socioeconomic conditions, becoming an important player in the state's high modernist project. The 1954 Counterrevolution terminated these projects and largely defunded the IING, and the high modernist project, which under the revolution had sought to further democracy, became an important tool of counterinsurgency for the authoritarian counterrevolutionary state. Thus, there was no real possibility for contemporaries to analyze the experiences of the IING or to revise indigenismo, as the counterrevolutionary governments dismissed it as a dangerous remnant of the revolutionary period. Likewise, intellectuals and activists during these decades began to critique indigenismo as a neocolonialist project, effectively ignoring the complexities and ambiguities of indigenismo as a discourse and as a practice. Despite these setbacks, indigenismo was a revolutionary work that was important in its historical moment and shaped the way that Guatemalans experienced and practiced the revolution.

Notes

1. Francisco Rodríguez Rouanet, interview, Guatemala City, August 12, 2014.

2. The terms *indígena*, *Maya*, and *ladino* each have extensive histories and independent meanings attributed to each one. In this chapter, I use the terms that the historical actors under question used in the 1940 and 1950s. I translate *indígena* to "indigenous" or "Indian," and I use the term *ladino/a* to refer to a nonindigenous person.

3. Francisco Rodríguez Rouanet, interview, Guatemala City, September 8, 2015.

4. James C. Scott, *Seeing Like a State: How Certain Schemes to Improve the Human Condition Have Failed* (New Haven, CT: Yale University Press, 1998), 4.

5. See the essays in Laura Giraudo and Juan Martín-Sánchez, eds., *La ambivalente historia del indigenismo: Campo interamericano y trayectorias nacionales 1940–1970* (Lima: Instituto de Estudios Peruanos, 2011); and in *Latin American Perspectives* 39, no. 5 (September 2012) for a variety of articles discussing the theme of "Rethinking Indigenismo on the American Continent."

6. Virginia Garrard-Burnett, "Indians Are Drunks and Drunks Are Indians: Alcohol and Indigenismo in Guatemala 1890–1940," *Bulletin of Latin American Research* 19, no. 3 (July 2000): 341–356; Diane M. Nelson, *A Finger in the Wound: Body Politics in Quincentennial Guatemala* (Berkeley: University of California Press, 1999), 86–90; Arturo Taracena Arriola, *Etnicidad, estado y nación en Guatemala, 1944–1985*, vol. 2 (La Antigua, Guatemala: Centro de Investigaciones Regionales de Mesoamérica, 2004), 41–50.

7. Jorge Ramón González Ponciano, "Diez años del indigenismo en Guatemala (1944–1954)" (MA thesis, Escuela Nacional de Antropología e Historia, México, DF, 1988); Abigail E. Adams, "Antonio Goubaud Carrera: Between the Contradictions of

the Generación de 1920 and U.S. Anthropology," in *After the Coup: An Ethnographic Reframing of Guatemala 1954*, ed. A. Adams and Timothy J. Smith, 17–48 (Urbana: University of Illinois Press, 2011); Abigail E. Adams, "El indigenismo guatemalteco: Atrapado entre la promesa de interamericanismo y la guerra fría," in *La ambivalente historia del indigenismo*, 99–132; Dennis F. Casey, "Indigenismo: The Guatemalan Experience" (PhD diss., University of Kansas, 1979).

8. James Ferguson, *The Anti-Politics Machine: "Development," Depoliticization, and Bureaucratic Power in Lesotho* (Minneapolis: University of Minnesota, 1994), xiv.

9. Archivo General de Centroamérica (AGCA), Ministerio de Relaciones Exteriores, *Memoria de la Secretaría de Relaciones Exteriores del año de 1938*, 15 and 133; "Breve historial," *Boletín del Instituto Indigenista Nacional de Guatemala* 1, no. 1 (October–December 1945): 7.

10. AGCA, Ministerio de Relaciones Exteriores, *Memoria de la Secretaría de Relaciones Exteriores del Año de 1940*, 383; "Discurso del Señor Ministro de Educación Pública, Profesor Manuel Galich," *Boletín del Instituto Indigenista Nacional de Guatemala* 1, no. 1 (October–December 1945): 14. President Ubico's minister of education had reported the official rationale for not sending a delegation, insisting that Guatemala had no "Indian problem." "Breve historial," *Boletín del Instituto Indigenista Nacional de Guatemala* 1, no. 1 (October-December 1945): 8.

11. Comité Organizador del IV Congreso Indigenista Interamericano, Inter-American Conference on Indian Life, *Actas finales de los tres primeros Congresos Indigenistas Interamericanos* (Guatemala City: Mayo 1959), 23–24.

12. Alexander Dawson, "From Models for the Nation to Model Citizens: *Indigenismo* and the 'Revindication' of the Mexican Indian, 1920–40," *Journal of Latin American Studies* 30, no. 2 (May 1998): 279–308.

13. Marisol de la Cadena, *Indigenous Mestizos: The Politics of Race and Culture in Cuzco, Peru, 1919–1991* (Durham, NC: Duke University Press, 2003).

14. María Josefina Saldaña-Portillo, *The Revolutionary Imagination in the Americas and the Age of Development* (Durham, NC: Duke University Press, 2003), 27.

15. A. Adams, "El indigenismo guatemalteco," 116.

16. Jorge Ramón González Ponciano, "'Esas sangres no están limpias': Modernidad y pensamiento civilizatorio en Guatemala (1954–1997)," in *Racismo en Guatemala? Abriendo el debate sobre un tema tabú*, ed. Clara Arenas Bianchi et al., 10–18 (Guatemala City: AVANSCO, 2004).

17. Joshua Smith, "Beyond Collaboration: Action Anthropology *as* Decolonization," in *Action Anthropology and Sol Tax in 2012*, ed. Darby C. Stapp, *Journal of Northwest Anthropology, Memoir 8* (2012): 82–83 and 79.

18. Goubaud to Redfield, January 29, 1945, box 11, folder 4, Robert Redfield Papers (RRP), University of Chicago Special Collections (hereafter UCSC).

19. Goubaud to Redfield, January 29, 1945, box 11, folder 4, RRP, UCSC.

20. Gobierno de Guatemala, Acuerdo Presidencial, August 29, 1945, accessed January 18, 2017, http://www.unesco.org/culture/natlaws/media/pdf/guatemala/guatemala_acuredo_28_08_1945_spa_orof.pdf; "Se crea el Instituto Indígena de Guatemala," *Mediodia*, August 29, 1945.

21. Mexico City, expediente "David Vela," Vela to Gamio, May 9, 1945, Archivo del Instituto Indigenista Interamericano (hereafter AIII).

22. "Discurso del Señor Ministro de Educación, Profesor Manuel Galich," *Boletín del Instituto Indigenista Nacional de Guatemala* 1, no. 1 (October–December 1945): 12.

23. Tax to Goubaud, October 3, 1945, box 85, folder 1, Sol Tax Papers (STP), USCS.

24. Francisco Rodríguez Rouanet, interview, Guatemala City, August 6, 2015; "Una Vida," unpublished memoir, 1999, with an addition in 2006, personal Archive of Francisco Rodríguez Rouanet (hereafter FRRA).

25. "Trayectoria de la Vida del Instituto," *Boletín Indigenista del Instituto Indigenista Nacional* 1, no. 1 (October–December 1945): 38; Goubaud to Redfield, September 14, 1945, box 4, folder 11, RRP, UCSC; Goubaud to Redfield, December 15, 1945, box 4, folder 11, RRP, UCSC; Goubaud to Redfield, January 15, 1945, box 4, folder 11, RRP, UCSC.

26. Olga Pérez Molina, "Desarrollo de la antropología guatemalteca: Influencias intelectuales e institucionalidad en la década de los cuarenta y cincuenta del siglo XX," *Estudios* (2010): 183–184; Francisco Rodríguez Rouanet, interview by Edgar S. G. Mendoza, Guatemala City, February 26, 1990, Archivo de la Oralidad, Escuela de Historia, Universidad de San Carlos de Guatemala.

27. With the exception of Cabrera, who responded to a job advertisement in a national newspaper, the Ministry of Education connected with these schoolteachers at a meeting in Cobán in July 1945, which the ministry had called to discuss the teachers' perspectives on the problems confronting indigenous towns and villages.

28. Francisco Rodríguez Rouanet, interview, Guatemala City, August 6, 2015. For comparative purposes, the quetzal was pegged to the dollar at the rate of one to one during this time.

29. Yanna Yannakakis, *The Art of Being In-Between: Native Intermediaries, Indian Identity, and Local Rule in Colonial Oaxaca* (Durham, NC: Duke University Press, 2008), 7. Yannakakis's book explores the role of indigenous intermediaries during colonial rule, yet there are clear parallels to the twentieth-century role of these intermediary figures as well.

30. Tania Murray Li, *The Will to Improve: Governmentality, Development, and the Practice of Politics* (Durham, NC: Duke University Press, 2007), 5.

31. George Murdock et al., *Guía para la investigación etnológicas*, trans. Radamés A. Altieri, private edition Publicación Número 250 del Instituto de antropología de la Universidad Nacional de Tucumán, Argentina; repr. Pátzcuaro, Mexico: Centro Regional de Educación Fundamental para la América Latina, 1952 (orig. pub. 1939).

32. James Scott, *Seeing Like a State*, 2–5.

33. Hélida Esther Cabrera, interview, Santiago Atitlán, September 19, 2015.

34. Ibid., September 24, 2015.

35. Francisco Rodríguez Rouanet, interview, Guatemala City, August 12, 2014.

36. IING, *San Bartolomé Milpas Altas: Síntesis socio-económico de una comunidad indígena guatemalteca*, special publications of the Instituto Indigenista Nacional no. 9 (Guatemala City: Ministerio de Educación Pública, 1949), insert prior to preface.

37. Ibid., vi–viii. Although the monograph does not record the occupations of the informants, survey methodology dictated that the ethnographers interview individuals from a variety of occupations and social classes.

38. Ibid., 3.

39. Ibid., 18–19.

40. Ibid., 10.

41. Ibid., 13.

42. Ibid., 14–15.

43. "Los orígenes del INCAP," *El Imparcial*, October 5, 1967, 11; "El Instituto de Nutrición (INCAP)," *El Imparcial*, September 28, 1967, 11; "El INCAP y su historia" (typed mimeograph, August 1954). INCAP was also under the direction of the Pan American Sanitary Bureau, which in turn was a subsidiary of the World Health Organization; "Función perenne del INCAP en Centroamérica quedó acordada," *El Imparcial*, December 19, 1959. See Corinne A. Pernet, "Between Entanglements and Dependencies: Food, Nutrition, and National Development at the Central American Institute of Nutrition," in *International Organizations and Development, 1945–1990*, ed. Marc Frey et al. (London: Palgrave Macmillan, 2014), 101–125, for an excellent overview of INCAP's importance in regional governance.

44. Entry from March 6, 1951, box 1, folder 1, Richard Adams Papers (hereafter RAP), Special Collections of the Benson Library at the University of Texas, Austin; Richard N. Adams, "Social Anthropology in INCAP," *Food and Nutrition Bulletin* 31, no. 1 (2010): 152–160.

45. Berta Pineda field notes, March 6, 1951, box 1, folder 1, RAP.

46. Ana Díaz's field notes, February 7, 1951, box 1, folder 1, RAP.

47. James C. Scott, *Weapons of the Weak: Everyday Forms of Peasant Resistance* (New Haven, CT: Yale University Press, 1985), xvi; Berta Pineda field notes, March 6, 1951, box 1, folder 1, RAP.

48. Richard Adams, interview, Panajachel, Guatemala, August 10, 2014.

49. Cabrera, interview, Santiago Atitlán, September 20, 2015. Despite her advanced age of ninety-four, Doña Hélida continues to be involved locally in health and education initiatives. She is a firm advocate for the use of the Tz'utujil language, which she speaks fluently, and she is frequently consulted by indigenous and ladina women on natural medicine.

PART IV
New Memories

CHAPTER 9

Water Power Promise

Revisiting Revolutionary DIY

Diane M. Nelson

What gives light is the organization, not the turbine.

Community member, 31 de Mayo Xecoyeu, in Colectivo MadreSelva, *El camino de la luz*

We slept where the paved road and electricity lines ended. The trip was grueling, but Ana, my traveling companion, told great stories about her years in Mexico studying anthropology, and we had reminisced about Chiapas in the mid-1980s when I had first come to Central America. The next morning, we coaxed the jeep up the steep dirt road, hugging close to the mountain on the barely single lane, the stark drop to the right affording an adrenaline rush and amazing views. Kids yelled and ran along beside us at the improbable sight of two *canches* (pale faces) so far from our usual haunts. Like many young people in Guatemala and elsewhere, in the 1970s Ana was questioning the militarized conservative Catholic status quo, including her class privilege. Mexico City and the university were full of exiles of different leftist movements from throughout the Américas—including the Partido Guatemalteco del Trabajo (Guatemala Workers Party; PGT), the very group whose support for President Arbenz helped justify the 1954 US intervention.[1] It was an exciting time and place. Transformations in consciousness and the organizing that were able to "give light" were apparent everywhere. My first introduction to Guatemala was a bit later and in a darker time. It was 1985 and also via Mexico City, through sectors of the peasant movement and Liberation Theology Church, some with (at the time unknown to me) ties to the revolutionary Ejército Guerrillero de los Pobres (Guerrilla Army of the Poor; EGP). It was then that I began to challenge my class and national privilege.

This was on the heels of the heat of the 1970s and early 1980s revolutionary projects in Central America. The revolution we were "revisiting" on that long ride was aimed at overthrowing a system of plantation-based accumulation-by-dispossession controlled by a small group of families in close association with US capital and its anticommunist political-military backing. The goal, as in the revolution of the 1940s and 1950s, was more independent development and more equitable distribution of its less bitter fruits. For a feminist such as Ana, it was also (*unlike* the focus in the 1950s) to create a transformation in gender and sexuality. As in the 1940s and 1950s, however, for many nonindigenous leftist Guatemalans and for many solidarity "gringas," the imbricated but not isomorphic consciousness about "race" privilege and the complex role of the Maya in the revolution/s have been harder to negotiate.

Severo Martínez Peláez's history *La patria del criollo* has served as a sort of bible for much of the educated Guatemalan Left.[2] In it, indigenous identity and practice are understood as at best epiphenomena—feathers and beads laid over ugly class relations. At worst, it is false consciousness—colonial distortions of lost practices mistaken for valid experience. Although Greg Grandin has shown the important role of the PGT in organizing indigenous people before and during the Guatemalan Spring,[3] the struggles and epic sacrifices made by urban, mostly ladino leftists in the 1970s and 1980s were—as they were in the 1940s and 1950s—for *nationalist* development.[4] They were for a living wage, basic infrastructure, representative democracy, and land reform, on the way to socialism. They were organizing to bring light. They were not so much focused on indigenous liberation per se, though the lives of the masses of poor indigenous people would improve as the bases of generalized economic exclusion were relegated to the dustbin of history. Like most whites who consider ourselves antiracist, these activists would never directly mistreat an indigenous person. It is more a matter of theoretical frameworks, emphases, priorities. Plus, radical ladinos' more general anti-imperial critique includes foreign anthropologists who often write as if half of Guatemala's population (the ladinos) do not exist. Fascinated with ceremonies, we seem to ignore exploitation—and our own complicity.[5] Ana is a wonderfully challenging travel companion. We found more common ground talking about how beginning to question some power structures had made many other assumptions tremble, including our religious beliefs. We discussed how it had been a hard but freeing journey to cast off the misogyny of the church and think on one's own as feminists.

But then there was also the question of how to deal with many Mayans' insistence that spiritual practices are central to their existence.

Ana had been grappling with these issues since returning from Mexico and as she accompanied participants in the exhumation of a mass grave in a Maya-Kaqchiquel town as a scholar and activist. I too was being schooled by Mayan interlocutors that struggles for land concern not just production and nutrition but also nested relations of give-and-take among people, soil, seeds, ancestors, and entities that might be considered deities. Ceremonies that accompany political organizing events or the seeking, digging, finding, and reinterring of loved ones' bodies are far more than just an opiate. Learning new sensitivities through such processes, we proud atheists had begun to feel something in the presence of the fire, the *pom* (pine incense), the candles, the mountains, the night, these women and men who could be both deeply serious and make uproarious jokes, as the hours wore on. I am aware of the siren allure of romance, essentialism, and the simplifying pleasures of the "New Age" to which the Maya have been subjected but also, increasingly, of my own problematic "enlightenment" epistemological assumptions—even when I think they are revolutionary.[6] It is an ongoing struggle to question one's privilege.

Sharing these stories engrossed us as we passed into the Zona Reina in northeastern Quiché Province, across an amazing ridgetop with views to what seemed forever, and down into a broad deforested valley town. It was a bit Wild West, with cantinas, sex workers, men packing pistols, and a small hospital serving some twenty thousand dispersed people. I later met a Cuban doctor who cared for patients there with no electricity. When they ran out of gas for the generators, they did surgery by the light of their cell phones. From there, many jolting hours later, we made it to 31 de Mayo Xecoyeu.[7]

Redoubt: From secret place (Latin), withdrawn, a safe or protected area

Adventurous as it felt, this journey was bitingly insignificant compared to the territorial passages undergone by the people we had come to see. In their original homes across northern Guatemala, they too had been part of the consciousness-raising movements that spread through the indigenous highlands in the 1960s and 1970s on the heels of the coup against President Arbenz. Through Liberation Theology, and in resistance to debt peonage and the land concentration and racialized labor exploitation embedded in their relations to local and national plantations producing for export, many became organized in the Comité de Unidad Campesina (Campesino Unity Committee; CUC). As the local- and national-level contradictions became more violently expressed, few took up arms—there just were not enough guns. In the early 1980s the Guatemalan Army designated the denizens of the entire ethno-bio-region—encompassing Maya-Chuj, Q'anjob'al, K'iche', and Ixil peoples and the mix of indigenous and ladino ethnicities who had colonized the Ixcán area farther north—as "internal enemies."[8] Deeply racialized relations of production mixed evilly with transnational Cold War training and financing to produce military-oligarch-backed scorched-earth counterinsurgency. Entire villages, including babies and pregnant women, were subjected to massacre. Sexual violence was systematically deployed against women and men, and anything that might autonomously sustain life—crops, food stores, tools, buildings, and domestic animals—was destroyed. Survivors fled into the surrounding mountains carrying what they could, including the trauma of such massive, sudden violence and loss—and all because they wanted to live with dignity and be able to feed their kids. In other words, for revisiting the revolutionary projects of Arévalo and Arbenz.

In the midst of intensive struggles to just survive, and to evade the sweeps by soldiers and civil patrollers ("forci-voluntarily" militarized survivors),[9] aided by the still fledgling and now reeling guerrilla movement, some of these people decided to remain organized. What emerged was an audacious and seemingly impossible project: the Comunidades de Población en Resistencia (Communities of the Population in Resistance; CPR). They would stubbornly remain within national territory (unlike the 200,000-plus refugees in Mexico) and try to maintain a cohesive community (unlike the million-plus people displaced elsewhere, mostly dispersed into the straggling fringes of urban areas). In part, this was a military tactic of the revolutionary organizations, an attempt to produce liberated territory that might be recognized under international law and figure in future negotiations. But it was also a deeply felt and reasoned project of the people themselves.[10] Without dismissing five hundred years of colonial history and deepening liberalism seeking to transform subsistence farmers into *mozos* ("those who work for nothing"), these are deeply biocentric people.[11] Through both lived experience and thoughtful, hard-won *conciencia*, they know, deeply, in ways both sacred and profane, that land is the only thing worth living for, worth dying for.[12]

So, they stayed put[13]—through sheer, almost unimaginable willingness to endure; through brilliance, ingenuity, and optimism of the will;[14] through networks of solidarity and tenuous lines of supply occasionally bringing in food, seeds, a bit of clothing, spiritual support; and through the good graces of the mountains themselves, the way their folds hid the *milpa* plantings, their caves gave shelter, their animals and plants gave sustenance, and their clouds would gather just as an army helicopter flew over. Perhaps most beloved was the Santa Malanga (*Colocasia esculenta*), a nutritious root related to taro that, rather like the people themselves, survives underground, even after its stem and leaves have been destroyed[15]—"The sacred forest saved us."[16]

Yet these resistance communities lived under constant threat of capture and murder as well as starvation and "natural" death. The mountains also house poisonous creatures, steep and unexpected drops, especially if you are fleeing at night and heavily burdened. Even a loose stone can twist an ankle and hobble you, or a stray thorn can open a wound and infection can set in. Women, sometimes pregnant or nursing without adequate nutrition themselves, carrying children, tending to the elders, their clothing slowly tattering on their bodies, making basic dignity even harder to sustain, deserve, I think, special recognition for their commitment to this liberatory project, paid for with so much suffering.[17] A woman named Maria said, "Tengo letras un poco. Pero me muero por mi organización. Mataron, quemaron por ello. Nunca olvido la organización" (I can't read or write but I will die for my organization. That's why they killed us, burned us. I will never forget the organization).

They managed, for over a decade, to maintain the CPR as a civilian presence outside of army control. They developed mechanisms for schooling children, maintaining their spiritual lives, managing supplies, and negotiating power struggles and interpersonal tensions. Not everyone could bear it, and some slipped away. In the rest of the country, while little information was circulating about anything happening in the highlands, the army was especially concerned that word of this autonomous zone not leak out.[18] But of course it did, forming an exciting imaginative space for those struggling for the dreams of the revolution in the aftermath of ferocious genocidal violence and insurrectionary defeat. They became almost mythical, and really, rightly so.[19]

Over time, existence slowly normalized a bit. Public recognition led to international accompaniers being stationed with them as human shields, which allowed a more settled life.[20] In the 1996 Peace Accords, the CPR were officially designated noncombatant actors and began to plan their return to "national" life. And that is when things got *really* difficult.

Redoubt: From Past Participle of *reducere*: to Lead Back

The government refused to accept CPR members' claims to the lands they had been occupying for over a decade and insisted they relocate to a plantation several mountains and large rivers away. It was not big enough for everyone, so they had to divide the community: one contingent resettled far away on the Pacific coast, another went north to Ixcán, and a few people returned to their original villages. The "plantation" turned out to be a cow pasture. It lacked the most minimal infrastructure, buildings, or a road, and it still had some big scary cattle roaming around. "I was afraid to walk among them, but we had no choice!" said one tiny woman. Claiming to want to ease the migrants' journey, the government insisted on transferring them by helicopter, meaning the migrants left behind what little domestic material they had managed to gather, including corn-grinding stones, animals, structures, and—for some, most important—the written materials they'd created and collected for their library.[21] Although several families in the area greeted the resettled CPR members with open arms, the region was heavily militarized, and their new neighbors had endured over a decade of army counterinsurgency propaganda denouncing the CPR as dangerous "reds." After all they had withstood and labored to build, they were once again starting from nothing, and in quite hostile territory, both socially and ecologically.

But they set to work, in collaboration with accompanying supporters from the Canary Islands and aid from Habitat for Humanity, and once they'd built a few rude shelters and put in some milpa they began to consider projects beyond adequacy.[22] After much discussion (and, as pragmatic people, feasibility studies and conferring with technical advisors), they decided they wanted electricity.

Electricity! After all those years of hiding—when a fire or even a candle were not only luxuries but dangerous, possibly revealing you to your army hunters—to propose, fearlessly, that yes, you desire that warm glow, that ease of flicking a switch, that human controlled elongation of daylight's possibilities for fine work such as weaving, for intellectual stimulation through reading, for conviviality, for doctors to see what they were doing at the health post, for children to learn to read and compute. What promise even a few cheap lightbulbs offer! And they would be powered naturally, cleanly, by a nearby river. Yet from that out-of-the-way cow pasture, these people—with their clothes made more of patches than fabric, their faces so eloquently revealing lifetimes of near starvation—weren't just proposing a more comfortable domestic life; they were always already thinking symbolically. We ourselves are light: our survival, our struggle, our work. We are always more than just ourselves. We are an example, a hope, a sign for the rest of Guatemala. They called their project "Light of the heroes and martyrs of the Resistance." Water. Power. Promise.

Redoubt: To lead back . . . but to where?

The revolutionary movements of the 1970s and 1980s were "revisiting the revolution" of the Guatemalan Spring in ways that struggled to include more emphatically the specificities of indigenous being (see Andersson [chapter 3], Foss [chapter 8], and Adams and Giraudo [chapter 7], this volume, on the complexities of this for both revolutions). Many sought (and were pushed by Mayan compañeros/as) to maintain this struggle as they were "led back" into aboveground and institutional life. But the military-oligarchs also sought to revisit the 1950s, specifically Colonel Castillo Armas's *counter*-revolution, in order to "lead the country back" to the very white supremacy and plantationocracy so many heroes and martyrs had died trying to overthrow. In the mid-1980s General Alejandro Gramajo, the architect of the transition from military dictatorship to nominal civilian government, declared, drawing on Carl von Clausewitz, that he was conducting "war by other means."[23] By this, he seemed to mean a number of things: governmentality and biopower (with necropower always hovering close); the strangling of revolutionary hopes via the belief in and struggle for liberal democracy and its institutions, including "human rights"; and phase 2 of the "shock doctrine" as mass murder gave way to neoliberal restructuring.[24] The Guatemalan guerrilla coalition, Unidad Revolucionaria Nacional Guatemalteca (the National Revolutionary Unity; URNG), backed by civil groups, made important gains in negotiations with the militarized state in the early 1990s: a truth commission, refugee return, indigenous rights. But on the socioeconomic aspects—the accords addressing land and money—the elite-backed state won its most transformative victory.[25] Land reform, the foundation—the ontology even—of every peasant revolt, the central plank of Arbenz's project for national development, was forced out of the political and into the economic realm (see Chassé [chapter 2] and Sierakowski [chapter 1], this volume). Only via market forces would the landless gain access to the means of production.[26]

Over the twenty years since, this "peace accord" let *finqueros* (plantation elites) dump both the costs of their ecologically destructive production (e.g., the squeezed-dry pasture sold to the CPR) and global market volatility (especially the early 2000s collapse of coffee prices), onto Guatemala's poor. This massive indebting, backed and enforced by the government, means that tax, international loan, and aid monies are also channeled to the rich. Via such gifts, the already wealthy gained a toehold in new capital-intensive forms of financialized accumulation. The Maya-K'ichee' anthropologist Irmalicia Velasquez Nimatuj chronicles people's unbearable spending on this spent land, the horrific logics of subprime debt, escalating interest, frantic labors, and constant abnegation of the flesh because one is always paying and paying and paying.[27] And around them, the local, regional, and global Cold War counterinsurgencies reaped their whirligigging Wall Street rewards, as leftist movements all over the world struggled to recover from the violence and their own limitations of verticalism, androcentrism, pigmentocracy, and "enlightenment" assumptions. Or they fell in with the new brutal extractivist regimes.

The former CPR of 31 de Mayo, so remote yet so firmly ensconced in these world-un-making projects, imagine electricity in their village. So simple a desire. So audacious a project! And they are aware that by doing so, they are also waging war by hydroelectric means. By DIY-ing, they will show precisely what the state refuses to do (or is incapable of doing) for its people—and what they can do, collectively, without it. As they did in the mountain, they will form an autonomous zone whose very being is an existential rebuke.

Redoubtable: Illustrious, eminent

The former CPR have not explicitly invoked President Arbenz, but he imagined something similar: the Jurún Marinalá national hydroelectric plant. It was meant to disrupt the US-owned electric cartel, a classic neocolonial gift that kept on taking: through monopoly pricing and by draining Guatemala's foreign currency reserves to purchase fossil fuels. The planned hydroelectric plant was a central piece of the massive nationalist public works planned by the revolutionary governments. Along with the Atlantic Highway and the new port in Santo Tomás Castillo, Jurún Marinalá would challenge the monopoly stranglehold of the United Fruit Company and its related businesses on Guatemala's independent development (see Bauer Paiz).[28]

Thus, revisiting the revolution-ary dreams of the 1970s through the former CPR's current DIY hydroelectric resonates with similar revolutionary projects for sovereignty in the 1950s. Just like the former CPR members, some sixty years later, Arbenz was thinking pragmatically—using local/national renewable resources for local/national needs. But they were also always acting symbolically: refusing imperial extractivism, seizing "power," organizing and bringing light and with it, autonomy and dignity. To follow these sparking connections, we will take a short detour before revisiting the 1950s war by hydroelectric means. And that is to revisit an even earlier revolution, of Carlos Herrera in the early 1920s, and a previous attempt at nationalizing that still rather newly domesticated, unruly force: electricity.

In 1894 Guatemala's first electricity project was founded by German immigrants, servicing Guatemala City and Escuintla from a plant in Palín. The project was expropriated by the state after World War I, a moment when many German Guatemalans lost their property (see Gibbings and Vrana, the introduction in this volume). However, El Señor Presidente Estrada Cabrera promptly ceded it as a ten-year lease to US Electric Bond and Share, a subsidiary of General Electric. In 1921, the Unionist government of Herrera tried to cancel the onerous contract (and that of the railway).[29] He was promptly overthrown by US-backed General José María Orellana. With Orellana in office, Electric Bond and Share, whose local subsidiary was Empresa Eléctrica de Guatemala (EEGSA), got the plant and distribution system back, and on much improved terms: a fifty-year concession with a tax of only about 2 percent on their declared earnings. The concession also included rights to both running and still waters and right of way over any property. It cost Q445,000. EEGSA built several hydroelectric projects over the next thirty years, but many of their plants ran on coal and oil, which had to be imported. Guatemalan electricity prices were quite high, often close to what US users paid (the same company electrified Cuba, where its gross earnings were the highest in the hemisphere).[30]

Under Arévalo, in 1948, in the wake of labor struggles with EEGSA and as part of larger efforts to collect back taxes and clarify audit procedures, the government opened an investigation into the electric company's practices, discovering multiple irregularities that had helped the company claim that it had been consistently operating at a loss. Many hoped this was a prelude to nationalization, though no further steps were openly taken in that direction.[31] As an alternative, Arbenz pushed Jurún Marinalá as a new, locally controlled hydroelectric source. With a promised 40,000- to 60,000-kilowatt production, Jurún would not only cut much of the nation's dependency on EEGSA but also offer power far in excess of current demand, creating a foundation for the enchanting promise of industrial takeoff Arbenz's economic planners hoped for.

By 1953, the studies had been done, plans were drawn up, money was being arranged, and congressional representatives and regular citizens were being invited to observe the site for the new hydroelectric project. Newspaper articles criticized EEGSA's terrible service, exposed electrocution deaths from falling wires, and denounced the uglification of Guatemala City due to the proliferating electric lines.[32] They also covered in detail the unfolding progress on Jurún.

It wasn't, of course, strictly DIY, any more than the folks in 31 de Mayo had the technical know-how or financial resources to build their hydroelectric facilities completely on their own. The government paid Westinghouse for the preliminary studies of several possible sites (including a plan to partially drain Lake Atitlán to power turbines on the Boca Costa), and it hired the American company Fluor to begin work at Jurún. The plan was for a "run of river" project, using the natural reservoir of Lake Amatitlán and its outflow, the Michatoya River, descending from an altitude of five thousand feet toward the Pacific Ocean, to power it. This would only require upgrading the lake's sluice gates for regulating the river's flow.[33] There would be no giant dam, no flooding, and little human displacement. Using the drop from the lake toward Palín, a second small reservoir would be built, diverting much, but not all, of the water at the confluence of the rivers Jurún and Marinalá with the Michatoya. Then, to increase the pressure, this water would be run through a tunnel built under the intervening mountain to drop over a thousand meters to Escuintla, where the turbines would be placed. The water would then return to (what was left of) the river.

Of course, Jurún, as one of Arbenz's "public works"—the infrastructures meant to lessen dependency and underdevelopment—was part of a larger project that included attacking the even deeper (infra)structure of socioeconomic exclusion: landholding. Decree 900 was the WMD of its day, becoming the CIA's justification for the 1954 coup.[34] As with the loss and suffering later endured by the CPR, I'd like to pause here for a moment to acknowledge what this *coup* (blow) meant for dreams for a dignified life, for feeding one's children, for acting as a symbol, a sign of hope for others.

Yet, not unlike the CPR, those who dreamed of nationally controlled power did not give up. Within a month of the coup, Jorge Bendix, chief of Arbenz's Department of National Electrification, was writing articles in *El Imparcial* bravely pushing for continuation of the Jurún project. "We must divide the technical from the political" and "This is not against private industry, nor will it harm EEGSA, this is a technologically proven way to improve Guatemala" (July 23, September 23, 1954).

In early 1956, flooding in the turbine room of an EEGSA plant led to power outages and public outrage. On January 11, *El Imparcial* called

EEGSA "an odious monopoly, in its slavering for profit it cares nothing for the rights of anyone else, nor will it cede a cent of its multitudinous gains to the government that hosts it. . . . Jurún might be expensive but it will be the basis for all other development."[35] On January 17, another unsigned article argued passionately for Jurún: "This is a primordial problem, a huge problem, *gravisimo* [*sic*], and also of a very complex technical nature, but Guatemalans must make sacrifices so that our future energy needs will not be dependent on a concessionary company." And on January 18 it denounced the special treatment received by the Novella cement company and a few other enterprises, who reportedly used 18 percent of all the electricity generated nationally, but covered only 6 percent of the costs.[36] By January 19, President Castillo Armas announced that he would build Jurún and it would be state owned (despite EEGSA maneuvering to take control).[37] It was clarified several times that although it was an Arbenz project, Jurún was in no way communist, but instead completely patriotic.[38] When a reporter asked a government promoter of the project what resources participants had to work with, he said, "Guatemalans' universal disgust and hatred for the Empresa Eléctrica!"[39]

Despite this, the uncertainty over political direction over the next few years—Castillo Armas's assassination in July 1957 led to a series of "acting" military leaders—and struggles over who would do it—Guatemalans or gringos—led to Jurún being back-burnered until 1959, while the new Instituto Nacional de Electrifición (National Electrification Institute; INDE) was being consolidated. Bendix was called before the Congress to discuss the plans, and things seemed again, at last, to be getting under way. Then, on May 14, under the banner headline "¡Sorpresa! Captura de Bendix," it was announced that he had been arrested leaving the Congress and imprisoned in the very scary Department of Defense against Communist Activities within the National Police. Congressmen literally ran up the street to the National Palace to beg President General Ydígoras Fuentes to release Bendix. They were successful, but it was a bad sign for Jurún. While the next military government, of Colonel Enrique Peralta Azurdia, continued with the plans supplied by Swiss consultants and some tunnel digging, the still-fledgling INDE lost a lot of its legal autonomy and dynamism.

Peralta Azurdia's successor, the civilian Julio César Méndez Montenegro, and his self-styled revolutionary government again took up the call for national development through infrastructure and set their sights back on Jurún. A loan was secured from the International Bank for Reconstruction and Development (part of the World Bank), and in March 1967 there was a big ceremony near Palín attended by representatives of all the government branches. This ceremony inaugurated construction in earnest on the reservoir, tunnels, turbine installations, transmission lines, substations, and control center. The National Electrification Institute oversaw the work while US, Swiss, and Spanish companies did much of the actual building. However, newspaper coverage based in regular on-site visits by journalists and politicians makes much of the many young, eager, National University–trained Guatemalan engineers at work on this project of national pride. (Frequent visitors to the construction site were supporters Gert Rosenthal and Alberto Fuentes Mohr, who went on to important roles in Guatemala's revolutionary history.[40]) The project helped reinforce the institutional bases of INDE as decentralized and autonomous, a state institution but enjoying its own guaranteed public funding stream.[41] The plan for Jurún was, via "reasonable and fair" rates, to cover upkeep and quickly pay back the loan, and then to direct the revenue stream to build new projects (Atitlán was still on the table). The goal was to electrify the country as a whole. Building Jurún employed over fifteen hundred men, including bringing back engineers who had been blacklisted by the post-Arbenz military governments (one was the father of a MadreSelva member). In one awful accident, an explosion in the tunnel killed a worker and seriously injured four more. Nevertheless, newspaper coverage frequently remarked on workers' commitment, their *mística* (a combination of esprit de corps and wholehearted faith and commitment), and even the *cariño* (love) that marked the proceedings (perhaps this is partly why, adding to the generalized pride, it was completed ahead of schedule). They were serving a collective need, working to improve their country as a whole. It was organization that brought light.

A spanner in the works was the ongoing fifty-year EEGSA concession—guaranteeing the foreign company rights to all waterways and riverbanks—signed over by President Orellana in 1921. The empresa claimed that using the river this way would affect the company's smaller hydroelectric projects near Palín, for which it demanded compensation. Officials of the company also insisted that the government pay for rights to the river itself, the Amatitlán sluice gates, *and* plantations they owned along the river's course, including all their buildings, as well as assuming responsibility for their workers' pensions, all to the tune of over US$3 million.[42] The company was backed by the transnational funders, as the World Bank refused to lend money to Guatemala until the state owned all the physical infrastructure needed for the project.

Finally, almost twenty years after it was first imagined by Arbenz, and with much fanfare, Jurún Marinalá was inaugurated on January 10, 1970. "A desire, cultivated for so many years, is finally made real," said President Méndez Montenegro. The director of INDE, Rolando Castillo Contoux, captured the mood:

> Today we inaugurate Jurún Marinalá! Jurún Marinalá! What a beautiful, resounding Guatemalan name! How many dreams, how many desires, how much effort? How much patriotic struggle, how much skill and sacrifice of our Guatemalan laborers! How many precious and patriotic lives were offered to build it, how much determination and revolutionary faith was needed to arrive at this moment! . . . Jurún Marinalá is not only a beautiful piece of engineering. It signifies the commitment and ratification by the Third Revolutionary Government, of a clear project for the integral, rational, and nationalist exploitation of our natural resources in service of the people. It also situates a national company, in which all of us are partners, at the vanguard of Guatemala's electrification. INDE has come of age and will tirelessly continue in its passion to electrify all of the Republic, and through such works to guarantee lower prices in the future for our nation. . . . Mr. President, I have the honor of delivering into your hands the Jurún Marinalá Hydroelectric Plant. I do it with profound satisfaction and intense feeling, I am well aware of the enormous joy that seizes us as your dynamic and patriotic government has allowed us to place a work of such national transcendence at the service of our beloved Guatemalan people.[43]

Here it is. Water. Power. Promise. Doing it yourself.

Yet it was at precisely this time that the Third Revolutionary Government had given the army a free hand to "use any means necessary" against the Movimiento Revolucionario 13 Noviembre (Revolutionary Movement 13th November; MR-13). Under the command of Colonel Carlos Arana Osorio, the army engaged in mass murder in the eastern portion of the country. An estimated fifteen thousand civilians, mostly ladino peasants, were killed by security forces between 1965 and 1970. Just three months before Méndez Montenegro took office, thirty members of the PGT were disappeared, and while he was president, his own cousin, the PGT member

César Montenegro Paniagua, was kidnapped, tortured, and executed by government forces. The systematic state terror that became institutionalized at this time, with wide-ranging support from the US government, laid the groundwork for the scorched-earth military practices that created the CPR, sending the current residents of 31 de Mayo, and so many others, into the mountains.[44]

Arana became president through nontransparent elections six months after Jurún was inaugurated. The subsequent governments, all run by army members until 1985, militarized INDE. The governments revisited the (counter) revolution by retaining the nationalist desire for sustainable sovereign energy (though financed by the World Bank) but with a deadly twist. The Chixoy hydroelectric project, started under General Kjell Laugerud García in 1976, was a dam, a huge one, and it was slated to displace thousands of Maya-Achi' people throughout the Río Negro valley in the province of Baja Verapaz. When the residents refused to leave, the subsequent military government of General Romeo Lucas García sent in soldiers and civil patrollers who erased ten communities in the basin, killing about five thousand people in the area between 1980 and 1982. Many of their remains are now under the rippling waters of the thirty-four-thousand-acre reservoir. The dam is the largest in the country, with over four times the capacity of Jurún.[45]

To return to *La patria del criollo* and my conversations with Ana, it is a bit too easy to say the counterinsurgency of the 1960s mostly targeted poor ladinos in the east and organized ladinos in the city, but it does look a lot like a class war, a revisiting of the 1950s revolutionary hopes and their counterinsurgent blightings. The military responses to the class *and race* formations that emerged in the 1970s, as organizing flowered from the indigenous western highlands, transformed counterinsurgency into genocide.[46] Its aftermath marks the appearance of a new historical actor, the Maya, as an increasingly self-defining subject, one without whom no future revolutionary projects will be possible.

I've taken the term "revisiting" from the title of this collection as an invitation to think about these processes as in some ways cyclical, revolutions, turning like a turbine perhaps, yet sending off sprouts of energy in unexpected directions, which of course makes it all more of a dialectic. It may seem like a repetition compulsion, first the United States blocking structural change and then increasingly powerful military oligarchic sectors within Guatemala doing the same (always with US support). Yet with each turn something different is happening. Amidst the bloodshed and loss, different constellations of *conciencia*, subjectivity, organizing, humans, water, cement, wire, and electric connectivity are being "infrastructured"—giving, despite everything, light.

Redoubtable: Formidable, valiant

As with Jurún, for the folks in 31 de Mayo, the idea of light—something so weightless, so fast—became materialized only through extraordinarily heavy labor at what felt like a snail's pace. Maybe we should call the pace and the labor "light years"? The course of the Lirio Putul River is over two kilometers from the village.[47] It is beautiful, rocky, fast moving, and loud, and in the rainy season rather torrential. Borrowing some of that power required siphoning a stream out while retaining the downhill flow. This meant men and boys digging a trench about a meter wide and a meter deep, through stony land and around curves, creating an earthwork that would control the water's flow without losing its own integrity. This meant collective effort, drawing on organizational forms they had carried from their villages and further developed in the mountains as people worked by turns, keeping careful track that it was fairly distributed. This meant women undertaking extra labors, getting up earlier to cook so they could also work the fields and tend children and animals while the men were digging, plus cleaning all the men's mud- and sweat-drenched clothing by hand in the river. This meant complex and ongoing negotiations with landholders in the channel's path and with the landscape, confronting the thingness of the ground itself, the woods and tree roots, clearing enough for the channel to pass while maintaining sufficient plant life to root and settle its walls. This meant transporting heavy bags of cement and each six-meter-long tube on men's backs for eight kilometers. Two men at a time to carry just one tube, through so much mud. Ay—it was exhausting! It would take all day to do. And the turbine: it took twenty men to lift it, and carrying it just a little way, they got tired so quickly. They even lost precious pack animals, their legs broken in the mud. This also meant constructing the holding tank and the building to house the turbine and generator, and digging and cementing the holes and cutting and erecting the posts for the wires that would finally deliver the volts to each home.

I try to imagine what this was like, as they were also remaking sociality around all those missing people—those lost to death in the war and in the mountain or more recently to the south coast and elsewhere. The apparatus of their larger organizational structure, the Consulting Assembly of the Uprooted Population, decamped to Guatemala City, the better to serve its members trying to reroot in communities dispersed around the country. All the while as they struggled to coax crops out of unfamiliar soil and construct houses, and amidst the everyday fraught negotiations with new neighbors, in this supposedly new (democratic, peace-treaty-complying) state, and the complex "*ofertas*"/offers of new supranational actors such as NGOs and their sometimes cloudy agendas.

At every stage, the people of the former CPR worked to practice their philosophy of autonomy and collectivity. The electricity project was chosen through a "community diagnostic" that measured hopes and desires while simultaneously producing shared understandings and responsibilities. They sent people to study other small-scale hydroelectric systems in Guatemala and to the Canary Islands for workshops. These representatives in turn reported back, sharing about the dangers of electricity and attendant safety measures, the rigors of administration and accounting. While only a few men received the intensive technical training needed to run the turbine and generator, they worked to distribute as much know-how as possible. They decided together not to use individual electricity meters, because they are potent condensations of the anathematic idea that if you can pay more you get more. They trusted that education would make clear that for everyone to have enough, no one could have more.

The state of emergency might be the rule, but *really* extreme situations can evoke solidarities that keep frustrations at bay and divisions more latent. When the emergency of displacement waned, fault lines emerged. An early crack materialized around the macromodern fractures between private and civic life; family, state ideological apparatus, and white-savior industry interventions; and how the past would be represented for the future—in other words, the school. While many families were proud of the teaching structures they'd developed in the mountains, including "barefoot teachers" (members of the community who gave classes, partly in Mayan languages) and a curricular emphasis on class consciousness and the reasons for struggle, others wanted their kids prepared for living in postwar Guatemala's national life. When a white South African arrived with a school project emphasizing Spanish language, science, and other "universal" offerings, many supported him. This angered others, who felt this outsider—and those who supported him—were dismissing their shared struggle and betraying the community's historic memory. There were also rumors he had counterinsurgency connections, and many families had racked up debts paying for such privatized education. The new school also began to create different play, study, and epistemic groups among the children. Meanwhile the state was insisting the people hew to standardized ruling structures such as elected mayors, bringing in party politics, which both revealed and created new divisions. In turn, newly official elected leaders began to undermine the authority of leaders from the old days.[48] As throughout postgenocide Guatemala, some people also came to find Evangelical Christianity more congenial to their spiritual seeking, rupturing both the Catholic Liberation Theology–infused polity and, as newly thrifty Protestant "ethnics," the collective investment portfolio.

Too, as Carlota McAllister found in her work with the similarly highly organized Maya-K'iche's of Chupol, decisions that people may have accepted during the war, yet were felt, nonetheless, as morally dubious or personally tragic—like setting traps for soldiers or being willing to smother your child to save others—create unruly emotions even decades later:[49] shame, resentment, anger, grief. People began to express these divisions jurisdictionally, creating first one and then three new hamlets, each with a separate set of leaders, separate relations to municipal government and NGOs, but not with separate space.[50] People still lived side by side, just in different towns. Resentments and disappointments also roiled domestic life, similar to what Paula Worby has documented with resettled refugees from the camps in Mexico.[51] There, as with the CPR, many men seemed to feel that radical gender equality was necessary during the war but "back at home" expected women to "go back to normal."

In part, people's expectations were, perhaps, unreasonably high, that once they resettled, life would change. Neither traditional leaders nor the new auxiliary mayors struggling to interact with the bureaucratic (and socioeconomic) structures (and officials who still viewed them as enemies) could fulfill those hopes. But people did not want to suffer anymore. Perhaps it was those unreasonably high expectations, but some people began to pocket collective monies. For instance, forty-two thousand quetzals (about US$7000) disappeared from the hydroelectric project. This led the folks from the Canary Islands, who had accompanied the community for years—from the mountains and through the electricity project—to withdraw from their solidarity work in frustration. Mimicking the stuttering process of building Jurún, the hydroelectric project was abandoned in 2001.

After 1997, the second phase of General Gramajo's shock doctrine kicked in. With the peace treaty, the Alvaro Arzú government began to privatize basic infrastructure, including electricity.[52] The National Electrification Institute still exists and runs nine major hydroelectric projects, but the door was kicked open for transnational companies to exploit Guatemala's rivers for industrial projects (such as the Canadian-owned Marlin gold mine and Cementos Progreso) and for export—as before the Guatemalan Spring—not for local needs. Over the next decade, several hydroelectric *mega-proyectos* (large-scale, corporate projects) were built on rivers in the region: Palo Viejo in Cotzal, and Xacbal I and II in Chajul. Well-heeled representatives of the dams did extensive PR work in the Zona Reina, promising cheap light without *any* labor, drawing in some community members (though no lines have yet been hung to *any* communities, and the voltage is too high for domestic use, so it is unlikely they ever will). Even as regional leaders talked down the communal project, saying it was worthless with the new high-tech hydroelectric systems, they tried to steal the commons by transferring the project to municipal control, a maneuver the community managed to quash. Despite being stuck, people felt that outside actors were jealous of their autonomy.

RE: Doubts

In the highlands of postgenocide Guatemala, an intense battle is being waged around "war by transnational financial means" and its often-enchanting promises. As the transnational scales down and up into and via these far-off redoubts, people grapple with both banal and existential doubts. Can one believe the promise of low-cost electricity, without any of the backbreaking labor? Will something really trickle down? Can one count on the politician, the *empresario* (businessman), the *finquero* (plantation owner) this time? They say they care about the Maya. Some of them are even one of us. More terrifying are those late-night worries, now voiced by day by neighbors, former companions in struggle: Were we duped by revolutionary hopes? The enchanting promises they struggled so hard to achieve together—jobs, roads, education, healthcare, and light—now only seem possible if provided by *empresas* (private companies).

But in 2005, several small Mayan communities over the mountains in the province of San Marcos held *consultas* (locally run referenda) that rejected large-scale mining and related extractivisms. The practice spread, and in 2010, 129 communities in the Zona Reina held consultas (2 of the 4 hamlets in 31 de Mayo participated). Over twenty-five thousand people said "no" to large companies installing hydroelectric and mining operations. The process of the consulta—partly producing the resistance it claims only to measure[53]—and knowing tens of thousands of their neighbors agreed (and would therefore need *local* power), buoyed the hopes of folks in 31 de Mayo, and they reignited the hydroelectric project. This entailed more labors and negotiations, making alliances with national organizations (which had also emerged or strengthened in the ensuing years, including Colectivo MadreSelva, and the new indigenous-radical Uk'u'x B'e), negotiating funding, displacing the corrupt committee members, and reconstituting their own organization, fixing the generator and clearing the channel. In 2012, electricity began to flow. New "light years" had begun.

Redoubtable: Formidable, worthy of respect

When I visited 31 de Mayo with Ana in 2013, we spent many hours hanging around the tiny building that housed the electricity office while a woman I will call Concepción, a village schoolteacher and project administrator, collected monthly fees and organized the technicians and work crews who were laboring feverishly to clear a series of landslides that had cut the flow. Concepción was gracious with the many queries about when the lights would come back on. Many visitors ended up settling on the bench beside us, watching the drizzling rain outside, and telling us their stories about the light, augmented as new people dropped by and took up the threads, mixing stories of their lives in the mountain with the pride in this amazing (if a decade-interrupted) accomplishment. Children could study. Women could weave after sunset rather than stealing daylight hours from childcare, cooking, gardening, marketing, and water carrying.[54] People could gather and make plans. In neighboring villages, people suspicious of those the army had warned would only bring trouble, saw that, instead, those scrawny folks in the raggedy clothes had captured that promethean promise of light in the darkness. And they were paying only twenty quetzals (about three US dollars) a month. "Fue sufrimiento faraónico, pero fue para nosotros. Todo cambió con la electricidad [It was epic suffering but it was for us. Everything changed with the electricity]," said don Paulino, an older leader. They had become redoubtable, "deserving of respect."

Ana and I were also invited to inspect the *zanja* (mill run) with don Paulino and the younger Miguel, and we spent a morning walking its length. Young and middle-aged men were engaged in great exertion (just walking up the steep incline had been exertion enough for me), clearing the mud and trees from its course (which, between March and July 2013, again "pharoanically," they had managed to line with cement—the whole two kilometers). They were well aware that every problem with the community power plant was fodder for their enemies and their enchanting promises of "modern" electricity. When we made it to the sluice gate at the river, don Paulino explained, "Now they are trying to screw us, saying the empresa will come and bring light. While we already have it! They come to screw us around, they won't leave us in peace. They are trying to destroy the project that all of us accomplished together. They are the same people who screwed up the cooperative. They don't want *lucha* [struggle], they don't want *bienes comunales* [common wealth], they want the empresa."

Many former CPR, like organized and *consciente* people throughout the country, see this as a con. Don Cirilo, another older leader from the time in the mountain, told us,

> They are lying if they say we can just solicit light from the *empresa*. First, we already have it cheap, only twenty quetzals for four lightbulbs, and you only pay more if you have things such as blenders, refrigerators. But in Uspantán they pay between Q250 and Q300 (about US$35) a month for light, even without *aparatos* [appliances]. Here people don't have it, so they don't know. There is very little information. And they also don't know that the energy the companies make here doesn't stay here, it goes to other countries. It's not for Guatemala. And the same family, the same ones who cheated us on the plantations, the Brols, now they are no longer just finqueros; they are empresarios, selling electricity. Where does the money go? Here we are always poorer.

Don Paulino added, "There is no *finquero bueno*."[55]

That evening—when the cheerful, golden, lovely light had come back—we shared a meal with Concepción's family, the gloom of the rainy dusk vanquished in the bare bulb's glow and in the camaraderie of a visit from family members now living on the south coast. We talked about the Ríos Montt trial, which CPR members had diligently supported—including giving testimony—and its similarity to their hydroelectric project. Both are pilot projects. With unity and hard work, community members could help extend the enchanting possibilities of enLIGHTenment: metaphorically to other perpetrators, through justice and clarifying what actually happened in the past, and materially to neighboring towns, by extending the cables from their turbine and creating new projects. Their generator had thousands of watts of capability more than they were even using, and they were developing the know-how to help others harness the rivers' powers. In fact, Ana was helping them put the finishing touches on the very DIY how-to manual I have been citing. At the dinner table they said, "This is a living possibility for other Guatemalans to emulate."

Enchantment is linked etymologically to *incantation*, but these were not mere words.[56] They are also deeds. The community members were actually living as if they *were* humans—rather than subsisting like animals on the plantations or forced to control and even torture and kill their neighbors as most rural men did through the Civil Patrols. In that same way, their labors to create the channel and provide electricity were "current engagements" (in both senses of "in the moment" and the charge of electric currency) aimed at future developments, a lot like Jurún.

When I saw Ana in the summer of 2015, she was excited about several things but also a bit down. On her last visit to 31 de Mayo, Concepción had asked for help to stem the many cases of domestic abuse. It was hard to know that the deeply consciente men she worked with and admired would drink too much and beat their *compañeras*, or that these proud, strong women were living with such fear and violence. Few women had options beyond the household, and improved legal protections for women had little traction, as some local leaders were also perpetrators, making it difficult for women to turn to them for succor. To revisit our conversations in the jeep on my first trip to 31 de Mayo, it is a complex thing to question class, race, *and* gender privilege. Feminism is not just about interrogating the patriarchal religious structures that inhabit our heads and hearts as we strive to be "good women"—and our companions struggle to be "good men." It is also a racialized and socioeconomic infrastructure. Revisiting revolutions too often shows where women have been left out, or provisionally included, only to be re-relegated to limiting roles—even as their struggles and suffering are essential to the sprouts of energy surging out in unexpected directions. We revisit so that there will be no future revolution without their full participation.

But there was also reason to be excited: the growing (and successful) movement to oust the country's president, Otto Pérez Molina; the new hydroelectric projects inaugurated in neighboring villages (as of 2020, there are four!); and how the former CPR had re-created a Council of Elders. Liberation Theology has been a powerful source of good in the world, but it was built on ethnocidal purification protocols that sought to root out "pagan" practices. The council was an older Mayan form, grounded in horology, engagement with telluric deities, and combined spiritual and practical community service. The Oedipal project of many of the young indigenous men (and some women) who had joined Catholic Action and then the revolutionary movements in the 1970s was not only to kill off the finquero and his political economic dominance but also to overthrow this local gerontocratic system.[57] Now, along with many indigenous folks around the country, people in 31 de Mayo are finding revolutionary possibilities in the identifications and organizing forms they thought they had overcome. The solidarity organizations 31 de Mayo had assembled to support revitalizing the electricity project—Colectivo MadreSelva and Uk'u'x B'e—connect class struggle, indigenous rights, and environmental activism in an emerging national infrastructure for future making.[58] Ana was delighted and bemused that Pepe—her partner, a member of MadreSelva, and a die-hard atheist—had been invited to serve on the council. They had schlepped up to the community and participated in the several-day initiation ceremonies, and Pepe was finding himself subtly transformed by his new responsibilities. In 2013, don Vicente, an older CPR leader who had become increasingly involved in Mayan spirituality since they had resettled in 31, had told me, "The power of Maya ceremony, and *costumbre* [traditional] religion, isn't like the others, that only come to divide us, ever since the Spanish arrived." Water. Power. Women. Maya. Promise.

Notes

"Do It Yourself." I would like to thank Ana Cofiño, José Cruz, the people in 31 de Mayo and MadreSelva (especially Andrea Rivera, Jorge Grijalva, and Rene Mérida), Fredy López and the people at INDE, Thelma Porres and CIRMA, Dorotea Gómez, Luis Solano, Judie Maxwell, Michal Osterwall, Mark Driscoll, and Oxidate. Fieldwork was funded by the US Department of Education/Title VI and the Andrew W. Mellon Foundation, awarded through the Duke Center for Latin American and Caribbean Studies, with special thanks to Natalie Hartman. I am very grateful to Heather Vrana and Julie Gibbings for their extraordinary commitment to this project, and to the other participants, especially Jonathon Peyton. I apologize for not fully responding to their excellent comments. All translations from the Spanish are by the author. Land Acknowledgement: the place I write is the ancestral territory of the Saponi and Catawba peoples. This essay is dedicated to Lois Nelson, who got me thinking about dams and socio-eco-systems back in the 1970s.

1. The PGT took various forms over the decades with some portions joining the armed revolutionary struggle. This did not save those who championed unarmed democratic tactics.

2. Severo Martínez Peláez, *La patria del criollo: Ensayo de interpretación de la realidad colonial guatemalteca* (Mexico City: Fondo de Cultura Ecónomica, 1970; repr. 2013).

3. See Greg Grandin, *The Last Colonial Massacre: Latin America in the Cold War* (Chicago: University of Chicago Press, 2004).

4. This is not the place to review the complex ways in which the Arévalo and Arbenz governments, or the different revolutionary organizations of the 1970s, engaged—and were engaged by—the majority indigenous population, but for

indigenous people it was a site of massive learning *and* of army-assisted divisions. There were very few indigenous commanders, and the idea that everyone would be the same in guerrilla fatigues (while partly true) also effaced the specificities of indigenous lifeworlds and hid entrenched racism. Organized indigenous women faced the added challenges of misogyny. When I analyzed jokes told about Rigoberta Menchú Tum when she won the Nobel Prize, I found that many Mayan men who were angered at the racism of jokes told by some leftist compañeros were happy to tell jokes I found sexist. See Betsy Konefal, *For Every Indio Who Falls: A History of Maya Activism in Guatemala, 1960–1990* (Albuquerque: University of New Mexico Press 2010); Diane M. Nelson, *A Finger in the Wound: Body Politics in Quincentennial Guatemala* (Berkeley: University of California Press, 1999).

5. See Jorge Ramón González Ponciano, "De la patria del criollo a la patria del shumo" (PhD diss., University of Texas, Austin, 2005); Diane M. Nelson, Beatriz Manz, Paula Worby, and Liz Oglesby, "Ricardo Falla S.J. y la antropología en tiempos de guerra," *Eutopia: Entrega especial Ricardo Falla S.J.*, 241–260 (Guatemala City: Universidad Rafael Landívar, 2018); Orin Starn, "Missing the Revolution: Anthropologists and the War in Peru," *Cultural Anthropology* 6, no. 1 (February 1991): 63–91; Víctor Montejo, "In the Name of the Pot, the Sun, the Broken Spear, the Rock, the Stick, the Idol, Ad Infinitum and Ad Nauseam: An Exposé of Anglo Anthropologists' Obsessions with the Invention of Mayan Gods," *Red Pencil Review: A Journal of Native American Studies* 9, no. 1 (Spring 1993): 12–16.

6. See Arturo Escobar, *Designs for the Pluriverse: Radical Interdependence, Autonomy, and the Making of Worlds* (Durham, NC: Duke University Press, 2018).

7. Like many settlements created through struggle the village was named for the date, May 31 1998, that people first occupied the site.

8. There are twenty-two Maya ethnolinguistic peoples in Guatemala.

9. See Jennifer Schirmer, *The Guatemalan Military Project: A Violence Called Democracy* (Philadelphia: University of Pennsylvania Press, 1998); Carlota McAllister and Diane M. Nelson, "Aftermath: Harvests of Violence and Histories of the Future," in *War by Other Means: Aftermath in Post-Genocide Guatemala*, ed. Carlota McAllister and Diane M. Nelson, 1–45 (Durham, NC: Duke University Press, 2013).

10. See Ricardo Falla, SJ, *Al atardecer de la vida*, vol. 5: *Pastoral de acompañamiento en área de guerra* (Guatemala City: AVANCSO/URL, 2018).

11. See Matilde González, *Se cambió el tiempo: Conflicto y poder en territorio K'iche' 1880–1996* (Guatemala City: AVANCSO, 2002); Eduardo Gudynas, *Extractivismos: Ecología, economía y política de un modo de entender el desarrollo y la Naturaleza* (Cochabamba, Bolivia: CEDIB, 2015).

12. McAllister shows that *conciencia* is the sense of what it means to be a moral person and the commitment to act on that awareness. Carlota McAllister, "Testimonial Truths and Revolutionary Mysteries," in *War by Other Means: Aftermath in Post-Genocide Guatemala*, ed. Carlota McAllister and Diane M. Nelson, 93–118 (Durham, NC: Duke University Press, 2013).

13. In a manner of speaking: The constant army incursions meant they frequently had to flee their positions, leaving behind what little they had managed to accumulate. When soldiers realized members of the CPR were scavenging the cans from the trash heaps of military outposts for cooking and storage, they began to put holes in them to deny them even this.

14. Someone discovered a way to excise the roosters' voice boxes so their crowing

would not give them away, and there were constant agronomical experiments in how to produce under such taxing conditions. See Carlos Santos, *Guatemala el silencio del gallo: Un misionero español en la guerra más cruenta de América* (Barcelona: Debate, 2007).

15. As part of the accompaniment project of the environmental justice collective MadreSelva, Ana Cofiño and Ana Eugenia Paredes worked with community members to create a document of their history, "The Way of the Light." My trip with Ana C. was part of the research, so I heard many of these stories and also draw on the beautiful book they published. Colectivo MadreSelva, *El camino de la luz: Historias del proyecto comunitario de energía eléctrica "Luz de los héroes y Mártires de la Resistencia"* (Guatemala City: Colectivo MadreSelva, 2014).

16. Alfonso Huet, *Nos salvó la sagrada selva* (Cobán, Guatemala: ADICI Wakliiqo, 2008).

17. I also have learned so much from Ana's feminist insistence on acknowledging these struggles. Those of a certain generation will remember the emotional last episode of *M*A*S*H*, when Hawkeye failed in his efforts to retain his sanity in the face of war. What hurt too much to bear was a woman suffocating her own child to keep its cries from giving away their position. Several women in the CPR made this same fateful choice.

18. On September 11, 1990, the anthropologist Myrna Mack was assassinated by the army in part for her work with the CPR and the organization's efforts to go public.

19. For example, figuring as a refuge in John Sayles's fictional film *Men with Guns* (Sony, 1998).

20. Public recognition included the army revealing they had captured the vestments and notebooks of Ricardo Falla the Jesuit-anthropologist who was living with the Jungle CPR, farther north in the Ixcán. Apparently red-baiting him took precedence over maintaining silence about the CPR.

21. While we were there, however, we were treated to a short concert and got to leaf through a carefully preserved notebook full of handwritten revolutionary songs and sketches of life in the forest.

22. See Maya Deren, *Divine Horsemen: The Voodoo Gods of Haiti* (New York: Vanguard, 1953).

23. See Héctor Alejandro Gramajo Morales, *De la guerra a la guerra: La difícil transición política en Guatemala* (México, DF: Fondo de Cultura Editorial, 1995). See also McAllister and Nelson, *War by Other Means*.

24. Greg Grandin, "Chronicles of a Guatemalan Genocide Foretold: Violence, Trauma, and the Limits of Historical Inquiry," *Nepantla: Views from the South* 1, no. 2 (2000): 391–412. See also Naomi Klein, *The Shock Doctrine: The Rise of Disaster Capitalism* (New York: Picador, 2008); and Joe Masco, *The Theater of Operations: National Security Affect from the Cold War to the War on Terror* (Durham, NC: Duke University Press, 2014).

25. Susanne Jonas, *Of Centaurs and Doves: Guatemala's Peace Process* (Boulder, CO: Westview Press, 2000).

26. Most owners got any price they asked, for often worthless land.

27. Irmalicia Velasquez Nimatuj, "A Dignified Community Where We Can Live," in *War by Other Means: Aftermath in Post-Genocide Guatemala*, ed. Carlota McAllister and Diane M. Nelson, 170–194 (Durham, NC: Duke University Press, 2013).

28. Alfonso Bauer Paiz, *¿Cómo funciona el capital yanqui en Centroamérica?* (Guatemala City: Editorial Fotopublicaciones, 1956).

29. It seems to have been a bit of a surprise that Herrera, whose family created the largest sugar mill in the country, Pantaleón—a seat for death squad and counterinsurgency support after the massive CUC strike on the southern coast in 1978—would have had such nationalist sentiments. See Elizabeth Oglesby, "Politics at Work: Elites, Labor and Agrarian Modernization in Guatemala, 1980–2000" (PhD diss., UC-Berkeley, 2002).

30. The rage of Cubans at this rip-off helped bring many middle-class consumers into the revolutionary alliance. See William J. Hausman, Peter Hertner, and Mira Wilkins, *Global Electrification: Multinational Enterprise and International Finance in the History of Light and Power, 1878–2007* (Cambridge: Cambridge University Press, 2009). In 1956 *El Imparcial* compared electricity prices in Puerto Rico, Washington, DC, and New Orleans and found they were higher in Guatemala.

31. Comité de desarrollo campesino (CODECA), *La privatización del derecho a la energía eléctrica: Impactos socioeconómicos y convulsión social creciente* (Guatemala City: CODECA, 2014); Jim Handy, *Revolution in the Countryside: Rural Conflict and Agrarian Reform in Guatemala, 1944–1954* (Chapel Hill: University of North Carolina Press, 1994).

32. *El Imparcial*, May 30, and June 1, 1953; see also Jorge Luján Muñoz and Daniel Contreras P., *Historia general de Guatemala*, vol. 6: *Epoca contemporanea de 45 a la actualidad* (Guatemala City: Asociación Amigos del País Fundación para la cultura y el desarrollo, 1997).

33. Empresa Eléctrica de Guatemala already had two small hydroelectric plants on the river.

34. The George W. Bush administration's trumped-up claims of WMDs, or weapons of mass destruction, were used to soften resistance to the disastrous invasion of Iraq in 2003, a strategy Joe Masco links to "national security affect" in ways very resonant with Cold War–era US-Guatemala relations (Masco, *The Theater of Operations*).

35. In ten years EEGSA invested about Q833,000 in electrical infrastructure, while its net profit from Guatemala went from Q2.5 million to over Q5.5 million (*El Imparcial*, January 26, 1956).

36. It was also argued that increasing electricity coverage would reduce deforestation, as electric stoves would replace wood-burning cooking. In turn, forest cover would encourage rain and water retention, in turn helping to power the new hydro electric facility (*El Imparcial*, January 18, 1956). There was also talk of building a nuclear plant. Cementos Novella has become Cementos Progreso and continues to use excess amounts of electricity while enjoying special low rates. It is also a flagrant abuser of human and indigenous rights and enjoys the use of the state security apparatus to defend its economic interests, leading to one of the many corruption charges that brought down President General Pérez Molina in 2015.

37. The president of Electric Bond and Share Company EBASCO and even the vice-president of its parent company, American and Foreign Power Incorporated, made personal visits to Guatemala to try to bully their way in on the project, offering to build Jurún and then sell it to the state after ten years.

38. The right-wing *Historia general de Guatemala* says, "Nothing could be further

from the truth than the story that the Liberation government turned back all the advances of the Revolution. It was not against development, it was just anti-communist. . . . the new constitution maintained the Atlantic highway and Jurún Marinalá" (Luján Muñoz and Contreras, *Historia general de Guatemala*, 36).

39. *El Imparcial*, June 5, 1956.

40. Rosenthal was serving on the National Planning Secretariat and went on to become Guatemala's UN ambassador and oversee implementation of the Peace Accords. Fuentes Mohr was Méndez Montenegro's finance minister. He later formed the Social Democrat party and served in Congress but was assassinated in January 1979. His murder convinced many people that nonviolent democratic change was impossible, greatly increasing the appeal of the armed revolutionary movements.

41. The same held true for the national university USAC and, later, the Academia de Lenguas Mayas de Guatemala (Guatemalan Mayan Language Academy; ALMG).

42. Luján Muñoz and Contreras, *Historia general de Guatemala*, 438. Fully buying out the concession in 1972 cost Guatemala over $18 million.

43. *El Imparcial*, January 10, 1970.

44. The practices included sending US military advisors and Green Berets, setting up computerized police archives, and funneling up to US$20 million by 1975.

45. See Barbara Rose Johnston, *Chixoy Dam Legacy Issues Study* (Santa Cruz, CA: Center for Political Ecology, 2005).

46. This was more a sublation, a carrying along of sporadic massacres of ladino peasants and the selective murder and disappearance of ladino activists along with the mass murder and scorched earth practiced against Mayan communities as a whole. As with the CPR, the PGT and other revolutionary activists who survived had to go underground or into exile.

47. There is a closer river, but it runs through an ex-PAC village where people are still "*encabronados* [pissed off] with the CPR because they fought on opposite sides of the trenches." Colectivo MadreSelva, *El camino de la luz*, 63.

48. This was exacerbated by the fact that several of the most respected leaders had opted to go to communities on the south coast.

49. McAllister, "Testimonial Truths and Revolutionary Mysteries," 93–118.

50. Struggles over control of fresh water, attempts to privatize things community members had bought or built together (cattle, a cardamom dryer), and complex dealings with outside powers—a conservative Catholic priest who thought they were all pagans, different political parties promising things from Uspantán, the municipal seat—all encouraged these divisions. Karla Holloway tells a similar story about Black-owned businesses in the US South, cultivated in the redoubt of segregation, but abandoned for white, supposedly superior, enterprises in the 1960s and 1970s. Karla FC Holloway, *Passed On: African American Mourning Stories. A Memorial* (Durham, NC: Duke University Press, 2003).

51. Paula Worby, "A Generation after the Refugee's Return: Are We There Yet?," in *War by Other Means: Aftermath in Post-Genocide Guatemala*, ed. Carlota McAllister and Diane M. Nelson, 330–352 (Durham, NC: Duke University Press, 2013).

52. Arundhati Roy says, "Privatization takes away the last weapon of the poor—the vote." Arundhati Roy, *DAM/AGE: A Film with Arundhati Roy*, dir. Aradhana Seth (BBC films, 2002).

53. Diane M. Nelson, *Who Counts? The Mathematics of Death and Life after Genocide* (Durham, NC: Duke University Press, 2015).

54. Weaving is an economic endeavor, creating goods for sale. But its practice and the fabulously intricate and beautiful clothing women create and wear are also fundamental elements of female identity as Maya.

55. These community leaders are struggling to convince their neighbors—who they thought were too clear-sighted to fall for such a scam—that it is just the same old story of rapacious exploitation they know so well. Elsewhere, in resettled CPR as well as "regular" communities, they are withholding payment from electric companies whose tariffs feel like extortion. Organized by the Comité de Desarrollo Campesino (Campesino Development Committee; CODECA), their denunciations strikingly revisit the complaints about the EEGSA from the 1950s.

56. Ann Burlein and Jackie Orr, "Introduction: The Practice of Enchantment: Strange Allures," *Women's Studies Quarterly* 40, nos. 3–4 (2012): 13–23.

57. Konefal, *For Every Indio Who Falls*.

58. It also bears mentioning that one of the two MadreSelva engineers is a woman, Andrea Rivera.

CHAPTER 10

Reclaiming a Revolution

Memory as Possibility in Urban Guatemala

Betsy Konefal

> It's in *our* hands [to ensure] that the revolution . . . returns to this country.
>
> La Batucada del Pueblo, October 20, 2017

On October 20, 2017, thousands of people made their way to the historic center of Guatemala City to mark Día de la Revolución (Revolution Day), a national holiday commemorating the beginning of the reformist Guatemalan Spring in 1944. Members of student groups, unions, and youth collectives congregated at El Trébol (a main highway "clover" intersection) to march together to Central Park, their matching T-shirts, banners, and chants proclaiming identities and demands simultaneously rooted in the past and pointedly of the present and future: they combined calls for equality and democracy symbolized by the October Revolution with demands for economic justice and an end to the corruption and impunity born of the bloody counterrevolution and decades of war that followed. Spectators lined La Sexta (Sixth Avenue) or followed marchers to the park for a day of speeches, music, and the venting of collective indignation.

Since the 1954 coup that toppled Jacobo Arbenz Guzmán, October 20 has been a date laden with symbolism and opportunity, tension and contestation. During the most repressive of the military dictatorships, security forces sought to contain the ferment through prohibitions, surveillance, and terror. But the symbolism and optics of the occasion meant that it was often difficult or unwise to do so entirely; not infrequently, state officials and politicians have used the symbolic date for their own ends. At the same time, generations of urban activists—and sometimes armed revolutionaries—have laid claim to commemorative public spaces and used

Revolution Day to shape social memory as a platform for resistance and demands infused with historical import.

Not coincidentally, October 20 marks another anniversary: the date when death squad assassins fatally shot student leader Oliverio Castañeda de León in 1978, after he delivered an impassioned speech at a Revolution Day rally near Central Park. Castañeda de León, an economics student at the Universidad de San Carlos de Guatemala (University of San Carlos; USAC) and the newly elected general secretary of the Asociación de Estudiantes Universitarios (Association of University Students; AEU), had used the occasion to defend mass protests against a doubling of bus fares and to condemn a government guilty of murders and disappearances. The timing of his assassination would prove to be a monumental political blunder on the part of security forces, as it wed the already symbolic anniversary of the 1944 Revolution with what would become annual protests in honor of Oliverio, and against terror and impunity.

His murder cemented October 20 as the most important date commemorating the reformist past while condemning the post-1954 reversal of its gains and the brutal repression of leaders who attempted to carry on its objectives.

Young People and Memories of Revolution: 1978 and 2017

The thirty-fourth anniversary of the Guatemalan Spring in 1978 came at the beginning of the vicious dictatorship of General Romeo Lucas García, who had taken power that July. In those first months of the Lucas García regime, university and high school students, unionists, and others from what is called the "popular" sector in Guatemala held mass urban protests and staged a strike against high transportation costs and incessant violence. State security forces responded in force, firing tear gas and bullets into crowds and singling out individual leaders. By late October, the AEU leader Castañeda de León had been under surveillance for months; police detectives reported on his activities with other students and unionists, and they listed his name as one of the "agitators of the marches" of August and September 1978.[1]

Even amid harsh repression, demonstrations continued in whatever spaces organizers could occupy, including on October 20. Castañeda de León delivered his speech in the Parque Centenario, an area heavily occupied by plainclothes police.[2] He paid tribute to the October Revolution for its achievements and its promise, and at the same time condemned ongoing violence that included mass killings of protestors: "They can kill the best sons of the *pueblo*," Oliverio declared, "but they never have and they never could assassinate the revolution. Because to do that, they . . . would have to kill six million Guatemalans. As long as there is a *pueblo*, there will be revolution!"[3] Moments later, as Castañeda de León and other AEU members and friends made their way across the park and onto La Sexta, assailants fatally shot him at the entrance to Pasaje Rubio.

On October 20, 2017, a crowd gathered at the very spot where Oliverio had been assassinated, as people do every year on that day, holding candles and red carnations, most in t-shirts bearing his photo and declaring the thirty-ninth anniversary of his murder. His most famous words were printed across the back of their shirts in all caps: "¡MIENTRAS HAYA PUEBLO . . . HABRÁ REVOLUCIÓN!"[4] Some people added a red bandana honoring the October Revolution and Arbenz, with the former president's image and the epithet *Soldado del pueblo* (Soldier of the People). Che hats, too, were a popular choice. Young people attended the memorial in force, alongside veterans of the struggles of the 1960s and 1970s. One older speaker and former compañero of Castañeda de León looked around and noted how important it was to see lots of young people at the commemoration, how vital it was to "fight arm in arm, the young people, all the generations." Bowing toward the site where his friend had bled and died nearly four decades before, he introduced the next generation: "Oliverio," he said, "here are the new *jóvenes* (young people) who fight for this country."[5]

One of those *jóvenes* soon accepted the small megaphone that was being shared by the speakers, a member of the drumming group La Batucada del Pueblo. "Batucada" refers to a Brazilian percussion style, and the group, which came together during the massive 2015 public uprisings against the corruption and impunity of the Otto Pérez Molina administration, uses drums and other instruments to set the rhythm of protests large and small.[6]

Seamlessly connecting themes of history and social memory, the speaker explicitly linked Castañeda de León and those who gathered to honor him in 2017 to the October Revolution and its aftermath, and also to pressing concerns in the present. October 20, 1944, was *so* important, the Batucada leader said, Guatemala's *fecha máxima* (the quintessential moment or turning point in the country's history), "and it should be honored as such." He continued: "In La Batucada when we say that power is in your hands and mine—*we* are the majority, *we* are . . . the people—at the

FIGURE 10.1. *Memorial for Oliverio Castañeda de León, Guatemala City, October 20, 2017. Photo by the author.*

same time we are . . . [exhorting Guatemalans] to carry the seed, so that 'as long as there is a *pueblo*, there will be revolution.' It's a call to say 'it's in *our* hands [to ensure] that the revolution . . . returns to this country.'"

One of the speaker's central aims was to remind the people honoring

Castañeda de León that real change was possible in Guatemala *because it had already happened*. The October Revolution itself proved that their dreams were attainable. The megaphone amplified his message as hundreds of people crowded the area: "The revolution already happened!" he reminded his listeners. "*Yes*, it was possible, *yes*, it happened in this country, a dignified revolutionary process, a total change in the structure of this system. Yes, it happened." But the future? "When will it return?" he asked the crowd. "In whose hands? . . . It's got me thinking . . . what did Oliverio feel when he woke up that morning, October 20, 1978? . . . What awaited us on that day? What are we going to build? What does this country deserve?" He wondered aloud whether Castañeda de León had had an inkling of what was coming his way. *Posiblemente, sí.*[7]

It was Oliverio's determination to act, he declared, despite the risks, that made him an example, and a martyr. "That spirit, that energy," he asserted, were evident in all he did; he was just a twenty-three-year-old *patojo* (kid) "but with wisdom, nerve, and so much bravery, . . . to plant himself in front of the *monstro* of repression, of terror, fear, and silence . . . and say, 'here is the pueblo of Guatemala, here we are, the youth of this country, here is the University of San Carlos, this is what we are, we are the pueblo, we are revolution, and we aren't afraid of anything.' He wasn't even afraid of death, and he met it that day, that same day, the 20th of October." The Batucada speaker urged his listeners to draw on the legacy of Oliverio to address the current crises in which Guatemalans find themselves. Just like in earlier times, a way forward, he said, needed "to be constructed with much nerve, with patience, with steadfastness and commitment," so that real change can come once again. "Oliverio is still here," he insisted, his memory an undying source of inspiration and guidance. His presence will not be erased by "more bullets, by more hate, . . . by those barbarous monsters who committed this crime," he continued. His legacy will never be diminished: "a legacy of struggle, of dignity, and of courage to change the order of things in this country."[8]

The speech was a rendering of almost three-quarters of a century of Guatemalan history—spanning Días de la Revolución from 1944, 1978, and 2017—but focused most urgently on what still needed to happen. Post-1954 history, a series of deadly struggles to rebuild what had been knocked down, represented loss and grief, but also *gigantesco* legacies and models for change personified by Oliverio and others like him. With a crisp nod to the rest of La Batucada, he passed the megaphone to the next speaker, and vigorous drumming filled the street.[9]

The speeches of Oliverio and the Batucada spokesperson, separated by almost four decades, demonstrate in similar ways how history and memory are closely related, but at the same time distinct from each other. In each case, the elements of the past that the speakers invoked—and the meanings they constructed of that history—reflected their most pressing demands and goals in the moment. As Elizabeth Jelin reminds us, it is important to differentiate history and memory in this way, to consider how "people construct sense or meaning of the past, and how they relate that past to their present in the act of remembering." She emphasizes conflicts that surround memories and, especially, "the active role of the participants in those struggles to make historical meaning."[10]

With Oliverio and La Batucada, we see young meaning makers actively shaping memories of Guatemala's past that could nourish contemporary social struggles, in contestation with a powerful state and other sectors. Efforts to harness the power of memory have unfolded on many other fronts as well: on other dates, in different streets and public plazas, in the press, through archives and exhumations, and at commemorative sites and their educational projects.[11] These "labors of memory" have tended to share a common thread: as outspoken Guatemalans since 1954 have reconstructed the past while demanding a *futuro distinto* (different future), the October Revolution has been a ubiquitous idea and example that contrasts sharply with the post-1954 history of marginalization, repression, and loss.[12] Against the backdrop of what followed, the Guatemalan Spring has been memorialized for its accomplishments, to be sure, but perhaps more powerfully as an example rife with possibility.

Invoking Revolution in Post-Coup Guatemala

Annual commemoration of the October Revolution, unsurprisingly, started during the Arévalo regime itself, with October 20 designated a national holiday in 1945 on the first anniversary of the coup against Federico Ponce that launched the Guatemalan Spring. In October 1951, during Arbenz's first year as president, Guatemalans enjoyed extra time off, with a decree officially extending the celebration. But even with the upending of the October Revolution just before its tenth anniversary, symbolic dates and individuals associated with it would continue to be recognized, at times openly, at other times more covertly. During the long series of dictatorships that followed, memories of the Guatemalan Spring would be invoked again and again, their significance and meanings asserted and contested, their commemorations sometimes opportunistic and sometimes risky.

In Carlos Castillo Armas's first few months in office after the 1954 coup, the new president tried to solidify the "counterrevolution" through conciliatory gestures toward urban, educated Guatemalans, sectors in which the revolution had found some of its most ardent support.[13] It was a move full of contradictions: even as the president met with students and professors, university-affiliated Arbencistas were being forced into exile or fled for their own safety in the post-coup crackdown against supporters of the revolution. Within two years, tensions between the Castillo Armas regime and students came to a head, and, not coincidentally, it occurred on the anniversary of the killing of a symbolic martyr of the October Revolution, María Chinchilla, a teacher shot during anti-Ubico protests on June 25, 1944.

During the furor that followed Chinchilla's death, the longtime dictator Jorge Ubico had been forced to resign, and just days later, in early July, the National Association of Teachers declared that June 25 would be observed in Chinchilla's honor as "Teachers' Day" in Guatemala. For students, especially, the day took on even greater significance in the post-coup context, as it came to represent not just the honoring of educators and of the October Revolution, but also opposition to dictatorship and repression. Aware of its symbolic power, the interior minister in 1956 prohibited public commemoration of Teachers' Day, suggesting that in the past, young people had "misunderstood their freedom" on the occasion.[14] Students from USAC nonetheless planned public commemorations at the university. They organized an art exhibition, a theater production, and a literary contest; they prepared a plaque recognizing students who had been active in the revolution, held a roundtable discussion at the law school on the revolution's impact, and organized a pilgrimage to Chinchilla's grave.[15]

Repression was swift and extensive: police raided USAC, took photographs of publications and promotional materials, and broke up the procession to honor the martyred educator. They invaded the roundtable discussion and arrested participants. The regime declared a "State of Alarm" and then a "State of Siege," suspending constitutional guarantees, establishing a curfew, and restricting travel and the right to assembly. A peaceful student march in defiance of the restrictions was met with police gunfire. The defense minister blamed student injuries and deaths—at the hands of the police—on the students themselves for unlawfully congregating.[16]

This banishing of the revolution would sometimes ease, if only temporarily. In fact, acknowledgment of the reform period would come in and out of favor in the coming years in direct relation to the politics of the moment. After the assassination of Castillo Armas in 1957, elections brought the more conciliatory Miguel Ydígoras Fuentes to power in 1958. Ydígoras was someone who would again half-heartedly court the university sectors—and, again, mostly fail to win their support or acquiescence—and, at the same time, would cautiously embrace revolutionary rhetoric, at least when it came to the presidency of Arévalo. While the more radical Arbenz and his supporters continued to be persecuted, the 1961 labor code under Ydígoras reinstated October 20—Revolution Day—as a paid holiday for all Guatemalans.

Arévalo himself briefly reentered Guatemalan politics, returning from exile on March 29, 1963, in an attempt to run for president. It was a move that Ydígoras appeared to tolerate, but one that prompted a military coup, bringing the hardliner Colonel Enrique Peralta Azurdia to power two days later. The coup eliminated any possibility of reform. For the first time since the Arbenz regime was overthrown, Guatemala was ruled by an administration that fully and explicitly rejected, in the name of anticommunism, a return to democracy. It would be "impossible to resolve [the country's] grave problems," the Peralta Azurdia regime declared, "within the constitutional framework, since the communists take advantage of the broad freedoms which the present constitution concedes; they have infiltrated the government and the different political parties, . . . with the logical result that they are empowered by the government within an apparent legality."[17] Peralta Azurdia suspended constitutional guarantees, established curfews, and required citizens to carry identification papers at all times. People feared appearing on lists compiled by the Committee of National Defense Against Communism. As Jennifer Schirmer explains, the military government "established a political strategy that effectively prevented opposition reformist parties from participating in politics for the next fifteen years by waging 'counter-terror' campaigns through clandestine groups 'designed to prevent any alteration—however minor—of the social and economic structure of the country.'"[18]

Democracy was over in Guatemala and, for the moment, so were symbolic public commemorations of its birth. In response, defiant celebrations of Revolution Day moved underground. The armed insurgency that had begun in 1960—and included officers who had remained loyal to Arbenz in 1954—took on the task of representing a nationalistic continuation of the Guatemalan Spring. The Partido Guatemalteco del Trabajo (Guatemalan Workers Party; PGT) and the Fuerzas Armadas Rebeldes (Rebel Armed Forces; FAR), for example, paid tribute to the revolution with propaganda bombs or by marking the streets of the capital with references to it on symbolic anniversaries. Their adoption of the October Revolution in effect rendered all Guatemalans who voiced a longing for democracy legitimate targets for repression in the eyes of the military—though that would likely have been the case anyway. What resulted was an almost complete criminalization of the revolution beginning in 1963. Stories circulate of cathartic shouts of "¡Viva Arbenz! ¡Viva la revolución!" during this time, but only voiced by drunks, who sometimes paid dearly for their nostalgia.

In the long series of dictatorships to follow, there was one interlude in which a civilian was allowed to assume the presidency: the regime of Julio César Méndez Montenegro (1966–1970). Predictably, the mood regarding the October Revolution shifted somewhat, with at least a rhetorical renewal of attention to revolutionary democracy. During Méndez Montenegro's first year in office, regime officials promoted the October 20 anniversary in flowery nationalist language. A congressional decree identified October 20 as one of three especially "glorious dates" in Guatemalan history: along with the "revolution" that ushered in Guatemalan Liberalism and the coffee state in 1871 and the declaration of independence in 1821, October 20, 1944, constituted one of the "fundamental social acts . . . by virtue of which [Guatemalan] nationality was reaffirmed." As the decree continued, "These [three] anniversaries mark the progressive stages in the social and economic structure of the country, when the human values were reaffirmed that would make it possible for Guatemala to become a democratic state."[19]

At the same time, a new degree of tolerance characterized commemorations. In a telegram titled "October 20 Happenings," the US ambassador to Guatemala described the relative calm at "well-controlled" government-orchestrated memorial events in 1967 and official restraint regarding counterdemonstrations, though he also noted the quiet arrests that took place afterward. Protestors with "anti-GOG [Government of Guatemala] and anti-'foreigner' posters" reportedly marched undisturbed for fifteen blocks "through heavily policed downtown streets," the ambassador noted. When they arrived in Central Park, demonstrators (led by USAC students) tore down a "huge placard" of President Méndez Montenegro, "to the glee of perhaps two thousand mostly casual onlookers." The event remained calm, however, and "occasional attempts to incite [the] crowd ('Yankees Out', Hoorays for Arbenz) were unsuccessful." Nonetheless, the police later arrested three students for "insulting" the president. The ambassador noted that more centrist politicians and intellectuals were permitted to commemorate the anniversary without incident: at one event, Partido Revolucionario

(PR) leaders proclaimed their party the "true legatee of [the] revolution"; the newspaper editor David Vela "elegantly eulogized fallen revolutionary heroes," while clarifying that "for him, promise of revolution was fulfillment of nineteenth century liberal ideals."[20]

The initial tolerance for such gatherings, however, soon diminished, as Méndez Montenegro, in a pact with the military, gave security forces a free hand in countering all kinds of opposition. A State Department "Internal Security Report" a year later signaled that October 20 (a Saturday that year) had become more tense and contested. "The twenty-fourth Anniversary of the October 20 Revolution passed in relative calm," the report noted, but then cataloged what "relative calm" meant in 1968:

> Four bombs exploded Saturday evening in Guatemala City causing some property damage but no injuries. Three devices were placed near police and military installations; one incendiary-type destroyed a police pickup truck. . . . Same night two bombs went off in Jalapa: one at the statue of Castillo Armas in a central plaza, the other at the home of [a] PR [Partido Revolucionario] Deputy. . . . Jalapa residents then witnessed the initials FAR emblazoned upon the hillside overlooking the town. Also on the 20th, a bomb reportedly exploded in front of the home of two Mormon missionaries in Chimaltenango but no one was injured.[21]

It was no accident that the likeness of Castillo Armas was chosen as the target of an explosion, or that US-based missionaries personifying imperialist foreign policy were singled out for reprisals on October 20. Amid the political upheavals of the late 1960s, the idea of the Guatemalan Spring as foundational never lost its resonance among Guatemalans.

They can kill the best sons of the pueblo, . . . but . . . they never could assassinate the revolution!

With a return to brutally repressive dictatorships beginning in 1970, protests over the next decade nonetheless grew in intensity and audacity, and the symbolism of the October Revolution continued to play a part. The 1970s would be an unprecedented period in terms of political mobilization: an earthquake in 1976 shook Guatemala politically as well as physically, and in its wake more and more people began to challenge the injustices that the disaster exposed. In 1977, the famous Ixtahuacán miners' march from Huehuetenango all the way to Guatemala City galvanized the public and linked campesinos in the western highlands—Mayas and ladinos—to growing national opposition movements. The brutal massacre of Q'eqchi's in Panzós in May 1978 shocked the country and filled the capital's streets with protesters.[22] In this crescendo of public outcry, references to the October Revolution appeared again and again on banners and signs, and figured prominently in speeches. It was in the midst of this crescendo that, on October 20, 1978, the student leader Castañeda de León headed to Parque Centenario to speak for the last time.

Oliverio's assassination may have deflated that great effervescence in opposition to dictatorship in the late 1970s, but as he had promised with his final words, it could not be eliminated entirely. In the early 1980s, October Revolution commemorations fell once more into the hands of *guerrilleros*, and the Guatemalan Spring again became a symbolic justification for revolutionary struggle. The two largest guerrilla groups at that time, the Ejército Guerrillero de los Pobres (Guerrilla Army of the Poor; EGP) and the Organización Revolucionario del Pueblo en Armas) (Revolutionary Organization of the Pueblo in Arms; ORPA), took to occupying *fincas* (plantations) or staging other high-profile public actions on October 20. The PGT would use the anniversary to mark its years of armed opposition: spray paint on boulders along the highway would announce, "PGT: 26 years of struggle." Other guerrilleros would jokingly mimic and update the roadside inscriptions: "PGT: 27 years of getting screwed."[23]

Yet despite the fact that the armed opposition had appropriated the symbolic October Revolution as its own, by the mid-1980s—with the counterinsurgency state entering its third decade—the stage was set for yet another rebirth of the revolution in official rhetoric. After the boundless corruption of Romeo Lucas García (1978–1982) and the extreme violence of counterinsurgency under Efraín Ríos Montt (1982–1983), more moderate (or politically savvy) military officers set a somewhat different tone, promoting the return of procedural democracy and the election of a civilian president in 1985.[24] When Vinicio Cerezo Arévalo was elected that year, the former president Juan José Arévalo made a lofty and overly optimistic prediction: "The October revolution is going to have a second chapter."[25]

That would not be the case under Cerezo, though his need to legitimize his administration did mean that certain revolutionary-era issues would at least come under discussion. The quintessential subject of the 1944–1954 period, land reform, for example, came up in negotiations around a new constitution. And peace negotiations began as Cerezo's term neared its end, proceeding in fits and starts under the next three presidents. As representatives of the civilian-led (but still militarized) democracy and the guerrilla forces slowly negotiated an end to armed conflict, the October Revolution was on its way to becoming once again a foundational symbol for the nation, but one whose meaning was as unsettled as ever.

The October Revolution after War

Even before the final peace accords were signed in 1996, full-throated shouts of "¡Viva Arbenz!" could once again be heard in the streets of Guatemala. Arbenz had died in Mexico in 1971 and was buried in his wife's native El Salvador. But on October 19, 1995, his body was repatriated to Guatemala with military honors and a cannon salute; at the airport, the defense minister announced that the former colonel had been restored to his military rank and that the medals stripped from him were returned. Thousands of people watched his horse-drawn casket pass on its way from the airport. Others accompanied it first to the University of San Carlos and then to the Presidential Palace, where an Honor Guard lowered its flags in tribute to the president who had been vilified for most of their lives. At the entrance, army personnel stood ready to take Arbenz inside, but as the weekly *CERIGUA* reported, "to the chants of 'murderous army out of power,' . . . students carried the coffin straight past the cadets, and before stunned guards could close the gates, streamed into the palace. For perhaps the first time since the fall of Arbenz, students filled the corridors of power. 'The same army that forced Arbenz from the palace, has no right to carry him in again,' explained student leaders."[26] The next morning, October 20, the belated return of Arbenz proceeded on its way. Students were joined by thousands of other Guatemalans—unionists, returned refugees, leftist politicians, housewives, and shop owners. "To the cries of 'Jacobo lives, the struggle continues!' and under a rain of blood-red carnations," *CERIGUA* reported, supporters carried Arbenz from the Presidential Palace to the General Cemetery where, ironically, he was buried just fifty yards away from Castillo Armas.[27] The juxtaposition was not lost on visitors. One eighty-three-year-old man, Matías Pérez, shared his thoughts with a reporter from the *New York Times*: If Arbenz had remained in power, Pérez asserted, more than thirty years of civil war might have been averted. "In Arbenz's time there were no guerrillas," he said, "because he loved the people and worked for them." As the *Times* recounted, "Mr. Pérez paused, and then began to sob. 'I loved him very much,' he said, wiping his eyes. 'And I hate that other one over there,'" gesturing toward Castillo Armas's mausoleum, adorned with the inscription "To the Liberator of Guatemala, Anti-Communist Martyr."[28]

During the next decade, spaces to debate the meaning of revolution expanded dramatically. At the same time, the return to democracy resulted in frustratingly little improvement in day-to-day realities for most Guatemalans—which in turn prompted more vociferous protest against continuing economic and political stagnation. A new era of mobilization unfolded in a context shaped, too, by the hopes and frustrations of the peace process itself, and the contestation over historical memory it engendered. The final signing of the peace accords in 1996 brought short-lived optimism, and truth commission reports provided an impressive level of detail on the history and causes of the war, while analyzing the horrific violence that had been justified in the name of anticommunism.[29] But this long-awaited historical clarity was ignored or denied by many in Guatemala's most powerful sectors, who continued to claim that the military had heroically saved the nation from the evils that revolution had unleashed. Proponents of the official narrative resisted at every turn the burgeoning recovery of a different historical memory and, especially, legal efforts to prove the criminality of counterinsurgency in court and bring accountability for extrajudicial violence and terror.

The army-as-savior narrative suffered a setback in 1999 with the leak of a "death squad dossier" compiled by the security forces themselves. Known as the *Diario Militar*, it contained identification photos and personal details of 183 political prisoners captured between 1983 and 1985 and documented their executions. Wendy Méndez, whose mother, Luz Haydee Méndez, was among the prisoners in the dossier, returned from exile and cofounded H.I.J.O.S. Guatemala, a collective of children of the dead and disappeared, "Daughters/Sons for Identity and Justice Against Forgetting and Silence." Eventually, Méndez and other families of the dossier prisoners and NGO representatives took their cases to the Inter-American Court of Human Rights. Such efforts for justice, while painfully slow, inched forward.

Within a few years, another groundbreaking discovery dealt another blow to the "forgetting and silence" decried by H.I.J.O.S. and to the long-standing practice of criminalizing histories of activism: the recovery of records from a police institution that had partnered with the Guatemalan military in post-1954 urban surveillance and counterinsurgency. The Archivo Histórico de la Policía Nacional de Guatemala (Historical Archive of the National Police; AHPN) houses millions of records from that now-defunct institution, administrative files that recorded everything from the most mundane police functions to the criminal activities of the Policía Nacional (National Police; PN), including officially sanctioned political kidnappings and assassinations.[30]

Since their recovery in 2005, over twenty-one million pages of National Police documents have been meticulously cleaned, ordered, digitized, and made public. The AHPN offers a site where Guatemalans and others can trace surveillance of reform efforts following the 1954 coup and witness the transformation of the National Police into a partner in state terror. In these files, the connections between the October Revolution and repression are unambiguous.

The first time I visited the AHPN in 2009, Che Guevara's 1954 exit papers were among the recovered documents prominently displayed in the entrance hall.[31] Expelling and turning back the revolution were central tasks of the National Police in the post-coup period, and in the 1970s, that work segued into full participation in criminal counterinsurgency. With the recovery of the documents, the AHPN became a key participant in the enormous task of exposing the criminality of the very institution whose records it holds, as well as documenting a longer and broader history of social contestation and repression. The archive also took on tremendous symbolic importance, occupying the very site of an infamous torture center known as La Isla (The Island). As Carlos Aguirre writes, the AHPN became "a model of what can be called archival activism: records ought to be considered not inert pieces of evidence but actual carriers of powerful symbolism and weapons in the multifaceted effort to create a more just society."[32]

The repression of the post-1954 period documented in the police files is directly related to the hopes and fears generated by the October Revolution itself; thus, these records help us understand the reform period and its undoing and provide evidence of some of the horrors that followed. As the AHPN explained in its 2011 report *From Silence to Memory*, "The PN [National Police] of the second half of the twentieth century emerged during a period of widespread political agitation and repression of the sectors that had gained strength during the revolutionary governments."[33] Specifically, the report showed, in the post-1954 Cold War context, that "persecution was unleashed against anyone demonstrating agreement with the Revolution (1944–1954), against former functionaries from that period, especially those belonging to the now proscribed Communist Party, and all those who defended and publicized the concept of a democracy with greater equality and opportunities for citizens."[34]

Police repression against such efforts would grow exponentially in the 1970s, when "political agitation" would be led by people such as student leader Castañeda de León. With the opening of the National Police archive, researchers located seventy-one documents relating to the Castañeda de León case, records that provide details about surveillance of student activists and the assassination itself, and also a great deal about the context in which Oliverio and his fellow students operated. For instance, a photograph of a march on September 20, 1978, features Castañeda de León leading a procession and carrying an AEU banner. Close inspection of the photo reveals a small cross—symbolizing death—penned onto his left leg. Oliverio was also among organizers "sentenced to death" by the Ejército Secreto Anticomunista (Secret Anticommunist Army; ESA), a death squad that published a hit list in their organization's bulletin two days before his killing. His specific targeting is clear: as the AHPN noted in a report, "The name of the student leader [Castañeda de León] stands out, as it appears underlined" in the document.[35]

Beyond providing evidence of specific crimes committed by state agents, the documents related to Castañeda de León and thousands of other leaders have another important and related function: by showing the incredible levels of surveillance, repression, and impunity that developed after 1954, they offer proof to today's activists that opposition struggles were—and continue to be—justified. As Kirsten Weld writes, "to *reivindicar* [rehabilitate/recognize/vindicate] Guatemalans' struggles against dictatorship would counter official narratives about the war and provide space in which those who had resisted could feel pride, not shame, for their actions." Many of the workers at the Archive had been closely involved in those struggles, some of them as former members of the EGP. "'The dignification of the *guerrillero*, . . . not of the assassin,' said [a] worker at the archives, an ex-combatant with the EGP, 'that is where the archive will contribute.'"[36]

The longtime AHPN director, Gustavo Meoño, himself a former commander in the EGP, also maintained a long view of histories of resistance and repression in Guatemala, and he positioned the archive and its educational outreach accordingly. Weld explains that that is why Meoño "prioritized the recovery of 'democratic memory'—which he defined as 'a focus on the history of the struggle for democracy in Guatemala'—as a distinct arm of the broader and more inclusive project of recuperating historical memory."[37] Casting the period from 1944 to the present as an unremitting struggle for democracy both resurrects the goals of the October Revolution and reveals the longer-term consequences of a revolution undone.

Postwar Politicians and the Guatemalan Spring

A wide array of political figures in the past few decades have tried to appropriate the symbolism of the October Revolution to burnish their own reformist credentials. When Arbenz's remains were repatriated as the country moved slowly toward a negotiated peace, members of the leftist Frente Democrático Nueva Guatemala (New Guatemala Democratic Front; FDNG) carried his body the final distance to the National Cemetery and pledged to carry on the unfinished tasks of the revolution.[38] At the other end of the political spectrum, the Guatemalan defense minister, as mentioned, paid his respects to Arbenz's body at the airport. As one observer commented in 1995, "This is an army that is trying to reinvent itself because it has a terrible image problem and is going to have to find something new to do once peace comes." Arbenz was a military man, he explained, and "provides one of the few positive memories people have of the armed forces."[39]

In 2011, a public ceremony honoring Jacobo Arbenz was staged by the office of the presidency itself. It was an event mandated by the Inter-American Commission on Human Rights as part of a dispute resolution between the government and Arbenz's family over the president's ouster in 1954. As the official representative of the Guatemalan state, President Alvaro Colom expressed regret for the overthrow of Arbenz fifty-seven years before. The ceremony—once again staged at the Presidential Palace on Revolution Day—featured Arbenz's son, Juan Jacobo Arbenz Villanova, and included a formal and public apology from the president, with a statement framed and presented to the Arbenz family. "A first step in achieving national reconciliation in Guatemala," the statement declared, "is the effective recognition of what happened in the past, given that a promising future for the country cannot be imagined if the violent acts of the past are forgotten and discarded."[40]

Colom lamented the terrible price paid when Arbenz was ousted in June 1954, labeling the actions against the president and his family "criminal acts of the State."[41] But at the same time, he argued, those crimes extended far beyond mere personal injuries. As Colom declared, the ouster was "a historic act against Guatemala" itself.[42] Connecting the past to the deeply troubled present, he remarked, "that day changed Guatemala and we have not recuperated from it yet."[43] The price paid for a revolution cut short, Colom went on, was ongoing conflict and unresolved crimes: over a half-century later, the prospects continued to look bleak. It was difficult to imagine, Colom pointed out just weeks before election day, either of the aspiring presidential candidates—the former general Otto Pérez Molina or the businessman Manuel Baldizón—willingly or effectively addressing human rights violations from the period of armed conflict.[44]

Perhaps the most audacious appropriation of the symbolic October Revolution was by Pérez Molina himself: that same year in his run for president, he identified Jacobo Arbenz—along with US president John F. Kennedy—as his role models, "symbols and *personajes de lucha* [figures of struggle] and examples to follow."[45] A former general, Pérez Molina as president would recriminalize the very struggles that took Arbenz as the revolution's symbol; at the same time, he stood firmly against efforts to address state atrocities, famously declaring during the genocide trial of former dictator Efraín Ríos Montt that "there was no genocide" during the armed conflict.[46] Alongside these blatant contradictions, tributes to the Arbenz period continued during Pérez Molina's tenure. In 2013—the same year as the genocide trial—the one-hundred-year anniversary of Arbenz's birth was publicly celebrated with speeches and parades, especially in Arbenz's hometown of Quetzaltenango, and an airport was renamed in his honor.[47] *¡Viva Arbenz!*

The October Revolution and Twenty-First-Century Youth

Other revolutionary commemorations have had far more political bite. For opposition activists, students, and artists, Arbenz's ouster has represented a wrenching reversal of revolutionary gains and promises but also the humiliation of imperialism. On the sixtieth anniversary of the coup in 2014, a riveting photographic piece in *Plaza Pública* featured Guatemalans paying tribute to Arbenz in the most empathetic way imaginable: by posing in the same comprised position Arbenz had been forced to endure at the airport in 1954—in their underwear.[48] As the photographer Alejandro Anzueto explained, the goal of the photo essay was to help Guatemalans recognize that "with the expulsion of Arbenz, not only did they throw him out, but also the whole revolution, and revolutionary Guatemala" more broadly.[49] The possibility of a more just society and a "futuro distinto," the photographer lamented, was exiled at the same time. Six decades later, Guatemalan young people—standing before the camera in their underwear—still shared the humiliating fate of Arbenz.

This kind of indignation also permeates the work of H.I.J.O.S. Guatemala, with their visually powerful and often provocative reimagining of Guatemala's twentieth-century history. The collective is led by, but not limited to, those who lost family members in the war, and it welcomes anyone committed to combating impunity and mobilizing for change; after all, H.I.J.O.S. insists, all Guatemalans "are H.I.J.O.S. [daughters and sons] of a shared history."[50]

It is their interpretation of that historical inheritance that the group so ingeniously frames, mostly in the streets of Guatemala City. Public art is their tool of choice: "We aim to retake the walls of the city," they write, "like blank pages of a silenced history."[51] Murals, graffiti, and stencils reveal and promote historical memory, envisioned as "art for the transformation" of society. The work that they describe as purposely "full of irreverence and rebellion" prominently features the violence and terror of the 1970s and 1980s, as the civil war period prompted their activism in the first place: the faces of the dead and disappeared that they wheat-paste row upon row on city walls are constant reminders of ongoing crimes and unpunished perpetrators. *¿Dónde están?52*

In a provocative move, H.I.J.O.S. Guatemala also identifies military officials with blood on their hands, insisting on a public accounting and the naming of names. "Wanted" posters feature individual military officers accused of human rights crimes, and their faces and names confront pedestrians right alongside the haunting images of the disappeared. The members of H.I.J.O.S. have been closely involved in human rights court cases, too, and they forcefully reject notions of moving on—personally or as a society—without justice: "No Olvidamos. No Perdonamos. No nos Reconciliamos" (We do not forget. We do not pardon. We do not reconcile).

At the same time, H.I.J.O.S. Guatemala's street art deftly places the injustices of the civil war within a longer time frame. As the structural causes of the war outlasted the signing of the peace accords, they have joined forces with current social justice struggles for economic rights, for example, the defense of communities fighting mining extraction.[53] They engage deeply, too, with lived histories of opposition since the 1940s as an "inexhaustible and essential source for learning." Such memories need to be rescued, they write, "as a foundation for transformative action toward the future."[54] They have firmly situated the activism of earlier generations—including those who led the October Revolution—as key to imagining new possibilities. With this, they have helped shape the thinking and interpretations of a broad sector of urban activists.[55]

In 2007, H.I.J.O.S. Guatemala included an "homage to the heroes of the revolution of 1944" in public and symbolic anti-impunity protests, part of a series of actions begun a few years earlier which they labeled "Ofensivas de la Memoria" (offensives or attacks of memory).[56] They envisioned

FIGURE 10.2. *"Heroes and Martyrs Day," June 30, 2017. H.I.J.O.S. Guatemala Memory Offensive: Not Afraid to Show Ourselves. Photo by author.*

these initiatives as "offensives," they explain, to respond aggressively to a deeply frustrating context: an unresponsive and corrupt judicial system, and repressive actions against their work, including two raids of their office. As a means of pushing back, they saw an urgent need to engage more forcefully in the arena of memory narratives and justice, with provocative language and action. Their responses were sometimes symbolic and sometimes literal. At the door of their own invaded office, H.I.J.O.S. Guatemala spray-painted, "*Señores* of the government, we have absolutely NO fear of you!"[57]

Since their founding, H.I.J.O.S. Guatemala has focused public attention on official June 30 "Army Day" commemorations, protesting the parades of military grandeur held each year in Guatemala City's center. They chose that symbolic national holiday to launch their collective publicly in 1999, and every year since then have staged their most visible actions on the occasion. In a stunning victory in 2007, their "Memory Offensive" demonstration actually brought an end to the annual military parade. The next year H.I.J.O.S. Guatemala reclaimed Central Park on June 30 for "Heroes and Martyrs" Day protests against violence and impunity.[58] To date, "Heroes and Martyrs" Day has continued. Army Day has moved behind closed doors.

H.I.J.O.S. Guatemala's confrontational "Memory Offensives" have continued as well. In 2015, their campaign unfolded in a particularly turbulent period of social upheaval, when nineteen weeks of mass protest brought down the presidency of Otto Pérez Molina and landed the president and vice-president in jail on corruption charges. Virtually every sector of civil society contributed to mass action, but young people played especially pivotal roles in maintaining pressure for weeks on end. The *Washington Post* reported that one protestor's sign prophetically declared that "they messed with the wrong generation."[59]

It was the ideal moment, H.I.J.O.S. members and other activists determined, to connect the politics of the present explicitly to 1944.[60] When Pérez Molina initially refused to resign, social media erupted with *#YoNoTengoPresidente*! (I don't have a president!), and protestors waved banners featuring Arbenz.[61] The logic later expressed in the 2017 Oliverio memorial was evident in 2015: fundamental change had happened in 1944 with the overthrow of General Ubico, activists told each other. People were in the streets and the plazas once again in 2015, in greater numbers than ever. "We're here, and it's possible again," they insisted, they could make it happen again. *Sí, se puede*.[62]

Pérez Molina did ultimately resign, and elections were scheduled for shortly afterward. But candidates did not represent the change protestors demanded. The artwork of H.I.J.O.S. Guatemala's "Memory Offensive" on that occasion was particularly potent. With vivid campaign posters pasted all over the walls of Guatemala City's historic center, they rejected the actual candidates who were running, and in their place, nominated past leaders—from the Guatemalan Spring and from the 1960s through the 1980s—most of them killed by Guatemala's security forces, as symbolic candidates for the nation's highest offices. They called their nominees a "Memory Cabinet," a governmental "cabinet symbolizing dignity" to counter the indignities of the present.

As candidates, they put forward the deposed Jacobo Arbenz for president, the poet and activist (during and after the October Revolution) Alaíde Foppa for vicepresident, and the teacher María Chinchilla for minister of education. At the same time, the campaign, which used the hashtag #LaRevoluciónFlorece (the Revolution blooms or flourishes), deliberately paired these mid-century leaders with martyrs of the armed conflict: Mamá Maquín (Adelina Caal), a Q'eqchi' land rights organizer killed by the army in the Panzós massacre of 1978, for "minister of sovereignty"; Luis Turcios, leader of the guerrilla FAR, for minister of defense; and Oliverio Castañeda de León for minister of finance.[63]

The impossible cabinet of the dead engaged with memory reconstruction in multiple, important ways. It forced people to confront the enormous political costs of a half-century of repression and to ask a crucial question: how would things have been different if these leaders had lived, if their visions for change and justice had been allowed to help shape Guatemala's twentieth century? It also countered the depoliticization of memory, the tendency to view the dead and disappeared as mere victims.[64] H.I.J.O.S. Guatemala's Memory Cabinet was filled with true leaders, they insisted, not victims. It was their militancy and activism, their visions and work for something better, that made these figures worthy of office. In morally bankrupt post-1954 Guatemala, it was also what had brought on their persecution. The political crisis and the vacuum in leadership in 2015 showed that society was still paying the price for a state that had criminalized efforts to create a just society since 1954.

The hashtag of the Memory Offensive—"the revolution flourishes"—underscores an important intervention of such memory work: with that slogan, H.I.J.O.S. Guatemala reinforced the message that Guatemalan resistance had a long, valiant, and ongoing history, one that needed to be resurrected and built upon. "Revolution" in the campaign most obviously referenced the leaders and thinkers of the 1944–1954 Guatemalan Spring, but with more recent leaders included in the "cabinet" alongside them, it would also connote the revolutionary armed insurgency. The campaign's intermingling of martyrs of both eras—bringing them all back from the dead to serve together—explicitly connected multiple generations of Guatemalans working for change and, in turn, linked them to today's protesters. It was a revision of an official historical narrative that had (eventually) come to commemorate one revolution—the October Revolution—while persecuting virtually all attempts at change in the years after its overthrow. In the tense political climate of 2015, it was vital, H.I.J.O.S. Guatemala declared, "to retake and rescue the thinking, the dreams, and the proposals for revolutionary political transformation" that all the leaders in the Memory Cabinet had stood for and to offer Guatemalans and the "generations of young people orphaned of political referents" a vision of distinctly different possibilities from those on the actual ballot. They sought to remember and memorialize not their deaths but their lives. "Memory is not a pure, static remembrance," they explained, "not the constant repetition of past sufferings, it is the seed of *ReVeldía* (rebellion)."[65] A teenager held a poster in the June 30, 2017, anti–Army Day / "Heroes and Martyrs" demonstration with the same essential message: "They can . . . disappear people but their ideas remain."[66]

This framing links generations, and at the same time is very much of the twenty-first century. In another striking graffiti series, H.I.J.O.S. Guatemala ties a deep history of militant resistance to ongoing demands for justice and, in the same gesture, provokes reflection on the part of the viewing public about changing tactics and changing times: on one wall in the historic city-center, graffiti artists inscribed the words, "We all know who the guilty are" . . . and three blocks down the street, the message continued, "The Guatemalan army." On another block, they scrawled, "We are re-arming" . . . and around the corner, "With Hope."[67]

Hope, to be sure, can be hard to come by in Guatemala's "post-peace" context. But the past is proving to be a surprising and indispensable source of it. References to histories of activism reverberate throughout Guatemalan social movements, and the October Revolution in particular has become ever-more emblematic. Another banner in a recent march, carried by four teens, featured a portrait of Arbenz and demanded in all caps, "ANOTHER REVOLUTION IS NEEDED, NOW!" The October Revolution, it proclaimed, "offered social progress and land for all."[68] When pressed, activist Guatemalans do not hesitate to acknowledge that the Arévalo and Arbenz regimes were imperfect, sometimes reflecting paternalistic sensibilities, as many of the chapters in this volume make clear. But like the creators of the banner demanding "*¡otra revolución ya!*," they point to the era's insipient social programs, aiming to alleviate inequality and expand participation in the nation, including for indigenous Guatemalans, as a legacy worth building upon.[69]

As H.I.J.O.S. Guatemala graffiti artists repurpose more "blank pages of a silenced history" with cans of spray paint, the walls of the capital convey their message unequivocally: resurrecting histories of struggle and resistance is "not . . . nostalgia . . . It's the memory of possibility."[70]

Notes

Many thanks to Ramón González Ponciano, Heather Vrana, and Julie Gibbings for their helpful comments on this chapter.

1. Archivo Histórico de la Policía Nacional (AHPN), *From Silence to Memory: Revelations of the Archivo Histórico de la Policía Nacional*, English translation (Eugene: University of Oregon Press, 2013; orig. Spanish 2011), 353.

2. See AHPN, *From Silence to Memory*, 361–365.

3. Quoted in Heather Vrana, *This City Belongs to You: A History of Student Activism in Guatemala, 1944–1996* (Oakland: University of California Press, 2017), 207. "Olivero's six million Guatemalans" represented the entire population at the time.

4. This message from his final address is inscribed on a plaque that marks the spot

where he was killed: "Podrán masacrar a los dirigentes, pero siempre que haya pueblo habrá revolución" (They can massacre the leaders, but as long as there is a *pueblo*, there will be revolution).

5. Speech at the memorial for Oliverio Castañeda de León, Pasaje Rubio, Guatemala City, October 20, 2017.

6. As one Batucada member put it, "La bulla llama a más bulla, la gente llama a más gente y el ritmo es un elemento esencial para aglutinarnos como colectivo" (Noise [a racket] attracts more noise, people [gathered] attract more people, and rhythm is an essential element to bring us all together as a collective). Roberto Caubilla, "La Batucada: El ritmo que movió la protesta ciudadana," *Soy 502*, www.soy502.com/articulo/batucada-ritmo-consiguio-sacar-gobierno-corrupto.

7. Possibly, yes. We learn from recovered police files that surveillance of activists was thorough and not exactly subtle. In one photograph of Castañeda de León at a demonstration, for example, two of his fellow protestors appear to be looking directly at the Detective Corps photographer's camera. AHPN, *From Silence to Memory*, 356.

8. Speech at the memorial for Oliverio Castañeda de León by member of La Batucada del Pueblo, Pasaje Robles, Guatemala City, October 20, 2017.

9. The percussionists/activists explain their role this way: "Sus tambores continuarán sonando por el tiempo que sea necesario, hasta conseguir los cambios que nuestro país requiere para florecer" (Their drumming will continue as long as necessary, until the changes our country would need to flourish are achieved). See La Batucada del Pueblo website, www.facebook.com/pg/Batucadadelpueblo/about/?ref=page_internal.

10. Elizabeth Jelin, "Public Memorialization in Perspective: Truth, Justice and Memory of Past Repression in the Southern Cone of South America," *International Journal of Transitional Justice* 1 (2007): 141.

11. A sampling of other Guatemalan organizations active in memory projects includes the Fundación de Antropología Forense de Guatemala (Guatemalan Forensic Anthropology Foundation; FAFG) and its Archivo de Historias Visuales; the Centro para la Acción Legal en Derechos Humanos (Center for Human Rights Legal Action; CALDH) and its educational project, La Casa de la Memoria "Kaji Tulam"; the Instituto Internacional de Aprendizaje para la Reconciliación Social (International Institute of Learning for Social Reconciliation; IIARS) and its "Exposición Interactiva ¿Por qué estamos como estamos?"; and as discussed in this chapter, the AHPN, and H.I.J.O.S. Guatemala.

12. For "labors of memory," see Elizabeth Jelin, *State Repression and the Labors of Memory* (Minneapolis: University of Minnesota Press, 2003).

13. For an in-depth study of the University of San Carlos and student activism in Guatemala, see Vrana, *This City Belongs to You*.

14. For more, see Vrana, *This City Belongs to You*, 80–83.

15. See Vrana, *This City Belongs to You*, 80–83.

16. Vrana, *This City Belongs to You*, 84–85.

17. Quoted in Jennifer Schirmer, *The Guatemalan Military Project: A Violence Called Democracy* (Philadelphia: University of Pennsylvania Press, 1998), 17.

18. Schirmer, *Guatemalan Military Project*, 17, quoting Jim Handy, *Gift of the Devil*, 394.

19. Guatemalan Congressional Decree 1618, October 14, 1966.

20. Department of State telegram, October 23, 1967: "Subj: October 20 Happenings," RG 59, entry 1613, Central Foreign Policy Files, 1967–1969, Political and

Defense, folder POL 23-8, 1967, National Archive Records Administration (hereafter NARA). The author of this telegram, Ambassador John Gordon Mein, would be assassinated less than a year later by members of the FAR.

21. Department of State Airgram, "Subject: Biweekly Internal Security Report: Oct 18–25, 1968," RG 59, entry 1613, Central Foreign Policy Files, 1967–1969, Political and Defense, folder POL 23 GUAT 1-1-68, NARA.

22. For the development of highland organizing in this period, see Betsy Konefal, *For Every Indio Who Falls: A History of Maya Activism in Guatemala, 1960–1990* (Albuquerque: University of New Mexico Press, 2010); for the Panzós massacre, see Greg Grandin, *The Last Colonial Massacre: Latin America in the Cold War* (Chicago: University of Chicago Press, 2004); for an overview of mobilization and its repression during the 1970s and 1980s, see Comisión para el Esclaracimiento Histórico (CEH), *Guatemala: Memoria del silencio* (Guatemala City: UNOPS, 1999), 12 vols., or its abridged English translation, *Memory of Silence: The Guatemalan Truth Commission Report*, ed. Daniel Rothenberg (New York: Palgrave Macmillan, 2012).

23. "PGT: 27 años de recibir pija," personal communication with former guerrillero. For nationalist positions of other factions of the guerrilla that paid homage to the October Revolution in the 1980s, see *Opinión Política*, first published in October 1984 as a periodical "for communication, exchange and debate among revolutionaries," and later as the "informative organ" of a group that had broken from the EGP in 1984 and eventually called itself Octubre Revolucionario (Revolutionary October; OR). As OR stated, that name paid tribute to two October Revolutions, in Russia in 1917 and Guatemala in 1944. While the Russian Revolution, they wrote, was the first victory of the international proletariat and the "dawning of humanity," the Guatemalan October Revolution marked "the beginning of the contemporary social struggles in our country." *Opinión Política*, no. 15, February 1989. See also *La Otra Guatemala* (Mexico).

24. For an examination of the Ríos Montt regime, see Virginia Garrard-Burnett, *Terror in the Land of the Holy Spirit: Guatemala under General Efraín Ríos Montt, 1982–83* (New York: Oxford University Press, 2010). For the military's transition in the 1980s, see Schirmer, *Guatemalan Military Project.*

25. Tim Golden, "Juan Jose Arevalo Is Dead at 86; Guatemala President in Late 40's," October 8, 1990, *New York Times*, https://www.nytimes.com/1990/10/08/obituaries/juan-jose-arevalo-is-dead-at-86-guatemala-president-in-late-40-s.html. The print edition omitted this quotation.

26. *CERIGUA Weekly Briefs*, nos. 40–41, October 27, 1995.

27. *CERIGUA Weekly Briefs*, nos. 40–41, October 27, 1995.

28. *New York Times*, December 6, 1995. To partisans of Castillo Armas's National Liberation Movement, to be sure, the return of Arbenz was seen quite differently: an "affront" that could only bring "bad results and national discord," in the words of Movimiento de Liberación Nacional (National Liberation Movement; MLN) leader Mario Sandoval Alarcón.

29. See Oficina de Derechos Humanos del Arzobispado de Guatemala (ODHAG), *Guatemala: Nunca más, Informe proyecto interdiocesano de recuperación de la memoria histórica*, 4 vols. (Guatemala City: ODHAG, 1998); CEH, *Memoria del silencio*, 12 vols. For the historical origins of the war, see vol. 1, "*Causes y orígines del enfrentamiento armado interno.*" An abridged and translated version of the history section is also available in Greg Grandin, *Who Is Rigoberta Menchú?* (New York: Verso, 2011), "Appendix: The Findings of the UN Commission for Historical Clarification—A State Racist in Theory and Practice," 99–149, and CEH, *Memory of Silence.*

30. The materials were found in 2005 by the office of Guatemala's human rights prosecutor. The existence of such records had long been denied, though they had been hiding in plain sight on an active police base, room after room of disordered bundles piled high, moldy, infested, and disintegrating. "For human-rights investigators," writes Kate Doyle of the National Security Archive, "the archive was the discovery of a lifetime, the long-abandoned scene of a terrible crime." Kate Doyle, "The Atrocity Files: Deciphering the Archives of Guatemala's Dirty War," *Harper's Magazine*, December 2007, 58.

31. Ernesto "Che" Guevara lived in Guatemala for nine months from late 1953 until several months after Arbenz's overthrow in June 1954, when he took refuge in the Argentine embassy. After witnessing the undoing of the October Revolution (he reportedly applied lessons learned in Guatemala to the Cuban revolutionary experiment a few years later), he was intent on traveling to Mexico rather than returning to Argentina. Guatemalan security forces processed his exit visa in September 1954.

32. AHPN, *From Silence to Memory*, xiii. The AHPN's "archival activism" has been both successful and aggressively challenged. Evidence from the archive has contributed to criminal convictions in high-profile cases in Guatemala, provoking the wrath of former military officers and their defenders. The political backlash has been particularly intense and devastating since convictions in the Molina Theissen case in 2018. At the time of this writing, the archive's longtime director, Gustavo Meoño, who was abruptly dismissed that August, is in hiding. See National Security Archive, "Guatemala Police Archive under Threat," August 13, 2018, https://nsarchive.gwu.edu/news/guatemala/2018-08-13/guatemala-police-archive-under-threat, and an update, "Imminent Threat to Guatemala's Historical Archive of the National Police (AHPN)," May 30, 2019, https://nsarchive.gwu.edu/news/guatemala/2019-05-30/imminent-threat-guatemalas-historical-archive-national-police-ahpn.

33. AHPN, *From Silence to Memory*, 459.

34. Ibid., 25.

35. Ibid., 359.

36. Kirsten Weld, "Dignifying the *Guerrillero*, Not the Assassin: Rewriting a History of Criminal Subversion in Postwar Guatemala," *Radical History Review* 113 (Spring 2012): 43.

37. Weld, "Dignifying the *Guerrillero*," 48.

38. *CERIGUA Weekly Briefs*, nos. 40–41, October 27, 1995.

39. *New York Times*, December 6, 1995.

40. *El Periódico*, October 20, 2011.

41. *Prensa Libre*, October 21, 2011.

42. Ibid.

43. *New York Times*, October 21, 2011.

44. *Prensa Libre*, October 21, 2011.

45. *El mundo.es*, November 6, 2011.

46. *La Prensa*, March 20, 2013.

47. For thoughts about the significance of the new attention to Arbenz, see Anabella Acevedo, "De cómo ahora resulta que todos quieren a Arbenz," *Plaza Pública*, September 13, 2013.

48. See "Pienso en Arbenz," *Plaza Pública*, June 27, 2014, https://www.plaza-publica.com.gt/content/pienso-en-arbenz.

49. Alejandro Anzueto in "Pienso en Arbenz," *Plaza Pública*, June 27, 2014.

50. See "Todas y todos somos hijos de una misma historia," accessed August 9,

2019, https://www.facebook.com/hijos.guatemala/photos/a.1630286387206481/1630290380539415/?type=3&theater. Guatemala is mostly an urban and ladino collective, and they would readily acknowledge that actual experiences of the war would vary across time and space.

51. H.I.J.O.S. Guatemala, *Todas y todos somos hijos de una misma historia: Sistematización de experiencias del colectivo H.I.J.O.S. Guatemala de 1999–2011* (Guatemala City: H.I.J.O.S. Guatemala, 2014), 63.

52. "Where Are They?," H.I.J.O.S. Guatemala, *Todas y todos somos hijos*, 10, 53.

53. Paulo Estrada of H.I.J.O.S. Guatemala, interview, Guatemala City, October 18, 2017.

54. H.I.J.O.S. Guatemala, *Todas y todos somos hijos*, 11. They dedicated the publication *Todas y todos somos hijos* to Alfonso Bauer Paiz, a leftist leader prominent during and after the October Revolution, who died in 2011 at the age of ninety-three, with "thanks for being our great *maestro* and teaching us to be persevering in life as in the struggle."

55. These ideas were echoed, for example, by La Batucada del Pueblo at the Castañeda de León memorial in 2017.

56. H.I.J.O.S Guatemala, *Todas y todos somos hijos*, 39–52.

57. Ibid., 39.

58. For more on repurposing the June 30 commemorations, see ibid.

59. *Washington Post*, September 5, 2015.

60. Paulo Estrada of H.I.J.O.S. Guatemala, interview, Guatemala City, October 18, 2017.

61. *Telesur*, August 24, 2015.

62. Paulo Estrada of H.I.J.O.S. Guatemala, interview, Guatemala City, October 18, 2017.

63. See www.facebook.com/pg/hijos.guatemala/photos/?tab=album&album_id=1714767908758328. Mamá Maquín had been in fact active in campesino organizing and leftist politics since the Arbenz era of the 1950s. For more, see Grandin, *The Last Colonial Massacre*, ch. 5.

64. Paulo Estrada of H.I.J.O.S. Guatemala, interview, Guatemala City, October 18, 2017. The tendency to strip the dead and disappeared of histories of activism in the process of seeking legal justice is mirrored in other transitional societies. For Argentina, for example, see Jelin, *State Repression and the Labors of Memory*, 53–55.

65. H.I.J.O.S Guatemala, *Todas y todos somos hijos*, 77. This word play on "rebellion" (*rebeldía/reVeldía*—"b" and "v" sound the same in Spanish) originated as a spelling mistake in 1999, when it was part of a message that read "*Las balas made in usa no mataron la semilla, nosotros somos reveldía* / Bullets made in USA didn't kill the seed, we are the rebellion." When they realized their mistake, they decided that the *v* would represent "victory," and have used that spelling—emphasizing the V with a capital letter or different color—ever since. H.I.J.O.S Guatemala, *Todas y todos somos hijos*, 79, note 35.

66. Photos 6 and 15, July 1, 2017, http://noticiascomunicarte.blogspot.com/2017/07/guatemala-fotoreportaje-ofensiva-de-la.html.

67. H.I.J.O.S Guatemala, *Todas y todos somos hijos*, 68.

68. "*URGE OTRA REVOLUCIÓN ¡YA!*," photo, January 19, 2018, *Comunicarte*, http://noticiascomunicarte.blogspot.com/2018/01/seguimos-de-mal-en-peor-comprobado-esta.html.

As the banner continued: "agribusiness," on the other hand, was to blame for present-day "destruction and poverty."

69. One member of H.I.J.O.S. Guatemala, for example, highlighted advances in healthcare, education, and land access as especially important. Paulo Estrada of H.I.J.O.S. Guatemala, interview, Guatemala City, October 18, 2017.

70. See street art at HIJOS Guatemala, #LaRevoluciónFlorece, October 21, 2015, www.facebook.com/hijos.guatemala/photos/00539813.1073741827.1630286343873152/1766338363601282/?type=3&theater.

Selected Bibliography

Adams, Richard N., ed. *Crucifixion by Power: Essays on Guatemalan National Social Structure, 1944–1966*. Austin: University of Texas Press, 1970.

———. "Political Change in Guatemalan Indian Communities: A Symposium." In *Community Culture and National Change*, edited by R. Adams, 1–54. Middle American Research Institute publication no. 24. New Orleans: Tulane University Middle American Research Institute, 1972.

Aguirre, Carlos, and Paulo Drinot, eds. *The Peculiar Revolution: Rethinking the Peruvian Experiment under Military Rule*. Austin: University of Texas Press, 2017.

Appleman Williams, William. *The Tragedy of American Diplomacy*. New York: Norton, 2009.

Archivo Histórico de la Policía Nacional (AHPN). *From Silence to Memory: Revelations of the Archivo Histórico de la Policía Nacional*. Translated by AHPN. Eugene: University of Oregon Press, 2013. Originally published 2011.

Arévalo, Juan José. *Despacho presidencial*. Guatemala City: Editorial Oscar de León Palacios, 2008.

———. *Discurso al asumir la Presidencia de la República de Guatemala*. Guatemala City: Tipografía Nacional, 1945.

———. *Guatemala: La democracia y el imperio*. México, DF: América Nueva, 1954.

Aybar de Soto, José. *Dependency and Intervention: The Case of Guatemala in 1954*. Boulder, CO: Westview, 1978.

Bauer Paiz, Alfonso, and Iván Carpio Alfaro. *Memorias de Alfonso Bauer Paiz: Historia no oficial de Guatemala*. Guatemala City: Rusticatio Ediciones, 1996.

Bethell, Leslie, and Ian Roxborough, eds. *Latin America between the Second World War and the Cold War: Crisis and Containment, 1944–1948*. Cambridge: Cambridge University Press, 1997.

Bourgois, Philippe I. *Ethnicity at Work: Divided Labor on a Central America Banana Plantation*. Baltimore, MD: Johns Hopkins University Press, 1989.

Boyer, Christopher R. *Political Landscapes: Conservation, Forests, and Community in Mexico*. Durham, NC: Duke University Press, 2015.

Cardoza y Aragón, Luis, Enrique Muñoz Meany, Arturo Taracena Arriola, Julio César Pinto Soria, and Arely Mendoza de Léon. *El placer de corresponder: Correspondencia entre Muñoz Meany, Cardoza y Aragón y Arriola (1945–1951)*. Guatemala City: Editorial Universitaria de la Universidad de San Carlos, 2004.

Carey, David, Jr. *Engendering Mayan History: Kaqchikel Women as Agents and Conduits of the Past, 1875–1970*. New York: Routledge, 2006.

———. "Guatemala's Green Revolution: Synthetic Fertilizer, Public Health, and Economic Autonomy in the Mayan Highland." *Agricultural History* 83, no. 3 (2009): 283–322.

———. *I Ask for Justice: Maya Women, Dictators, and Crime in Guatemala, 1898–1944*. Austin: University of Texas Press, 2013.

———. *Oral History in Latin America: Unlocking the Spoken Archive*. New York: Routledge, 2017.

———. *Our Elders Teach Us: Maya-Kaqchikel Historical Perspectives. Xkib'ij kan qate' qatata'*. Tuscaloosa: University of Alabama Press, 2001.

Casey, Dennis. "Indigenismo: The Guatemalan Experience." PhD diss., University of Kansas, 1979.

Chomsky, Aviva. *West Indian Workers and the United Fruit Company in Costa Rica, 1870–1940.* Baton Rouge: Louisiana State University Press, 1996.

Colby, Jason M. *The Business of Empire: United Fruit, Race, and U.S. Expansion in Central America.* Ithaca, NY: Cornell University Press, 2011.

Colectivo MadreSelva. *El camino de la luz: Historias del proyecto comunitario de energía eléctrica "Luz de los héroes y Mártires de la Resistencia."* Guatemala City: Colectivo MadreSelva, 2014.

Comisión para el Esclarecimiento Histórico (CEH). *Memory of Silence: The Guatemalan Truth Commission Report.* Edited by Daniel Rothenberg. New York: Palgrave Macmillan, 2012.

Crafts, Lydia. "Sanitizing Interventions: PHS VD Research in Guatemala and the Rise of International Health." MA thesis, University of Texas at Austin, 2012.

Cueto, Marcos. "International Health, the Early Cold War and Latin America." *Canadian Bulletin of Medical History* 25, no. 1 (2008): 17–41.

Cullather, Nick. *Secret History: The CIA's Classified Account of Its Operations in Guatemala, 1952–1954.* Stanford, CA: Stanford University Press, 2006.

Dawson, Alexander. "From Models for the Nation to Model Citizens: *Indigenismo* and the 'Revindication' of the Mexican Indian, 1920–40." *Journal of Latin American Studies* 30, no. 2 (May 1998): 279–308.

Dosal, Paul J. *Doing Business with the Dictators: A Political History of United Fruit in Guatemala, 1899–1944.* New York: Rowman and Littlefield, 1993.

Ebel, R. H., and Harry S. McArthur. *Cambio político en tres comunidades indígenas de Guatemala.* Guatemala City: Editorial José de Pineda Ibarra; Ministerio de Educación, 1969.

Espada, Rafael. *Consentir el daño: Experimentos médicos de Estados Unidos en Guatemala, 1946–1948.* Guatemala City: Comisión Presidencial para el Esclarecimiento de los Experimentos Practicados con Humanos en Guatemala, 2011.

Evans, Sterling. *The Green Republic: A Conservation History of Costa Rica.* Austin: University of Texas Press, 1999.

Farley, John. *To Cast Out Disease: A History of the International Health Division of the Rockefeller Foundation, 1913–1951.* Oxford: Oxford University Press, 2003.

Ford, Anabel, and Ronald Nigh. *The Maya Forest Garden: Eight Millennia of Sustainable Cultivation of the Tropical Woodlands.* New York: Routledge, 2015.

Forster, Cindy. "The Macondo of Guatemala: Banana Workers and National Revolution in Tiquisate, 1944–1954." In *Banana Wars: Power, Production, and History in the Americas,* edited by Steve Striffler and Mark Moberg, 191–228. Durham, NC: Duke University Press, 2003.

———. *La Revolución indígena y campesina en Guatemala.* Guatemala City: Editorial Universitaria, USAC, 2012.

———. *The Time of Freedom: Campesino Workers in Guatemala's October Revolution.* Pittsburgh, PA: University of Pittsburgh Press, 2001.

———. "Violent and Violated Women: Justice and Gender in Rural Guatemala, 1936–1956." *Journal of Women's History* 11, no. 3 (2003): 55–77

Gaddis, John Lewis. *The Cold War: A New History.* New York: Penguin, 2005.

———. *The Long Peace: Inquiries into the History of the Cold War.* Oxford: Oxford University Press, 1989.

———. *The United States and the End of the Cold War: Implications, Reconsiderations, Provocations*. Oxford: Oxford University Press, 1994.

Galarneau, Charlene. "'Ever Vigilant' in 'Ethically Impossible': Structural Injustice and Responsibility in PHS Research in Guatemala." *Hastings Center Report* 43, no. 3 (May–June 2013): 36–45.

García Ferreira, Roberto. "La revolución guatemalteca y el legado del presidente Arbenz." *Anuario de Estudios Centroamericanos* 38 (2012): 41–78.

Garrard-Burnett, Virginia. "Indians Are Drunks and Drunks Are Indians: Alcohol and Indigenismo in Guatemala 1890–1940." *Bulletin of Latin American Research* 19, no. 3 (July 2000): 341–356.

Gibbings, Julie. "Mestizaje in the Age of Fascism: German and Q'eqchi' Maya Interracial Unions in Alta Verapaz, Guatemala." *German History* 34, no. 2 (June 1, 2016): 214–236. https://doi.org/10.1093/gerhis/ghw017.

———. *Our Time Is Now: Race and Modernity in Postcolonial Guatemala*. Cambridge: Cambridge University Press, forthcoming [2020].

Giraudo, Laura, and Juan Martín-Sánchez, eds. *La ambivalente historia del indigenismo: Campo Interamericano y trayectorias nacionales 1940–1970*. Lima: Instituto de Estudios Peruanos, 2011.

Gleijeses, Piero. *Shattered Hope: The Guatemalan Revolution and the United States, 1944–1954*. Princeton, NJ: Princeton University Press, 1991.

González, Matilde. *Se cambió el tiempo: Conflicto y poder en territorio K'iche' 1880–1996*. Guatemala City: AVANCSO, 2002.

González Orellana, Carlos. *Historia de la educación en Guatemala*. México, DF: Colección Científico Pedagógica, 1970.

González Ponciano, Jorge Ramón. "De la patria del criollo a la patria del shumo." PhD diss., University of Texas, Austin, 2005.

———. "'Esas sangres no están limpias': Modernidad y pensamiento civilizatorio en Guatemala (1954–1997)." In *¿Racismo en Guatemala? Abriendo el debate sobre un tema tabú*, edited by Clara Arenas Bianchi et al., 10–18. Guatemala City: AVANSCO, 2004.

Gould, Jeffrey L., and Aldo A. Lauria-Santiago. *To Rise in Darkness: Revolution, Repression, and Memory in El Salvador, 1920–1932*. Durham, NC: Duke University, 2008.

Gramajo Morales, Héctor Alejandro. *De la guerra a la guerra: La difícil transición política en Guatemala*. México, DF: Fondo de Cultura Editorial, 1995.

Grandia, Liza. *Enclosed: Conservation, Cattle, and Commerce among the Q'eqchi' Maya Lowlanders*. Seattle: University of Washington Press, 2012.

Grandin, Greg. *The Blood of Guatemala: A History of Race and Nation*. Durham, NC: Duke University Press, 2000.

———. "Chronicles of a Guatemalan Genocide Foretold: Violence, Trauma, and the Limits of Historical Inquiry." *Nepantla: Views from the South* 1, no. 2 (2000): 391–412.

———. "Everyday Forms of State Decomposition: Quetzaltenango, Guatemala, 1954." *Bulletin of Latin American Research* 19, no. 3 (2000): 303–320.

———. *The Last Colonial Massacre: Latin America in the Cold War*. Chicago: University of Chicago Press, 2004.

Grieb, Kenneth J. *Guatemalan Caudillo, the Regime of Jorge Ubico: Guatemala, 1931–1944*. Athens: Ohio University Press, 1979.

Guzmán Böckler, Carlos, and Jean-Loup Herbert. *Guatemala: Una interpretación histórico-social.* México, DF: Siglo XXI Editores, 1970.

Handy, Jim. *Gift of the Devil: A History of Guatemala.* Boston: South End, 1984.

———. "'The Most Precious Fruit of the Revolution': The Guatemalan Agrarian Reform, 1952–54." *Hispanic American Historical Review* 68, no. 4 (1988): 675–705.

———. "National Policy, Agrarian Reform, and the Corporate Community during the Guatemalan Revolution, 1944–54." *Comparative Studies in Society and History* 30, no. 4 (October 1988): 698–724.

———. *Revolución en el área rural: Conflicto rural y reforma agraria en Guatemala, 1944–1954.* Guatemala City: Centro de Estudios Urbanos y Regionales de USAC, 2013.

———. "Revolution and Reaction: National Policy and Rural Politics in Guatemala, 1944–1954." PhD diss., University of Toronto, 1985.

———. *Revolution in the Countryside: Rural Conflict and Agrarian Reform in Guatemala, 1944–1954.* Chapel Hill: University of North Carolina Press, 1994.

———. "'A Sea of Indians': Ethnic Conflict and the Guatemalan Revolution, 1944–1952." *The Americas* 46, no. 2 (1989): 189–204.

Harms, Patricia. "'God Doesn't Like the Revolution': The Archbishop, the Market Women, and the Economy of Gender in Guatemala, 1944–1954." *Frontiers: A Journal of Women Studies* 32, no. 2 (2011): 111–139.

Hatcher, Rachel. *The Power of Memory and Violence in Central America.* Cham, Switzerland: Palgrave Macmillan, 2018.

H.I.J.O.S. Guatemala. *Todas y todos somos hijos de una misma historia: Sistematización de experiencias del colectivo H.I.J.O.S. Guatemala de 1999–2011.* Guatemala City: H.I.J.O.S Guatemala, 2014.

Holden, Robert H. "Communism and Catholic Social Doctrine in the Guatemalan Revolution of 1944." *Journal of Church and State* 50, no. 3 (2008): 495–517.

Immerman, Richard H. *The CIA in Guatemala: The Foreign Policy of Intervention.* Austin: University of Texas Press, 1988.

James, Daniel. *Red Design for the Americas: Guatemalan Prelude.* New York: John Day, 1954.

Jelin, Elizabeth. *State Repression and the Labors of Memory.* Minneapolis: University of Minnesota Press, 2003.

Jonas, Susanne. *Of Centaurs and Doves: Guatemala's Peace Process.* Boulder, CO: Westview, 2000.

Joseph, Gilbert M., and Jurgen Buchenau. *Mexico's Once and Future Revolution: Social Upheaval and the Challenge of Rule since the Late Nineteenth Century.* Durham, NC: Duke University Press, 2013.

Joseph, Gilbert M., and Greg Grandin, eds. *A Century of Revolution: Insurgent and Counterinsurgent Violence during Latin America's Long Cold War.* Durham, NC: Duke University Press, 2010.

Joseph, Gilbert M., and Daniel Nugent, eds. *Everyday Forms of State Formation.* Durham, NC: Duke University Press, 1994.

Joseph, Gilbert M., and Daniela Spenser, eds. *In from the Cold: Latin America's New Encounter with the Cold War.* Durham, NC: Duke University Press, 2007.

Klubock, Thomas. *La Frontera: Forests and Ecological Conflict in Chile's Frontier Territory.* Durham, NC: Duke University Press, 2014.

Konefal, Betsy. *For Every Indio Who Falls: A History of Maya Activism in Guatemala, 1960–1990.* Albuquerque: University of New Mexico Press, 2010.

Kraft, Douglas W. "Making West Indians Unwelcome: Bananas, Race and the Immigrant Question in Izabal, Guatemala, 1900–1929." PhD diss., University of Miami, 2006.

López Larrave, Mario. *Breve historia del movimiento sindical guatemalteco*. Guatemala City: Editorial Universitaria, 1979.

Lovell, W. George. "Surviving Conquest: The Maya of Guatemala in Historical Perspective." *Latin American Research Review* 23 (1988): 25–57.

Luján Muñoz, Jorge, and Daniel Contreras P, eds. *Historia general de Guatemala*, vol. 6: *Época contemporánea de 45 a la actualidad*. Guatemala City: Asociación Amigos del País Fundación para la cultura y el desarrollo, 1997.

Martínez Peláez, Severo. *La Patria del Criollo: An Interpretation of Colonial Guatemala*. Translated by Susan M. Neve and W. George Lovell (shortened from original); edited by W. George Lovell and Christopher H. Lutz. Durham, NC: Duke University Press, 2009.

Marx, Karl. *Capital*. Vol. 1. Translated by Ben Fowkes. London: Penguin Classics, 1990.

McCreery, David. *Rural Guatemala 1760–1940*. Stanford, CA: Stanford University Press, 1994.

Monteforte Toledo, Mario. *Guatemala: Monografía sociológica*. México, DF: UNAM Instituto de Investigaciones Sociales, [1959] 1965.

Nelson, Diane M. *A Finger in the Wound: Body Politics in Quincentennial Guatemala*. Berkeley: University of California Press, 1999.

———. *Reckoning: The Ends of War in Guatemala*. Durham, NC: Duke University Press, 2009.

———. *Who Counts? The Mathematics of Death and Life after Genocide*. Durham, NC: Duke University Press, 2015.

Nelson, Diane M., and Carlota McAllister, eds. *War by Other Means: Aftermath in Post-Peace Guatemala*. Durham, NC: Duke University Press, 2013.

Oficina de Derechos Humanos del Arzobispado de Guatemala (ODHAG). *Guatemala: Nunca más, Informe proyecto interdiocesano de recuperación de la memoria histórica*. 4 vols. Guatemala City: ODHAG, 1998.

Opie, Frederick Douglass. "Black Americans and the State in Turn-of-the-Century Guatemala." *The Americas* 64, no. 4 (April 2008): 583–609.

Pastor, Robert A. "A Discordant Consensus on Democracy." *Diplomatic History* 17, no. 1 (1993): 117–128.

Pernet, Corinne A. "Between Entanglements and Dependencies: Food, Nutrition, and National Development at the Central American Institute of Nutrition." In *International Organizations and Development, 1945–1990*, edited by Marc Frey et al., 101–125. London: Palgrave Macmillan, 2014.

Presidential Commission for the Study of Bioethical Issues (PCSBI). *"Ethically Impossible": STD Research in Guatemala from 1946 to 1948*. Washington DC: PCSBI, 2011.

Putnam, Lara. *The Company They Kept: Migrants and the Politics of Gender in Caribbean Costa Rica, 1870–1960*. Chapel Hill: University of North Carolina Press, 2002.

Reverby, Susan M. "Ethical Failures and History Lessons: The U.S. Public Health Service Research Studies in Tuskegee and Guatemala." *Public Health Reviews* 34, no. 1 (2012): 1–18.

———. "'Normal Exposure' and Inoculation Syphilis: a PHS 'Tuskegee' Doctor in Guatemala, 1946–1948." *Journal of Policy History* 23, no. 1 (2011): 6–28.

Roseberry, William, Lowell Gudmundson, and Mario Samper, eds. *Coffee, Society and Power in Latin America*. Baltimore, MD: Johns Hopkins University Press, 1995.

Schirmer, Jennifer. *The Guatemalan Military Project: A Violence Called Democracy*. Philadelphia: University of Pennsylvania Press, 1998.

Schlesinger, Stephen C., and Stephen Kinzer. *Bitter Fruit: The Untold Story of the American Coup in Guatemala*. Garden City, NY: Doubleday, 1982.

Schwartz, Norman. "Colonization of Northern Guatemala: The Petén." *Journal of Anthropological Research* 43, no. 2 (1987): 163–183.

———. *Forest Society: A Social History of Petén, Guatemala*. Philadelphia: University of Pennsylvania Press, 1990.

Scott, James C. *Seeing Like a State: How Certain Schemes to Improve the Human Condition Have Failed*. New Haven, CT: Yale University Press, 1998.

Smith, Carol. *Guatemalan Indians and the State, 1540–1988*. Austin: University of Texas Press, 1990.

———, ed. "Local History in Global Context." *Comparative Studies in Society and History* 26 (1984): 193–228.

Smith, Timothy J., and Abigail E. Adams, eds. *After the Coup: An Ethnographic Reframing of Guatemala 1954*. Urbana: University of Illinois Press, 2011.

Starn, Orin. "Missing the Revolution: Anthropologists and the War in Peru." *Cultural Anthropology* 6, no. 1 (February 1991): 63–91.

Streeter, Stephen M. "Interpreting the 1954 US Intervention in Guatemala: Realist, Revisionist, and Postrevisionist Perspectives." *History Teacher* 34, no. 1 (2000): 61–74.

———. *Managing the Counterrevolution*. Columbus: Ohio University Press, 2000.

Taracena Arriola, Arturo. *Etnicidad, estado y nación en Guatemala*. Antigua, Guatemala: Centro de Investigaciones Regionales de Mesoamérica, 2004.

Todorov, Tzvetan. *Hope and Memory: Lessons from the Twentieth Century*. Princeton, NJ: Princeton University Press, 2003.

Toriello Garrido, Guillermo. *La Batalla de Guatemala*. México, DF: Cuadernos Americanos, 1955.

Trouillot, Michel-Rolph. *Silencing the Past: Power and the Production of History*. Boston: Beacon, 1995.

United States State Department. *Intervention of International Communism in Guatemala*. Washington, DC: Department of State Publications, 1954.

Velásquez Carrera, Eduardo Antonio. *La Revolución de Octubre: Diez años de lucha por la democracia en Guatemala, 1944–1954*. Vol. 2. Guatemala City: USAC Centro de Estudios Urbanos y Regionales, 1994.

Villagrán Kramer, Francisco. *Biografía política de Guatemala: Los pactos políticos de 1944–1970*. Guatemala City: FLACSO, 2009.

Vrana, Heather. *This City Belongs to You: A History of Student Activism in Guatemala, 1944–1996*. Oakland: University of California Press, 2017.

———. "'Our ongoing fight for justice': The Pasts and Futures of *Genocidio* and *Justicia* in Guatemala." *Journal of Genocide Research* 18, nos. 2–3 (2016): 245–263.

Wakild, Emily. *Revolutionary Parks: Conservation, Social Justice, and Mexico's National Parks, 1910–1940*. Tucson: University of Arizona Press, 2011.

Wasserstrom, Robert. "Revolution in Guatemala: Peasants and Politics under the Arbenz Government." *Comparative Studies in Society and History* 17 (1975): 443–478.

Way, J. T. *The Mayan in the Mall: Globalization, Development, and the Making of Modern Guatemala.* Durham, NC: Duke University Press, 2012.

Weld, Kirsten. "Dignifying the *Guerrillero,* Not the Assassin: Rewriting a History of Criminal Subversion in Postwar Guatemala." *Radical History Review* 113 (Spring 2012): 35–54.

———. "The Other Door: Spain and the Guatemalan Counter-Revolution, 1944–54." *Journal of Latin American Studies* (January 2019): 1–29. https://doi.org/10.1017/S0022216X18001128.

Wilkinson, Daniel. *Silence on the Mountain: Stories of Terror, Betrayal, and Forgetting in Guatemala.* Durham, NC: Duke University Press, 2004.

Contributors

Abigail E. Adams is a sociocultural anthropologist, professor at Central Connecticut State University, and former journalist. She writes on Maya cultural revitalization, US–Central American relations, "voluntourism" and *indigenismo*, with new research on food justice. Among other publications, she coedited with Katherine Borland *International Volunteer Tourism: Critical Reflection on Good Works in Central America* (Palgrave Macmillan, 2013) and Timothy Smith, *After the Coup: An Ethnographic Reframing of Guatemala 1954* (University of Illinois Press, 2011).

Anthony Andersson teaches courses on global environmental history at DePauw University and was a postdoctoral fellow in the Program in Agrarian Studies at Yale University. His current book manuscript, "Environmentalists with Guns: Conservation, Revolution, and Counterinsurgency in the Petén, Guatemala, 1917-2017," examines the intersections of authoritarian state building, popular insurgency, and forest management in the tropical woodlands of northern Guatemala. His latest research probes the troubling ways that popular myths about the Ancient Maya and swidden agriculture have informed scientific studies of climate change in the neotropics.

David Carey Jr. is Doehler Chair in History at Loyola University. In addition to writing some two-dozen peer-reviewed articles and essays, he is the author of *I Ask for Justice: Maya Women, Dictators, and Crime in Guatemala, 1898–1944*, which was corecipient of the 2015 Latin American Studies Association Bryce Wood Book Award. His most recent book is *Oral History in Latin America: Unlocking the Spoken Archive*. He has authored three other books and has edited or coedited three volumes. Among other entities, the Fulbright, American Philosophical Association, and John Simon Guggenheim Foundation have supported his research and scholarship.

Patrick Chassé received his PhD from the University of Saskatchewan in 2017 and is a Social Sciences and Humanities Research Council postdoctoral fellow at the University of Guelph. His research interests include indigenous, environmental, and agricultural issues around the world. His research combines historical methods and digital techniques, such as historical GIS, to analyze how agricultural modernization has affected indigenous food systems and ecosystems across Latin America.

Sarah Foss is an assistant professor in the Department of History at Oklahoma State University. Her research focuses on the politics of Cold War–era international development projects in Latin America and the ways in which indigenous people interacted with, and often appropriated, these projects. Her current book project, *Making the Modern Indian: Development, Indigenismo, and Citizenship in Cold War Guatemala*, focuses on a diverse set of actors who utilized discourses of international development to redefine the category of "the Indian" in an attempt to integrate the indigenous population into the nation.

Julie Gibbings is a lecturer in the School of History, Classics, and Archaeology at the University of Edinburgh. Gibbings is the author of *Our Time Is Now: Race and Modernity in Postcolonial Guatemala*, forthcoming from Cambridge University Press; "In the

Shadow of Slavery: Historical Time, Labor, and Citizenship in Nineteenth-Century Alta Verapaz, Guatemala," in the *Hispanic American Historical Review*; and "Mestizaje in the Age of Fascism: Interracial Sex, Germans, and Q'eqchi' Mayas in Alta Verapaz, Guatemala," in *German History*. Her research interests include gender, race, and class; the cultural history of cartography; and indigenous history.

Laura Giraudo is a researcher at the School of Hispanic American Studies of the Spanish National Research Council (EEHA-CSIC) in Seville, Spain, and the coordinator of the INTERINDI Network (www.interindi.net). Her current research focuses on the Indian question and *indigenismo*; cultural and racial categories; and inter-American networks, projects, and institutions. Her publications include *Anular las distancias* (2008); *La questione indigena in America Latina* (2009); and the edited volumes *Ciudadanía y derechos indígenas* (2007), *Derechos, costumbres y jurisdicción indígenas* (2008), and *La ambivalente historia del indigenismo* (2011), as well as a special issue of *Latin American Perspectives* (2012) and several recent essays on indigenismo.

Jorge Ramón González Ponciano holds degrees in anthropology from Stanford University (MA) and the University of Texas at Austin (PhD), and was the Tinker Professor, a visiting scholar, and a research affiliate at the Center for Latin American Studies of Stanford University. He has been a professor at the Universidad Nacional Autónoma de México, Universidad de Ciencias y Artes de Chiapas, and Universidad Autónoma de Chiapas and in the University of California's Education Abroad Program. His current research focuses on human rights, genocide, racism, humor, borderlands, tourism and exoticism, laziness, dictatorship, and plebeian studies in Latin America.

Jim Handy is a professor of history at the University of Saskatchewan. He is author of foundational histories of the Guatemala Revolution, including *Gift of the Devil: A History of Guatemala* and *Revolution in the Countryside: Rural Conflict and Agrarian Reform in Guatemala, 1944–1954* (University of North Carolina Press, 1994). His current research interests include human rights, dispossession, environmental history, and peasant livelihoods.

Betsy Konefal is an associate professor of history and Center for the Liberal Arts Fellow at the College of William and Mary. She is the author of *For Every Indio Who Falls: A History of Maya Activism in Guatemala, 1960–1990* and numerous articles and book chapters, including "Subverting Authenticity: *Reinas indígenas* and the Guatemalan State, 1978" in the *Hispanic American Historical Review*.

Diane M. Nelson is a professor of cultural anthropology at Duke University. She is author of *A Finger in the Wound: Body Politics in Quincentennial Guatemala*, *Reckoning: The Ends of War in Guatemala*, and *Who Counts? The Mathematics of Death and Life After Genocide*, as well as numerous articles. Her current research focuses on capitalist extraction in highland Guatemala, particularly hydroelectrics, and eco-ontologic resistance movements.

Ingrid Sierakowski completed her PhD from Yale in 2014. She teaches world history and Latin American history at the Trevor Day School in New York City. She is also an adjunct instructor at the NYU School of Professional Studies. Her research centers on the study of race, labor, and migration in modern Central America and the Caribbean. She was a contributor to Henry Louis Gates Jr. and Franklin K. Knight, eds., *Dictionary of Caribbean and Afro-Latin American Biography* (Oxford University Press, 2016).

Arturo Taracena Arriola is a research professor at the Centro Peninsular en Humanidades y Ciencias Sociales of the Universidad Nacional Autónoma de México en Mérida, Mexico. He is the author of more than a dozen books and numerous articles, most recently, *Guatemala, la República Española y el Gobierno Vasco en el exilio, 1944–1954* (UNAM-CEPHCIS, 2017). His research interests include political history of the nineteenth and twentieth centuries, the nation-state, citizenship, social movements, and interethnic relations.

Heather Vrana is an assistant professor of modern Latin America in the Department of History at the University of Florida whose research focuses on disability, human rights, photography, youth, and student movements in Guatemala, Nicaragua, and El Salvador. Vrana is author of the monograph *This City Belongs to You: A History of Student Activism in Guatemala, 1944–1996* (University of California Press, 2017) and the anthology *Anti-Colonial Texts from Central American Student Movements 1929–1983* (Edinburgh University Press, 2017), as well as several articles and book chapters.

Index

Note: Italic page numbers refer to illustrations.